W9-BRD-805

★ THE ★
PRESIDENT'S
MAN

★ THE ★
PRESIDENT'S MAN

The Memoirs of Nixon's Trusted Aide

DWIGHT CHAPIN

WM

WILLIAM MORROW

An Imprint of HarperCollinsPublishers

Grateful acknowledgment is made to the following for the use of materials that appear in the front matter and the appendix: courtesy of the author (pages viii–ix and x); Department of Justice, "Watergate Investigation—OPE Analysis," July 5, 1974, file 139-4089, Federal Bureau of Investigation (pages 419–23); Department of Justice, "Summary of Investigation, Washington Field Office," August, 28, 1972, file 139-4089, Federal Bureau of Investigation (pages 446–48); and The Dwight Chapin Private Collection (pages 449–52).

Grateful acknowledgment is made to the following for the use of the photographs that appear in the art insert: The Dwight Chapin Private Collection (page 1, top and middle; page 2, top left and right; page 4; page 5, top; page 6, top left; page 14, middle; page 15, bottom; and page 16, top); Courtesy of the USC Digital Library. The *Daily Trojan* Collection (page 1, bottom); Richard Nixon Foundation (page 2, bottom: A10-024.49.3.4; page 15, top right: NF Opening 2016 e_057); Bob Fitch Photography Archive, Department of Special Collections, Stanford University Library (page 3, top left); Photograph by Jack Robinson, *Vogue,* © Conde Nast (page 3, top right); Richard Nixon Presidential Library and Museum, Ollie Atkins Collection (page 3, bottom: 0642-05); Lyndon B. Johnson Presidential Library (page 5, bottom: D3114-22); Richard Nixon Presidential Library and Museum (page 6, top right: 0728-22; page 6, bottom: 1923-31; page 7, top: 6791-3A; page 7, bottom: 8567-08; page 8, top: 7642-02; page 8, middle: 7641-01; page 8, bottom: 8479-21; page 9, top: C8476-15; page 9, bottom: C8476-06; page 10, top: 8568-17; page 10, bottom: C8472-08; page 11, top: C8498-17; page 11, middle: 8528-01; page 11, bottom: 8482-23; page 12, top: 8569-02; page 12, bottom: 9207-31; page 13, top: 9257-09; page 13, middle: 3144-06a; page 13, bottom: 5364-18; page 14, top: D0018-14a); Courtesy of the Associated Press (page 14, bottom); AFP/AFP via Getty Images (page 15, top left); and Courtesy of Liza Segretti (page 16, bottom).

FIRST EDITION

Designed by Bonni Leon-Berman

Library of Congress Cataloging-in-Publication Data has been applied for.

ISBN 978-0-06-307477-4

22 23 24 25 26 LSC 10 9 8 7 6 5 4 3 2 1

With Love

TO OUR GRANDCHILDREN

Jack & Emily

Chase & Matthew

John, Billy, Tommy, Andrew & Kate

Teddy, Ollie & Henry

Everett, Amelia & Eliza

———————————

Let Your Light Shine

Love, Pipps

★ CONTENTS ★

White House Staff Chart viii
White House West Wing First Floor Plan x
Preface xi

1 1
2 20
3 40
4 68
5 91
6 110
7 133
8 154
9 178
10 203
11 225
12 253
13 277
14 299
15 328
16 348
17 367
18 385
19 399

Acknowledgments 407
Recommended Sources on President Nixon 417
Appendix 419
Index 453

WHITE HOUSE STAFF CHART

Chart Limited to the Principal Individuals
or Groups Mentioned in *The President's Man*

President Nixon

Rose Mary Woods
President's Secretary

[Presidential Assistant Level]

John Ehrlichman
Counsel to President '69
Director Domestic Council

Patrick Moynihan
Director of Urban Affairs '69
Counselor to President

Dr. Henry Kissinger
Director Natl. Security Council

David Young
Assistant to Dr. Kissinger

Winston Lord
Assistant to Dr. Kissinger

General Alexander Haig
Deputy Director of NSC

DOMESTIC COUNCIL
MEMBERS:
(Partial List 1969 -1973)
Pam Bailey
James Cavanaugh
Charlie Clapp
Ken Cole*
Henry Cashen*
Jeff Donfeld
Mike Duval
Lew Engman
John Evans*
Dick Fairbanks
Jim Falk
Bobbie Green
Ed Harper
Tod Hullin
Egil "Bud" Krogh*
Will Kriegsman
Dana Mead
Walter Minnick
Ed Morgan*
Henry Paulson
John Price
Andy Rouse
John Whitaker
Roger Semerad
Geoff Shepard

William Rogers
State Department
Secretary of State

John Mitchell
Justice Department
Attorney General

Melvin Laird
Defense Department
Secretary of Defense

George Shultz
Labor Department
Secretary of Labor '69
Director of OMB '70

Admiral Thomas Moorer
Defense Department
Chairman Joint Chiefs

Admiral Rembrandt Robinson
Admiral Robert Welander
Yeoman Charles Radford
Pentagon White House Office
Liaison to NSC

President Nixon

↕

Herbert Kalmbach
President's Personal Attorney

Mr. Kalmbach was not a
White House staff member.

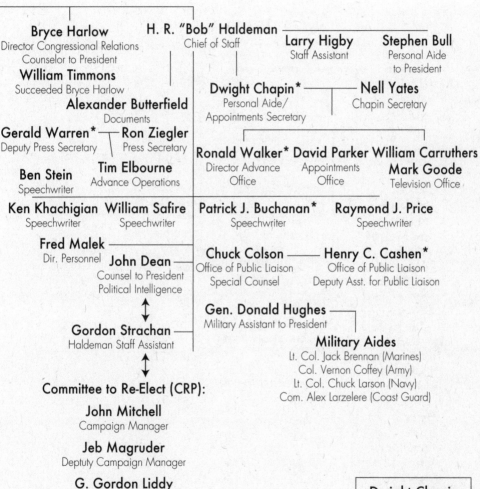

Bryce Harlow
Director Congressional Relations
Counselor to President

William Timmons
Succeeded Bryce Harlow

Alexander Butterfield
Documents

Gerald Warren* — **Ron Ziegler**
Deputy Press Secretary   Press Secretary

Ben Stein
Speechwriter

Tim Elbourne
Advance Operations

Ken Khachigian
Speechwriter

William Safire
Speechwriter

Fred Malek
Dir. Personnel

John Dean
Counsel to President
Political Intelligence

Gordon Strachan
Haleman Staff Assistant

Committee to Re-Elect (CRP):

John Mitchell
Campaign Manager

Jeb Magruder
Deptuty Campaign Manager

G. Gordon Liddy
Director of Security

E. Howard Hunt
Consultant to G. Gordon Liddy

Hugh Sloan
Assistant Treasurer

H. R. "Bob" Haldeman
Chief of Staff

Larry Higby
Staff Assistant

Stephen Bull
Personal Aide
to President

Dwight Chapin*
Personal Aide/
Appointments Secretary

Nell Yates
Chapin Secretary

Ronald Walker* **David Parker** **William Carruthers**
Director Advance   Appointments
Office   Office

Mark Goode
Television Office

Patrick J. Buchanan*
Speechwriter

Raymond J. Price
Speechwriter

Chuck Colson
Office of Public Liaison
Special Counsel

Henry C. Cashen*
Office of Public Liaison
Deputy Asst. for Public Liaison

Gen. Donald Hughes
Military Assistant to President

Military Aides
Lt. Col. Jack Brennan (Marines)
Col. Vernon Coffey (Army)
Lt. Col. Chuck Larson (Navy)
Com. Alex Larzelere (Coast Guard)

Dwight Chapin
Gordon Strachan
↕
Donald Segretti
Pranksterism

Mr. Segretti was not a
White House staff
member.

WHITE HOUSE WEST WING FIRST FLOOR PLAN

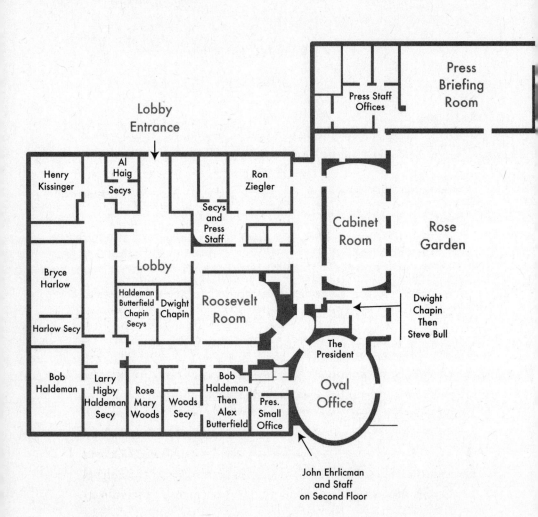

Press Briefing Room

Press Staff Offices

Lobby Entrance

Henry Kissinger

Al Haig Secys

Ron Ziegler

Secys and Press Staff

Cabinet Room

Rose Garden

Lobby

Bryce Harlow

Haldeman Butterfield Chapin Secys

Dwight Chapin

Roosevelt Room

Dwight Chapin Then Steve Bull

Harlow Secy

The President

Bob Haldeman

Larry Higby Haldeman Secy

Rose Mary Woods

Woods Secy

Bob Haldeman Then Alex Butterfield

Pres. Small Office

Oval Office

John Ehrlicman and Staff on Second Floor

★ PREFACE ★

We were visiting my daughter Tracy. Early one evening I heard several soft, hesitant knocks on the guest room door. When I opened the door, my grandson Matthew, already in his pajamas, was looking up at me. With the innocence of a seven-year-old he asked, "Pipps"—that's what my grandchildren call me—"did you work for a president?"

I nodded. "I did."

"Did you have to go to prison?"

"Yes, Matthew, I did."

He considered that, giving it the mighty weight "prison" conveys to a child. He tilted his head and pursed his lips. "Did the president go to prison too?"

"No, Matthew. No, he didn't." I took a step back. "Come on in." We sat side by side on the bed. "It's very complicated," I said. "When you get a little older, I promise, I'll explain the whole story to you."

The whole story? Explain what happened to me? What happened in America? That would require explaining, understanding Richard Nixon, the thirty-seventh President of the United States. Richard Nixon was the most complex man I've ever known. He was an enigma wrapped in a cocoon of contradictions. He was a man of extraordinary intelligence and vision. He could take you around the entire world with his words, country by country, detailing the political dynamics, the shifting winds and the power players in each place, while at the same time concerning himself with petty slights. He could be warm and gracious, cold and off-putting. He was a political genius but he missed completely the dangers of Watergate. He was a man of great emotions, but he took pride in containing them. He was a public man, who drew sustenance from the crowds, yet he was happiest in a room by himself, a briefcase on his lap, recording his thoughts and ideas by hand on yellow legal pads.

I met him when I was so young, and still today, many years later, my life reverberates from our relationship.

★ 1 ★

"... WHEN MY LIFE CHANGED FOR THE BETTER AND FOREVER..."

I knew Richard Nixon well. I started working for him as an organizational field man during his 1962 California gubernatorial campaign. I served him as an aide as he wandered in the political wilderness, planting a forest of favors in anticipation of another run for the presidency. I became an advance man at the beginning of the 1966 off-year election cycle and then his personal aide in 1967. In the White House, as his appointments secretary, I had the office next to his. My door opened into the Oval Office. Then I was given responsibility for the logistics and arrangements for the president's historic 1972 trips to China and the Soviet Union. And I was the first of the Nixon men to go to trial because of Watergate, although I had no involvement in it.

We spent thousands of hours together, from small hotels in New Hampshire to the Forbidden City in Beijing. I knew him so well; but as I have continued to discover through the decades, in many ways I barely knew him at all.

Still, today, right now, I can close my eyes and visualize him standing a few feet away from me, acknowledging defeat in that 1962 California gubernatorial election, beads of sweat on his forehead as he bitterly tells reporters they don't have Nixon to kick around anymore. I can see him alone in his New York apartment, making endless notes as he plans his political future. I can see him in the backseat of a car in the early-morning sunrise, lost on a one-lane road searching for a small radio station to do a campaign interview. I can see him, arms outstretched, reaching to the heavens, luxuriating in the roar of a packed Republican convention hall in Miami Beach. I see him tapping the schedule I've prepared for him with his forefinger, pointing out to me, "Dwight, it says here that when I'm finished speaking, I will dance with this lady. People running for sheriff dance. I don't dance." (Or, as I was later reminded, wear a silly hat.) And there he is in his bathrobe, a satisfied, vindicated smile on his face, as I tell him he had been elected President of the United States.

I also can visualize myself sitting across from the president in a helicopter, circling Washington, D.C., on a glorious early June night in 1972. Below us the city was twinkling into the night. The First Lady, Pat Nixon; the Chief of Staff and my best friend, Bob Haldeman; and Press Secretary Ron Ziegler were with us, as was the president's physician, Major General Walter Tkach. We had just returned to America from a triumphant trip to the Soviet Union, where Nixon and Russian leaders had signed the historic Strategic Arms Limitation Treaty (SALT), among the first significant efforts to limit the spread of nuclear weapons. We were flying from Andrews Air Force Base to the Capitol, where the president was to address a joint session of Congress. During that short flight I briefed him on the preparations that had been made for his arrival there, his escort into the building, and the extent of the media coverage. We circled once over the White House, then passed the Washington Monument, as Lincoln watched stoically from a distance. The city had never looked more beautiful to me. The symbolism of that flight aboard *Marine One* was unmistakable. Richard Nixon had taken me to the height of power. Me, a kid from the American heartland, from the Kansas plains, who at times had struggled through school; a young man with seemingly unlimited energy, a drive to please, and an abundance of unfocused ambition, sitting inches away from the President of the United States, the man I was certain would be remembered as one of the great leaders in the history of this country.

At that moment, for me, everything seemed possible. I was already beginning to consider my post–White House future. A few months later I would be honored as one of the Ten Outstanding Young Men in America. I was a phone call away from reaching almost any successful and important businessman in the country. And few my age had a résumé that could match mine, a résumé that might include recommendations from the president, from Secretary of State Henry Kissinger, from Bob Haldeman, and from so many other American leaders.

Having "everything" included things I would never have imagined possible. Eighteen months later, though, I would be indicted on four counts of perjury, supposedly because of my involvement in the Watergate break-in and cover-up, a crime about which I knew nothing and to which I had absolutely no connection. Within a couple of years I would be serving time in prison.

It was an extraordinary journey, and it had been made possible by one man: Harry Robbins Haldeman. H. R. "Bob" Haldeman was my mentor, the most demanding boss I ever had. He was at times the source of incredible frustration, dismay, and anger; and yet he was my closest friend. I never knew how Haldeman saw the possibilities within me, but he did. He took me and shaped me. Together we walked into history.

By the time I met Bob Haldeman I was ready and eager to be molded. I had been raised in Wichita, Kansas. My maternal grandparents, the Helenas, had Norman Rockwell covers of the *Saturday Evening Post* hanging on their walls depicting the perfect American family, gathered around a Thanksgiving table or depicting Dad doing something silly while everyone gathered around him is grinning with love and understanding. That's what our family was supposed to be, though no family is exactly that way. My parents had been the darling couple at East High School, which was a big deal back then. He was the handsome quarterback of the football team. She was the beautiful young woman, a diver, from Crestview Country Club. He was an incredibly smart man, an aeronautical engineer, a hardworking man.

I struggled in school. My father spoke the language of numbers;

numbers made no sense to me. He was an artist with a slide rule; I couldn't figure out how the damn thing worked. At that time there was no such thing as a "learning disability." You were smart or you were slow. I couldn't sit still. I didn't listen. I couldn't focus. To compensate I was loud and funny and nice. I wanted to be liked and did whatever was necessary to make the other kids like me. As a teacher noted correctly on my report card, "Dwight is always the class clown." I actually had to repeat third grade. Years later I would be diagnosed with dyslexia, a condition that made reading difficult for me. The combination of poor grades and deportment issues created a wall between my father and me. He believed in spanking. He would hit me with his Sigma Chi paddle from Purdue. I can remember sobbing and shaking in fear as he was telling me I was smart, I just had to work harder. But I knew the truth: I wasn't smart. I couldn't keep up.

I did whatever was necessary to survive. I even learned how to forge my parents' signatures on the disciplinary notes I brought home. My mother had no idea how to deal with me. When I was out of control she would threaten me: "I'm going to tell your father." All that accomplished was that it added to my fear of him. I needed what he was never capable of offering me. It left a part of me empty. Near the end of his life as I stood at his bedside, the two of us alone in that room, he said, "Son, I love you." It was the only time I ever remember him telling me that.

I was three years old when my baby brother, Sheldon, was born. He was a "blue baby," born with a defective heart. My parents traveled around the country trying to save him. All their travel had to be by train because Sheldon's condition prevented him from flying. They would be gone weeks at a time, to the Mayo Clinic in Minnesota, to Johns Hopkins in Maryland. I stayed with my wonderful Aunt Nan, but I couldn't understand why my parents would abandon me. At the age of twenty months Sheldon died. My mother told me at that Christmas I asked to be taken to his grave so I could share my toys with him.

I was named after my paternal grandfather, Dwight Chapin, a man driven by a strong work ethic and an entrepreneurial spirit. After graduating from high school, he went to New York City—a daring decision—

and worked his way through electrical school by sweeping up horse droppings on Fifth Avenue. He went home to the Midwest and opened the first electrical lighting plant in Lyons, Kansas. His business grew, and while others were trying to just survive during the Great Depression, he became a millionaire by building power lines across the plains to the new Hoover Dam in Nevada. With his fortune he built one of the largest hog farms in the nation. To feed his hogs, he got the contract to collect the garbage in Wichita. When the city council prohibited raw garbage from being fed to pigs, he created a system that piped steam into his trucks, which quickly cooked the garbage. Eventually he built a slaughterhouse and packing plants to process the meat, then he sold it all to the Swift meatpacking company.

Grandmother Chapin was a real Methodist hard-liner. When she found out there was alcohol in Geritol she thought she was going to hell. That's a family joke, but it's true. There wasn't a lot of flexibility in her value system. When I was thirteen years old she introduced me to Dr. Norman Vincent Peale's classic bestseller *The Power of Positive Thinking*. She conveyed his message to me: I could do it. Whatever it was, I could do it. It was the positive reinforcement I so needed and appreciated. She believed in me. She believed I could do it. In fact, for a time while I was in high school, I wanted to become a minister. At one point I attended a Presbyterian youth conference, and while I was not especially religious, I was enthralled by the ability of a great minister to carry a congregation along with him on the strength of his words. I admired men like Dr. Peale and the Reverend Billy Graham for their abilities to give me an inner strength, a spirituality, not in any biblical sense but in my daily life. Even at that young age I began to appreciate the value of a great sermon or, as I really learned, a great political speech. Both Dr. Peale and Billy Graham would become personal friends in the years ahead. In fact, at the 1988 Republican Convention in New Orleans, Susie, my wife of twenty-five years, and I restated our wedding vows with Billy Graham doing the officiating. I am told it was the only time he ever conducted the renewal of a couple's vows.

My mother's parents were Christian Scientists, a group that believes in the power of the mind to cure. They do not go to medical doctors. My mother taught Christian Science Sunday school classes—but we also would go to doctors, so we were somewhere in the middle. I was always taught it's Christian *and* it's science—a combination of the two—and both are to be respected. Bob Haldeman was a Christian Scientist, but he adhered more strictly to the principles. Maybe that background was one of the things that brought us together.

When I was eleven years old, my five-year-old sister, Linda, and I moved with our parents out of Wichita to a 160-acre farm near Derby, Kansas. My parents thought the change might be better for me, meaning I would be easier to handle. Dad had a day job, working for the Garrett Corporation selling components to the aircraft industry. I was responsible for the daily farm chores. I hated it. We were isolated, away from everything and everyone I knew. I desperately missed my friends. Once again I felt that great sense of abandonment. I cried all the time. But then I would suck it up. I would be the good soldier, doing as I was told. The themes that would govern my life were developing: Suck it up. Smile and do what you're told. Work hard. People will like you.

As much as I hated being on the farm, it taught me responsibility. I joined the local 4-H club and started raising my own animals. Within a year I was driving an old two-ton military jeep around the farm. On Saturdays I'd work with my father digging post holes to put up a barbed-wire fence or go over to Granddad Chapin's to pick up the right kind of big pipe wrench to work on the tractor. During the week, when my father was at work, I took care of our cattle. In the winter I fed them at four thirty in the freezing windy morning. In the summer I would mow the alfalfa and then pick up the sixty-pound bales from the fields and stack them in our feedlot. Maybe I wasn't great with numbers, but I could drive a tractor and care for the cattle. Our neighbor across the road, a farmer named John Rick, was impressed by my work ethic. He invited me to noon dinners with his farm crew of six. We feasted on Mrs. Rick's fried chicken, mashed potatoes, gravy, rolls, vegetables, and two or three home-baked pies and conversed about farming. I felt connected. I loved the talk about the business of farming and the recognition of being with the farm crew.

A family friend, Wichita oil man Ed Bradley, visited one evening. I talked with him alone for half an hour. After our conversation he told my dad he was impressed by the fact I was earning money to buy a horse; and that when we spoke I stood tall and looked him right in the eyes. Mr. Bradley was so impressed he decided to give me a horse. This horse had been bred as a polo pony, but he was too small to be ridden in a match. The horse was a direct descendant of the great Man o' War and high-spirited, and he was mine.

I learned the intended lessons on that farm: How to accept an unpleasant situation and make the best of it. How to stand up for myself and say what was on my mind. How to do a job and follow instructions to the best of my ability. And most of all, I developed the work ethic that would make the big difference in my life.

If we had stayed there, I would have lived a different life. We didn't, though. My father was offered a better position in Southern California and, when I was fourteen years old, we moved to Brentwood, in western Los Angeles. In 1955 California was the Golden West, a place where dreams came true. Kansas was flat, sparse, colorless in the winter. California was green, rich, and sophisticated. It had its own culture. There was an energy and optimism there unlike anything I had ever experienced. It would have been nearly impossible for me to have felt any more out of place.

My clothes were funny. My Kansas twang was foreign. I was a kid from the country tossed into this West Coast world. In Derby, Kansas, my school had so few students that two grades shared one classroom. My school in Brentwood had two thousand students. In Kansas my classmates had been farm kids, or their parents worked the line at Boeing. Nancy Sinatra was a fellow student at Emerson Junior High in Brentwood, and most of the other kids came from wealthy families.

My parents had always been very social. They quickly met other couples from Kansas who had made similar moves to California. Not me. At this point, once again, I was an outsider, the stranger in a strange land. None of the values I had learned in Kansas seemed to apply in California. That became clear to me when I found out a group of neighborhood kids were making counterfeit coins to buy ice cream and food in school. I reported them to the principal—not to my parents, but to the authorities. Don't ask me why. I suspect I just needed some approval from an authority figure for having done the right thing. Next moment I was in the principal's office being interviewed by FBI agents. It escalated from there. My parents were furious that I hadn't talked with them before going to the principal. My belief that I had done the right thing, just as I had been taught, was in question.

Everyone knew I had "ratted out" the popular kids. The FBI was in our school. The situation got very tense. Threats were made, which cemented my parents' decision to move over the Santa Monica Mountains to Encino. It was, in retrospect, the move that changed my life. As it turned out, there was no better place in the world for me to be. My parents bought a beautiful home. We lived right across the street from the flamboyant and very popular pianist Liberace. Actor William Talman, the D.A. on *Perry Mason,* was next door. Clark Gable would drive by in his Mercedes convertible. Phil Bonnell, one of my best friends in high school, would become a fraternity brother, USC roommate, and best man at our wedding. Phil's mother was the television celebrity Gale Storm, who starred in the popular sitcom *My Little Margie.* A year earlier I'd been raising my baby beef for the 4-H club. Suddenly this glamorous world had opened to me.

When we'd left Kansas I sold Brad, the horse Mr. Bradley had given me. Dad matched that money, and with it I bought a Model A Ford. Dad put only one condition on it: I had to take the engine completely apart and then put it back together. It took a few months to get it running. I was fifteen years old, the only kid in the neighborhood with a car that I couldn't drive until I was sixteen.

But for the first time in my life, I felt as if I fit in. I had a new best friend, Mike Kramer, and several other neighborhood friends, people who liked me. I had teachers who recognized my capabilities and encouraged me, especially my history and political science teacher at Birmingham High School, Mr. Ramirez. Lou Ramirez was a character. On every test he asked the same two questions: "What happened in 1880?" and "What is the best fraternity in the world?" The answers were "USC was founded" and "Sigma Chi." If you answered them correctly you were guaranteed at least a D. Mr. Ramirez liked me a lot. He was a straight-arrow type guy and I was a straight-arrow type kid. For the first time learning was fun for me. Mr. Ramirez loved to talk and his tests were based on what he said, not what was in our books. That was perfect for me. If I heard it, I remembered it, and for the first time I was getting better grades. Maybe I wasn't so dumb after all.

I gained confidence I'd never had. The prettiest girl in my class, Susie Howland, became my girlfriend. Susie and I were inseparable, the class couple. My grades improved marginally, but more important, I became a student leader. The summer between my junior and senior years I was selected to attend Boys State in Sacramento, an American Legion leadership development program. At this convention we were assigned to "political" parties. I was elected chairman of our party. Stacy Keach, who would become a celebrated actor, was from Van Nuys High. He became chairman of our rival party. His candidate won the gubernatorial election, but the campaign allowed me to develop political organizing and communication skills. I loved every minute of it. I loved the attention. I loved exercising authority. I loved the challenge. It was my first real connection to elective politics, and it stuck.

My senior year I was elected student body president, a job I took so seriously that I made myself an expert on *Robert's Rules of Order,* the book of rules governing organization proceedings. I read it over and over, intrigued by the nuances. And to the dismay of our advisors, I never hesitated to display my knowledge. Whatever the faculty wanted to do, I often just tabled their motions. I had an independent streak. Even with my poor grades, I was permitted to speak at our graduation. I proudly advised my classmates, as if revealing the most solemn wisdom,

"We have to decide from the lumber of our lives if we are going to build a tavern or a temple."

That certainly applied to my own life.

As a result of my high school experiences, I had become fascinated by elective politics. My father's family were staunch Republicans, while my mother's parents were Democrats. In my family we loved President Eisenhower and hated Harry Truman. And emerging in the middle of it all was controversial, combative, resilient, brilliant Richard Nixon.

Richard Nixon was then the vice president of the United States. Before that he had been the congressman from the district we'd moved into and then a senator. Even then he was a controversial figure. As a member of the House Un-American Activities Committee, he had earned a national reputation for his interrogation of the Communist Alger Hiss, which led eventually to the successful and highly controversial prosecution of the senior State Department official. Nixon had confirmed editor Whittaker Chambers's claim that Hiss had been a Soviet spy. At the outset, Chambers only charged Hiss with being a Communist. Hiss upped the ante by denying it. That forced Chambers to produce his ace (or pumpkin) in the hole, that being microfilm of stolen documents that proved Hiss was a spy. Nixon's relentless pursuit of Hiss had earned him the enmity of the Democrats. (Democrats on the left despised Richard Nixon his whole career for his stance against Communism.) More important, perhaps, was the enmity of the liberal elite of media, artists (including actors), and academics, most of whom were also Democrats. Nixon's 1950 senatorial campaign against Helen Gahagan Douglas had been especially bitter, partially because of his tenacity and her leftist views. World War II hero and five-star general Dwight Eisenhower picked Richard Nixon as his running mate in 1952. At the time Ike told Nixon one of the reasons he had chosen him: "You got Hiss fair and square." (Ike said this because unlike many rabid anti-Communists, Nixon's approach had been methodical and reasonable, and, therefore, more devastatingly effective. That was what appealed to Ike.) After winning the presidency, Ike solidified Nixon's

Republican standing by giving him power few vice presidents had ever enjoyed. He sent him around the globe to meet with world leaders; then directed him to attack Senator Joseph McCarthy, who had gotten out of control with his charges of widespread Communist subversion. The assignments Ike delegated to Nixon gave him opportunities and experiences that were unique in the history of a vice president. It gave him considerable public exposure and awareness. The Eisenhower assignment to take down Joe McCarthy made Nixon very unpopular with the conservatives who continued to support McCarthy and didn't want him taken down. It was an example of how Nixon sacrificed his own interests in order to carry out Ike's wishes.

The Chapins admired Nixon. He had made headlines in 1958 when his motorcade was attacked violently by protesters in Venezuela, and again a year later when he stood up to Soviet Premier Nikita Khrushchev in an exchange of political and economic "debates" that took place in a showplace American suburban home built for an exhibition in Moscow.

The first politician I worked for was Democrat (at the time) Sam Yorty, the independent maverick and outspoken mayor of Los Angeles. I went door-to-door for him, the bottom rung of politics. But there was no better place to start in politics than slipping pamphlets under a door or looking someone in his eyes (smile, always smile) and telling him why he should support your candidate. Until you've had a door—or many doors—slammed in your face, you won't understand politics. This is the best political course anyone can take: You and me, one-on-one, why you should vote for my guy.

Although I had been accepted by USC—thank you, Lou Ramirez, for your recommendation and my parents' ability to pay the tuition—my father insisted I attend Menlo College, the equivalent of a junior college, to learn how to study. My English teacher there was Mr. Heck, who had me read Conrad's *Heart of Darkness*. I received a C on my book report. I was furious about that and went immediately to his office. The darkness of a winter afternoon set in as we sat there and

I carefully explained my interpretation of the book. He listened. He actually heard me. When I was finished, he changed my grade to an A. That was such a big deal for me. After that I started enjoying small successes in the classroom and most of the things I tried. I began taking a serious interest in the world. A close friend at Menlo, Bart Noone, and I would quiz each other on everything in that week's *Time* magazine. We gambled a dollar per question. That challenged me to focus on current events, particularly politics. I was blossoming into the person I was capable of being. I wanted to know everything, I wanted to understand it all. I had proven to myself that I could do college work, and I never had academic problems again. Dad had been right: Menlo taught me how to study, and I no longer felt "dumb."

In 1960 I was going to join Susie at USC for my sophomore year. That was an election year, handsome and charismatic Kennedy vs. the experienced Nixon. That summer my mother's best friend, Kathleen Hite, a woman who had attended college with her in Wichita, had years before moved west to write for radio and television. She was the creator or co-creator of the Western series *Gunsmoke,* which was both on radio and then television. She arranged for me to work for CBS News at the Democratic Convention in Los Angeles. My job was to clip the stories that were printed by the teletype machines, go into the studio while the correspondents were on the air, crawl up to the end of the anchors' desk on my hands and knees to avoid the cameras, and deliver them to the producers. It was an exhilarating experience. Rotating in and out of the studio were the giants of early news broadcasting: Edward R. Murrow, Charles Collingwood, Eric Sevareid, Douglas Edwards, and Walter Cronkite.

I became infatuated with the hubbub of it all, the importance of being in the middle of the excitement. I was there when Kennedy came to the convention hall to accept the nomination. I was nineteen years old, witnessing this and feeling this extraordinary euphoria in the hall. There is an expression usually applied to relatives of politicians, that politics is in his (or her) blood. For me, this was where I got my transfusion.

At USC I became a Sigma Chi and got involved in student politics. Both my dad and Uncle B. R. had been Sigma Chis at other schools. Lou Ramirez, as I knew so well, had been a Sigma Chi at USC. Among my fraternity brothers were Ron Ziegler, who would become President Nixon's White House Press Secretary; Sandy Quinn, who also would work for Nixon and later serve as Governor Ronald Reagan's assistant executive secretary and chaired his inauguration; and Tim Elbourne, who would work for Ziegler in the White House press office, managing logistics.

Sandy Quinn, only a couple of years older than me, was one of my first mentors. He took me to several Los Angeles Young Republican events. On campus I served as president of the fraternity for two semesters, as well as treasurer. I was part of an incredible group that revived the dormant Trojans for Representative Government Party (TRG). A high school friend and fellow USC student, Harvey Harris, came to me with his plan to resurrect TRG from the political graveyard. It took us two years, but we elected Bart Leddel as student body president. Bart ran against another good friend of mine, Dan Moss. Both of them were Jewish. Our campaign slogan, "There's a Jew for you," drove the USC administration nuts. We could not have cared less. Then we ran Ken DelConte, a football star and my fraternity brother, to succeed Leddel. Our opponent in that election for student body president ran on the slogan "Think Twice," meaning if you took the time to really think about it, you'd vote for him. To help get out the vote the night before the election, our pledges painted "Think Twice Jocks!" in bright red on the front of fraternity and sorority houses. Highly motivated and deeply angry Greeks turned out to vote—for our candidate DelConte, who won in a landslide.

Many news stories later misrepresented our TRG efforts and their relationship to Watergate. At USC, TRG was made up of good guys. We were a positive campus political force. We were not "ratfuckers" as some have tried to characterize us. My roommate the semester Leddel won was a smart, personable young guy named Don Segretti. Don was the person I would eventually hire to play political pranks before the 1972 election—the decision that led directly to stays for both him and me at the Lompoc correctional facility, though at different times.

When my reputation as a campus activist kept me out of Skull and Dagger, an honor organization, I joined with Mike Paulin and several of our TRG pals to announce that the sixty-third Annual Ballers Banquet would be held. This came as a great surprise to many people because, until that announcement, there had never been a Ballers organization, let alone a banquet. With considerable laughter, fun, and ridicule, we had made the whole thing up. This, in the opinion of the USC administration, added one more event to a long list of things that were not at all popular with them. Approximately seventy-five Ballers attended the dinner, where we honored the memory of our mythical founder Hiram Ball, although admittedly that was not the derivation of our society's name.

Early in the summer of '62, I still had not landed a summer job. My father arranged an interview for me with a key member of the Richard Nixon for Governor campaign. I walked into the Wilshire Boulevard headquarters and met with a man named Herb Kalmbach. He was a USC alum and a young lawyer. Almost instantly we formed a relationship, a kinlike friendship, that would last more than half a century. After a half-hour discussion he left the office, returning minutes later to invite me to the office of a perfectly groomed, snappy, crew-cutted, California-tanned, smiling man in his mid-thirties. "I want you to meet our campaign manager," he said, "Bob Haldeman."

Few people have the gift of being able to point to one moment and say, "There, that's it, that's when my life changed for the better and forever." That was my moment.

I spent my summer vacation and the fall semester of 1962 as a paid Nixon "field man." Having lost the 1960 presidential election, supposedly because Chicago Mayor Richard Daley "found" the number of votes Kennedy needed to carry Illinois and win the electoral vote, Richard Nixon was relaunching his political career by running for governor of California. His opponent was Pat Brown. My job was to help local organizers, mostly women, set up campaign offices in the San Fernando Valley area of Los Angeles, Ventura, and Santa Barbara counties. I found the office space, filled it with rented tables and chairs, then recruited volunteers to do the work and on Election Day help get out the vote. Maybe I didn't know exactly what I was doing, but I was good at it. I believed I was doing something important. I was dedicated and honest and willing to listen and learn. Herb Kalmbach was a great teacher, who treated me like an experienced campaign worker, giving me responsibilities and gently correcting me or, perhaps more accurately, advising me.

I met Richard Nixon for the first time that August. We were told to be at the campaign headquarters to meet "the former vice president." My desk was in the bullpen area. Sitting near me were Sandy Quinn, Ron Ziegler, and some other staff. Mr. Nixon's extraordinarily competent secretary, Rose Mary Woods, had her own office, as did John Ehrlichman, who was in charge of the advance operation—which meant preparing a designated place for a campaign rally, from setting up and creating the event to bringing in a crowd—and Nick Ruwe, who ran scheduling. Standing around that day, with no desk, was an advance man named Pete Wilson. Pete would go on to become mayor of San Diego, California State assemblyman, two-term United States senator, two-term governor of California, and a presidential candidate. When "the former vice president" arrived, Bob Haldeman introduced each of us to him, adding a brief description of our responsibilities. I don't really remember it well, but as I was to see so many times in the future, I'm quite certain Nixon looked each of us directly in the eyes, shook our hands firmly, and muttered a few supportive and believably sincere words.

I did my job well. Starting in junior high school, I had learned how to make friends as a way of overcoming my academic difficulties. Those skills proved invaluable in this job. People considered me a nice guy. I could move easily through our satellite offices and do whatever needed to be done without any drama. (Anyone who has ever worked on a political campaign may be smiling now at the memory of his own dramas.) Near the conclusion of the campaign, we didn't have anyone to advance the former vice president's scheduled rally in Panorama City, which is located in the San Fernando Valley. Nick Ruwe, a veteran of the 1960 presidential campaign and head of candidate scheduling in '62, turned to me. "Odd Job"—his nickname for me because I would do any task that needed to be done—"we want you to be the lead advance man on this one."

I was sort of dumbfounded. I wanted to do it, but I was a realist. I had never advanced an event. I admitted that, telling Nick, "I have no idea what I'm supposed to do."

"I'll go out there with you," he said. "You'll learn. The main thing is to get people organized and make sure the event goes right." We went to the campaign office in the San Fernando Valley, which was being run by a very competent woman named Lenore Yeamans. Nick and Lenore held my hand but made me feel like I was in control. I started planning this major rally, feeling as if the fate of the entire campaign— maybe even the former vice president's political future—rested on my shoulders. What time will the candidate arrive? Who will speak? But mostly: How am I going to get several thousand people to show up?

The rally was being held in a shopping center parking lot. We erected a stage. We set up barriers, then created the illusion that this was going to be a larger than anticipated event with a huge crowd by having to extend the barriers as the crowd size grew. I was beside myself. I had no idea how many people would show up. I followed a campaign-issued how-to advance manual and, knowing their parents would come to see them perform, invited the Girl Scouts and the Boy Scouts to say the Pledge of Allegiance. I did everything I could think of to build that crowd. We announced it for 11:30 A.M., planning on the candidate's arrival at noon.

I never let any doubts surface. Whatever problems arose, we solved them. The result was one of the biggest rallies of the entire campaign. It was nearly flawless. People showed up early and stayed. When I met the candidate's car, thousands of people were waiting. It was a perfect day. Finally, I breathed. Unbeknownst to me, Nick told John Ehrlichman that this kid Chapin had done a phenomenal event in Panorama City, and Ehrlichman told Haldeman. In the Nixon world, nothing is more important than a successful event. Word spread among the campaign staff of the event's success. It meant I had paid attention to all the details, which, in advance work, is the essence of the job. The candidate radiates because of the work done before his arrival. To Nixon and Haldeman, crowd size mattered. My dad always said, "You make your own luck." So my diligence on the assignment paid a huge dividend in raising my profile, especially with Haldeman.

The campaign was going extremely well. I was convinced we would win. Only later did I come to believe that Richard Nixon had no real interest in being governor of California and he really never had a chance of winning. As some reporters had suggested, his intention was to use that position as a platform to launch another run for the presidency, again against Jack Kennedy, in 1964. In fact, the night before the election he gave a speech in which he made a Freudian slip: "Tomorrow, I'm hoping you elect me president of California."

I was confident, even though the polls never had Nixon ahead. I went to the planned Election Day party that night in the ballroom of the Beverly Hilton with another college roommate and TRG member, Mike Guhin, who eventually worked in the White House for Henry Kissinger on multilateral arms control and nuclear nonproliferation. While some of the veteran members of the campaign were prepared for the loss, I wasn't. When the results started coming in, I was stunned. Throughout the night I continued to believe that somehow we would pull it out. When it became obvious we had lost, I was devastated.

Early in the morning we heard rumblings that Nixon was coming down to speak in the hotel's ballroom. Suddenly an elevator door flew open and a group of people piled out. Bob Haldeman said later that he had tried to prevent Nixon from coming down, but the former vice president wouldn't be stopped. He had been up all night. I suspect he was in mild shock, and I have no doubt he'd had a couple of drinks. That's when he allowed his emotions to spill out in public. He was angry, furious. He was a tough, proud man who'd been battered by the media throughout his entire political career. Finally, his political career seemingly over, he felt free to express his feelings.

I was standing no more than ten feet from him as he made what was to become one of the most memorable speeches of his career. It was the first time in my life I had been present at a historical moment. I couldn't possibly have realized it at the time, but the sentiment of "them versus us" expressed at that moment eventually would become the key to the entire Watergate scandal. Forever after, Nixon would be pleased that he had finally let it all out, all his anger and frustrations. "Now that all the members of the press, I know, are so delighted that I lost, I'd just like to make [a statement] myself . . ." He concluded: "As I leave you, I want you to know, just think how much you're going to be missing. You don't have Nixon to kick around anymore. Because, gentlemen, this is my last press conference, and it will be one in which I have welcomed the opportunity to test wits with you. I have always respected you. I have sometimes disagreed with you. But unlike some people I have never canceled a subscription to a paper . . . I believe in reading what my opponents say, and I hope that what I have said today will at least make television, radio, and the press recognize that they have a right and a responsibility to report all the news and, second, recognize that they have a right and responsibility, if they're against a candidate, to give him the shaft; but also recognize if they give him the shaft, put one lonely reporter on the campaign who will report what the candidate says now and then. Thank you, gentlemen, and good day."

I wish I could remember what I thought about Richard Nixon at that moment, but I don't. I suspect I saw him through a distant prism. I was watching a remarkable figure making his last public appearance. Personally, I was devastated. I couldn't believe my candidate had lost.

I stood outside the hotel with several other staff members watching Nixon getting into the front seat of a car and being driven away.

We watched until the car disappeared. I had been up all night. I was exhausted. At eight thirty in the morning I got into my mother's black-and-white Ford convertible and spent the rest of the day driving around Los Angeles with tears streaming from my eyes.

Months later, I learned that the defeated candidate had returned briefly to his Trousdale Estates home, then disappeared. Vanished. No one, including Mrs. Nixon, knew where he had gone. His family and friends were frantic. There was great concern for his safety, but they managed to keep it out of the media. After a week of personal seclusion, he surfaced. Speculation was he had been at the beach house of LA TV personality Tom Duggan.

Most people assumed this marked the end of his political career. On November 11, five days after the election, ABC's Howard K. Smith hosted a news special titled "The Political Obituary of Richard Nixon." To add insult to injury, Alger Hiss, the Soviet spy who had been imprisoned as a result of Nixon having identified him, was brought on the show as a guest. In fact, for the former vice president, his political life briefly appeared to be over. But to paraphrase Mark Twain, reports of Nixon's political death were greatly exaggerated. The '62 defeat was only a temporary setback, a learning experience, a painful step on a long journey. Nixon was a man of resolve and resiliency.

An extraordinary period of American history was about to begin, and I was going to be right in the middle of it.

★ **2** ★

A LOVE OF POLITICS TAKES ROOT

Politics is _____.

One thing I've learned is that there are an infinite number of ways to fill in that blank. For me, initially, politics was a world of intrigue, competition, teamwork, and winning. It was not ideological then. Those people whom I met during that 1962 campaign, and what I learned from them, would shape my life for decades.

Soon after the '62 campaign I returned full-time to USC and my studies. One afternoon Herb Kalmbach called, essentially asking if I wanted a job working for Bob Haldeman, who was running the West Coast office of the J. Walter Thompson (JWT) advertising agency. Maybe Haldeman asked Herb to call so that if I said, "No," I wouldn't be turning him down. At that time the advertising industry was considered the hot place to work. It was the world of *Mad Men,* and JWT was the gold standard of the advertising world. Marketing was King Kong in that era, like investment banking would become, and tech and the biosciences are today. I leaped at the opportunity. I was assigned by Haldeman to the media department, and I worked there part-time until graduation in June 1963. Haldeman also hired my fraternity brother Ron Ziegler, who was two years older than me, to be his assistant.

I have often wondered why Bob Haldeman took me into his world. I suspect he saw evidence during the campaign that I was a hard worker, competent, ambitious, and willing to learn. Our politics and our values were similar. Maybe he saw a younger version of himself, and he believed he could bring out those abilities that I possessed. He became my mentor and eventually my closest friend. So much of the person I am today is because of Bob Haldeman. He shaped me.

Bob Haldeman was unbelievably intelligent—a member of Mensa—and an unfailingly decent man. He also was incredibly self-confident. His values were deeply rooted in his Christian Science beliefs and the power of truth and God. He and his mother, Betty, who had also worked on the '62 campaign as our office manager, both radiated that clarity, as does his wife, Jo.

He was not the cold, dispassionate figure depicted by the media. In fact, while he completely supported President Nixon and believed he was accomplishing great things, very early in our friendship he admitted to me that he had some qualms about Richard Nixon. Bob could be judgmental. I believe the reservations he held were simply because Nixon was a politician, and Bob didn't really care for the politician side of "political people." Of course, he advocated and believed in good government, but not in politicians. It was the phoniness of politicians that could turn him off.

Like Nixon, he did not believe in great displays of emotion. He laughed easily, but he never cried in front of me until one fateful day years later when at Camp David he had to tell me I was to leave the White House. I remember when his father died during the 1968 campaign. We were in New York. He came into my office and said matter-of-factly, "Dwight, my father just died." Then he said, "Let's go for a walk." We spent three or four hours walking aimlessly around the city while he reminisced about his father. He was very sad and trying to comprehend the loss of a parent. His words poured out, but he was more guarded with his emotions.

In the office he was considered to be a no-bullshit, stern boss, a man who demanded quality and was not shy about correcting people when he felt it was necessary; but with me he was always warm and open. It was only years later, after we had achieved our mutual dreams and reached the White House, that I saw this other side of him directed at me.

I loved working at JWT. One of my first assignments was to assist our Chicago office. One of our clients, the pet food company Ralston Purina, had been contacted by a woman who claimed her dog was perfect for a commercial because it could actually say the name of the company's dog food. They wanted me to check this out. I asked the woman to bring in her pet for a demonstration. Supposedly it had appeared on Johnny Carson's *Tonight Show,* but this was before the availability of video. I was nervous about this because I'd never interviewed an animal before. It was a small dog, slightly bigger than a Chihuahua, and not especially photogenic. She put it on our conference table. "You have to listen carefully," she warned me.

That was the first clue.

"Say 'Hello.' Say 'Hello.'" The dog barked. It sounded like a bark to me. "Hear that?" she exclaimed. I smiled wanly. "Say 'That's good,'" she ordered, although in this instance she repeated those words in sync with the dog's barks. A couple of office secretaries whom I had invited in to watch this audition confirmed my conclusion. That dog didn't talk.

Advertising was easy. It also was challenging and interesting. I worked with Ron Zeigler on the Disney account. Walt Disney was an old friend of the Haldeman family. Their Palm Springs homes were near each other. One afternoon Bob, Ron, and I went to the Burbank studio and Walt Disney—yes, the man himself—took us on a tour of a replica of the amusement park, Disney World, that he intended to build in Orlando, Florida. The model had been built on a soundstage. They hadn't even broken ground on the project, but Walt Disney spoke as if it already existed. Looking at the future with visionaries was a common experience in the world to which Bob Haldeman had introduced me.

Each day I learned a little more about Haldeman. After I had been working at JWT full-time for several months, Susie and I decided to get married. I felt I deserved a raise. I went into his office and explained the situation: I was working there full-time, doing a good job, getting married. I was confident Bob would agree with me. He sat across his desk from me listening intently. When I had finished my pitch, he said pleasantly, "So what you're really telling me is I'm not doing my job."

I immediately started backpedaling. "No, that's not what . . . I'm just saying that now that I'm here full-time I have added responsibilities . . ."

"No," he corrected. "Basically, you're saying that I'm not managing the office correctly." The idea that I had decided I had earned a raise did not sit well with him. I did not agree with his comment, but I got the message that was to form a foundation to our relationship: My duty was to perform; and when I did, his duty was to reward me for it. Haldeman Management 101.

It was an important insight into his managerial style. Maintaining control was important to him. While Bob would not have called himself a creative person, he was running an important office in America's most creative industry. He didn't create the advertising, but he understood it. At times he could improve it, but he knew how to run his shop and maintain its profitability while giving the creative people the flexibility they needed. He also understood fully the business of every client in the Los Angeles office and how and why they needed advertising. As with everything he did, it was a total involvement, always a deep understanding of "what makes the watch tick."

He chose to become my mentor. He picked me, and I was grateful to be picked. He advised me, trained me, protected me, and nurtured me. I had a need to be liked, to be respected, and he understood that. He began creating opportunities for us to meet and talk. We would have lunch or an early dinner after work and eventually we would go down to his in-laws' house on Balboa Island, about an hour from the office. This was not the officious, buttoned-down Bob Haldeman who was later described by the media as running the White House with an iron fist. We'd sit on the beach sharing a big bowl of popcorn, drinking Cokes or beer, sailing on his Sunfish and talking. What began as brief discussions evolved over months into hours upon hours of long discussions. He would speak to me as if I were a management consultant.

At first it was just me listening, then he began asking my opinions, and gradually I became more comfortable and more conversant. He'd use me as his sounding board. We would discuss all aspects of the office, including strategy, management, and personnel. He never held back, telling me about people getting promoted or fired, or of coming changes. Eventually he began asking my opinions about things far beyond my junior management position. I sort of assumed that my thoughts were valuable to him because I had a good, logical mind and no vested interest in the outcome. More important, he would thank me for my insights. He would tell me my advice was helpful, useful, and that added greatly to the relationship. My confidence zoomed. He would talk through issues with me, but his closing line would often be, "Don't tell Ziegler."

Don't tell Ziegler. That certainly made me feel special, yet awkward. It was really unfair. Ron was a fraternity brother and friend. When something started bubbling in the office, Ron would ask me if I knew anything about it. I never lied. I would reply, "I'm not supposed to get into that," which would infuriate Ziegler. Bob purposely pitted us against each other. I don't know why. I realized that and I could handle it. Ron understood it too but, understandably, he had a more difficult time accepting it.

My conversations with Haldeman always had a focus on politics. He quickly figured out I shared his passion for "all things political." Eventually we spent far more time discussing American politics than business. One of the first gifts he gave me was a copy of Machiavelli's *The Prince*. "If you're going to be in politics," he inscribed it, "you have to read this book." How prophetic this gift. Bob's most intriguing and interesting conversations were always about Richard Nixon. After his defeat in the 1962 campaign, Nixon had moved back east into an apartment on Fifth Avenue in New York City, but Haldeman remained in continuous contact with him. Even at that lowest point, after Nixon had experienced two devastating defeats, Bob told me that he felt "the former vice president" was determined to run for the presidency again.

I was twenty-two years old, a kid, thrilled and riveted by this inside information. Other than that perfunctory meeting in our campaign office, I had never spoken with Nixon. I'd never spent a moment alone with him. And yet Bob was bringing him to life for me. He was painting a picture for me of a fascinating, accomplished, sometimes difficult man. A man of great potential but with very human flaws who, Bob believed, was destined to lead the nation. Through Bob I began meeting other people who clearly were in the Nixon decision-making universe, including Bob Finch, who had served as the vice president's aide in the Eisenhower years; and Murray Chotiner, who had been a key advisor since Nixon's 1946 congressional campaign.

At 4:00 P.M. the afternoon of August 18, 1963, Susie and I were married in the garden of her family's home in Hope Ranch, outside of Santa Barbara, California. We had known and dated each other since the ninth grade, and virtually everyone expected us to marry. The wedding was attended by all of our family and friends. My uncle B. R. Chapin and aunt Nan even brought my five cousins by van on a car-train from Toronto, Canada. It was a happy, joyous wedding. I was set at JWT and Susie was teaching second grade in a Reseda public school. We had no idea where life was about to take us, but we were in it together.

There was strong speculation that Nixon wanted a 1964 rematch against Kennedy. While in history Kennedy has become almost legendary, at that time he was politically vulnerable. That discussion ended on November 22, 1963. I was working on the production of a fundraising brochure for Republican Associates, a support group for Republican candidates, when Haldeman's secretary, Dorothy, opened the conference room door and said emotionally, "President Kennedy's been shot."

Bob was away. Dorothy and I went into his corner office and watched, with disbelief, the news on his small black-and-white television. We stayed there for hours. An image I will never forget was glancing out his window, down Wilshire Boulevard, as one by one the flags atop each building were lowered to half-mast.

But while the nation was still in mourning, journalists had already begun speculating on the political impact of this tragedy. No one had any idea how the country would respond to Lyndon Johnson, or how strongly Americans would embrace the growing myth of Kennedy's "Camelot."

A lot of discussions took place. Nixon called Bob and a select group of insiders for a secret summit in New York. Bob shared the details from that "secret" meeting with me. Within weeks Nixon had decided he would not challenge Johnson, leaving a clear path to the Republican nomination for Barry Goldwater, the superhero of the growing conservative wing of the Republican Party. Bob laid it out for me: In winning the California Republican gubernatorial nomination in 1962, Nixon had defeated a popular conservative candidate, a man named Joe Shell. That victory had cost him the support of conservatives. Few men were better at political calculations than Richard Nixon. He realized he could rebuild that trust, which he would need eventually, by backing Goldwater without reservation. He also was certain that the Goldwater campaign, especially in light of President Johnson's popularity after the Kennedy assassination, was going to be a train wreck, which would serve his purpose by eliminating a formidable future opponent.

As we watched from Los Angeles, Nixon worked tirelessly for Goldwater. No one could doubt his commitment. The 1964 Republican National Convention was held in San Francisco. Haldeman invited me to attend, without giving me any specific assignments. On the Sunday afternoon before the convention officially opened, Nixon held a reception at the St. Francis Hotel. All of those state delegates who had worked so hard on the previous 1960 Nixon vs. Kennedy campaign were invited. Officially it was a "Dick and Pat Nixon want to thank you for your efforts on their behalf" event. But in fact, it was the beginning of Richard Nixon's quest for the 1968 nomination. Several hundred delegates showed up to see the Nixons once again. It was a smashing success.

That was the first time I worked directly for Richard Nixon. I was stationed at the head of the receiving line, next to Mr. Nixon; Mrs. Nixon was on his other side. As each person reached me, I would introduce myself and shake hands. In turn they would introduce themselves to me, loudly enough for the seemingly distracted Nixon to hear, enabling him to greet each guest personally, as if he were a close friend—as many of them were.

It was a simple job, but it put me physically right next to Nixon. None of the guests knew who I was, but they likely made a mental note that I must have some connection to him to have been given that assignment. It was the beginning of my public connection to Richard Nixon and the first small step toward his being comfortable with me by his side.

The following Tuesday afternoon Nixon was scheduled to address the convention in the Cow Palace. Haldeman wanted me to go with him and be available if I was needed. We all squeezed into a car. Bob and I were in the front seat with the driver. Nixon, Bob Finch, and Paul Keyes, the great comedy writer and producer of the popular show *Laugh-In,* crammed into the back. My job when we got to the convention was to escort Nixon from the holding room to the backstage area, from which he would go to the podium. Once again it was a minor assignment, a job anyone could do. As long as we didn't get lost on the way, I would be successful. But what I didn't realize was that Bob had a plan. Bob generally had a reason for everything he did. He wanted me to be with Nixon. He wanted Nixon to recognize me, to be comfortable with me, to trust me to do my job. I knew my place: At that time it was wherever Bob Haldeman told me I was supposed to be.

Nixon was warmly greeted. The conservatives controlling the convention wanted to make it obvious that they recognized and appreciated his efforts. He gave a good speech, loyally extolling Barry Goldwater and the Republican Party platform. Then we packed back into the car and returned to the hotel laughing out loud, with tears streaming from our eyes, as Paul Keyes entertained us with joke after joke, mostly at Goldwater's expense. Nixon kept repeating that soon-to-be famous line from Goldwater's speech, "Extremism in the defense of liberty is no vice. And moderation in the pursuit of justice is no virtue." Nixon was predicting that the hard-line rhetoric would be the news lead and it would cause Goldwater problems with the broader political center of the electorate. As usual, Nixon's instincts were right.

Although I enjoyed working with Haldeman at JWT, I wasn't satisfied. I had always thrived on challenges, and my job at the agency had become repetitive. So when I was offered a job in the sales department of the local ABC-TV affiliate, at more than double my current salary and with a chance for substantially more in commissions, I was very interested. Susie had given birth to our daughter, Kimberly, and we certainly could have used the additional money. I immediately told Bob that ABC had approached me. He asked only that, before I made my final decision, I discuss it with him.

When we finally sat down by the pool in the backyard of his Hancock Park home in Los Angeles, I didn't think there was much he could do to make me change my mind. The salary ABC was offering would make a significant difference for Susie and me, and the prospect of getting involved in television was enticing. But Bob Haldeman had a plan.

Bob didn't raise his voice, or argue or plead. That was never his style. Instead, after I had told him the details of ABC's offer, he said, "I've been in touch with our human resources team in New York. So that you can really learn the advertising business, we'll move you, Susie, and Kimberly to New York. There is no better place to learn the business than New York." Bob had started his career there, commuting into Manhattan from Riverside, Connecticut, and had enjoyed the experience. The move came with a 20 percent raise and a commitment that, after two years, we would move back to California. Normally J. Walter Thompson required account rep applicants to have an MBA, but he had convinced them that my work at JWT in LA was the equivalent of going to graduate school. In fact, in the perfunctory application I had to fill out (i.e., that I could operate a typewriter, calculator, and film projector), I noted: "Mr. H. R. Haldeman suggested I consider advertising as a possible career."

All of this had been going on without my knowledge. It was incredibly flattering. But then he added the real clincher to his New York plan for us. "It looks like the old man"—Haldeman usually referred to Nixon as "the old man"—"is going to gear up for the '68 presidential race. With Nixon now in New York, we can get you more exposure to him, so you'll be able to work on that campaign." He didn't say "work with me on the campaign," but I knew that's what he meant. Bob had a pad on his lap, and he helped me write down the pros and cons of the two offers. At ABC there would be "no opportunity for extracurricular activities"—working for a presidential candidate, for example. I would be peddling a lousy product and get "no intellectual stimulation"; and worse, there would be "no prestige, visibility, or community stature."

Then he ran the numbers: two pages of long columns in which he somehow managed to show me that, even though ABC would be paying me a higher salary, if I stayed at Thompson I would end up netting $1,088 more a year. I can't explain it today, but somehow it made sense to me then. The bottom line: I opted for the career experience that J. Walter Thompson offered me.

When I think back to that day I find myself smiling. Only Bob Haldeman could make the lesser of two offers sound more appealing. And I couldn't turn down the long-range prospect of working for Nixon in a presidential campaign. As I prepared to leave Los Angeles in September 1965, I wrote to Bob: "I am very much aware of how fortunate I have been to have begun my career under your watchful eyes . . . I admire so many of your qualities and through my association with you . . . it seems my mind has improved and my ability to reason is keener."

In response, he wrote: "I told you that there would be a place for you in anything I do and anyplace I go. I meant that literally . . . I feel that you and I complement each other to a remarkable degree—and the two of us as a team were considerably stronger than that of each of us separately."

As Bob had suggested, Susie, Kimberly, and I moved to Cos Cob, Connecticut, and I entered JWT's exclusive training program. I was assigned to the Scott Paper account, specifically to a new product, Cut-Rite plastic sandwich bags. The objective was to introduce plastic bags to the public through advertising and promotion. Bob had provided a list of people he knew in the New York office whom I should contact, and he reminded me, "Don't try to be anything but yourself as you start opening the many new doors in this challenging phase of your career."

Haldeman and I were three thousand miles apart, but in so many ways we were closer than ever. I never questioned why he had taken such an interest in my life. There was no reason to. But as anyone who has ever had a powerful mentor would understand, knowing he was there provided a real sense of security.

New York was hard—not the job, but the life. I became a daily commuter on the New Haven train line, hating every minute of it. I was just another part of the herd, one of millions of people being processed through the system, from standing in the freezing cold on the Cos Cob train platform in the winter to sweating in the crowded, non-air-conditioned cars in the summer, then squeezing into an elevator that took me to my cubicle at the JWT office. It was all very foreign to me. Growing up in Kansas and in California I had become accustomed to open spaces and to commuting in my own car. In New York, masses of people were rushing and pushing their way through life in a manner to which I never aspired.

Haldeman would come to New York on business regularly and we would meet for dinner. Soon after Susie and I were settled, he suggested I call Richard Nixon's secretary and office manager, Rose Mary Woods, and volunteer. It was that general: Just volunteer. They'll find something for you to do. Rose had been with Nixon since she joined his congressional staff in 1951, and, as I was to learn, she was extraordinarily protective of him. She was almost a member of the Nixon family. She was very close to Mrs. Nixon and their two daughters, Tricia and Julie. In fact, the girls would refer to her as "Aunt Rose."

Nixon was a private citizen, a very private citizen for such a well-known public figure. He was keeping a relatively low profile, working as a senior partner at the law firm of Nixon, Mudge, Rose, Guthrie & Alexander. In 1967 the firm added another senior named partner, Mitchell—the "Mitchell" being John Mitchell, who would later become his attorney general. I began going to the office at 20 Broad Street after work two or three evenings a week. Also working in that office, in addition to Rose Woods, were Pat Buchanan and a young woman named Shelley Scarney, who would later become Mrs. Buchanan. Mrs. Nixon also had a desk there.

I began working for Richard Nixon by writing responses to his mail, piles of mail. Whether it was a letter of support hoping he would run for the presidency in 1968, or a question or a comment on LBJ and Democratic policies, every letter got a friendly response. The letters would be signed by Rose as Mr. Nixon's secretary or, on occasion, she would sign his name. (Rose learned to do a very good Richard Nixon signature.) The office was run like a congressional operation, dutifully making "personal" contact with constituents and Nixon insisting that every single letter get a personal response.

The person tutoring me on how to respond to the letters was none other than Mrs. Nixon. We worked in a small conference room two or three floors down from Mr. Nixon's office where all the incoming mail was handled, both of us typing responses. I learned there that Pat Nixon was nothing like the indifferent political wife standing quietly in the background, as she was often pictured to be. She was a strong woman with terrific political instincts. At times she was the force pushing "Dick," as she always referred to him. Pat Nixon was a fighter, and she believed deeply in her husband. In 1952, for example, after Dwight Eisenhower had selected Nixon as his running mate, there was an effort to remove him from the ticket because of the scandal resulting from a phony charge that he had a political slush-fund. Nixon decided to give a national television speech, the "Checkers speech," to put the matter to rest. Tom Dewey, a former Republican governor of New York and unsuccessful presidential candidate, called Nixon and suggested that if the response to Nixon's speech wasn't sufficiently supportive he should resign and withdraw for the good of the party and let Eisenhower pick somebody else. Nixon had even dictated a withdrawal telegram. Murray Chotiner tore it up. Pat Nixon stepped in to support Chotiner, telling her husband, "We're not going to be pushed around like this." She put some backbone into the decision-making process, which eventually led to Nixon giving his historic "Checkers speech" and remaining on the ticket. Mrs. Nixon didn't always win. After the contested results in the 1960 election, I learned she wanted to fight back rather than concede. She truly believed, to her core, that Chicago Mayor Richard Daley had conspired with the Kennedy campaign to steal the 1960 election from Nixon. There were also egregious abuses in Texas where LBJ had a record of manufacturing "landslides" out of thin air, which was where LBJ got his nickname, "Landslide Johnson."

History has underrated both Pat Nixon's intelligence and her political instincts. She was a very smart woman, and her husband often turned to her for advice. While the Nixons rarely showed affection in public, from my vantage point they had a loving, mutually supportive marriage. The concept of Pat Nixon sitting quietly in the background just isn't accurate.

I enjoyed working with her, even though we were together in a small room and she liked to smoke. She was somewhat formal. When she came to the office, she always wore a dress and her hair was coiffed. She was very warm and always very nice to me. We'd talk about my family, about how Susie was adjusting to East Coast living, about our daughters. (Everyone in the office knew Susie was expecting our second child, and they were excited for us.) We would also chat about life in Connecticut and about my work at JWT. There was always a certain distance between us. We both knew my place.

Gradually we got to know each other better and, most important, she began to trust me. I suspect she mentioned my commitment and my capabilities to Mr. Nixon, which was how I got on his radar. In gaining acceptance with this prominent family, no single factor was more important than trust. Mrs. Nixon trusted me.

While officially this was a law office and Nixon was earning his living as a practicing attorney, it actually was headquarters for an as yet undetermined campaign. I had no doubt Nixon wanted to run for the presidency again, believing he could provide the critical leadership the country needed, especially in foreign policy. That's why Nixon intended to run again, and Pat Nixon was encouraging that, but he also was a realist. The question was timing. An opening had not yet appeared. President Lyndon Johnson had taken some bold steps: passing a major civil rights bill, instigating welfare reform, and expanding our country's role in the Vietnam War. In 1964, having succeeded JFK and launched the Great Society legislation, LBJ was politically very formidable. By 1965 he was becoming controversial. As the country grew more divided because of the Vietnam War, he still retained substantial political support. Running against him in 1968 would have been a difficult challenge. If there was an emerging favorite for the Republican nomination, it was probably the popular governor of California, Ronald Reagan. The charismatic former movie star had repackaged and moderated some of the more radical Goldwater language in an attempt to find a niche between the conservative and the more centrist wings of the party.

My volunteer work was rewarded with the opportunity to do even more volunteer work. Welcome to politics. In the approach to the 1966 midterm elections, Republican candidates across the country were inviting Richard Nixon to campaign for them. Barry Goldwater and his conservative movement had been soundly repudiated by voters in 1964, and few candidates wanted to be associated with him. Nixon, on the other hand, remained popular, including within the Goldwater faction, and could draw both large crowds and deep-pocketed contributors. So Nixon crisscrossed the country, piling up political IOUs.

Whatever was happening, I wanted to be part of it. Politics was far more exciting than sandwich bags. I reached out to Bob, asking for advice: "I would like to establish myself as a trouper for Nixon's cause." But whether it was with Nixon or not, I wanted to be involved. "How does he feel about Rocky?" I asked Bob. "Rocky" was New York Governor Nelson Rockefeller, who also was maneuvering for the '68

Republican nomination and whom I was thinking of supporting. That naive flirtation of an idea was quickly discarded, as Bob knocked some sense into me immediately. He felt that because I was helping out at the law firm and their reliance and trust in me then, in no way did I belong in the Rockefeller orbit, let alone should I even consider it. He was right. I was acting solely in an opportunistic way, and that Rockefeller thought never entered my mind again.

In 1966, I was invited to work as an advance man for Nixon, to help stage some events where he would appear. I arranged with JWT to utilize all my vacation time on Fridays and Mondays through the campaign season. On those days, added to Saturday and Sunday, I would work for the Republican Party—for Nixon, actually. In September, the Nixon team held a two-day advance man training school run by John Whitaker, another former 1960 advance man and Nixon loyalist. It was held in New York at the Statler Hilton hotel. Officially this was known as an Ohio Art Company sales meeting, because W. C. Killgallon, the owner of that company and a Nixon supporter, paid some of the bills. Mr. Killgallon's son Bill was one of our new advance men and he oversaw all the arrangements. However, the Nixon team did not want the media to know about it—because if it was known publicly that Nixon was putting together a campaign staff, including advance people, then sure as hell he was running for the Republican nomination. Nixon was not ready to make that commitment. It was much too soon, so our cover was the Ohio Art Company.

The manual we used was an edited version of the "Advance Man Manual," written by Haldeman for Nixon's 1960 campaign when he had been chief advance man. The manual was based on the strategies developed by the incredibly successful Billy Graham crusades. Haldeman had visited Graham's operation in Montreat, North Carolina, to learn how large rallies were organized, promoted, and executed in large cities. Bob then adapted those practices to Nixon's campaign. The result was the essential guidebook on how to smoothly arrange and carry out a candidate's appearances.

A good advance man, we were taught, has to take control from the local leaders on the ground. He has to gently sell them on the operating style of our candidate. We didn't have a candidate; we had Mr. Nixon coming in to help their candidate. And if they wanted that help, there were rules that had to be followed. For example, Mr. Nixon was not going to sit through an entire dinner. Doing the job correctly required attention to a thousand minor details while being creative enough to instantly solve the unexpected problems that popped up, doing it all without ruffling any feathers or visibly sweating.

The first morning of the advance school, Nixon gave a brief but enthusiastic speech, telling us this election was a tremendous opportunity for the Republicans to pick up several House seats. He was so good at making each of us feel we were playing a significant role in a great movement that would affect the entire country. That was an aspect of Richard Nixon's complex personality. While he could be awkward in a one-on-one situation, in a group he could make you feel as if he was relating only to you.

The first appearance I advanced by myself took place in Waterville, Maine, a small city with a population of about fifteen thousand people on the west bank of the Kennebec River. While I was setting up, President Lyndon Johnson was in the Philippines, in Manila. At a press conference there he had responded somewhat angrily to remarks Nixon had made about the conduct of the Vietnam War. Johnson had referred to Nixon as "a chronic campaigner." It was a political mistake by Johnson, because it presented a wonderful opportunity for Nixon to get national TV time. I was at the Waterville airport, waiting for Nixon's plane to arrive, when CBS correspondent Mike Wallace called. I took a deep breath. Mike Wallace? The closest I had ever come to a network correspondent was crawling under their desks at the Democratic Convention in 1960. After introducing himself, Mr. Wallace told me he was ready to fly to Maine to interview Mr. Nixon when his plane landed. He was essentially asking me to hold Nixon at the airport until he got there.

What he didn't know was that Nixon was still in New York, at LaGuardia Airport, because his flight had been delayed. I didn't know what to do, so I followed the first rule of advancing: Don't panic. I called John Whitaker, who quickly got back to me. Nixon would talk to Wallace. I should go ahead and make the arrangements.

Wallace rented a Learjet and arrived in Waterville before Nixon. I took him to an unoccupied room and his crew began setting up. Just as they finished, Nixon arrived, and I escorted him into the room to meet Wallace. It all worked as smoothly as if I had done it all before. Nixon was pleased with the way it turned out, and I was invited to fly with him to his next appearance, in New Hampshire. This was my first flight on a campaign plane. I sat quietly and watched and listened, and I knew I wanted to be part of it.

Bob flew in late on Election Day in 1966 and invited me to join the Nixon team to watch the returns that night. Nixon was there. At that point he was getting used to seeing me around. We were in a hotel room—not a suite, just a room—sitting on two queen beds watching the results on TV. Pat Buchanan and two Nixon law firm partners, Len Garment and John Sears, were with us, along with Peter Flanigan, an investment banker and fundraiser. I was watching a master politician at work, up close. Each time it was announced that a Republican had won his election, Nixon would immediately call him to offer congratulations. He was very smooth on the phone—which was sincere. He loved politics, just loved it, and there was no feeling quite like sharing in an election victory. "I remember how that crowd cheered you," Nixon would tell the winner—thus sealing the reminder that he had played a role in the victory being celebrated. He also was relentlessly building the personal relationships that would become vital in the next election cycle. I remember hearing a lot of laughter that night.

That campaign season introduced the "New Nixon" to America. This was an upbeat, optimistic, experienced former vice president, a man who was comfortable with world leaders and understood the complexities of foreign relations. A man capable of getting this country out of the mess in Vietnam that the Democrats had gotten us into.

The story within the story of the 1966 off-year elections was remarkable. Nixon and John Sears, his expert on congressional districts, had studied the map to determine where Republicans could win and how they would. They understood the issues and devised a recovery approach for the GOP. Nixon campaigned harder day in and day out than most of the candidates on the ballots. The year 1966 was his proving ground. Since Nixon lost the presidency in 1960 and the California governorship in 1962, the biggest problem he faced was being stuck with the label "loser." The 1966 elections played a vital part in his "I am a winner" theme in preparation for the 1968 campaign.

It worked. The Republicans did well in the off-year elections, and Nixon had successfully reestablished himself as a viable candidate for the 1968 nomination. I also had done my job efficiently, without any screwups, and people in the Nixon orbit now knew my name. Thank you, Bob. He was in my corner even when I didn't know I had a corner.

Bob was in New York the next month, December 1966. We had dinner and he had big news. "You are going to get a call from Rose to go down and see the old man," he told me. "He wants to talk to you about being his personal aide for the campaign."

Everything I had done since working in that 1962 campaign had added up to this. I didn't know what the duties of a personal aide (which has now become popularly known as a "body man") entailed, but certainly I was excited about the opportunity.

Rose Woods called me in mid-January to tell me "the Boss" wanted to meet with me. That's what she called him, "the Boss." We met in his law office in the early evening. I knew what it was about, and I was very nervous. This was potentially a life-changing meeting. Pat Buchanan was there. As I waited, Pat and I spoke, and Rose asked me about Susie and the girls. Finally I was called into his office.

Nixon was sitting behind his desk. We shook hands, and I sat down. There was no preamble, no small talk. To my surprise, he never asked me if I wanted to work for him or even explained the job. Instead, he told me what we would be doing. "I think I'm headed toward running for the presidency. What we'll be doing is traveling around the country, meeting people." At most the meeting lasted ten minutes. He offered no details, not even when I would start or what my duties might be. From his tone it seemed he just assumed I was aboard with the plan. It was likely that Bob and Nixon had arranged the whole thing before I was ever invited to meet with him. As I left, Rose told me she would be in touch, with no hint of when.

I called Bob immediately. Nixon had never mentioned any salary, I told him. He didn't even tell me if I had the job or even asked if I wanted the job. He didn't say anything about when I would start, what I would do. I was feeling upset because my expectations had not matched anything I'd been told in that meeting. Bob let me get it all out, then said knowingly, "Relax. It'll all work out."

Leaving what was evolving into a promising career in advertising for an undefined job with a politician claiming to be unsure about his future didn't seem like the wisest choice for a young man with a family, but I never hesitated. It was what I wanted to do. Susie was supportive, although she knew I had already made up my mind. I don't know what I would have done if she had taken a stand against it.

My father, always the responsible parent, cautioned me to be careful. "You're burning an important bridge. Nixon might not run. Or if he does, he might lose." My father had worked for the same company for more than three decades. By nature he was conservative, a company man. I'm not quite sure he understood or agreed with my decision. But I was going with the flow. The course was set.

In January Bob laid out the details. I would begin work in March. My salary would be $5,200 a year, less than I was making at J. Walter Thompson. I would share an office with Rose and Pat Buchanan. "Wait until February before you give notice," Bob advised me.

Apparently, it had taken several weeks to figure out exactly how I was going to be paid. There are very specific laws about campaign financing, and for reasons I never understood, I could not be a political employee, nor could I work for the law firm. Eventually Nixon's close friend and financial supporter Bob Abplanalp, who'd made his fortune from inventing the aerosol valve, paid my salary through his advertising agency, Feely and Wheeler. How that accounting worked I never knew; it was another of the great mysteries of politics.

March 1, 1967, was my first day as former Vice President Richard Nixon's personal aide. I was given my own desk at the law firm, sharing a room with Rose Woods and Pat Buchanan. Actually, I took over Mrs. Nixon's desk. There were five file cabinets, each five drawers high, in front of Buchanan's desk. These cabinets contained the DNA of a political campaign. They were filled with information and letters from key supporters and donors. Information about any prominent American who had touched the Nixon universe was in those cabinets. My very first assignment was to learn the names of all the people in those files, and the way I did that was to do all the filing, which enabled me to become acquainted with every name in the cabinets.

What was going on? I was furious. I expected to be in politics, and instead I was filing papers for Rose Mary Woods. I barely saw Nixon for more than a few seconds. This went on for a couple of months. It turned out, though, to be ingenious. Richard Nixon always believed that one important key to political success is inclusion. Nixon wanted every supporter and friend to have a role in the campaign. He was adamant on this subject. The people whose names were in those cabinets eventually would play significant roles in the campaign and later in the administration. Filing and learning the names and relationships was my introduction to many people who would populate my world for the next decade.

★ **3** ★

GROWING INTO THE JOB

Even as I got physically closer to Richard Nixon, he remained a distant and elusive figure. He was practiced at revealing very little of himself. After I'd become familiar with those files, Rose began sending me into his office to discuss his upcoming events. I was learning how to make arrangements and set up a schedule. I was learning the very particular rules: no dinners, no dancing, no hats. (No hats? On a trip to Jerusalem he visited the Wailing Wall. As was customary at that site, he had to wear a black Homburg. There was no way to avoid it. As he knew, the photos of him looking uncomfortable in that hat would appear in newspapers around the world.) I learned how to deal with people in receiving lines, what notes to take, what to pass along to another staff member, how to seemingly relate personally to a great number of people at the same time. These were all the lessons Richard Nixon had perfected during more than two decades of political life. People at that time didn't have cell phones, let alone cell phones with cameras. But, using their cameras, I took hundreds, probably thousands, of pictures of eager supporters with Nixon.

Included in the advice Haldeman gave me was to be completely honest with the old man. "If he asks you something to which you don't know the answer, don't try to bullshit him. Don't even think about going down that path. The right answer is, 'Sir, I don't know, but I'll find out.' He doesn't mind if you don't know, and he likes the fact that you'll find out. What he doesn't like is being surprised to find out your answer was not correct." It may sound rinky-dink, but with Richard Nixon, if you contrived a story, you were finished. Eventually I think he knew I was a truth-teller. I do remember that there were many times over the years when I had to say, "Sir, I don't know, but I'll find out."

Nixon trained me to be the person he needed me to be. He never turned over to anyone, not even Rose Woods, complete authorization to plan his events or trips. He was always involved in the planning. As I learned very quickly, he controlled the reins and held them tightly. It made sense. Years of experience had taught him how to emphasize his strengths and downplay his weaknesses. I can hear him: "Dwight, it says here on the schedule that we'll arrive at dinner at six thirty. I don't do dinners. We'll go in for dessert, and I'll make my speech. Make sure that I'm introduced in one minute—one minute, do you understand?" We became very good at reading each other. He could tell by looking at me if I got it, and I was learning to read him too. Sometimes I would hear: "Dwight, you don't understand, do you?" That was a hard one. But if he was right and I didn't understand the instruction, I just had to say so. I hated hearing "You don't understand," usually said with frustration on his part.

When I began traveling regularly with him, I learned more rules. My job on the road was to be prepared to do anything at any time. Before each trip Rose gave me as much as two hundred dollars in cash. I was told it was unseemly for Nixon to take out his wallet. That was my job, and I was cautioned to leave an appropriate tip when necessary—but not an excessive tip. I also carried Nixon's sleeping pills, which he took on a regular basis. Rose counted those pills carefully, keeping track of how many she gave me and how many I gave back to her when we returned. While Nixon always packed his own suitcase, I carried a sunlamp and his goggles with me. After the debacle of his pale and washed-out appearance in the 1960 debates, Nixon had become focused on how television made him look. This was underscored by Nixon knowing that in the first 1960 debate, those people who had heard him on the radio thought he had won, while those who saw him on television thought he had lost.

The camera did not love him. Even if he shaved immediately before a broadcast, his translucent skin made him look haggard. When possible, he would spend time tanning in the sun at his close friend Bebe Rebozo's home in Key Biscayne, Florida. When we were on the road in the winter, he used that sunlamp every day. My job was to make certain we had it with us and to religiously set it up.

I was, wrote the *Washington Post,* "responsible for getting Nixon up in the morning, putting him to bed at night, and looking after his wardrobe, meals, and schedule." The *Post* was mostly accurate, and I considered it all a significant responsibility, not menial staff work. My understanding of the "you have to work your way up" attitude ended up serving me well.

We spent countless hours together, and while I learned his needs and his habits, it was difficult to get beyond that shell that Nixon wanted to show to the world. I didn't push him at all. I didn't pry. I just let the relationship mature. But every once in a while, he would expose a little piece of himself. There was one memorable flight that has proven over time to have been very impactful on me. We were flying across the country. We were sitting together in first class. He was next to the window. He liked sitting inside because my presence formed a barrier between him and people who wanted to speak with him, take a picture or get an autograph. We had finished eating and were talking. He was in somewhat of a reflective mood. We were discussing something about education and life, and he said to me, "Dwight, as you go through life, just always remember the key thing is keeping your learning curve vertical." It was personal advice, as close to giving me that advice as he would get. Never stop learning, was what he meant. He lived that in his own life. I have always remembered it and have always considered it to be wise counsel.

I grew into the job. One stormy afternoon we were on an Eastern Airlines shuttle flight from D.C. to New York. We taxied to the end of the runway and stopped there, pounded by buckets of rain. The pilot announced that, because of the weather, we couldn't take off; in fact, we might be sitting there for more than an hour. The pilot apologized and asked everyone to remain seated. Nixon turned to me and said, "Get me off this plane."

Get me off this plane? I had heard what the pilot said, but I unbuckled my seatbelt and stood up. The stewardess immediately repeated the pilot's request that we remain seated, adding that the plane might move suddenly. I walked right up the aisle to the front and told the flight attendant, "Mr. Nixon is scheduled to address a group at the United Nations, and he has to get to a telephone. We have to get off this plane."

The UN? I have no idea where that came from, but I felt sincere when I made it up. "Let me speak to the captain," she said. A few minutes later she returned to our seats. "We're going to take you back to the terminal," she said.

The pilot made an announcement that we would be returning to the terminal but would not lose our place in the takeoff line. But when we got up to leave the plane, several people actually hissed at us. To me that was the sound of success.

I made mistakes, and when I did, Nixon corrected me. We went to the Mayflower Hotel and checked back into the suite we had checked out of two hours before. He told me, "I want to speak to Ev Dirksen." Everett Dirksen was a powerful Republican senator from Illinois and a good Nixon friend. As the minority leader of the Senate, he had great sway in the Republican Party. Rose Mary Woods had put together an elaborate phonebook, with contact information for key people around the country. As I began calling Dirksen's office, Nixon went into the restroom. Dirksen wasn't in his office. I left a message with his secretary and hung up. When Nixon came back, I told him Senator Dirksen wasn't there. "So you hung up?" he asked, almost incredulously. I nodded. I mean, what else was I going to do? "Dwight, let me tell you something." He shook an index finger at me, meaning I should pay attention. "It's more important I talk to Dirksen's secretary than to him. If I talk to his secretary, and I'm nice to her, she'll tell everybody around the Capitol. They'll all know it. If I talk to Ev, he's the only one who'll know it and he won't tell a damned soul." Lesson: Be especially nice to staffers. It is more important that Nixon talk to the staff, because they talk, gossip, and spread the word.

When we weren't on the road, I would work out of the law office or the Nixons' Fifth Avenue apartment. Richard Nixon had been a talented and successful lawyer. He had even argued an important privacy case in front of the Supreme Court, based on a home invasion that had become the basis of the Humphrey Bogart movie *The Desperate Hours*. But by this time he was moving into campaign mode. Many of the other attorneys working at the firm were also working on the campaign on a part-time basis. John Mitchell had the office next to Nixon's and was becoming his most important advisor. Mitchell was an expert on financing municipal bond projects and had worked for years with key governors, mayors, and city and state politicians in the 1968 primary battle states. Mitchell's connections were worth "political gold." That was one reason Nixon had helped to attract him to becoming the newest named partner in the firm.

Len Garment, a Nixon law partner; Ray Price, a former newspaper editorial writer who would become Nixon's chief speechwriter; and Bill Safire, a public relations professional who would also become a White House speechwriter, were of the liberal-moderate persuasion. Those three pulled, or anchored, Nixon into the political center, serving as a counterbalance to Pat Buchanan, who was pulling hard from the right. Buchanan had great sway. He was incredibly intelligent, grounding his views in solid conservative ideology, and Nixon respected him. Buchanan was very up front with Nixon. One never had to wonder where he stood on anything. But, to his credit and advantage, what Nixon did from the outset was surround himself with staff and advisors holding a variety of different views.

John Sears may have been the smartest of them all, though, and he was an expert on the needs and trends of every congressional district in the country. Years later, as manager of Ronald Reagan's campaign for the presidency in 1980, John would be fired. He thought he was smarter than Nancy Reagan—not a wise position to have taken with candidate Reagan.

In the Nixons' apartment at 810 Fifth Avenue, I had a small desk in a walk-in closet. That gave me a place to hang out and allowed me at the end of the day to leave my work there and close the door. Among my responsibilities, when I was there, was to go down to the lobby to greet visitors and bring them up. Then when their allotted time was over, I was to politely barge in and tell Nixon that his next appointment was there or that he had a call. It was not unusual for Nixon to say, "Dwight, I want you to tell Rose . . ." and he would give me a follow-up assignment related to the guest I was about to usher out. I was the escape valve. We had many techniques to make a guest believe they were receiving very special treatment. That became another area of my expertise. I'd say, "Your next appointment is here, sir," and then I would manage the follow-up instructions related to what Nixon and the guest had been discussing. Nixon always cared about how people were treated. He knew that little things mattered. The bigger and more prominent the person was, the more the little things they did mattered to those they encountered. Nixon taught me this political truism.

Mrs. Nixon was always very nice to me. She would come to their guest room where my tiny closet office was located and ask, "Can I make you a sandwich, Dwight? You have to eat." Not wanting to impose on her, I would try to say no, but she would insist. She'd take me into the kitchen and make me a peanut butter and jelly sandwich. Or she might ask Manolo or Fina Sanchez, the Spanish-born couple from Cuba who worked for the Nixon family for many years, to make my sandwich. The feeling in the apartment was very friendly and considerate. It was always quiet, no music playing and never a TV on anywhere. This was the era before cable news, the Internet, and social media.

More and more, Nixon's life became Susie's and my life. It was far more difficult on her than on me. I was in the middle of this exciting, wonderful experience while she was living it all with me through my nightly phone calls and the stories I would tell when home. But it was hard on her, living vicariously, while taking care of our two little girls. She had many friends, but she missed my presence. It was an abnormal situation for us, because for years we had never been away from each other for days at a time. Plus, as anyone with young children knows, two little girls can be a handful.

Nixon and I traveled during the week and also campaigned every weekend, usually with Mrs. Nixon and their two daughters. David Eisenhower, a grandson of President Eisenhower who was dating Julie, joined us on most weekends. It was truly a 24/7 job. Everything centered around Nixon. I was so focused on what I was doing that I didn't worry about Susie. While we were together and she was my wife, this was my job. Since ninth grade it had been "Dwight and Susie," "Susie and Dwight." That was my identity. It was her identity. I think we knew, if only intuitively, the campaign and what we were experiencing was a once-in-a-lifetime opportunity. The uniqueness of our lives at that time fueled our ability as a couple to work our way through it, even though it was becoming "Nixon and Dwight" or sometimes "Dwight and Nixon" in our family. We lived in the moment, not wanting to jinx things by imagining how it would be to live in Washington.

I found myself doing things I couldn't have imagined. If Nixon was taking an early morning flight, I'd have to get a train out of Connecticut well before dawn. I couldn't be late. One very cold winter's morning, I remember, I was stuck on a train that wasn't moving just outside the 125th Street station in Harlem. There were frozen signals or something. I kept glancing at my watch, panicking about missing the flight. I had to be at the Nixons' apartment so Manolo could drive us to the private air terminal at LaGuardia. After forty-five minutes I literally pushed open the doors, got off the train with my suitcase, climbed over the electrified tracks, and took a cab to the apartment. It seemed part of the job requirement—it even felt exciting.

Nixon was unofficially running for the presidency, but certainly we were on a very fast track. It was a uniquely American political campaign, as we were creating the image of the reluctant candidate, considering whether or not to run. Meanwhile, we crisscrossed America in 1967, meeting with state legislators, supporters, and contributors, supposedly seeking advice to help Nixon make up a mind that had long ago been made up. Often as I escorted someone out of the hotel suite, I would hear the guest's parting advice: "You've got to run." And Nixon's reply: "Oh, we'll decide sometime before the end of the year."

It seemed like we were constantly on the road. I got to see him at work every day. Our trips often included small gatherings in private homes or clubs, with carefully selected "insiders" relishing the opportunity to meet the man who might be president. In those meetings he would spend ninety minutes outlining a new American foreign policy, his unstated objective being to tell his audience, "This is why I want to be your president." He would typically take issue with the decisions of his probable opponent, Lyndon Johnson, especially concerning Vietnam. He always emphasized his respect for traditional values and upholding law and order, and he would add a dose of political gossip to create the illusion of sharing inside information. He always took questions because, as he explained, "That makes those people participants."

I was getting an extraordinary political education. And while Nixon did not especially love the travel or the necessary glad-handing, there was no doubt he enjoyed the intellectual aspect of these meetings. He was talking about global issues and domestic politics, which he savored. The people constantly telling him "The country needs you as president" supported the dream he harbored.

Nixon used a handheld IBM dictating machine and dictated dozens of memorandums daily. Rose Woods would transcribe and distribute them. Filled with campaign strategy and suggestions, these memorandums were highly confidential. Many recipients were somewhat startled to receive a copy addressed to them from "D.C." When the first person asked me about these memos, I told Rose, "Someone is using my initials for their memorandums."

"It's R.N.," she said. "If any of them end up in the press we'll just say you wrote them." That was my first experience with "plausible deniability." I was twenty-seven years old at the time, and these memos were politically very sophisticated. I doubt anyone believed I wrote them, but it never became an issue. In fact, it became a joke among the senior staff: "Have you read Chapin's latest memo?"

At one point that year Nixon suddenly announced a "moratorium on politics," a pause in most political events while he assessed the situation. I remember being both perplexed and disappointed by that decision. I didn't immediately understand the strategy. In fact, I didn't realize it was a strategy. Then I got it: That announcement enhanced the speculation about his plans and created even more interest. The volume of mail received shot upward, with thousands of letters encouraging him to run. Meanwhile, the decision to run had been made and we were gearing up for the primary campaign.

We would meet in his law office and he would run through his daily lists of instructions and questions. This was retail politics at the highest level. His national image as "the New Nixon" had to be honed and reinforced. A fundraising organization capable of attracting tens of millions of dollars from supporters had to be formalized. Nixon, however, never asked people for money. He was his own worst fundraiser. It bothered him. He loved dealing with policy, issues, writing and strategy—such as strategies to win the nomination against George Romney, Nelson Rockefeller, or perhaps Ronald Reagan—anything besides fundraising, He would host a prospective contributor for a "business" or "support" meeting and then let one of his fundraising committee people follow up later to solicit the contribution.

He spent part of those early months building alliances. Among those people whose support he wanted was Illinois Republican Senator Chuck Percy, who was rumored to be considering running himself or more probably was positioning himself as a perfect fit for vice president on the ticket. At that time Percy's daughter Sharon had just married Nelson Rockefeller's nephew Jay Rockefeller, so people assumed the popular Illinois senator would support Rocky. Nixon wanted him to wait before going public with any endorsement, so a secret meeting was arranged by President Eisenhower's brother Milton, who was then president of Johns Hopkins University. As we drove to the campus in

Baltimore, Nixon reiterated to me that this meeting had to remain confidential. We were taken to a house with a small gravel courtyard. It was Dr. Eisenhower's campus home.

Percy arrived alone, driving a Jaguar. I wondered why a U.S. senator was driving a foreign car, since at the time driving a foreign car was considered by many to be unpatriotic. This meeting was real inside politics, hush-hush, nobody could know about it. I felt like I was in the middle of the popular Allen Drury political thriller *Advise and Consent*. I sat in a waiting room as they met privately for more than an hour. I have no idea what transpired in that room, but it worked: Percy held back on announcing his support for Rockefeller.

That was only a beginning. Nixon was constantly meeting or speaking on the phone with friends and political acquaintances he'd made throughout his career. He insisted, "Everyone who has worked in a past campaign or volunteers in this one must be given an assignment. They have to hear from us and be told we need them, even the ones who are a pain in the ass." He waved that index finger again. "Inclusion," he said, "always practice inclusion." What that really meant was give them something to do but, for God's sake, keep them away from Nixon. Everyone feels they need to give a candidate advice, but he didn't have time to hear it all. He wanted to infuse this campaign with younger people who would not be so obviously connected to past campaigns, particularly 1960. He wanted the positive energy and the hunger to win that young people, new to politics, bring to the table.

As I was to learn many years later, he could be unsentimental in his use of people. There was a time and a place for those who assisted him, and to those people at that time he was intensely loyal. And then he wasn't. This was not so much a character defect as it is a harsh fact of political life; a successful politician must, when necessary, make the painful decisions to cut his losses. As I was to find out, it can be very personal—and when it happens, it can feel very unfair.

Coming out of the 1964 Goldwater for President campaign, Nixon slowly and carefully picked his core advisors. The three on staff were

Rose Woods, Pat Buchanan, and Ray Price. Four members of his law firm also played key roles: John Mitchell, Len Garment, Tom Evans, and John Sears. Bob Haldeman and Bob Finch advised on political matters, and Maurice Stans and Peter Flanigan had fundraising responsibility. There were several dozen other important players in time, but this was the original core group.

Rose Woods, who had been with him in those earlier campaigns, was given the task of handling those former players, "the old friends." Nixon wanted Bob Haldeman to supervise the new people, telling him, "Rose doesn't understand or appreciate all these new people we need." Management of Nixon had for years been Rose's responsibility. Nixon's attitude was this: "We can't let her manage the operations. That's what I want you to do, Bob." That was the beginning of a territorial conflict between Rose and Bob. She saw Bob as usurping her powers, and later her access, and she did not like it. Nixon never gave her the full authority she had once enjoyed. This would lead to years of resentment by Rose and many of our mutual friends, most of whom could never place the blame, if one were to call it that, where it actually belonged. They preferred to think that Haldeman was usurping power, while the truth was that Haldeman was simply abiding by Nixon's instructions.

That kind of conflict was not at all unusual in that campaign or that administration. It's the situation in any administration when new staffers deal with those of longer tenure. Nixon recognized how best to utilize the talents of both of them.

In late 1967, it was Bob Haldeman who laid out a shift in campaign strategy for Nixon to consider, writing him: "A candidate for any city-wide, statewide, or national office can't afford the old 'tried and true' methods of campaigning: six speeches a day, plus several handshaking receptions, a few hours at factory gates, and a soul-crushing travel schedule. Just because it has always been this way doesn't mean it always has to be." What Bob was proposing was the forerunner of the modern political campaign, a mix of old-fashioned meet-and-greets combined with greater utilization of media, especially television. Nixon had been entrenched in traditional campaigning, but he quickly saw the wisdom of Haldeman's strategy and bought into it. The acceptance of Bob's counsel is testimony to Nixon's respect for Bob's strategic thinking, particularly regarding the role of political communications. Television was the key to this new strategy. Nixon's other "media advisors"—including Frank Shakespeare, a president of CBS; law partner Len Garment; speechwriters Ray Price and Pat Buchanan—all supported the Haldeman strategy.

Nixon had no idea of the depth of my friendship with Haldeman, but he regularly bounced his feelings about him off me. In 1967 and early 1968, Nixon wanted to bring Haldeman aboard. Naturally, I concurred because I saw the organizational problems that I knew Haldeman could fix. But Bob was very reluctant to quit J. Walter Thompson to join the campaign. Timing was everything, and Haldeman was not about to jump officially onto the Nixon bandwagon until it was just the right time.

I was a fully committed Nixon man by this point, and I believed strongly that we needed Haldeman running things. I did everything I could to encourage him. "If you come in," I wrote, attempting to sway him,

> the publicity will center around your administrative skills . . .
> You should enter on a high plane and structure your efforts
> so as to have contact and work with the cream of the top
> echelon businessmen around the country. This will not hurt
> you . . . To be in the White House; you could serve your term
> of duty and then cash in on the fruits of your labor. And I
> think RN has a better-than-even chance at the nomination.
>
> Oh, I wish I could be there in the hot California sun
> contemplating what it would be like to have control of the
> White House. In 1960 you must have, on occasion, wondered
> at the power which was so near—and it is hard for me
> (knowing you) not to feel it is still an exciting thought.
>
> You are needed and you know you are wanted. You have
> made it big in Southern California, now let's take it national.

Haldeman finally made his decision and decided not to accept the offer to join the campaign. I was surprised. We all were. If Nixon should win, I wrote, "To have been Chief of Staff to a President, deeply immersed in World Affairs and national politics, what excitement it would have been."

Finally, I staked out my own position: "I am loyal and I believe the office should come his way . . . To those who are here blistering themselves for the cause I offer all that is possible for me to give. Victory would be so very sweet. But more than this cause, and especially for the Presidency, I look forward to working for a man [*sic*]. (Someday we are going to put our Man into the White House and the feeling I will have toward him, my allegiance, is bound to be something which up to this date I have not felt.)" I believe what I was feeling when I wrote those words back in 1967 was a loyalty more to Bob than Nixon. While I was committed to Nixon, Haldeman joining the campaign would have made my commitment stronger. After all, I too considered Bob and myself "a team," as he had written me many months before when I was moving to New York.

As for the mystery of why Bob turned down this early opportunity to officially join the Nixon team, I wondered if it involved, as he described it, "activity in the Disney area." It was rumored that Walt Disney wanted Bob to take control of the studio. I concluded, "Someone is trying to tell you something."

As the campaign unofficially began, a group of loyalists would gather often at Rose Woods's midtown Manhattan apartment in the evening. Drinks were served and people would voice their opinions. There was considerable resentment over the new advisors to whom Nixon was listening. Rose was the leader of the group. She was the Nixon veteran and was highly respected by the group, but her opinions were impacted by listening, day in and day out, to the complaints of many old friends, those who no longer were on the inside of the candidate's circle.

Although Bob was not onboard, I kept him informed. He advised me to stay away from the get-togethers at Rose's. I was walking a fine line, and to Rose's great credit, she never took out on me any animosity she might have felt toward Bob. This tension between Bob and Rose never dissipated.

We began gearing up for the primary campaign by going to Brooks Brothers early one morning when it opened, in order to avoid as many other shoppers as possible. We were ushered into a special area of the store for private, personalized tailoring. I was told, in fact, that Abraham Lincoln had had his suits made by Brooks Brothers. Nixon bought several new suits, an overcoat because it was going to be cold in New Hampshire where the campaign would begin, and a lined tan raincoat. He wanted a lighter color because in photographs it would stand out against darker coats. We always carefully considered how he and Mrs. Nixon would look, especially in photographs.

We also continued building a campaign staff. In retrospect—not just for the upcoming campaign but for the future world of television news—everything changed on January 9, 1968. It was Nixon's fifty-fifth birthday. After lunch at his Fifth Avenue apartment, we drove to Philadelphia, where he was to appear on the Mike Douglas afternoon talk show, to be blatantly coy about his political plans.

We arrived at the studio about two o'clock and were escorted to the greenroom, the waiting room. And we waited. Waiting patiently was not one of Mr. Nixon's attributes. Time was meant to be used. After a while, he sent me to find someone to brief him. I found the twenty-seven-year-old executive producer, a man named Roger Ailes, and introduced him to Richard Nixon. It was the beginning of a beautiful friendship. The two men hit it off as if they had been waiting to meet each other. In words something like this, Roger said, "Sir, here is how you should think of television. Television is what you need to get elected. You have to make television your friend." And then the selling line: "And I'm the man who can show you how to do that." Roger was young, but he was a pro—even at that point. He had thought through the exact words that would get Nixon's attention. It was as if he had rehearsed a script. He delivered his lines perfectly, with passion and believability. That was because Roger really believed what he was saying, and he liked Nixon. You could feel it. It worked big-time.

On our drive home, Nixon told me to arrange for Ailes to come to New York right away to meet with Ray Price and the campaign's television advisors. By the end of January, Roger Ailes had become known to the media as Nixon's television producer. He proved to be invaluable to Nixon, especially during the campaign. His connection to Nixon proved equally valuable to Roger Ailes, who went on to legendary status as head of Fox News. Roger and I remained good friends through thick and thin. If you were Roger's friend, and loyal, you were always Roger's friend. I ran into him on an Eastern shuttle flight years later, after he had been exiled from the 1992 Bush '41 campaign. He told me, "The difference between me and those other Washington consultants is I will die for my clients."

It was Ailes, working with Len Garment, CBS President Frank Shakespeare, and producer Al Scott who created the "Man in the Arena" formula we used throughout the campaign. It was called that because it was roughly based on one of Nixon's favorite quotes, from a Teddy Roosevelt speech about questing after great goals, even though it often means suffering defeat and rising again:

> *It is not the critic who counts, not the one who points out how the strong man stumbled or how the doer of deeds might have done them better. The credit belongs to the man who is actually in the arena, whose face is marred with sweat and dust and blood; who strives valiantly; who errs and comes short again and again; who knows the great enthusiasms, the great devotions, and spends himself in a worthy cause; who, if he wins, knows the triumph of high achievement; and who, if he fails, at least fails while daring greatly, so that his place shall never be with those cold and timid souls who know neither victory nor defeat.*

We utilized the Man in the Arena concept in local and regional television markets. Nixon would stand in the middle of a seated group, behind a stand-up mic with no notes and no podium. In some cities the participants would be local media. In others it would be supportive citizens. In most cases we also had an audience, and Mrs. Nixon sat with the audience. There was also a moderator. The moderator who was usually brought in for the occasion was the very recognized and beloved legendary University of Oklahoma football coach Bud Wilkinson. Bud added a great celebrity aspect to the event, and his midwestern style fit nicely with Nixon's informal style. Without notes, Nixon would respond to questions. This format was revolutionary at that time, but it has become a staple of political campaigns and known as a "town hall."

Nixon never really trusted the broadcast media, but he learned how to tame them. During the primary campaign, we were on a soundstage filming commercials in New York when a network crew showed up and requested an interview. Nixon sent me to find out exactly how much time they wanted. I reported back, "Three or four minutes."

He shook his head. "Dwight, they won't use three or four minutes. I want you to ask them how long the segment with me will be."

Again I reported back, "They said about ninety seconds."

"Then that's exactly the amount of time I'll do." The reporter sat down with him and the entire interview lasted ninety seconds. It was as if he had a stopwatch in his head. He was determined that no one was going to edit his remarks to fit his own agenda. Instead, he did his own editing. Whatever the length of the segment was going to be, that was the amount of commentary he provided for them. It guaranteed that the essence of what he wanted to say would be broadcast. That happened numerous times. I learned to pin down the media—What do you need? Thirty seconds? One minute?—before we granted any interviews.

Whatever resistance Nixon had to TV, Ailes and Haldeman had convinced him it was necessary for him to embrace it. While during this period Haldeman still had not accepted any official role, he was readily available and Nixon sought his advice. As Haldeman pointed out to him, if he went through an entire campaign, making two or three stops a day that were filmed by local TV, by the end of the day he would have reached at most two million people. In contrast, every national network TV appearance would reach tens of millions of people a night. There was only one game in town: network television. Nixon got it.

Although we had been unofficially campaigning through the winter, the plan was for Nixon to make the official announcement that he was running for the presidency in New Hampshire. We were supposed to fly from New York to Boston, but a snowstorm grounded our flight. Five of us squeezed into one car: Nixon, myself, Pat Buchanan, Ray Price, and advance man Nick Ruwe. We arrived in New Hampshire late that evening. Nixon announced his candidacy the next morning by saying, "What America needs most now is what it once had, the lift of a driving dream."

Most people remember Richard Nixon as a world leader, opening China to the West, negotiating nuclear agreements with the Russians, and later as the main figure in the middle of a historic scandal. What I remember as much are those long, often late night drives and the early, cold mornings trudging through rain and snow, fighting for the Republican nomination. At night he would slip a note under my hotel room door reminding me what time he needed to be up. I usually set three alarm clocks to be certain not to oversleep. There are people who glamorize political campaigns. There is nothing glamorous about watching the sunrise on a January morning from a hotel room window or from the backseat of a car on the way to another breakfast.

Through experience I became competent in the mechanics of campaigning. From the moment we left the hotel in the morning, Mr. Nixon was public property. He couldn't walk into a diner without boom mics and cameras being pushed in front of him. My job was to keep the candidate moving. The schedule dictated everything. We took great pride in staying on schedule, being on time. When we were late for something, it was because we intended to be late, to let the anticipation build. I had to find that line between moving people back and letting them close enough to create good pictures. I learned how to move him along a rope line, politely deflecting people inclined to time-consuming conversations.

Every day and every night brought new and unique problems. Part of my responsibilities was to make arrangements and prepare Nixon for whatever was about to happen. No surprises. For example, we'd be getting ready to leave the hotel room and I would tell him I had given the local Republican candidate, for whatever office, permission to meet us by the elevator to be photographed shaking hands. Once we were in a little Wisconsin town, and as we got ready to depart for an early evening appearance, the campaign advance man, Ed Morgan, told me, "You're not going to believe this. We got a guy here who wants to show Mr. Nixon a little pig." His son was the local 4-H winner and this was his prized pig. Ed had a great sense of humor so, when he first told me, I thought he was joking. It was like a story from the advance man's school of what not to allow. "A baby pig? You've got to be kidding me."

If Richard Nixon did not want to be photographed wearing a hat, the thought of him being photographed holding a pig did not seem promising. But we were on the second floor of a motel. There was no elevator, and the father and son were waiting with their pig at the bottom of the stairs—with a photographer.

I wasn't looking forward to explaining this to Mr. Nixon—but on this day, thank God, he was amused by it. When we got to the bottom of the stairs, the man was waiting with his son and the piglet. Nixon dutifully put on his campaign smile and said, "It looks just like a dog."

He got it. The American political system sometimes requires being photographed with a pig to get to the White House. Nixon alumni laughed about the little-pig-looking-like-a-dog story for years.

My personal life ceased to exist. I was an adjunct of the campaign. I knew my family, friends, and neighbors were impressed—"Dwight is traveling with Richard Nixon!"—but my reality was quite different. I was not Richard Nixon's pal. I wasn't an advisor. I was a young man who had a role, and I performed it well. I had been taught by Dad, Mother, and my grandparents to respect older people and follow instructions. I had been raised to call people "sir" (which angered John Mitchell, who often told me he did not want to be addressed that way).

We lived on the road, grabbing as much sleep as we could, Nixon shaking thousands of hands every day. The primaries were all about basic retail politics. We visited every small town in New Hampshire. One town faded into the next. One week felt just like the previous week. Meet the people. Shake every hand. Two weeks before the New Hampshire primary, the campaign made a great strategic decision. We mailed invitations to every single registered Republican voter in the state. We told no one the number of invitations sent out. Over two hundred and fifty thousand people were actually invited to a reception: "Dick and Pat Nixon want to meet you." We were told it was the single biggest mailing in the state's history. Julie and Tricia were there with their parents. The reception line was blocks long, on an absolutely gorgeous, mild, winter afternoon. The Nixons shook every single hand. They stood there for hours. The crowd size was a clue that something big was happening. The media, local and national, were blown away by the overwhelming outpouring of support. It paid off: Nixon won 77 percent of the vote in New Hampshire and was on his way to the nomination.

The California primary in June served as the bookend to the primary season that had begun in New Hampshire. Another "Meet Dick and Pat" reception was held at the Century Plaza Hotel in Los Angeles. It was noteworthy because again the crowds were so large. Held on a Sunday, it lasted six full hours. Thousands moved through the fast-paced receiving line that included Mr. and Mrs. Nixon and me, working as I had in San Francisco at the Republican Convention, four years before. We had to stop the reception line every two hours for restroom breaks. The highlight for me was looking toward the back of the hotel ballroom and seeing my very proud parents. They had come to witness the big event, deciding to watch but not to come through the receiving line. At the very end of the reception, they did come over to say hello to the Nixons.

At times during the primaries I didn't even know where we were. One night we were in the car driving from Madison, Wisconsin, to Lake Geneva, supposedly less than a two-hour drive. It was the middle of the winter, and it couldn't have been darker. As always, I was watching the clock. Roy Goodearle was driving, and I was riding in front with him. Two hours became two hours and twenty minutes. Two hours and forty minutes. Mr. and Mrs. Nixon were in the back. Nixon had his briefcase open, a yellow pad on his lap, reading by the overhead car light, making notes. Finally, Roy tapped my leg. "Get the map," he whispered.

We were lost. That was a helpless feeling. There were no cell phones, no GPS. Just us somewhere in Wisconsin. Us and Richard and Pat Nixon. As unobtrusively as possible, I took the map out of the glove compartment and tried to figure out where we were. Finally Mrs. Nixon, realizing the situation, asked politely, "What's the matter, Earl? Are we lost?"

From that night forward, Roy Goodearle became affectionately known as "Earl."

Nixon spoke right up: "Goddamnit, Pat. His name is Roy. He'll figure it out." Roy and I did, but it took us a couple of hours. That was typical Nixon, though. He let the people with the responsibility figure it out, though he wasn't happy about it.

We arrived at our Lake Geneva hotel at about ten thirty. The advance man's job in this situation was simply to move us through the lobby without being stopped. He didn't do the job. The hotel manager greeted us and asked Nixon to look at a beautiful ice sculpture surrounded by fresh shrimp and lobster. The hotel chef had put time and energy into this, and a crowd of people had been waiting. That brings up another rule of campaigning: Don't ever be publicly obnoxious. We could have either begged off or been considerate of the chef. As always, we opted to be considerate.

As my responsibilities increased, I was permitted to speak to certain reporters about a very limited range of subjects. Nixon was not hesitant to delegate authority to get things done. In fact, at times, he would delegate the same task to several people, telling each of them they were the only ones to know about it. But there was no room for mistakes. If you overstepped your authority, if you did anything potentially damaging to the campaign, there weren't a lot of second chances.

We campaigned relentlessly. Day and night. Weekdays and weekends. We never stopped. We had no choice. Unlike the other two most likely candidates, California Governor Ronald Reagan and New York Governor Nelson Rockefeller, we couldn't afford to lose a primary. We were selling our candidate as "the New Nixon." (I think Mike Wallace gave him that nickname, and it stuck.) "The New Nixon" meant shedding the loser image of his presidential run against John Kennedy in 1960 and his gubernatorial run against Pat Brown in 1962. So we couldn't lose a primary. We needed massive turnouts and lopsided victories.

The campaign took a toll. We were all absolutely exhausted. One Friday night we left Wisconsin on a Learjet. We were going to Florida for some sun. It was a very small plane, and I was sitting on a back benchseat with Buchanan. Nixon and Ray Price were directly in front of us, inches away. They were working on some speech ideas and they started talking about a trip to Asia they had made the year earlier. We'd all had a few drinks and Nixon looked out into the night, then began reminiscing—talking about people, talking about Asians. He got sad. He said he thought it was wrong that liberals seemed to identify with Europeans while those in Asia got the short end of the stick in terms of an understanding of their heritage, their value. He didn't think Asians were taken seriously as human beings. Ray Price was later to document this in his book *With Nixon*. Nixon talked of the dismissed Asians as "little brown people." "I love those people," he said, letting his tears flow without embarrassment. It was a remarkably intense moment for the three of us. I remember Buchanan and I looking at each other with concern. Then Nixon cleared his throat to regain his composure and returned to the discussion. It was only many years later, when we had gone through so much more, that Ray, Pat, and I even spoke openly about it with others.

We were in the middle of an incredibly intense primary season, literally and figuratively. Reagan was running to our right and Rockefeller was running to our left. We were fighting George Romney, the governor of Michigan (and Mitt Romney's father), for the middle. Romney was middle-left while we were middle-right, although Nixon believed Romney was a stalking horse for Rocky. Months earlier Romney had told an interviewer that he had been "brainwashed" by his military hosts while visiting Vietnam, an incredibly naive remark to make that destroyed any chance he might have had for the nomination, but he stayed in the race. In fact, when Nixon heard about the "brainwashing," he asked incredulously, "He said what? That's it. He's dead." No one was going to support a candidate who so blatantly admitted to being manipulated.

So-called "dirty tricks" have been a fact of life throughout our political history. Nixon had been the butt of many of them, especially those played by the well-known Democratic operative Dick Tuck. Tuck had been plaguing Nixon for almost three decades, beginning in 1950 during the Senate campaign, when he somehow managed to schedule a Nixon appearance for which he booked a large auditorium—then invited very few people to attend, thus giving the appearance that a large and expected crowd had failed to show up. Tuck once arranged for a train to leave the station while Nixon was standing on the back of the train's caboose, giving a speech. Later in this campaign he hired a very pregnant woman to appear at a Nixon rally, holding a big sign bearing our campaign slogan, "Nixon's the one." Those were classic Dick Tuck tricks, treated as pranks, and there were many more.

We had our own Dick Tuck moments in 1968. One favorite that Nixon knew nothing about was directed at Nelson Rockefeller. Knowing Nixon, if he had been aware of this he would not have permitted it. Rocky was considering running for the nomination but hadn't yet made a decision. He had the money to run a formidable campaign. We tried to help him make his decision. Rocky's dalliances with women were reasonably well known. We uncovered the name of a girlfriend he had at the time. In those days when a politician did a press event, reporters or commentators would lay their tape recorders on the podium or on the ground next to the podium to record whatever was said. So when we learned that Rocky was having a press conference, we were prepared. We had someone place our recorder next to the podium, not to record what was being said but to play our previously recorded tape. The player was timed, so minutes after the press event began, at full volume, a voice shouted from our recorder: "Who is [the name of his girlfriend]?" It repeated over and over, "Who is [the name of his girlfriend]?"

That remains one of the briefest press conferences in history. When Rocky heard that question being shouted from in front of the podium, he looked right, looked left, and then excused himself and was out of that room faster than a speeding bullet.

During every campaign there are going to be unexpected challenges. Often the way a candidate responds to them proves to be far more important than his day-after-day appearances. During the primary campaign the most significant event we had to deal with was the assassination of Dr. Martin Luther King Jr., on April 4, 1968. His murder was devastating to the country. Nixon was having limited success attracting African American voters, and his reaction to this tragedy had the potential to reverberate throughout the entire campaign.

We were in New York when Dr. King was killed in Memphis. We had to be realistic. Nixon had to consider the political consequences of his response. We spent a significant amount of time trying to decide what he should do, or not do. Pat Buchanan was focused on the effect this might have in southern states because George Wallace, a segregationist, also was running. Buchanan was adamant that Nixon should not attend the funeral. John Mitchell agreed with Buchanan. Len Garment and Ray Price believed that if Nixon wanted to be the president of all Americans, he had to attend the funeral. His top advisors got together in the Nixons' apartment to talk about it. What I didn't know at that time was that Richard Nixon had a personal relationship with Dr. King and his wife, Coretta Scott King. He had known them for a long time. The couples had met during the 1957 independence celebrations in Ghana while Nixon was vice president, and Nixon later facilitated Dr. King's introduction to President Eisenhower.

Nixon finally decided he should go to Atlanta and pay his respects to Mrs. King and the family privately. Under no condition did he want to appear to be grandstanding. This aligned with his low-key Quaker tradition beliefs. This sincere approach matched his responsibility as a public figure, while maintaining the dignity provided by privacy. From the outset, Mr. Nixon wanted to avoid what he thought would be the possible "carnival" atmosphere of all the political people attending the funeral.

Most important, by "private" he wanted it off the record and out of the newspapers. Nixon was adamant about that. Nick Ruwe flew to Atlanta to make the arrangements for the visit with the family. Nick asked the King family to keep it private, presumably to emphasize the fact that this was not about politics. My belief is that Nixon was certain news of his "private" visit would leak to the American public.

Nixon and I flew to Atlanta on the plane of his good friend Bob Abplanalp. Since it was not a political trip, no one else went with us. We were met on the tarmac by Ruwe, who had arranged a car and driver that took us directly to the King home. It was in a black neighborhood not too far from Dr. King's Ebenezer Baptist Church. It was modest and well maintained, very similar to all the other homes on the block.

Nick escorted us up a walkway to the screened-in porch and front entrance. The King children, two daughters twelve and five years old and two boys ten and seven years old, were waiting on the porch with a family friend. Nixon introduced himself to each of them, shook hands, then offered some very personal words for each and his condolences. Then we went down a hallway to the master bedroom, followed by a family friend who had a camera and took the pictures that exist of the visit. Coretta King was lying on the bed, fully dressed, propped up by a pillow. There was a chair next to the bed. Nixon went inside, sat down, and took her hand. "Hello, Coretta," he said, "I am so sorry . . ." I left the room and went back to the porch and talked with the children. Nixon was with Mrs. King about ten minutes. He then went back to the porch and spent a little more time talking with family members, after which we got back in the car.

I assumed we were going back to the airport. Instead, he asked the driver if he knew where Dr. King Sr., "Daddy" King, and MLK's mother lived. We drove to their home. It was quite a contrast to their son's more modest home. It was larger and in a more upscale neighborhood. The front door was open. People were moving in and out. We stopped in the entrance foyer. Looking into the living room, Mr. Nixon spotted Dr. King and went across the living room to him. Other guests seemed surprised to see Nixon arrive. Few people were aware of their relationship. Nixon and Dr. King put their arms around each other and embraced. Again, unbeknownst to me, Dr. King Sr. and Nixon had known each other far longer than Nixon knew his son. We stayed there less than half an hour. Nixon spent time with Mrs. King Sr. and other members of the family and friends who had gathered there. He was warmly welcomed.

We then flew from Atlanta to Miami, staying at the Key Biscayne Hotel and Villas. Nixon was very pleased with his visit to see the King family. We had pulled off a difficult feat, visiting the family without the media finding out. Later that evening Nixon called and asked me to come over to his villa. When I walked in, he was sitting on the couch with his friend Bebe Rebozo and Bebe's girlfriend, Jane Lucky. They were watching a ballgame. Nixon turned and asked me, "Dwight, how's our trip to Atlanta playing?"

I was surprised. We had been told specifically no media, no publicity. "I don't know," I said, "I'll find out." I called John Whitaker, the head of scheduling who had sent Ruwe to Atlanta, and told him, "Mr. Nixon just asked me how our trip to Atlanta is playing."

"What do you mean?" Whitaker asked. "Nobody's supposed to know."

"I think he expected that it would leak."

John checked by phone with Nick. "Nope, you told me specifically that nobody was to know about this."

Whitaker called me back. "You're going to have to tell him that nobody knows."

"Sir," I explained—that was a good time for "sir"—"remember your instructions that no one was supposed to know we were there? Well, we did it. There hasn't been a single news report about it."

He considered that. "If nobody knows," he said, shaking his head, "we're going to have to go to the funeral."

I was stunned. Nixon had had a great plan. The only problem was that it had worked. He had thought his visit would leak. But no one, including the King family, had said a word about his being there. I called Nick directly and asked him to see if he could get the word out. Nick called the largest local radio station anonymously and told them he was sure he had seen Richard Nixon with the King family. A short time later Nick got a call from the King family: "The media called us wanting to know if Richard Nixon had been here. Don't worry, we told them we knew nothing about that."

Now if anything leaked we would be betraying Dr. King's family. He decided to return for the funeral. We flew back to Atlanta, again on Abplanalp's plane. This time Bebe Rebozo was with us. We all stayed at the Hyatt on Peachtree. I shared a room in our small suite with Bebe. Bobby Kennedy was in the same hotel. There was no way our presence could be overlooked. The entire hotel morphed into what felt like a gigantic Irish wake. By morning the hotel had run out of liquor, every single bottle.

The same driver from our earlier private visit drove us to the church the next morning. It was a very sunny, hot and humid spring day. We walked a half block from the car to the front door of the church, where more than a thousand people were gathered. They surrounded us and very quietly started clapping. It grew into an unexpected but welcoming soft-clapping ovation, a different feeling from what we had been expecting. I found it incredibly moving. As we entered the church, an usher met us and escorted Nixon to a seat in the third-row pew, directly in front of Teddy Kennedy. The same usher escorted former First Lady Jackie Kennedy to her seat. Bebe and I were directed up to balcony seats. The church was filled with politicians, both elected and ambitious.

An aside: A month later we were back in Atlanta for an event, and at the airport on departure, I spotted that usher who had escorted Nixon and Mrs. Kennedy to their seats for the funeral. He was an unusual-looking guy which is why I remembered him. The man was standing two or three rows back on a rope line Nixon was walking. I immediately brought him to the attention of Bill Duncan, our lead Secret Service agent. It was discovered, I was later told, that the fellow had recently walked out of a mental hospital. This was a huge lapse in security at the King funeral.

The funeral for Martin Luther King Jr. was a long and moving service. Afterward we assembled in the church basement, which was filled with dignitaries and civil rights leaders. Nixon talked to many, including Democratic presidential candidate Eugene McCarthy and basketball icon Wilt Chamberlain. Soon we were taken outside and positioned behind the caisson carrying the casket, which was headed to the cemetery.

The caisson started moving and we all started walking behind it. The entire walk through downtown Atlanta was four miles long. I could see ahead that we had three or four long blocks and then it looked like a left turn toward the cemetery. We had previously told the King family that Nixon would not be attending the burial. Nixon and Bebe Rebozo were walking in the center of the street along with Chamberlain, who towered over everyone. I was walking along the side of the procession. Nixon waved me over and whispered, "Dwight, get us out of here." He knew we were due at the airport and if we didn't extricate ourselves, we would be walking all the way to the cemetery.

I moved ahead to where I saw Nick Ruwe. "Nick, you need to get us out of here." Nick left and returned in four or five minutes. "When we get to that dogleg turn ahead," he said, "bring Nixon and Bebe right through the crowd. I have a car waiting." I relayed the message to Nixon, and as we approached the left turn I said, "Sir, follow me."

Wilt Chamberlain saw what we were doing. He had heard Nixon say to others nearby, "We need to get to the airport. I need to be in New York."

"Can I ride with you?" Wilt asked Nixon.

"Yes," Nixon replied, "come on."

We plowed through the crowd that was five or six rows deep, with people packed at the turn observing the procession. With Wilt walking with him there was no way that Nixon's departure wasn't noticed. We found Nick standing next to an ancient black Cadillac sedan with the doors open. Nick had stopped the car and told the driver he would give him a significant amount of money to drive "some folks" to the airport. We all piled into the car. Nixon, Wilt, and Bebe squeezed into the backseat, "squeezed" being the operative word. I rode shotgun with Nick in the center. You can imagine the look on the driver's face as he glanced in his rearview mirror and saw Richard Nixon and Wilt Chamberlain in the backseat. He appeared to be dumbfounded, but he got us to the airport.

The next day the Associated Press photograph of Nixon getting out of the car in front of the Ebenezer Baptist Church ran across the country. In the end, Nixon felt good about returning for the actual funeral. Maybe he realized it was the right place for a future president to be.

With the exception of the Massachusetts primary, which Rocky won, and California, where we did not compete against favorite son Ronald Reagan, Nixon swept the primaries on his way to the nomination. The events of the 1968 political campaign were being scribed indelibly into American history. There had never been a primary campaign season like it.

4

CAMPAIGNING FOR THE PRESIDENCY AND WINNING

An extraordinary chain of events began on March 31, 1968, when Lyndon Johnson announced he would not be running for reelection. His presidency was another consequential casualty of the Vietnam War. As we had been gearing up to run against him, this announcement was a real jolt to our campaign. At the same time, it was promising, because running against an incumbent president during a war is an incredibly difficult proposition. Now we were left wondering who our opponent, the Democrat candidate, would be.

While Eugene McCarthy, who was running for the Democratic nomination, had mobilized the antiwar movement, his lead diminished once Robert F. Kennedy had decided to enter the race after the New Hampshire primary. There was great enthusiasm among Democrats about putting a Kennedy back in the White House, but their hopes ended on June 5, 1968, the night Kennedy won the California primary. Later that night, immediately after declaring victory, Bobby Kennedy was assassinated in the kitchen of a Los Angeles hotel. Soon thereafter, with Johnson out of the race, Vice President Hubert Humphrey became the Democratic front-runner.

Even after all these years it is difficult to describe the anger, the hatred running wild in the streets of America. The war was ripping the country apart. It was setting the World War II generation, which generally supported the war, against their children, who were joining the growing protest movement. The 1964 and 1965 Civil Rights Acts, eliminating legal segregation in public places, job discrimination, and attempts to prevent black Americans from their right to vote, had infuriated many southerners. In addition, Alabama Governor George Wallace was running for the presidency as a third party candidate, with a platform that essentially sought to repeal that legislation. The assassination of Dr. King, and the nationwide riots that followed, set cities on fire across America; and the murder of Senator Robert Kennedy compounded the political chaos. There literally was blood in the streets.

The morning after Bobby Kennedy was shot, LBJ ordered Secret Service protection for all presidential candidates, including Nixon. At ten thirty that morning, I arrived at the Nixons' Fifth Avenue apartment. Nixon introduced me to Jim Rowley, the Director of the Secret Service. Technical crews were already present, installing cameras and emergency alarm systems. Two agents, Bill Duncan and Chuck Zboril, were also present. Those two agents would be with us for the rest of the campaign and would then be assigned to the presidential detail after the inauguration.

We didn't talk about it, but no one doubted Nixon was potentially a target. Throughout his political career, he had provoked intense emotions. People had strong feelings about Richard Nixon. There certainly were crazy people out there who might act on those feelings.

Nixon never faltered. Never hesitated. I was still learning about his character. Whatever fear or anxiety he might have been feeling inside, it never showed.

With Secret Service protection came our code names, which we used throughout the campaign and the White House years. Nixon was Searchlight. Mrs. Nixon was Starlight. Haldeman became Welcome and I was Watchdog. Ron Ziegler was Whaleboat, a handle he detested because he thought they were making fun of his weight. He asked to have it changed, but Haldeman and the Secret Service refused to change it. Eventually the head of our advance operations, Ron Walker, became, appropriately, Roadrunner; and Tim Elbourne, my USC fraternity brother who worked for Whaleboat, became Snapshot.

I remember having to deal with two significant security issues during the campaign that involved Nixon's personal safety. We were staying at the Century Plaza Hotel in LA. Nixon liked staying there because the presidential suite had a baby grand piano, and even if he didn't have time to play, he liked having the piano available. Early in the morning, Bob Taylor, lead senior agent, who became head of the president's Secret Service detail upon his inauguration, knocked on my door, which was unusual. Taylor asked me to find Haldeman, who at this point had joined the campaign and was always traveling with us.

"There's a guy with a rifle," Taylor told us, "who has made a threat against Mr. Nixon. We have confirmed the threat with his family, but we can't find him. We believe his plan is to assassinate Mr. Nixon, and we believe he's going to be at the rally today at Panorama City. We'd like you to cancel the event."

Haldeman left my room and went into the living room of the suite to speak with Nixon. He came back shaking his head. "He won't cancel it. He's not going to let this stop him." The rally proceeded as scheduled, but it was tightly controlled by the Secret Service. The fact that it was outdoors made it an even bigger challenge for the agents. To ensure that Nixon would be exposed as briefly as possible, they pulled the limo up right next to the set of stairs leading to the stage from which he would be speaking. When we arrived, Nixon hopped out of the car and was up those stairs in an instant. He waved, spoke for three minutes rather than the usual twenty-five, and got back into the car. It was the fastest rally in political history.

In another instance, when Nixon was president, we were campaigning in Columbus, Ohio. We were with Ohio Governor James Rhodes. The appearance was being protested by a large group of demonstrators from Ohio State University. As Nixon left the Capitol building steps after speaking, he impulsively decided he wanted to walk over to the demonstrators and speak with them. I think his hope was to bridge the gap between the younger and the older generations. He wanted to connect with that group of young people. When I told Bob Taylor about Nixon's plan, the color drained from his face. "He can't," Bob said. "We haven't secured that area."

This time Taylor turned to Nixon and said, "Sir, I need to talk to you in the car." They got into the backseat of the limousine. I was peering through one open window. Haldeman had gotten into the car and was on a jumpseat facing Nixon and Taylor. "Dwight says you want to walk over to that crowd," Taylor explained. "I can't let you do that." Taylor took a card out of his wallet and read it aloud. Basically it said that the president would be taking an action that might jeopardize his life and that the Secret Service formally objected to it. If he walked over to that crowd of young people, the Secret Service could not be responsible for his safety or for the safety of others. This time Nixon listened and accepted that he shouldn't try to talk to the demonstrators, but his desire to do that set the stage for a remarkable event that was to take place at the Lincoln Memorial in 1970, after a firestorm of protests over the killing of students by the Ohio National Guard at Kent State.

As we piled up victories in the primaries, it became obvious that Nixon was going to be the Republican nominee. The biggest decision he had to make leading up to the convention was the selection of his running mate. There were many good candidates. Obviously, Rockefeller was out because, among other things, both he and Nixon were New Yorkers. We went on tour, meeting viable candidates, including Massachusetts Governor John Volpe, the former Governor of Pennsylvania William Scranton, and the then-current Pennsylvania Governor Ray Shafer. Richard Ogilvie, then running for governor in Illinois, might have been an interesting choice, as he was very popular in a key electoral state, but he lacked political charisma. There were some political advisors pushing for a "coalition ticket," meaning either Reagan or George Romney. Then we went to Annapolis, Maryland, to spend time with Governor Spiro Agnew.

I had been with Nixon when he first met Spiro Agnew several

months earlier in New York. It was a glorious spring day in the city. We walked from the Nixons' apartment on Fifth Avenue to the Park Avenue apartment of Louise Gore, of the Maryland Gores (not the Tennessee Al Gores). Mrs. Gore, a wealthy and influential woman who was a member of the Republican National Committee, had invited Nixon to a gathering of all the female Republican National Committee members at her apartment. Louise Gore was a wonderful person and an early 1968 Nixon supporter. Mrs. Gore wanted Nixon to meet several people who might prove valuable during the campaign, one of them being her governor, newly elected Spiro "Ted" Agnew. This was the first time the two men had met. Agnew was tall and good-looking, and immaculately dressed. In all the years I knew him I never saw a single wrinkle in his coat or pants. In fact, that's probably my most significant memory of him. Nixon did his usual meet-and-greet and spoke for about thirty-five minutes. Then Agnew spoke to the group about what he intended to do as Maryland's new governor.

As we were walking back to his apartment, Nixon uncharacteristically asked me what I thought of Agnew. It was obvious to me then that Agnew had made an impression on Nixon. "Well, he seemed pretty astute," I said, then added, "His remarks were articulate and the women sure seemed to be attracted to him." As I recall, Nixon responded, "I liked him."

We next visited Agnew at the capital in Annapolis at the start of summer. It was a humid, overcast day. The Agnew people had done a great job turning out an unexpectedly large crowd. Crowd size was not especially important in these visits with governors. It was the TV time that mattered more, but someone had done a very professional job of advancing our visit. It made an impression on Nixon.

As far as I know, those were the only two times Nixon had met Agnew before selecting him as his vice presidential running mate. They certainly had no relationship, no friendship at that point. and that never changed. But Nixon chose Agnew as his running mate for 1968.

The actual VP selection supposedly took place in Miami just before the convention opened. I say "supposedly" because I believe it had probably been decided the previous week. We'd spent that week in Montauk, New York, at the eastern end of Long Island. While he was there, Nixon relaxed, worked on his acceptance speech, and taped several television segments for possible use in campaign commercials.

That Montauk week was important. He was resting, getting his acceptance speech honed, and meeting with top advisors on how the post-convention campaign launch would unfold. Also, he was thinking of how the convention itself would position him as "presidential" with the millions who would watch on television.

At the convention, my desk was situated by the door to the presidential suite. About eleven o'clock on Tuesday night, after Nixon had clinched the nomination, the Republican power structure convened to discuss the vice presidential selection. There probably were thirty-five people in the room, including senators, loyal contributors, Barry Goldwater, even Billy Graham. I think that meeting was mostly for show—that is, Nixon was being inclusive, making people believe they were playing a role in helping him make a decision that had already been made.

I think Nixon selected Agnew because he was the safest choice. He was a strong speaker. He bridged nicely between the conservative and the more moderate Republicans; he was popular with other governors; plus he always looked as if he could be modeling for a men's fashion magazine. He certainly would be loyal, and it appeared he didn't have a lot of political baggage. What was generally considered the main reason was Agnew's response to the riots after MLK's death. Agnew had received recognition for dressing down a meeting of black leaders who arrived expecting to be cajoled. Agnew instead publicly criticized the leaders for their failure to control the more radical elements and failing to contain the rioting and lawlessness. This was at a time when a majority of Americans supported the law-and-order effort, and candidate Nixon had placed that issue squarely as a central piece of the domestic agenda he embraced.

The highlight of the convention for me was being invited into the presidential suite with the Nixon family and several close friends and advisors, among them Rose Woods, Pat Buchanan, Bob Haldeman, and Ray Price. On the second night we watched from the suite as the delegates placed the nominations on the floor, after which they proceeded to vote. The surge of excitement I felt when the delegates' votes took Nixon over the top to clinch the nomination is impossible to describe. It seemed a lifetime ago that I had been interviewing a dog. Now I was in a suite with the man who might well be the next President of the United States.

When Nixon received the magic number of delegates to win the nomination, we all clapped and cheered. As the cheering died down, Nixon thanked each of us; then he reminded us this was just the beginning and that we needed to get to work immediately. About forty-five minutes later, after the room had emptied, he turned to me: "Get Haldeman and Mitchell." The nomination now won, he had important things to accomplish.

Nixon had worked hard on his acceptance speech, which was well received. Two parts of it remain with me to this day. He talked of being a little boy, lying in his bed at night, listening to a train going to far-off places, and wondering where he would travel in his life. It painted a poignant picture of the dreams of that little boy, how far he had traveled, and how far he was yet to go.

The second memorable aspect of the speech was when he addressed the rioting and unrest in the nation's streets and asked if we had traveled so far for this—and that we, as a nation, had to do better. "We see Americans hating each other, fighting each other, killing each other at home. And as we see and hear these things, millions of Americans cry out in anguish, 'Did we come all this way for this?'"

He concluded his speech and then, to the surprise of every delegate in the hall, the presidential nominee and Mrs. Nixon stood for the next two hours on the podium of the convention hall, shaking the hand of each delegate and thanking them. I dutifully stood there too. Thanking every delegate in the convention hall had never been done before, and I don't believe it has ever been done since. It was an expression of the tremendous appreciation both Mr. and Mrs. Nixon felt for their supporters. Remember the Nixons' "thank you" handshake back in San Francisco in 1964 and the long receiving lines in the primary states? Shaking hands with the delegates was Nixon Retail Politics 101.

The 1968 Democratic Convention in Chicago a week later was a sharp contrast to the Republican National Convention. It was plagued by antiwar demonstrations and police clubbings—all of which was aired on national television late into the night on each of the four evenings. While Nixon spent the week in Key Biscayne, out of public view, Pat Buchanan and Congressman Don Rumsfeld sent firsthand political reports from Chicago to Haldeman, who was with the candidate in Florida. Haldeman shared the reports with Larry Higby, his assistant, and me as we hung out on the beach and, more important, with Nixon, who was staying at Bebe Rebozo's home. No one was unhappy to hear of the Democratic dissension and turmoil coming from Chicago.

Nixon's point men with whom I interfaced the most were Ehrlichman, Haldeman, and occasionally John Mitchell. Mitchell ran the nuts and bolts of the campaign, everything from fundraising to organizing the national and state political operatives. He was based in Nixon's New York campaign headquarters at 521 Fifth Avenue for a while and then 457 Park Avenue. Haldeman and Ehrlichman were on the road almost full-time with Nixon. John Ehrlichman was in charge of the advance operation and daily logistics on the road. Haldeman oversaw Ehrlichman and everything concerning the candidate. While he was not yet known as Nixon's chief of staff, that was his function.

My relationship with Haldeman, which had been remarkably cohesive heretofore, got complicated very quickly. Communicating with him was one thing when I was on the road with Nixon and Bob was talking with me from his office in Los Angeles. It was another when he was with us on the campaign trail and overseeing every detail of every moment. I wasn't prepared for all the responsibilities that came my way as the campaign ramped up. Nor was I prepared to have my off-hours behavior scrutinized at all times. The staff worked hard and, needing to blow off steam in our free time, played hard too. Haldeman, on the other hand, lived by his strict Christian Science moral code and was not inclined to join in the partying. I felt I was letting him down. "I guess I've made my disillusionment pretty clear," he wrote.

While he was exceedingly proud of what we had accomplished as a team, and the fact that Nixon had gained trust and confidence in me, he continued to emphasize our shared objective; "Let's just never lose sight of our objective, and let's not let _anything_ get in the way of achieving it. It's not only the most important thing in your life and mine, I truly believe it is the most important thing in the world."

He told me that he was in it "101% and I'm totally _dedicated_ to winning," and no one or anything was going to disrupt that objective.

As I was beginning to understand, I was serving a lot of different purposes. In public Haldeman could never afford to show his emotions; so in private, I became an outlet for his frustration and his anger, not just with me, but with whatever was going on that bothered him. The next many years of our personal friendship, as well as our working relationship, were a roller coaster. But no one in the campaign—or later in the White House, including Nixon—knew the depth of our friendship. As upset as he might have been with me at times, Bob protected me throughout the campaign and into the White House years.

For our former White House colleagues, the relationship Bob and I shared, which had begun in our J. Walter Thompson days, will be a surprise. Looking from just the White House perspective, it might not have appeared to be as close as it was. But in fact, we shared a strong bond, both personal and professional.

The fall campaign was a single blur of appearances: from the American Legion in New Orleans to B'nai B'rith in New York; from a three-day train tour through Ohio, Michigan, and Illinois to airport "prop stops" (meaning propeller planes) in North Dakota, South Dakota, and Idaho—then on to Seattle on the same day. We never paused, never slowed down. State after state, city after city, speech after speech. It was a grueling schedule, but Nixon never faltered, never hesitated.

His smile was always in place, his determination propelling him forward. It's hard to tell the difference between Cleveland and Omaha from a hotel suite. If I had been collecting soap and shampoo, I would have been set for life. Nixon always found an easy chair in those hotel suites. Most often he had his suit jacket on, his feet up, his briefcase on his lap with six, seven, eight yellow pads around him. Several books would be open on a table, a hassock, or on the floor. He never stopped reading. His glasses would be hanging from his mouth as he scribbled notes with a pen. He always had one finger covered with ink. This was not Jack Kennedy, adored by the press, throwing a football to his brother Bobby as cameras captured his every move. This was the real Richard Nixon, hard at work.

Running against Jack Kennedy in 1960, Nixon was his own "chief cook and bottle washer," exhausting himself trying to run everything. We kept a solid pace of campaigning in 1968, but Nixon had learned a lesson from 1960 and, as a result, in 1968 he delegated. He truly trusted Mitchell, as our "campaign manager," to run the campaign. Likewise, Nixon delegated to Haldeman, who was the gatekeeper in determining who actually needed to meet or talk with Nixon. Haldeman set up schedules, specific windows, for those meetings. He made certain Nixon only had to focus on those things that were necessary for him to know or where his input was needed. All this allowed Nixon precious preparation time, the ability to focus on the next important thing he would be doing, free of interruption. My role was to implement the candidate's schedule with a calm demeanor—well, as "calm" as a presidential campaign could allow.

We were running on a law-and-order platform. "The wave of crime is not going to be the wave of the future in America . . . We shall reestablish freedom from fear in America. To those who say law and order is the code word for racism, this is our reply: Our goal is justice for every American . . . Let us build bridges to human dignity across that gulf which separates black America from white America . . . We are on the wrong road. It is time to take a new road."

But the key issue of the campaign was the Vietnam War. The

American people had grown tired of watching coffins come home every week from a war they didn't understand that seemed endless.

At some point during the campaign a reporter had written that Nixon had a "secret plan" for ending the war. Much of the public accepted that as fact—but it wasn't true. Nixon was a patriot. He was a World War II veteran. If he actually had a workable plan that he failed to share with the government, it would have been an extraordinarily self-serving and disloyal act.

Throughout the entire campaign Nixon carefully avoided claiming he had a plan to win the war. So that all his options would be open when he became president, he was specifically ambiguous about any strategy. As he said when accepting the Republican nomination, "The first-priority foreign policy objective will be to bring an honorable end to the war in Vietnam. We shall not stop there. We need a policy to prevent more Vietnams . . . To the leaders of the Communist world, we say: After an era of confrontation the time has come for an era of negotiation . . ." His mission: "Peace with honor."

Later it would be written that Lyndon Johnson was trying to end the war with the North Vietnamese before leaving office, and in fact he had ordered a partial halt to the bombing of that country. In that context, it was also written that Nixon, through Anna Chennault, who had been active and effective as a fundraiser in Nixon's 1960 presidential campaign, had effectively torpedoed any chance of a pre-election peace in Vietnam by using an emissary to convince South Vietnam's President Thieu to not send a delegation to the Paris peace talks that had been jumpstarted by Johnson's bombing halt. It was an enormously complex situation. Peace talks had begun in Paris and American negotiator Averell Harriman was rumored to be optimistic that an agreement could be reached before the November election. Conversely, it also was rumored that the South Vietnamese were against any agreement that would result in American troops leaving South Vietnam. I would not have been privy to the specifics of such conversations, but chances are if Nixon had been working secretly with Anna Chennault, I would have heard bits of the larger puzzle. I didn't. Not a word. When the controversy surrounding this story was brought to the attention of Theodore "Teddy" White, author of *The Making of the President 1968,* White investigated the matter and rejected it. And Hubert Humphrey said in his memoirs that there was no evidence of Mr. Nixon's involvement.

Back during the New Hampshire primary Nixon was asked a question about Vietnam after a UPI reporter had attributed the phrase "secret plan" to him. Nixon never said he had a "secret plan." It came from that reporter looking for a lead to a story summarizing Mr. Nixon's promise to end the war without losing it. The continual press questioning about the matter is a perfect example of the media prolonging a negative Nixon story rather than reporting the truth. Those kinds of dishonest attacks on Nixon by the press were endless.

I did witness a fascinating moment of power politics, of presidential strategy played out at the highest possible level. The Democratic nominee was Hubert Horatio Humphrey, LBJ's vice president. Humphrey was caught between wanting to be loyal to Johnson, who couldn't seem to get us out of the war, while at the same time wanting to satisfy the antiwar movement, who demanded we leave Vietnam immediately. It was an untenable position.

Nixon was leading in all the early polls. In late September 1968, we were just checking into the Cadillac Hotel in Detroit, where Nixon was scheduled to address the American Legion the next day. As we were settling in, Buchanan entered the suite and said, "Sir, Humphrey just gave his speech in Salt Lake City. He's breaking with Johnson on the war." Humphrey had separated himself from Johnson, setting out his own policy to end the war.

This was a huge gamble by Humphrey, and it required a response. It was potentially a make-or-break moment in the campaign. Nixon thought about it for a very few moments, then told me, "Get President Johnson on the phone." While the decision was made quickly, it was not impulsive. Richard Nixon did not make impulsive or emotional decisions. Everything he did was considered and weighed. Sometimes he had to be pushed to finally make a decision, but not in this instance.

He and Johnson had known each other for a long time, and this was a phone call he felt he needed to make.

My job was simply to get President Johnson on the phone. But I realized I didn't have the slightest idea how to get the President of the United States on the phone. I went down the hall to Rose Woods's room. "202-456-1414," she said, as if it were a number that everyone knew. "Call and tell them that the former vice president wants to talk to President Johnson."

I dialed the number and followed Rose's instructions. The White House operator who answered paused, then asked me to hold on. Seconds later she returned, "Can you please put Vice President Nixon on the phone so we can identify him?"

I gave Nixon the phone. "They would like to identify you, sir." I heard his end of the conversation. "Hello." Then: "Milly, how are you? How are Sally and Betsy? Give them my best, please." He knew the switchboard staff well because every Christmas, as vice president, he and Mrs. Nixon would go to the switchboard to share holiday wishes with the women who worked there in shifts around the clock. Few if any other White House staffers, much less at the vice presidential level, took the time to visit the operators in person, and as a result these people were especially appreciative and attentive to Nixon's needs. I would come to learn an important lesson from this. Although Nixon's motives were pure because he respected and appreciated the important work these unseen women did, it was also a wise strategic move on his part. The White House operators are legendary for their ability to find and bring on the line in short order anyone anywhere in the world. To have them in your corner is a brilliant strategic move that served Nixon well all the way to the end of his life when, as a former president, he would occasionally use the White House switchboard to connect him with someone who was otherwise impossible to find.

Nixon chatted with the operator pleasantly. Several seconds later: "Hello, Mr. President. Dick Nixon." While their political philosophies were quite different, both President Johnson and former Vice President

Nixon were accomplished men who shared an understanding of the political realities of this country, as well as a competitive regard and, let's call it, a "cautious respect" for each other. "Hubert's announcement," Nixon said, "will be interpreted, as I'm sure you know, as a dramatic move away from the position of your administration." Nixon continued: "It's my intention not to move in that direction." Nixon was suggesting to President Johnson, essentially, that Humphrey had betrayed him and that he, Nixon, was the candidate still supporting Johnson's Vietnam policy.

There could have been many reasons for this call, but I've always felt Nixon's primary objective was to try to keep Johnson from pulling some type of "October surprise" to assist Humphrey's candidacy just before the election. No one will ever know if that call swayed Johnson at all, but he certainly was not as active in his vice president's campaign as he could have been. Humphrey's running mate, Senator Walter Mondale, also expressed the view that LBJ was not as active as he should have been. No matter, the Nixon call did not achieve its full purpose, with LBJ declaring a bombing halt five days before the election.

After breaking with Johnson, Humphrey's poll numbers began improving dramatically. While polling then was not nearly as sophisticated as it has become, it still was useful as a snapshot of the moment. We did our own internal polling, while also paying attention to the two major polling organizations at that time, Gallup and Harris. One day early in the campaign, Nixon asked me to "make contact with the Harris people and see if we can get on their list to get a preview of their polls in advance." Lou Harris was basically a Democrat pollster who had done very good work for Jack Kennedy. I asked on our behalf and was flatly turned down. "Only political associates of Mr. Harris are allowed to get the polls early," I was told.

Nixon wasn't surprised by the Harris organization's response. He listened, then instructed me to call the Gallup organization. I spoke with George Gallup Jr., who was happy to provide us with their polling information, even before it was given to the Johnson White House.

Mr. Gallup told me he believed that a man running for the presidency ought to know what the American people are thinking, especially about the war.

This was actually the beginning of our very beneficial relationship with the Gallup organization. After Nixon's election and throughout his administration, I would meet with George Gallup Jr. and John Davies, a top Gallup lieutenant, at the Hay-Adams hotel, across the street from the White House. They would allow us to preview the questions they were polling and to make suggestions as to how to frame those questions, and they listened to our suggestions of what questions they should ask in their surveys. Often they would incorporate our suggestions. The Gallup organization allowed us this participation for patriotic reasons, I was told, and that the firm had extended the same courtesy to the Johnson administration.

Bob Teeter was our internal pollster. Days before the election in 1968, the public polls as well as Teeter's internal polls were telling us the same thing: The election was going to be very close. Humphrey's last-minute decision to turn on LBJ's policy had worked. The antiwar vote was moving Humphrey's way, reluctantly, but there was considerable movement and there was nothing we could do to blunt it. We were generating enormous enthusiasm, but the confidence that we, the campaign staff, had felt a few days earlier was dwindling. The closing polls, however, didn't discourage Nixon. He simply worked harder. The race was so close that if the campaign had lasted a few more days, the result might have been a win by Hubert Humphrey.

We woke up on Election Day at the Century Plaza Hotel in Los Angeles. Nixon had closed his campaign the evening before with a nationally televised telethon, answering questions from around the nation. We spent the main part of Election Day flying on the "Tricia," the chartered campaign plane that was named after his older daughter. The second chartered campaign plane was named the "Julie," the name of his younger daughter, and it carried the press. As we crossed the nation, the citizens below us were going to the polls. While the mood on the plane was anxious, at the same time, our expectations were high for a victory. I made notes on the plane that day and shared them with Teddy White for his book *The Making of the President 1968*. (See Exhibit 6 in the Appendix on page 449.)

It was raining when we landed in Newark, New Jersey. As we rode into New York City there were crowds along the streets to greet Nixon. After everything he had been through in his political career, I can't imagine what he must have felt to once again be that close to winning the presidency and to hear the cheers of support from the crowds. Streets had been blocked off around the Waldorf Astoria, where we would be spending the night. We were causing gridlock.

Polls were still open when we got to the hotel. We gathered in a large suite to wait for the returns. Mrs. Nixon, Tricia, and Julie had their own suite just down the hall. People moved in and out throughout the night, but Haldeman, Mitchell, Ehrlichman, and Larry Higby were in the suite with us the entire evening.

There was an attached bedroom in which Nixon spent most of the evening, meeting with senior campaign staff or trying to catch a quick nap. A couple of times when I went in, he had propped himself up in bed, his robe on over his slacks and undershirt with, as usual, his briefcase and yellow pads. There was a TV in the room, which he didn't turn on. There was only one other television in the suite, in the living room. It was set mostly to ABC, though I don't know why. We all stayed busy working the phones and dealing with messages for Nixon, letting him know who had checked in. He spent much of the evening on the phone, returning many of the calls. He spoke with Billy Graham several times. He called various governors to get reports. Mitchell and Haldeman were busy calling state coordinators and totaling figures on yellow pads, trying to get some sense of what was going on. Food came in, dirty dishes went out.

About one thirty in the morning the phone rang. I answered. It was Mike Wallace of CBS News, wanting to speak with John Mitchell. He told Mitchell that he had spoken with Chicago Mayor Richard Daley, who controlled the whole state of Illinois. Daley had told Wallace that they hadn't yet received all the ballots from southern Illinois. We were prepared for that news. We were not going to allow him to repeat his questionable 1960 tactics.

Mitchell replied firmly, as if he had been waiting for this call: "That's fine, Mike. But you can tell the mayor that when he brings in a box of ballots, we'll bring in our own box of ballots." Bottom line: Instead of presenting all of our votes first, as we had in 1960, giving the Democrats the opportunity to present just enough votes to defeat us, in 1968 we were holding back our totals until we heard from the Democrats. Nixon hadn't asked for a recount in 1960 because he didn't believe the country, at such a critical time internationally, could afford several months of uncertainty about who was president. Our campaign was not going to let that happen again. Shortly after that conversation, it was projected that Illinois had been won by Nixon.

The election results rolled in through the early morning on Wednesday. Nixon was in the bedroom, the TV in that room still off, when ABC finally announced, maybe around eight thirty, that "Richard Milhous Nixon has just been elected the thirty-seventh President of the United States." I practically ran into the bedroom. How often does someone have the opportunity to tell a person he has been elected President of the United States? "Sir," I said, "ABC just announced that you've won."

Nixon, still wearing a bathrobe over his slacks and undershirt, literally jumped out of bed. Mitchell, Haldeman, and Ehrlichman were all in the bedroom with him by that point. Everyone piled into the living room and was cheering. Nixon's eyes were fixated on the television screen, an incredible look on his face: a mixture of satisfaction, pride, relief, joy, determination, and gratitude. (I was the only person present with a camera, and I was able to document the moment.)

Then Nixon turned and went down the hall to tell his family.

Several minutes later he returned, carrying a crewel embroidery of the presidential seal that his daughter Julie had been secretly making for him throughout the campaign. He shook hands with everyone;

then looked at Mitchell. "John, we're going to Florida this afternoon and we're going to start putting the government together."

I saw John Mitchell's eyes start to tear up. "Mr. President-Elect," he said—the first time I had heard anyone use that title—"I'm going to have to meet you there." We all became very quiet, looking at Mitchell and wondering what was going on. "I've got to go up to Connecticut first to see Martha." For many years, the outwardly gruff and unemotional Mitchell had been struggling to cope with his wife's emotional and mental problems, which were seriously exacerbated by alcohol. Rather than being with us on that momentous night, she was at Silver Hill in New Canaan, Connecticut. At that time, Silver Hill was known as a "nervous tension" treatment center. Martha was there, trying unsuccessfully to deal with the problem that was to plague not only the Mitchells but also the Nixon administration for the next several years. It was a very sad few moments as the new president-elect told Mitchell to take his time in seeing Martha and that he should come to Florida when the time was right.

With the election having been declared for Nixon, the phone began ringing off the hook. We'd had our few minutes of private celebration. It had been a tension-filled all-nighter for everyone. Rumors of who would be the likely winner, Nixon or Humphrey, had been swinging back and forth throughout the night. After ABC's midmorning call for Nixon, it wasn't until around eleven that Hubert Humphrey called to concede. Now it was time to get to work. Nixon shaved and showered in order to go downstairs to thank our campaign volunteers—and to address the nation around noon.

We all went to our respective rooms to clean up. It was the first time I had been to the room that Susie and I were given. She had spent the night with all the advance men and their wives.

A couple of hours later I went to the Waldorf ballroom with the Nixon family. I was standing a few feet from him when he made his victory speech, closer to him in victory than I had been six years earlier when he gave his bitter "You won't have Nixon to kick around anymore" speech. Nixon had lost before, he told the crowd of supporters, in 1960 to Kennedy and in 1962 to Governor Pat Brown. "Winning is a lot more fun." In his comments he flashed back to events he recalled from the campaign. He was on cloud nine. The whole family was. It had been a very long journey to that moment.

I can't imagine anyone could have been better prepared for the presidency than he was. There was no learning curve, as we used to say. He knew where all the bathrooms in the White House were. He had learned the mechanics of the job from watching Eisenhower and learning from him. He knew how to select a cabinet and how to conduct high-level meetings. He knew how to handle relationships with the Pentagon, how to develop policy and then how to work with Congress to get it implemented.

More than that, though, he knew how he wanted to conduct his presidency. He had thought about it for years. He was a reader, especially about the great men of both recent and distant history. I'd see him reading about Churchill of England, de Gaulle of France, Adenauer of Germany, Lee Kuan Yew of Singapore, Ben-Gurion of Israel, and Shigeru Yoshida of Japan. For him these weren't just names on a page. He knew them all. Even after losing to Kennedy in 1960, he kept going to Europe and to Asia, meeting with world leaders. He also made trips to South America and Africa. From his earliest foreign trips as a congressman, he had also insisted on meeting leaders outside the official circles—military personnel, political opposition, academics, and so on. Having started doing this so early in his political and diplomatic life, in many cases when he returned, the people he had met in opposition were now in power. That was the unique basis of his knowledge of both nations and leaders from the 1940s through the 1990s. It is representative of Nixon's amazing discipline and experience.

He learned from those men how they "think," how they reached decisions, how they initiated action. He loved to talk about thinking. He asked those leaders, personally, how they thought, why they governed as they did. Nixon was intellectually curious. He was a seeker of the "hows" of leading, of political life. For him a great Saturday night would be spent discussing geopolitical relationships or in conversation with a Kentucky senator about the political situation in that state. If a senator or someone else was not available, then he would read.

But above all, he believed completely in the magic of mystique. All great leaders have an aura that seems to set them apart. General de Gaulle, in the 1930s before becoming a general, had written a small book, *The Edge of the Sword*. Nixon read the book, and in his copy he marked many sections throughout with a yellow highlighter, including several different sections on leadership that explain how a leader has to keep himself reserved and, despite the occasionally necessary "crowd baths" among them, to keep a distance from the people. This was not Nixon learning to isolate. He was creating his personal leadership style. In today's political world, leaders believe they must be celebrities, always in front of the crowd. Nixon had a "precious resource" view of leadership. It was not to be wasted. He created and nurtured the Richard Nixon he showed to the world, conducting himself in a way that he believed added to that mystique.

I remember him talking about an aspect of leadership that had a unique twist: "Dwight, the most important thing in conducting foreign policy is consistency." Yet, for mystique, he didn't care if Kissinger told the Russians that Nixon was a little out of his mind. Project stability—but keep 'em guessing.

He entered the White House knowing how he intended to conduct his presidency. He had a unique understanding of the role of the president. He certainly appreciated and respected all American institutions. This was a man who was prepared.

Just hours after Richard Nixon was declared America's next president, Susie and I, both exhausted, running on adrenaline and beyond excited, along with the Nixon family and other senior Nixon staff and their spouses, boarded a large government jet with no windows provided by President Johnson. We flew first to Andrews Air Force Base, near Washington.

I then proceeded with Nixon and limited staff to Walter Reed Army Medical Center, where President-Elect and Mrs. Nixon visited former President Eisenhower, who was gravely ill. Nixon's relationship with Eisenhower was complex. Dwight Eisenhower had made Richard Nixon's presidency possible. However, there was a time during the 1952 presidential campaign when Eisenhower's support wavered. It might have been politically expedient for Eisenhower to take Nixon off the ticket during the crisis over the phony slush fund. However, Nixon saved the day with his "Checkers speech." Ultimately, Ike trusted his vice president enough to send him on important missions around the world and to assign him major responsibilities at home. But the age and experience gap between them was huge. While Eisenhower had commanded the entire European Theater during WWII, Nixon had merely served in the navy. I was told that during the eight years of the Eisenhower administration, other than official state occasions, the Nixons were never invited to the official Residence. I did know Rose Woods, who was with Nixon throughout those years, did not like the way President Eisenhower had treated the Nixons and was always critical of Ike.

On the other hand, I had seen firsthand the deep respect Nixon had for President Eisenhower. Months before the primaries began, we'd flown to Washington, then driven to former President Eisenhower's office in Gettysburg, Pennsylvania. Nixon spent several hours with the former president, presumably discussing the campaign and world events, specifically the Vietnam War. Before we left he introduced me to the general, saying, "General, I want you to meet another Dwight." Later that evening I excitedly called my parents and grandparents: "Guess who I met today."

In addition to their eight years (1953–1961) in the Eisenhower White House, Eisenhower and Nixon had been drawn closer together by the impending marriage of Julie Nixon to Eisenhower's grandson David.

I do know that Nixon had a deep, steadfast respect for the general. And I thought that visiting Eisenhower on Nixon's first day as president-elect was a beautiful gesture and a sign of great respect.

From Washington we flew on to Key Biscayne. We would return a few days later for the president-elect to meet with President Johnson at the White House. On that occasion the president-elect entered the Oval Office through the Rose Garden patio entrance. As Nixon would do later when we'd meet the Pope at the Vatican, after shaking hands with Johnson he introduced each of us individually. Johnson greeted us warmly. While Johnson and Nixon conferred, we were briefed by the White House staff.

I think most of us were feeling a combination of exhilaration and trepidation. We were beyond thrilled at what we had accomplished, but very few of us had served in government before and had no idea of what was to come. However, we had tremendous confidence in Nixon, who displayed complete calm and resolute determination.

Eight years earlier, after losing the presidency to John Kennedy, Nixon offered to visit Kennedy. But Kennedy insisted on traveling to see Nixon at the Key Biscayne hotel where Nixon was resting and unwinding after the close and bitter campaign. Their intention was to demonstrate national unity after having experienced an excruciating campaign. Now Hubert Humphrey was making that painful trip to see Nixon. About four days after the election, Humphrey and Nixon met at the secure Opa-locka Airport, near Miami. Because Johnson spitefully wouldn't give him a jet, Humphrey arrived in a prop plane. Humphrey's wife, Muriel, and vice presidential candidate Ed Muskie and his wife were also on the plane.

Nixon arrived at the base minutes before Humphrey's plane landed. They were meeting on the second floor of a barracks-like building, certainly nothing fancy. In the room where they were to meet, there were two easy chairs facing each other, separated by a coffee table, on which there were glasses and a pitcher of water. When Humphrey and his group arrived, Nixon greeted all of them. The two former candidates posed in front of the cameras for the requisite photographs. The others went to a reception room for coffee while I led the vice president and president-elect upstairs to their meeting room. The two of them met privately, while Secret Service remained outside.

Before the meeting I had been told by Nixon, the president-elect,

"Give us ten minutes and then you come in. Ten minutes, do you understand me?" He was a little anxious, it seemed to me. Knowing that Humphrey could be highly emotional, I believe he wanted to keep what was going to be an uncomfortable meeting as short and as painless as possible for Humphrey. However, the second they were together, it all changed, as Nixon sensed the feelings and fatigue of Humphrey. I kept my eyes on my watch. After ten minutes I opened the door. The two men were sitting opposite each other in discussion. Nixon waved me off with a nice "Give Hubert and me a few more minutes."

Ten minutes later I again opened the door, and again he asked for more time.

When I opened the door once again, after roughly thirty minutes, they were standing together. Nixon had his arm around Humphrey's shoulders, embracing him. Humphrey was sobbing. Tears were streaming down his face and Nixon was consoling him. "Dick," Humphrey said, "I want to do whatever I can to help you."

Nixon continued patting him on the shoulders. "Hubert, I'll be in touch. You and Muriel go have a good vacation." Humphrey took out a handkerchief to wipe his face, and the two men walked out of the room.

Nixon was a man who was instinctively uncomfortable with public displays of emotion. Seeing a tearful Humphrey, as Nixon comforted him with words and touch, was an image I've never forgotten. There was something magnificent about it. These were two warriors, the contest over, loyal Americans both, basically embracing one another.

We all walked out to the gate and they shook hands one last time. I stood next to Nixon as we watched Humphrey board his plane. We didn't move. As the plane started to taxi, Nixon took a deep breath and said, "Dwight, believe me, that is so, so hard. I remember." A few seconds later he looked at me again and added, "But I didn't cry."

5

TRANSITIONING TO THE WEST WING

Starting with Christmas 1963, Bob Haldeman and I exchanged holiday letters. Bob's 1969 New Year's letter, with the inauguration on the horizon, held great meaning:

"We're on the brink of more than we have any ability to realize," Haldeman wrote to me as he set to work creating the Nixon administration. "We've both, in our way, gained and surpassed the wildest dreams of most men. And much more lies ahead than behind." Awesome thought!

As we began this extraordinary adventure, Bob would use our correspondence to set down his most private thoughts. Unlike the buttoned-down confident man seen by the public, he shared his hopes and fears with me. It was not the awesome power he had been given by the president that so humbled him, he wrote, but rather the mammoth responsibility. While admitting his own doubts, "there are times when I really seriously doubt that I am the right one . . . ," he understood that this power "used well and wisely . . . can bring about some good for the world."

As to what was to come, he warned me, "Don't let my daily harangues get you down. I can't help pushing for perfection—and since none of us will ever make it, the critiques will go on. Well, here we go . . ."

Susie too wrote to me, reminding me, "We all have adjustments to make, and as long as we are considerate and thoughtful and patient toward one another, there will be no problem." Susie was referring to my total absorption in the campaign and transition and the need to pay attention to her, our girls, and our marriage. I tried to hear her, but she obviously felt the need to write to me.

Richard Nixon may well have been planning his entire political lifetime for this, but the rest of us had seventy-five days to put together the new government of the United States of America. Imagine replacing the entire leadership of the largest corporation in the world with people new to their jobs, who were expected to have their shops up and running within seventy-five days. It was a Herculean task. But as long as we kept moving forward and didn't pause to think about the complexity of this transition, it seemed doable. As Haldeman had expressed, it was an awesome responsibility; so rather than looking at the whole of it, we were more focused on making sure there was enough coffee and ensuring that the president-elect's next meeting started and ended on time. We set up the transition office in New York's Pierre hotel. We would joke about that location and question who was responsible for finding the single most expensive place in New York to put our headquarters. I remember looking at a menu and seeing that a hamburger cost $25.00. At that time in 1968 a McDonald's cheeseburger cost $0.19, and there was a McDonald's less than three blocks from the Nixons' apartment.

The transition process initially consisted of working with President Johnson's staff as they began to turn their offices and responsibilities over to us. At the same time, we were also building our own team. Nixon had to recruit a cabinet, a subcabinet, and a White House staff. When administrations change, the only people who typically remain in their jobs are the White House professional staff, from the ushers, telephone operators, and certain career secretaries to the butlers and maintenance people. No one had told me what my job was going to be, so I just kept doing whatever I was told to do. That has always been my area of expertise. I sat at a small desk just outside the entrance into the hotel's presidential suite in a small alcove, setting up appointments, escorting visitors in and out, watching the Nixon administration being formed.

The third day we were in operation, FBI Director J. Edgar Hoover arrived for a meeting. At that time Hoover was still a legend. I'd grown up in Kansas hearing all those incredible stories about the G-men and their boss, J. Edgar Hoover. As a boy growing up in Kansas, one of my favorite radio shows, a program I never missed, was a fifteen-minute daily drama called *The FBI*. And here I was, meeting Hoover himself. As it turned out, Nixon didn't especially like the director and kept him waiting in our small anteroom for almost an hour. Hoover sat right next to my desk on a small couch. I remember he looked like a little toad, waiting patiently. Certainly I don't know, but I suspect that Hoover was not used to waiting for many people. He was one of the most powerful men in the world. Whatever Nixon's reasons, he seemed to be letting Hoover know that he was not intimidated by this very powerful man waiting outside his office. Hoover sat patiently, showing no indication to me that this treatment made any impression on him. We made small talk while he waited.

Nixon was making the point from this first meeting that Hoover was not going to have the same relationship with him that he had enjoyed with President Johnson. The FBI director and Johnson were friends and neighbors. Johnson had used the FBI to investigate rumors of Communist involvement in the antiwar movement, specifically checking to see if Senator William Fulbright was receiving information from subversives. He had asked the Bureau to "look into members of Senator Barry Goldwater's staff" and whether some of the results "contained derogatory information." We later learned that to placate Johnson, the FBI had been spying on our campaign to determine if Nixon was using Anna Chennault to take messages to the South Vietnamese government.

At the time I didn't know any of that, of course. I just knew I was sitting with the legendary J. Edgar Hoover and that Nixon, for whatever his reasons, appeared to be deliberately keeping him waiting.

While I felt I had earned a doctorate in campaigning, I was surely inexperienced and naive when it came to governing. I trusted in the sanctity of most of the core American values; as well as the professionalism and honesty of foundational institutions such as the FBI and CIA and, to some degree, even the media.

I was sitting at my small desk when two men in dark suits showed up, and each handed me a notebook with a black-and-white insert in the cover reading: "Top Secret, Eyes Only." I'd never seen anything like this outside of a movie theater. But okay, I took the notebooks and told the two men I'd give the notebooks to the president-elect when he was free. I didn't think anything more about them until Haldeman asked with astonishment, "They just left them with you?" "Yes," I replied.

When Nixon found out he asked with equal astonishment, "They just left them with Dwight? Is Dwight cleared?" "No." All hell broke loose. Nixon even called President Johnson, letting him know what had happened. Those notebooks that were left with me contained the most consequential presidential intelligence concerning the Vietnam War. That action served as a harbinger of other things we would learn regarding how sloppy the Johnson administration and our intelligence agencies could be concerning intelligence.

But in this instance it seemed it was my fault for accepting those documents that I didn't know I shouldn't have accepted. Bob Haldeman had warned me he was going to be tough on me, and we'd already struggled through some issues, but he came down hard on me on this one. I pushed back a little. This was one of the first times I heard what was to become a not uncommon refrain over the following very stressful months: "I'm disappointed in you, Dwight."

One day, I remember, I was told to get hold of this fellow I'd never heard of, a Harvard professor named Henry Kissinger. I asked the White House Communications Agency operator to please get Dr. Kissinger on the phone. They found him in a meeting with Nelson Rockefeller. I introduced myself by phone and explained that the president-elect would like to meet with him. Kissinger had been Rockefeller's foreign affairs advisor and was very loyal to Rocky. Nixon and Kissinger didn't know each other well. Apparently they had only met briefly at a cocktail party given by Ambassador Clare Boothe Luce many years before, in 1957, at the Luce Christmas party when one was leaving and the other arriving. Kissinger had contributed a couple of papers on foreign policy issues to our campaign. Nixon had also read Henry's book *Nuclear Weapons and Foreign Policy*.

Henry loves to tell the story of his first official meeting with President-Elect Nixon and his hiring. When they met at the Pierre hotel, they had a long, somewhat in-depth conversation about world affairs. I can imagine Nixon's delight in finding someone who understood the complexities of global relationships and the use of power as much as Henry did. They talked at length during this meeting, but Nixon never mentioned the possibility of a job. Several days later John Mitchell followed up with Henry, asking if he had made up his mind. "Made up my mind?" he responded in his heavily accented voice. "He never asked me to join his staff."

Mitchell clarified that he had, in fact, been offered the position in the West Wing as head of the National Security Council (NSC). Henry equivocated, asking for some time. In telling Rockefeller about the offer, he said, "I told them I wanted to think about it."

Rockefeller reacted: "The President of the United States is asking you to join his staff. You don't think about it. You do it." Kissinger became one of the first new members of the administration, accepting the position of National Security Advisor.

Kissinger's legendary wit and concern over his public image became evident once we were in office, as demonstrated by a meeting he had with William Safire. Bill Safire, a speechwriter who was media savvy and also very witty, would tell the story of a conversation he had with Kissinger, during which Henry accused him jokingly of having no convictions. Bill responded immediately, "True, Henry. I've had a lot of arrests but no convictions." "That's a good line," Kissinger said, an impish smile on his face. "Why don't you call Maxine Cheshire at the *Washington Post* and attribute it to me."

It was fascinating to watch Nixon shift effortlessly from tireless campaigner to tireless executive. He was in his element. He ran things incredibly smoothly and had mastered the art of making all the necessary decisions. He worked in the suite at the Pierre hotel during the day and in the evening at his apartment, attending only those events that were politically necessary while exercising complete control over the transition. It was a lesson in disciplined leadership.

The most important decisions he had to make during this period involved putting together his cabinet. He knew who he wanted and he went out to get them. We were in California, at the Century Plaza Hotel, in early December 1968. I was sent downstairs to the lobby to find this professor from the University of Chicago whom few had heard of. His name was George Shultz. I escorted Shultz upstairs to the suite for his first ever meeting with Nixon. Shultz wasn't a politician. He was an academic. It was Richard Nixon who brought him into the public domain, where he distinguished himself many times over, first as U.S. Secretary of Labor, then Director of the Office of Management and Budget, and finally as Secretary of the Treasury in the Nixon administration. Later in his career Shultz would become President Reagan's highly respected Secretary of State.

Mel Laird was part of the Republican leadership in the House of Representatives and had absolutely no intention or desire to leave the House. On the same trip to California that December, Laird flew with us from Los Angeles to a governors' conference in Palm Springs. While on the very brief flight, Nixon extended to him an invitation to join his administration, while twisting Laird's arm to the breaking point to get him to say "Yes." Just before we landed, while holding up a bottle of champagne, Nixon announced to all of us that Mel Laird had accepted his invitation to become Secretary of Defense.

The cabinet was filled with other seasoned executives; among them John Volpe, Governor of Massachusetts, who was appointed Secretary of Transportation; George Romney, Governor of Michigan, who was appointed Secretary of Housing and Urban Development; loyal political aide Bob Finch, who was appointed Secretary of Health, Education and Welfare; and campaign manager John Mitchell, who was appointed to the important position of U.S. Attorney General.

Nixon had learned the effective use of television. Rather than announcing each appointment separately, which would have had much less of an impact, he waited until he had assembled his entire cabinet. He then introduced them as a group in a prime-time television event from the Shoreham Hotel in Washington, D.C. It aired on all three of the networks at the time, ABC, CBS, and NBC. Nothing like this had been done previously. "Another historic first," we would proclaim. There were two things Nixon really liked: achieving "Firsts" and pulling "Surprises" in terms of creative policy implementation.

At this announcement all the new cabinet members were seated along with their wives in rows on a stage. As the president-elect introduced each nominee in turn, they appeared on the television screen. Nixon explained in detail why he had selected that person, thereby building the public's confidence in the new administration. Nixon being Nixon, he had memorized everything he wanted to say about each cabinet member and spoke with no notes. Unfortunately, he accidently skipped one of the people who had worked hardest to get him elected, his chief fundraiser, the new Secretary of Commerce, Maurice Stans. It was a mistake for which Nixon felt terrible and it took place on live television. It must have been crushing to Stans, who was a distinguished public accountant. That evening 25 percent of the U.S. population listened and watched as Nixon introduced his cabinet choices.

Nixon appointed five assistants to the president, each of whom quickly grabbed his bailiwick. Haldeman was Chief of Staff, responsible for running the office of the presidency. Henry Kissinger was the National Security Advisor, responsible for foreign policy and security. Bryce Harlow was assigned Assistant to the President for Legislative and Congressional Affairs, responsible for communicating with the legislative branch. John Ehrlichman, who was initially appointed to be the White House Counsel, was moved within a year to the newly created position of Domestic Affairs Advisor, responsible for all domestic issues. Daniel Patrick Moynihan, a Democrat, was originally supposed to run that department but after a few weeks became Urban Affairs Advisor. (That shift in responsibilities was done quietly. Moynihan didn't know beforehand that the decision had been made, or he might have quit. When he did learn of this decision, he was not a happy camper.) Arthur Burns, who was later to become Chairman of the Federal Reserve, was a conservative who was appointed Counsellor to the President and sparred with Moynihan on domestic policy.

The president also appointed Air Force Lieutenant General Don Hughes to be his assistant with responsibility for the White House military aides operation. Hughes had been Nixon's military aide when he was vice president.

Within a few days my appointment and that of Ron Ziegler, my fraternity brother from USC, were announced. I was named Special Assistant to the President. Actually, at the beginning I was his appointments secretary, meaning I was responsible for planning his schedule. I coordinated his meetings, his travel, pretty much whatever he did on a daily basis. I was also given responsibility for several other things that fit nowhere else, including coordinating with the television office and overseeing use of the White House tennis court and swimming pool. While Ron Ziegler did not have the press credentials of many former press secretaries, he was given the position of White House Press Secretary. Nixon purposefully chose a man without a press background because of the little regard in which he held "the media." Ron did a tremendous job as press secretary. He was, without question, one of the hardest working members of the White House staff—he had to be to just survive the daily grind of serving the media in the Nixon administration. He wasn't an easy person for the rest of the staff to get along with, but he was very loyal to the president.

Nixon warned his cabinet secretaries that they had no more than sixty to ninety days to set up shop and make any significant changes before the Establishment and the media would box them into the status quo. Any changes they wanted to make had to be made very quickly because the bureaucracy, which never likes change, was far more powerful than they realized. The entrenched powers, essentially comprised of Democrats (a.k.a., our "political enemies"), Nixon warned, would fight to maintain the system. We were to learn quickly that Mr. Nixon's warning was not an exaggeration.

We had a day-long seminar outlining expectations, dos and don'ts, and operating procedures in the White House. It took place in the ballroom of the Pierre hotel. It was a required meeting for anyone appointed or awaiting appointment. The "faculty" that day included Bryce Harlow and Arthur Burns, both of whom had served in the Eisenhower administration; and Daniel Patrick Moynihan, from the Kennedy administration. They shared with us their experiences in the administrations in which they had served. Haldeman also spoke and told the group that he understood and accepted the enormity of his position and how different it was going to be from running a small office in an advertising agency.

Bryce Harlow had been appointed the Assistant to the President for Legislative and Congressional Affairs, a difficult challenge, as both the Senate and House would be controlled by the Democratic Party. Harlow was our coolest hand. He had been through the political wars of the Eisenhower years. He was a small man in stature but a giant in terms of wisdom and common sense. Will Rogers was from Oklahoma, and so was Bryce. Will Rogers was a natural entertainer, and so was Bryce. The stories Bryce told, as he stood on a box behind a podium, had his audience roaring with laughter. When he turned serious, everyone took note.

Bryce's message: The White House is brick and mortar, but when you call somebody and the operator says to them, "The White House is calling," it's not a building on the phone. You are representing the President of the United States. Whatever you say will sound as if it's coming from the president. Be careful. Be judicious. And the most important thing for you to remember is that the position to which you have been appointed is temporary. Don't start thinking that you are something special. You are there, by the grace of God, for a brief period of time. Don't fall into the trap of thinking your life is going to be like this forever after. This isn't about you. It is about the power and majesty that comes with the Office of the Presidency in which you have been given the privilege to serve. Bryce's talk was practical and sobering that day. I've always remembered it.

Given all the power he was warning us about, it was inevitable that problems would arise. The White House is no different from any other office. There are always rivalries and personal conflicts. These were all very successful people, running their own operations before they arrived at the White House, and so there were a lot of big egos in the administration.

Two weeks after the inauguration I had to speak to Henry Kissinger about the scheduled visit of Anatoly Dobrynin, the Soviet Ambassador to the United States. He met me outside his office and escorted me to a different one. When we were alone, he shook his head ruefully and said, "I have five egomaniacs in there." (Kissinger himself, of course, would have been the sixth.) But what his joke underscored is important. It is at the heart of the relationship he and I established with each other in the first days of the administration, which has carried through to this day. I joke that I have not only earned a doctorate in campaigning, but I've also earned one in Kissinger management. I cannot think of one time in all of the opportunities over the years that I've had to work with him that there have been harsh words. Our relationship was initially based on humor and camaraderie, which led to trust. Some former colleagues were critical of Kissinger's maneuvering and what they saw as his "propensity to eclipse" the president. I never saw it that way. Nixon towered over Kissinger, in my view. I dismissed Kissinger's need for gratification as being just that: a need for gratification. I never saw him as anti-Nixon. I've always felt tremendous affection, admiration, and respect for Henry Kissinger.

The jockeying for power between Haldeman and Rose Woods continued into the White House, but this was a fight she couldn't win. Rose, having been with the president for so long, was upset when her access to Nixon was curtailed. At one point she complained of feeling like "a fifth wheel," and once, when Nixon refused to take an old friend's call, she complained that he was "kicking old friends in the teeth."

The administration rapidly took shape. John Ehrlichman, who had been appointed the Counsel to the President, immediately began looking for ways to expand his influence, eventually becoming head of domestic affairs. His relationship with Kissinger was not always copacetic, which actually turned out to benefit me a few years later, when the China trips were being planned.

Kissinger also clashed with Secretary of State William Rogers, which was almost inevitable. As Nixon had learned as vice president, the State Department was a huge bureaucracy that operated as its own fiefdom. Other presidents had tried to tame it. President Nixon intended to conduct foreign policy himself from the White House, using Kissinger and the NSC as his agency. To have more control over the State Department, he appointed his old friend Bill Rogers, who had no background in foreign affairs. Nixon considered him a loyalist who would help rein in the influence of the State Department. While Kissinger and Rogers jockeyed for position, Rogers never had a chance to emerge the victor.

Yachtsman Bus Mosbacher, who had twice successfully defended the America's Cup, was appointed Chief of Protocol. The president expected Haldeman and me to exercise control over his schedule and travel; and the last thing he intended to do was to give the State Department, let alone Protocol, any authority to run things. This set up an awkward relationship with Mosbacher, who wasn't popular with the president or our staff.

Mosbacher's primary mission, it appeared, was getting his picture in the newspapers. I never knew why he was given the position at Protocol but, in order to handle him, Haldeman appointed Nick Ruwe Deputy Chief of Protocol. The Chief of Protocol is supposed to make certain that national and international traditions and customs are upheld. Haldeman put out a presidential directive that all events, with the exception of official state visits, were to be handled by Nick, whom he trusted implicitly. Many years later Nick would become former President Nixon's chief of staff in New York. Nixon would then recommend to President Reagan that Nick be appointed U.S. Ambassador to Iceland, which capped his career.

I'm confident Nixon was aware of most of these interpersonal issues. He enjoyed hearing all the gossip, but he carefully kept himself out of it. He assiduously avoided personal confrontation. If he wanted to get involved in an issue, his directions would go through Bob, who had learned how to provide deniability. So while the directive about Nick Ruwe came from Haldeman, Bob wasn't the person who had made that decision.

Similar to the placing of Nick Ruwe at Protocol, Roy Goodearle, an advance man and one of my great friends and mentors, was placed by the president and Haldeman as Vice President Agnew's Chief of Staff. Roy was loyal to the vice president, no question. But his first and foremost loyalty always remained with President Nixon.

Nixon was inaugurated on January 20, 1969. That morning, Haldeman, Ziegler, and I went with the Nixon family to the church service at St. John's Episcopal Church, across the street from the White House. Known as "the president's church," St. John's was established in 1816, and every president since James Madison has attended services there.

After the service it was then on to the White House for coffee, a special and memorable experience. The Johnsons and their staff could not have been more gracious. Everything about the morning was perfect. We were over-the-top excited. I have an indelible image of President Johnson and President-Elect Nixon, standing that morning in the Blue Room. Johnson is bending Nixon's ear with a last piece of advice, while, framed in the background through the Blue Room's large window, stands the Washington Monument.

I went to the Capitol in the motorcade. Susie was waiting for me. We watched the ceremony together in a reserved staff section. At the conclusion of the inauguration, we made our way through crowds to the Hay-Adams hotel, where we met our parents for lunch. They had come from California to attend the inauguration and the inaugural balls and to be present at my swearing-in with the White House staff, which would take place the next day. Later that afternoon we were invited into the presidential viewing booth in front of the White House. The parade, organized by the Washington Military District, ran unnecessarily late into the early evening. Had we been running the parade, it would have been on time.

It was approaching five o'clock and we were in the reviewing stand. Susie and I were getting ready to go to the hotel to change into our formal attire for the inaugural balls, when Bob suggested that, while Susie was getting ready for the balls, he and I go inside to check out our new offices. While we had been occupied with the ceremonial events, our offices were being set up, and here we were, getting ready to walk into the West Wing of the White House together for the first time.

I'm going to pause here and savor those words: ". . . the West Wing of the White House together for the first time." All these years later, those words still have the power to stir my emotions. They are words that few people have the privilege of uttering.

Haldeman and I walked across the White House lawn on sheets of plywood over the squishy lawn. It had been raining, and the lawn was soaked. We were ready to move into the White House but, as it turned out, the White House was not ready for us. As if it were an ant colony, eager GSA (General Services Administration) workers were all over the place. With the exception of the Oval Office, the West Wing was a mess, and they were trying to make it habitable. Viewed for the first time through the critical eyes of two about-to-be occupants, it was run-down, torn up, battered, and abused. Paint was peeling. There were holes and darkened spaces where framed pictures or documents had been hung. Wires attached to nothing were coming out of the baseboards. The carpets were worn threadbare. The Johnson folks had not been overly concerned with the appearance or upkeep of those hallowed spaces. Within a day or two it had been cleaned up, refreshed, and repainted, but that first look was unsettling and disturbing.

The phones on the president's desk in the Oval Office spoke volumes about the differences between the outgoing and incoming chief executives. LBJ's phone, which had approximately thirty-six direct lines to administration officials, was replaced by Nixon's phone, which had two White House outside lines and four small buzzer buttons: Haldeman to issue orders, Rose to dictate memos, the navy steward for coffee, and me ("odd job") . . . for everything else.

LBJ was obsessed with media coverage. Johnson's large TV console with three side-by-side monitors that allowed him to keep track of the three major networks had been removed, as were the AP and UPI wire tickers. He also had manually controlled tape recorders in the Oval Office, Cabinet Room, Executive Office Building (EOB), under the bed in the White House Residence, and at the LBJ ranch in Texas.

Nixon kept one small TV in a small office directly off the Oval Office. The fireplaces in the West Wing, which apparently had not been used by the Johnson team, had been reactivated. Nixon loved fires, and thanks to air-conditioning he could keep the fires going even during the hot Washington summers. The serenity of the fires probably brought him peace.

Nixon greatly appreciated the majesty of the White House. In fact, he authorized a makeover of the interior to bring it up to a standard expected by the American people. He used the Oval Office mostly for ceremonial purposes and for meetings, but he much preferred to work in his EOB office, which was directly across West Executive Avenue and just a short walk from the West Wing. It afforded him the privacy he wanted.

I had been assigned prime real estate, literally the office next to the president's in the West Wing. (See the West Wing First Floor Plan on page x.) One door opened into the Oval Office. Another two doors opened onto the Rose Garden. The Cabinet Room was on the other side of my office. Bob Haldeman had the space on the other side of the Oval Office for the first few months and then moved to a much larger Chief of Staff office farther down the West Wing hall but still just steps from the Oval Office.

When Haldeman and I walked into my new office we were both

stunned to find one of the largest desks I had ever seen, positioned directly beneath a huge, beautiful brass chandelier. Bob was not happy; I was horrified. The GSA had selected the desk. It was completely out of proportion, not just for my position as an aide but for the room itself. It was overwhelming and was just the kind of thing that would understandably upset Haldeman. By the next morning, that desk was gone forever replaced by an appropriately smaller desk.

Bryce Harlow had recommended that Nell Yates be my secretarial assistant. Nell had begun working in the White House during the Truman administration. She was competent and trustworthy beyond description, and she knew how everything in the building worked. She wore her hair in a bun, always had a beautiful smile on her face, and looked as if she could have stepped out of an episode of *Little House on the Prairie*. Nell being assigned to work with me was one of the most fortunate gifts I could have been given. She was wonderful and an amazingly loyal assistant. However, her assignment created a minor crisis.

Harlow had said to Haldeman, "Dwight needs Nell." He was right: I absolutely needed Nell. But in those first few days Bob learned that Nell had been working in the White House for several administrations and, in fact, had worked for my Democratic direct predecessor in the Johnson administration. Bob was a cautious man. Nell couldn't work for me, he told me, because she would see so many documents moving among Nixon, Haldeman and me that were political and confidential. "You have to get rid of her," he told me.

When Bryce was informed, he approached Bob, saying something to the effect of, "You don't understand the secretarial staff here. These aren't political people. They're professionals." Whatever he said, it worked. Nell was able to continue as my secretary. She helped me survive.

The first morning on the job I arrived in my new office around seven thirty. When I opened the door into the Oval Office, President Nixon was standing right in front of his desk, perhaps just savoring the moment. There were times I wondered what he was thinking. This was one of them. He had been through so much, the victories and the defeats, the extraordinary highs and the soul-wrenching rejections. It had all come to this moment. He was standing in the Oval Office as the President of the United States.

"Good morning, Mr. President," I said for the first time. I may have been the first person to speak to him in the Oval Office.

"Can you ask Rose to come in," he said.

Rose had not yet arrived. "Then get me Haldeman," he said. I had heard that "Get me Haldeman" often—but this was the first time he said it as president.

Later that morning in the East Room, President Nixon and Chief Justice Earl Warren swore us all in. "The people who will be sworn in," the president said, "are members of the White House staff. They are supposed to be faceless men and women. For faceless men and women, I think they look very good, though, don't you, Mr. Chief Justice?"

We all laughed, appropriately and appreciatively.

We would work long hours, he said, "but I try not to call after midnight . . . As far as the wives are concerned, of the husbands who are here, if they are away after midnight, don't blame me. Blame them."

We laughed again, but nervously this time. Spontaneous humor was not a Nixon skill.

During our first week in the White House, when most of us were still stumbling around, trying to find the bathrooms, Haldeman was already at work trying to make our operations more efficient. Bob remained focused on details. We had three Haldeman buttons. If the telephone button showing green was lit, it meant Haldeman could be interrupted; the yellow button signaled we could interrupt but only if urgent; and a lit red button meant no interruptions allowed under any circumstance. Haldeman was responsible for turning the three lights on and off, and he did so religiously. One of the lights was always on when he was in his office.

The president's locator board was a light system that told us precisely where he was at any given moment. Physically, it was located in a walnut box (3" x 12" x 3") with five labels on the front and five small red lights above each label. The box was located high in our offices above a doorway, so as not to be visible to a guest. The board would very softly chime when the president moved within the White House or off the White House grounds. The small red light would move along with the chime, indicating where he was: "Now Moving" (within the buildings) in "EOB Office," "Oval Office," "Residence," or "Off Grounds" (away). For example, if he was in San Clemente at the Western White House or at Camp David, the "Off Grounds" red indicator would be lit. The locator board and the switching of the red indicator lights was controlled by the Secret Service. There was a locator board in all the Secret Service offices in the White House and the Executive Protective Service guard stations, Haldeman's and my offices, and the offices of Nixon aide Steve Bull and Alex Butterfield, Haldeman's deputy. We used the boards constantly.

To "increase efficiency" in the use of the hotlines that connected us to Bob's office he sent a memo: "If you are able to answer the hotline yourself when it rings, just come on and say 'hello' or 'yes,' or something to indicate you are alive and breathing and we can get right to the subject from there." If we were not there, whoever answered the phone should not waste time saying hello but rather simply state where we were.

He also established the ethical culture. One day very early in the administration, Don Kendall, the chairman of Pepsi, an important Republican fundraiser and one of the president's close friends, called. "Dwight, I'm down here in Costa Rica," he said. It may have been another South American country, but he apparently was somewhere on Pepsi business. "The president of Costa Rica is going to be having dinner in my suite tonight at seven thirty. It would be very helpful if I could get a call from the president. He could say hello to the president of Costa Rica."

I sent a note to Haldeman repeating the request. "What did you tell him?" Bob asked.

"Well, I didn't give him an answer," I said.

"You should have said 'no' immediately," he scolded me. "This is not happening." I had to politely let Kendall know that we were not in the business of using the presidency for others' business purposes.

Like all the rest of us in those first few weeks, Haldeman was finding his footing. During our second week in office, he sent me a note providing "rules of thumb," a random set of ad hoc thoughts. Among those guiding principles:

The president must always come first. "He was born to do this job—and he's perfect."

Our job was to make certain that at the end of every day the president left his office feeling confident that he had achieved his objectives.

Admitting to his insecurities. "I'm afraid I do feel sorry for myself way too often." The one thing about which he was certain was the strength of our friendship, adding, "and it sure helps."

Every day brought a new learning experience. I started writing to my friends and family on the very light green White House stationery. That letterhead, "The White House," was impressive. The heavily embossed presidential seal in gold made it even more special. One day Rose Woods walked by and saw me writing. "Where'd you get that?" she asked.

"From the president's desk," I replied.

"Dwight," she said, admonishing me, "that's only for use by the President of the United States."

On another day Haldeman called Ron Ziegler, the White House Press Secretary, and me into his office. The way we worked was that Bob would meet with the president first thing every morning and make long lists of everything that needed to be done. He'd fill literally a dozen or more pages of a yellow pad with notes and tasks. Then he would distribute the responsibilities. Ron and I were sitting at Bob's conference table listening as he went through his list. Suddenly he stopped and looked at us. "Wow," he said. "You guys must be geniuses." I looked at Ron. Smart, yes, but . . . Bob continued: "I don't want you ever coming in here again without a pad and pen, and I want to see you taking notes. I'm not sitting here, going through this list, to entertain myself."

I learned. I got better at my job. We all did. And while some people eventually got jaded, I never did. I loved working in the White House for Richard Nixon. I believed in the man and I believed in our mission. It felt like we were going to make the United States a better place, which was surely Nixon's intention.

During our swearing-in ceremony, Chief Justice Warren took a moment to tell us about Washington, "the Capital of the World," as he called it. "Enjoy it; savor it while you are here. You will look back on it later and remember what a wonderful experience it was."

He was right. Many days I would leave my desk in the West Wing around noon and go out through the Northwest Gate to the front of the White House and walk all the way around to the Ellipse, just marveling that I was there. I felt a deep sense of gratitude to be in Washington, D.C., working in the White House. I loved it, loved every minute of it. Even these many years later, I've never lost that pride, the special feeling that I felt in those days.

$\star$ **6** $\star$

SETTLING IN FOR THE HARD WORK

"February 1st, 1969. It is ten days since the Inauguration," I wrote in my diary. "The president's mood has been excellent. He has been keeping long hours and loves the work."

We were settling in, figuring out how to get the job done. Ever since FDR coined the concept and the phrase "the first hundred days" back in 1933, the media had treated the first hundred days of an administration as a kind of benchmark by which it might be measured. It was sort of a honeymoon period during which a new administration crosses the threshold, begins hanging the curtains, and setting its tone and pace. We experienced the same first hundred days. We knew we had a period of time to get our people and policies in place. But as the initial excitement faded, the daily issues began surfacing. We had a lot to learn. Bob Haldeman, for example, almost set fire to the West Wing when he used the fireplace in his office for the first time. Apparently it hadn't been used since who knows when, and as the chimney did not draw smoke properly, it billowed into his office. The windows couldn't be opened because they had been painted shut. Bob noted that Rose was furious about not being able to open the windows, which may have had as much to do with her unhappiness about her perceived lessening of responsibilities as the smoke.

"In their own way," I wrote in a memo to him, "these first few days have been harder than those that will come later. We all have to learn our way and our role . . . Now you must evaluate the situation and see that people are following the proper patterns. This should be done before people grow accustomed to the roles they are developing which may be incorrect, unworkable, or unsuitable." My observation must have been sparked by some level of personal confusion or by what I was seeing others doing.

During the campaign, few of us had been together for more than brief periods of time. We had been scattered around the country, crossing paths as we worked together for the election of Richard Nixon. But suddenly we were all finding ourselves in one place together. Most of us had absolutely no understanding of what was to come, no preparation for it.

And then people started settling in, and their personalities began emerging. Everyone began carving out their fiefdoms. We all watched each other as we figured out how we fit into this great White House puzzle. Carefully heeding Bob's advice, I kept a low profile, kept my eyes on the next task at hand, and smiled agreeably at all the right times.

Perhaps more than with anyone other than Bob, I forged a strong working relationship with Henry Kissinger. From those first days, he never hesitated to voice his opinions to me. I liked him. He was unlike anyone I'd ever met. He was extraordinarily knowledgeable, off-the-charts smart, funny, insightful, and decent. And he was dedicated to working with President Nixon in his quest to end the Vietnam War. At the outset of the administration, however, Henry seemed insecure in terms of his relationship with the president. This was understandable since Henry was a Harvard man, a Rockefeller man, totally unfamiliar with Nixon, and Nixon wasn't an easy man to read.

Henry and I were standing in my office one afternoon when I was first getting to know him. He told me that the president was not acting like a president. Or, better said, he was not acting as Henry believed a president should be acting. He was too nice, Henry said. His comment had come in response to my telling him that the president wanted to see him "but not if he's busy with something else." Nixon, conscientious about interrupting someone who might be otherwise engaged, would say this often. Actually, I thought it reflected a positive attribute for the world's most important executive. However, Henry felt that if the president were to be effective, he had to ask for things more firmly. He felt that when the president wanted to speak with someone, he should expect that person to respond instantly, regardless of what he was working on. "After all," Henry said, "I am his expert on foreign affairs, and how do I know what he is thinking if I'm not there when he asks for me?"

I suspect few journalists would have agreed that Nixon was too nice. But, of course, they didn't really know the president. Nixon's relationship with the media had been, at best, combative. However, as the administration began, the situation had changed, at least temporarily. Nixon had become president and the press seemed to be granting him, if only grudgingly, the traditional honeymoon period. After all, reporters needed access to the White House as much as we needed them to carry our message.

There were a few reporters the president trusted. Theodore H. White, for example, who was finishing his book *The Making of the President 1968,* was among the first journalists invited into the Oval Office. Although White wrote frequent journalistic pieces and had no problem getting anything he wrote published in a newspaper or magazine, by 1960 he was a full-time author rather than a journalist. The phenomenal success of his groundbreaking and Pulitzer Prize–winning *The Making of the President 1960,* followed by a similarly titled book on the 1964 election, had moved him into the stratosphere as a sort of oracle on the subject of the mechanics and demographics of presidential campaigns. Nixon knew that White had a wide circle of friends and acquaintances and that working journalists would be looking to White for the approach to take with him. He also knew that White would be producing another book on the 1972 campaign.

Nixon spent several hours working with White, trusting him to get the details of the recent campaign right. But White was the exception. During a discussion on how to deal with the media at the very first cabinet meeting, the president said adamantly that he did not want anyone in the White House talking to the highly influential, independent, and widely syndicated investigative reporters Drew Pearson and Jack Anderson. Nixon had a history with them, and it wasn't a friendly one.

That created a problem for me a couple of weeks later when I glanced at Vice President Agnew's schedule and noticed "a background meeting" with Jack Anderson. Nixon and Agnew didn't have a bad relationship; they simply had no relationship at this point. Nixon was most comfortable with people he had known for a long time, people who had proven their value to him. Agnew was still an unknown. I immediately went to John Ehrlichman, the White House Counsel. Since the scheduled meeting was in opposition to our stated policy, Ehrlichman was surprised to hear about it.

This definitely was not a good way for Agnew to begin building his relationship with the president. Ehrlichman called Roy Goodearle, Agnew's Chief of Staff, to make sure the vice president understood the no-meeting-with-Jack-Anderson policy. Next thing I received a phone call from Agnew, sounding upset and asking for an appointment to see the president.

The president agreed to see him that afternoon. This was the first time the two men had met privately in the Oval Office. Evidently Agnew used the opportunity to complain about the way he was being treated by Ehrlichman. It was obvious that the vice president had little understanding of the president. Nixon trusted Ehrlichman, while he barely knew Agnew, so I'm not sure whose side Agnew thought the president would be likely to take.

The relationship between Nixon and Agnew never got better, only worse. Agnew had no clear role in the administration. Initially he was assigned to be the liaison between the White House and the nation's governors, but once the governors realized he lacked influence with the president, they would bypass him and go directly to Ehrlichman. Agnew never figured it out. He would complain to people loyal to Nixon about the situation, and the more he complained, the worse it got. He didn't have the ability to track with us; or, if he did, he failed to demonstrate it at the beginning, which cost him with Nixon. Where the president was concerned, the saying "You only have one chance to make a first impression" was true. It never took the president long to conclude that a person either had it or he didn't. And once the president locked on to an opinion about someone, he wasn't likely to change his mind. The few times the president asked for my opinion, I was always very careful. Not that I had sway on his opinions, but I knew from being around him for years that I had earned some credibility with him. If I was negative in any comment about an individual, Nixon would remember it, and the impression I might leave would be next to impossible to change once uttered.

I do think the president came to believe his selection of Agnew as his running mate was a mistake. But he stuck with him. The staff understood very quickly that the vice president wasn't relevant. He was utilized mostly for political purposes, such as appearing in the hinterlands for GOP candidates and, eventually, for attacking the media, at which he did a good job. Agnew had an office in the West Wing for less than a month until he was moved to an office in the EOB. But officially his office was at the Capitol. I doubt that he saw Nixon more than once or twice a month at a cabinet meeting or at some political event.

One afternoon during this early period, for example, Nixon was taking a quick nap. An aide woke him to tell him that Agnew was calling. An hour later we received a warning from Haldeman that when the president was taking a nap, he was never to be awakened unless it was a national emergency—but especially not for a call from the vice president.

My own relationship with the vice president was good, but there were awkward moments. One morning Agnew was at Andrews Air Force Base aboard his plane, taxiing on the runway. I was called into the Oval Office, where the president was reading the remarks the vice president was to deliver later in the morning. I believe this was Agnew's famous "nattering nabobs of negativism" speech about the mainstream media, which had been written by Nixon speechwriter Bill Safire. "Stop his departure. Tell him to wait till we get back to him." I immediately called Agnew's Chief of Staff Roy Goodearle: "Roy, wait. The president says don't take off. We'll get back to you." I then went about my morning. About an hour and a half later, my secretary, Nell Yates, said, "Mr. Goodearle is on the phone." "We're still waiting," he said. "The vice president is anxious to take off."

Whoops! I quickly got permission for Agnew's plane to take off. Agnew's waiting had completely slipped my mind. A few days later in the White House mail I received an autographed picture of the vice president. "To Dwight Chapin: Can I take off now? Regards, Ted Agnew."

My own relationship with the media was respectful, at least in the beginning. I had worked with many of them during the campaign. Although at times I saw how unfairly they could report, I understood that we, and they, all had jobs to do. Whatever my initial feelings about the media, they changed forever in May 1969. Haldeman buzzed me into his office. John Ehrlichman and Larry Higby were there, along with White House Communications Director Herb Klein. "We have a problem," Bob said. In fact, it was a huge, consequential problem.

Within minutes we were joined by Attorney General John Mitchell, who began: "Gentlemen, I've just met with the president. I'll explain what he wants us to do. But first the situation." Herb Klein provided the background: "I got a call from Jack Anderson. He's getting ready to go with a story that there is a homosexual ring in the White House. It involves the four of you"—meaning me, Haldeman, Ehrlichman, and Higby. It turned out that Anderson had one of his staff named Joe Trento and a photographer follow us when we were in Key Biscayne. The photographer had taken pictures of the four of us going into and out of each other's villas late at night. From that activity, they leaped to the conclusion that we were homosexual. Anderson was getting ready to break the story. While the story wasn't true, at that time it could have been a career ender, given the bias that existed against homosexuals in that period of our history.

I had learned from an episode in the Johnson administration that accusations can stick. Several years earlier Lyndon Johnson's closest friend and aide through his entire political career, Walter Jenkins, had been arrested with another man by a park policeman in a public bathroom and charged with loitering. The FBI started investigating. While Johnson demanded that the FBI "bring pressure to bear" on the park policeman making the accusation, once the story broke, Jenkins had to be fired—not only because the story was true, but because he was at risk of being blackmailed. So we knew how damaging accusations could be. I was terrified. This was way beyond my comfort zone. I literally felt my life was at stake. All four of us were disturbed. Someone was playing very dirty politics with our lives. Again, this was fifty years ago, a less enlightened and a highly homophobic time, when the accusation itself could ruin a life and end a career.

Had the story about the four of us been printed, it could have cost the president his two top aides, Haldeman and Ehrlichman, as well as Higby and me. Mitchell and the president had agreed in their meeting that they would have Herb Klein call Anderson and ask him what we could do to prove his story was not true. Anderson's response was simple: We could be interviewed by the FBI.

The next day I went into the Cabinet Room for my interview. There were four or five people waiting for me. I recognized the short burly man seated on one side of the cabinet table waiting to question me. It was J. Edgar Hoover, the Director of the FBI himself. I put my hand on the Bible, swore to tell the whole truth, and I did. Hoover's secretary did my swearing-in. Then Hoover and one of his agents asked me questions. I answered every question directly and honestly. A day later I was presented with a written copy of my statement which, under oath, I swore to be true, and signed. What an irony that Hoover, who is now widely assumed to have been a closeted gay man, was sitting in judgment on this issue.

John Ehrlichman was questioned by FBI Associate Director Mark Felt. I don't know who interviewed Haldeman, although I believe it was probably Hoover. Fortunately, the interviews by Hoover and Felt were sufficient for Jack Anderson. He dropped the story.

Our depositions disappeared. Haldeman told me that when Hoover's body was found in 1972, someone had searched unsuccessfully for them in his home safe, which is where he supposedly kept highly sensitive documents.

Next we learned that Rowland Evans and Robert Novak, two other well-known Washington investigative columnists, were planning a similar story. Their information, we were told, had come from "a very reliable source in the White House." The stories were likely planted to hurt Haldeman and/or Ehrlichman, rather than Larry or me. They were patently false, but it was dispiriting to recognize that someone with his own agenda, and maybe someone in the White House, was leaking them. The administration had decided that if such a story were to be published, we were going to sue for defamation of character. Fortunately Herb Klein talked Evans and Novak out of running with theirs, and it didn't come to that.

Those two episodes served to toughen me. Apparently there were people who disliked me—and us—enough to smear us with the intention of having us fired. The fact that people, presumably in the White House, could stab people in the back so viciously was chilling.

The president stood by us. He must have suspected who was behind the accusations. I had gotten used to people maneuvering for power, but this was different. Whatever remained of the naive kid I had been when I started working for Richard Nixon was evaporating.

Like just about everyone else on the staff, I was struggling to figure out exactly where I fit. In the initial scrambling for power I was sent a fairly strong message. The president announced he would be taking a trip to Europe to meet with allied leaders. I was completely left out of the preparations and scheduling. The advance operation and logistics were going to be handled by John Ehrlichman. While this matched his role during the 1968 campaign, it was incredibly depressing for me. For the past two years I'd essentially handed my life over to the president and now, for the first really exciting trip, I was being left out, left home. The message I got was that I was not needed. "I must realize," I wrote in my journal, "how fortunate I am and not expect everything at once. But it is hard knowing I won't be a part of it." Thankfully, though, the way it all turned out over time was to accrue to my benefit. Ehrlichman wanted higher-level responsibility, for example, to serve as White House Domestic Affairs Advisor. His appointment to that position a few months later created an opening for me to assume management of the foreign trip advance operations.

Meanwhile, I was continuing to figure out my job. Throughout the campaign Nixon had settled into a pattern. I knew what to expect from him and how to best facilitate his needs. In contrast to his style during the campaign, the president was inconsistent about the way he wanted his time allotted in the White House. He gave me a set of rules to follow, and within a day or two he would be breaking his own rules—and complaining about it. Keeping up with him was frustrating. In truth, he was feeling out and testing the optimum way to manage his own time. As vice president he had watched President Eisenhower up close. There were areas of governing that he enjoyed, as well as duties he didn't enjoy but was obligated to assume. He was looking for that right formula between handling official presidential ceremonial obligations and dealing with the more substantive issues, such as the Vietnam War, domestic and foreign intelligence, foreign policy, congressional relations, the economy, and a whole range of other matters.

The presidency is an all-consuming, complicated job. Bob was responsible for listening to the president and helping to figure out the formula for the optimum use of his time. My job was to provide options to both men and then to implement the decisions they made. This responsibility was beyond stimulating for me. It was very exciting.

Everything we did created ripples in the world. The decisions the president was making had the potential to affect millions of lives. I was learning that even the smallest decisions were fraught with potential political consequences.

In early February, Coretta Scott King and a foreign affairs minister from the United Nations were scheduled to meet with Henry Kissinger. It was a simple enough meeting, but planning it took a great deal of time. The president decided this meeting should take place in the Roosevelt Room, directly across the hall from the Oval Office. He wanted the doors to both the Oval Office and the Roosevelt Room to remain open. That way the participants in the Coretta Scott King meeting would see that the president wasn't there, so they would know he wasn't snubbing them. He wanted the King group to enjoy the prestige of meeting in the Roosevelt Room, which would give it far more importance than Mrs. King's meetings at the White House during the Johnson administration had been given.

Sounds simple enough. However, the president was going to be working in his small anteroom office, and I was afraid he might forget Mrs. King and Dr. Kissinger were there and walk out in the middle of their meeting. Also, the Secret Service, for its own reasons, did not want the minister from the UN to be in the Roosevelt Room with doors open to the Oval Office. After lengthy discussion, Kissinger threw up his hands in frustration and decided to meet with the group in his own office. It seemed even a simple meeting in the West Wing had its complications.

All White House staffs have to negotiate around the idiosyncrasies of the president they're serving. Bob Haldeman had learned how to handle President Nixon's temper. No one was more loyal to the president than Haldeman, but he had the difficult responsibility of determining when Nixon was serious and when he was just blowing off steam. He described it to me as "saving Richard Nixon from Richard Nixon." For example, after reading a particularly unflattering or unfair column, the president might say to Haldeman, "Bob, you understand this cannot go on. I want you to have Ziegler tell that little bastard he is no longer allowed in the press room. That story is just a repeat of the goddamn crap that SOB has been writing since the campaign. I want him out of there today. I mean it. Do you understand?"

And when he said that, he did mean it. Kinda. Haldeman would tell Ziegler what the president had said. Ziegler's eyes would pop open, and Bob would tell him, "Don't do anything yet. Sit tight."

Later, when the president asked Haldeman if he had spoken to

Ziegler, Bob could answer, "Yes." A day later, after the president had calmed down, he would say to Bob, "I've been thinking about tossing that reporter out of the press room. Ziegler probably shouldn't do it."

This kind of incident happened often. It was characteristic of Nixon. Sometimes out of anger or his own frustration or whatever his emotion, he just spouted off. He would say things he didn't really mean. Some historians have overlooked that very human trait—that he was subject to the same passions and shortcomings as the rest of us. The staff understood it, accepted it, and found ways to work around it. It was Haldeman's job to filter out those rash comments and decisions while instituting administration policy.

This pattern of the president's was accentuated in a negative way when the secretly recorded Oval Office tapes, in which at times he made unpleasant, controversial remarks, were released in later years. The public heard presidential remarks and demands that were, shall we say, "unvarnished." Great damage was done to President Nixon's reputation by his inclination to issue knee-jerk orders or demands that he really didn't expect to be carried out. These impulsive reactions, when taped and then replayed by the media, served to undermine his character and created a false impression of the man I knew.

Just like the rest of us, Bob was feeling his way into his job. He had power that the rest of us didn't have, so when the president told me to do something that I believed might cause problems, I did what Bob did: I waited, always informing Haldeman, who would at the opportune time ask the president if that was really what he wanted done. Sometimes these Nixon outbursts could be funny. As an example: At an airport rally during the campaign, something happened that frustrated Nixon. Once we had taken off, Nixon called the lead advance man to the front of the plane. In all seriousness he said, "This plane is never, ever again, to land at another airport. Do you understand?" "Yes, sir," came the response.

Another task I was given for which I had no preparation was handling Martha Mitchell. Martha was married to John Mitchell, a fine man, an intelligent man, and a loyal Nixon supporter. He had served on PT boats in the South Pacific during WWII. He was a very good lawyer and was disinclined to accept Nixon's offer to become United States Attorney General. This was, at least in some part, because he loved his wife, Martha, and was concerned that her drinking and neurosis could become a problem. Nixon had to pressure him to take the cabinet position. In retrospect Mitchell's instincts to not take the position were probably right. Martha was an alcoholic. I'm not sure I understood what "alcoholic" meant at that point. On television, drunks were good people who said funny things. We were just beginning to understand there was nothing funny about it, that it was a disease that destroyed lives. The White House switchboard was told that when Martha called in drunk, she was to be routed to me. Those calls came sporadically. She might call four times in one day, five times in an hour, then I wouldn't hear from her for two weeks. "Dwight, I want to talk to my president," she would tell me.

"Mrs. Mitchell," I replied politely, "he's busy working right now. He's in a meeting and can't take a call."

She was insistent. "I really need to talk to him. Have him call me back."

I would call the attorney general and tell him she had called again. He would do his best to take care of it, but it weighed heavily on him. Dick Moore, whose role as "special counsel" was to be a calming and wise voice for all of us, had been a classmate of Mitchell's at Fordham and did his best to help. The president knew about Martha's issues, but they didn't really become a political problem until she began drunk-calling reporters late at night. The reporters enabled and emboldened her. They used her and turned her into a character who became well known to the public. Mrs. Mitchell loved the attention. She became "the celebrity wife" of the administration, but not in a good way. Eventually, people stopped laughing with her and began laughing at her. There was nothing we could do about it, and it devastated John Mitchell. Later, as Watergate began to unfold, Martha Mitchell spoke of things she claimed to know—and in some cases actually did know—which caused huge problems for our administration. There was no question she was a woman with a serious problem on the verge of a breakdown. Building her up into a folk hero whistleblower created great copy and hastened Martha's deterioration. Nixon believed it was done purposely and ghoulishly.

My frustration in understanding the parameters of my role was shared by—well, by pretty much everybody. In early March, for example, Haldeman had to deal with the first of the many times Henry Kissinger threatened to quit. Bob would have to talk Henry out of leaving. "That's it," he would say, "I'm leaving!" His assistant, Al Haig, would tell Haldeman, "Henry's quitting again," and Haldeman would tell me, almost as a punch line, "Henry's quitting again." Bob treated those threats as simply Henry's need for attention. All of us, including the president, understood this. He would share many of these stories with me. In the first such instance, Secretary of State William Rogers had met with Soviet Ambassador Dobrynin and apparently had agreed to much more than the president had offered. As a result, Rogers had given the Russian the impression that Nixon was not fully backing the South Vietnamese government. Henry was furious because he believed that impression could lead to the loss of Saigon. He immediately flew to Key Biscayne, where the president was staying for the weekend, to personally confront him on his policy and, no doubt, his decision-making.

All the other issues we had inherited paled in comparison with the Vietnam War. We were looking at the same pictures of young soldiers killed in the war that the rest of America was seeing every day on the news. And we were feeling the anguish just as deeply. The media was starting to convey the impression that Nixon was cold-blooded, that he didn't care, that he fought the war for some political advantage. That was infuriating and totally unfair. That wasn't Richard Nixon.

Nixon was a Quaker, a sensitive and private man. Florida Senator George Smathers liked to tell a story about the time he introduced then-Senator Nixon to Smathers's close friend Bebe Rebozo. Nixon was going to visit Florida and Smathers asked Bebe to take Nixon fishing. This was the first time Nixon had ever met the man who was, over time, to become his best friend. Rebozo did take Nixon fishing; then called Smathers to tell him about it. "I got to tell you," said Rebozo, "you can't take Nixon out fishing. If the fish dies, he gets upset. There's nothing that Nixon abhors more than killing something."

Bebe Rebozo was President Nixon's best friend. Understanding that relationship is important to understanding Richard Nixon. Of Cuban heritage, Bebe was movie-star handsome, with the disposition of a teddy bear. He was perpetually Florida tanned and totally at ease in any situation. He was one of the few people able to get Nixon to fully relax, a very difficult feat. There were people who joked that Bebe was not especially bright, but they completely missed the essence of the man. He was sharp, clever, cunning, and calculating. He had come from a family of nine; he had worked his way up from owning a small gas station to owning the Key Biscayne Bank, becoming a wealthy man through hard work and good fortune.

Bebe understood the way the world worked. He had few illusions. He had widespread relationships and could use them without arousing a ripple of curiosity. Bebe's operational philosophy could be summed up in one word: discretion. And Richard Nixon trusted him, as he did no other person outside of family, without exception.

I experienced an unforgettable Vietnam-related moment with Nixon in the early days of his presidency. He buzzed for me to come into the Oval Office. He was standing in front of his desk. He had finished writing personal notes to families who had lost a son or daughter in the war. Standing there wiping away tears in his eyes, he reached out to me and said, "Please give these to Rose." Rose would make copies of his letters for the presidential files, then mail the letters. The Vietnam War was very personal for the president, and it weighed heavily on him. There was never a doubt in my mind that Nixon sincerely wanted to find a way out of the war that maintained the strength and honor of the United States. He knew we couldn't pack up and fly away, as the antiwar protesters wanted, because of the ramifications that would have on all American foreign policy, not to mention the lives of South Vietnamese men and women and families who had believed our reassurance of support and worked with us and for us.

Other than the president, Kissinger, and a handful of other people, no one in the White House knew we were going to attack sanctuaries in Cambodia. The first week of March 1969, I was with Haldeman in Key Biscayne. The president had just returned from the NATO meetings in Brussels. Kissinger and his assistant, General Alexander Haig, along with Bob Haldeman, had been with Nixon on that trip. What Haldeman had to tell me was so secret he asked me to walk with him on the beach so we could not be overheard. He warned me to not even write down what he would say. (I disobeyed Bob, as these notes were in my journal.) Kissinger and Haig had developed a new master plan. We were going to go over the border into Cambodia to bomb the North Vietnamese sanctuaries and kill the Viet Cong top command. This was because the enemy would retreat into their vast network of bases they had established over many years in Cambodia. The stated purpose was to stop the enemy from using sanctuaries in a neutral nation to supply their forces in South Vietnam. The bombing would be described as "an accident." When the State Department would not agree to this cover-up, Nixon decided to go ahead with it anyway. The Cambodian leader Prince Sihanouk denied publicly, as he had to, that he had given Nixon his approval. But privately Sihanouk had welcomed the bombings to maintain the integrity of his nation and the safety and lives of his citizens.

A few days after that walk with Haldeman, I learned from the president himself that we had expanded the war into Cambodia. About five thirty on the afternoon of March 17, 1969, I walked into the Oval Office, as the president had instructed me to do, to interrupt a meeting between himself and Dr. Kissinger. I informed the president that his next meeting was waiting. He looked at me and said, "Tell him I'll be able to meet him later. Right now we have a strike going on." Haldeman told me soon afterward they had been able to reestablish the cover, and the bombing had been announced as an accident. It wasn't necessary. Unlike other classified information that had been leaked to the press, this remained secret. In fact, two days later Hedrick Smith wrote in the *New York Times,* "Indications from other official sources were that President Nixon was still delaying for the present any retaliation against North Vietnam itself, such as a limited air strike against reported North Vietnamese troop build-ups just north of the demilitarized zone." It only remained secret until May 9, when William Beecher exposed it on the front page of the *New York Times*.

This was only the beginning, though. The war had already brought down the Johnson administration. A few weeks later Henry Kissinger would tell a guest, "Richard Nixon is determined he will not be the first American president to lose a war." More than that, Henry said the president wanted the war settled diplomatically in two months. If not, he would make certain it was settled militarily. Haldeman told me he doubted the president was willing to wait that long and predicted we would be bombing Cambodia again within days.

The war hung over the administration like a great dark storm cloud that never moved. It was always there, usually embodied by the antiwar protesters who showed up wherever the president went. The president was determined to end the war, partly to end the killing and partly to be able to get on with restructuring our foreign policy and relations. He wanted to begin shaping the Asia-after-Vietnam that he had foreseen in his *Foreign Affairs* article in 1967. He was prepared to make major concessions to the enemy. These were up to but not including betraying our South Vietnamese ally, which was imperfect but wasn't as bad as the totalitarian, subversive, and brutal North Vietnamese Viet Cong. He thought it would take about a year. He was prepared to use a combination of carrot and stick, applying the stick when the carrot didn't work or when momentum flagged. What he didn't anticipate was that the enemy wasn't prepared to settle for anything less than total victory. And what the enemy understood was that the U.S. antiwar sentiment and protests would develop apace, and eventually (even if it took to the 1972 elections) an antiwar candidate, if he were to win, would withdraw from the war and thereby deliver victory to the North Vietnamese.

Meanwhile, we gradually got comfortable in the White House. We got used to the fact that it was *our* office and we weren't just visiting.

The White House, the physical building, had been loosely maintained by the Johnson administration. As I've mentioned, when we moved in, the West Wing offices had been given a coat of paint, but it was in desperate need of remodeling. It was the president's trip to several European capitals in February of 1969 that led him and Haldeman to compare the lackluster West Wing to the official offices of European leaders. Upgrading the appearance of the White House was not about grandiosity. Rather, it was the idea that every American president should have an office complex exemplifying the significance and dignity of the presidency of the United States. A remodeled West Wing would serve Nixon and all future presidents, and, most significant, would be a worthy representation of our nation.

The West Wing of the White House as it exists today remains a tribute to the decision to refurbish it and to the work done by Haldeman and his assistant Larry Higby. The White House is among the most historic buildings in this country, and changing it was a tricky matter. Bob and Larry brought in experts from Colonial Williamsburg, who understood modernizing while maintaining tradition. The Williamsburg architects and interior decorators did magnificent work over several months. They met with each of us and helped us plan our offices. They suggested paint colors, moldings, lighting, and carpeting, and once decisions had been made, they brought in crews to implement the changes. The actual construction work, papering, and painting would all take place during off-hours, on weekends, or when we were out of town. The transformation of the White House was spectacular and, to my knowledge, did not receive a single negative news story. Everyone, press included, eventually felt the changes were appropriate. At first, the press were upset with the changes because the press lobby—where they would hang out, watching and talking with visitors arriving and departing—had been eliminated. But shortly they got used to their larger press accommodations which had been constructed over the White House swimming pool. The pool was now gone. I was disappointed personally, as I was one of the few who used the pool a few times a week.

However, there was one instance in which we went too far. The purpose of the European trip had been to firm up relations with our allies while sending a clear message to the Soviets that the allies were united and strong. This trip reflected the president at his best. It was a tremendous success. However, in Brussels one of our staff had been impressed by the attire of the official Belgian guards and security people, who were the equivalent of the White House Executive Protective Service police, who protect the White House complex. The guards in Brussels were dressed in hats with feathered plumes and some sort of broad coat. They looked theatrical, as if they had been costumed for some kind of period Broadway play. In contrast, our officers at the White House wore traditional police uniforms. Someone among our staff—I never learned who—decided that, compared to those security people in Brussels, our security officials looked "sloppy" and should be spiffed up. Certainly, both the president and Haldeman were aware of this and approved the plan. A month or so after the European trip, there was a White House ceremony welcoming a visiting dignitary. It was at that ceremony that our police turned out in their new uniforms. It was a disaster; actually, it was hysterically funny. The *Times* described our new uniforms as "operetta-like," including "double breasted white tunics trimmed with gold braid and gold buttons, and stiff plastic shakos decorated with the White House crest. The headgear vividly resembles that worn by American drum majors and West German traffic policemen. The next boldest silhouette is the black holstered pistol hung from a black belt." The new uniforms were gone that night, never to be seen again, which is to say that not everything we tried worked.

Those first few months were exciting and challenging. We had started to establish a routine to follow. Once the Haldeman family, Jo and their four children, moved from California to join Bob in Washington, our routine became more predictable. In the morning a White House car would first pick up Larry Higby, then Haldeman, and finally me. In the car, we always worked, no matter if we were headed into the White House in the morning or headed home in the evening.

I'd be in the office every morning by seven thirty at the latest. Before leaving the office the previous night, we would have finalized the president's schedule for the next day and put it on his desk in the Oval Office. However, the schedule was always flexible. When I got into the office the next morning, there would usually be notes waiting for me detailing the changes to be made.

In the evening, usually around six o'clock, a chime would go off in my office. That meant Haldeman and the president had left the Executive Office Building, The chime was the signal to Larry Higby and me that we had five minutes—no more—to collect whatever we needed to take with us and meet Bob in the car. Often, by the time we were in the car, Nixon would have walked from the EOB to the Residence—and thought of several more items he needed to speak with Bob about. As we climbed into the car, sure enough the car phone would ring and the president would discuss his most recent thoughts. Usually that conversation would end after five or ten minutes and Bob would go through his long list of to-dos with us. I usually felt for Larry, because he typically had more instructions than I did. Has this been done? Why hasn't somebody checked back on that? Who's responsible for this? Tell this person that. Bing. Bing. Bing. It was high intensity the whole drive home. As usual, Bob didn't waste a minute. Occasionally we would have a ride where laughter prevailed, but that was unusual. I would get home by six thirty or so and hop on the phone to get my additional assignments underway.

The president had settled in too. I wouldn't say I ever saw him express excitement about becoming president. I never got the sense that holding the office thrilled him, but rather he had embraced it as the very important job for which he had been preparing—was prepared—to do. He appeared to feel satisfied, contented, and dedicated. He understood his role completely and never seemed overwhelmed by any of it. I think that was brought home to us at the end of March, when President Eisenhower died.

Haldeman informed him of the former president's death. As Eisenhower's death had been anticipated, the White House had already been making funeral preparations. According to Bob, when the president was told about Eisenhower's passing, he reviewed the White House plans for the funeral, then stood up, turned around, and started crying.

After regaining his composure, he walked into his small West Wing office by himself.

A bit later he traveled in a motorcade to Walter Reed to spend time with Mrs. Eisenhower. Once again, I was told, he became very emotional with the Eisenhower family. That side of Nixon was one he never wanted to show to the public. Maybe he thought it showed weakness. In reality, though, the public image of Richard Nixon as cold and unfeeling simply isn't accurate. The president was, in fact, a very sensitive man. He had suffered great personal losses as a young man. Two of his four brothers had died from tuberculosis. However, showing his emotions publicly and crying was not his way.

Complicating matters, the president was sick, probably with the flu. At times his temperature spiked to 104, but he insisted on working on his Eisenhower eulogy. Over that weekend we were invited to the presidential retreat, Camp David, me for the first time. President Franklin Roosevelt had founded the camp and named it Shangri-La. President Eisenhower renamed it after his grandson, David Eisenhower. (David, having married Julie Nixon just before President Nixon took office, was at this point the president's son-in-law.)

Before becoming the presidential retreat under FDR, the camp had been a military commanders' base and included several cottages, a pool, a bowling alley, and other recreational facilities. We were shown the bomb shelter and instructed that there were two entrances to it, just in case. The president spent the weekend working on his eulogy, while we enjoyed exploring the retreat we would revisit many times in the next four years.

In his eulogy, Nixon said that General Eisenhower "was probably loved by more people in more parts of the world than any American president has ever been." There was a reception that night at the White House for foreign dignitaries. I remember looking around the room and realizing I was present among these great men who had led the Allied nations to victory in WWII. Among them were Charles de Gaulle, standing rigidly as he represented France; and Britain's Lord Mountbatten. Eventually even working in the White House feels routine, but there were always times when it was impossible not to recognize that I was standing in the middle of history. This was one of those times.

Throughout this whole period Haldeman continued working to get the White House under control. The only office Bob had run previously, at J. Walter Thompson in Los Angeles, consisted of fewer than a hundred people. Now he was charged with running the operations of the president and his entire staff, sometimes including the various department heads. The pressure, in addition to his natural quest for perfection, took a great toll on him. For the first few months of the president's term, Bob's family had remained in California to complete the school year. That essentially left me to be the shock absorber, taking a lot of the brunt of his anger when things went wrong.

And they did go wrong. Every single day. Small things, but irritating things to Haldeman. Again Haldeman was under enormous pressure and the smallest screwup by me or others could set him off. And, of course, my job required getting the smallest details right, all the time, which was a great goal but next to impossible to achieve at the pace things were happening. For example, my job was Appointments Secretary. One morning I made the mistake of putting an uncorrected schedule on the president's desk. Bob was rightfully furious. At our morning meeting he ripped into me. Later he sent me a note. While it continued the criticism, it also outlined what he was trying to achieve. "This particular incident is unforgiveable," he wrote. ". . . you have lots of ideas for big planning, but first you've got to do your job . . . I've gone way out on a limb in my all-out backing of the 'eager but inexperienced young crew,' and I am determined not to let that limb be sawed off . . . either we do things right or we don't do them. If we can't rely on the systems or the people—then we have to abolish them or revise them . . . What may appear to you to be over-reaction is in reality the expression of a deep concern that things be done right and an assumption of responsibility to see that they are."

Unfortunately, that was not a one-time experience. My relationship with Bob got worse, not better. What made it even worse for me was the presence of Larry Higby, Bob's assistant. Larry was a few years younger than me and a wonderful guy. His skills fit Haldeman's needs much better than mine did. Larry and I were—and still are—good friends. "This fellow is so good," I wrote to Bob in a memo, "I am starting to think I found him . . . If there is any problem, it is that he is leaps and bounds ahead of everyone else on your staff." For me, the problem was that Larry rarely made mistakes, which made my mistakes more apparent. There came to be a saying that underscored Larry's value: "Everyone needs a Higby." Not everyone appreciated Larry, which was not Larry's fault. Larry represented Bob, and rather than directing one's anger toward Bob—something not wise to do—people would direct their anger at Larry. He was an easier target. Many of our staff called him "Haldeman's Haldeman."

As for me, I benefited from Haldeman's tough image. This was about contrast. My personality and style wasn't one of being tough. In fact, the *Washington Post* published an article about me titled "Mr. Nice Guy." I was congenial by nature. A key to my role was getting along with everyone. I did not have the burden of responsibility and accountability to the president that Bob carried. I was not, nor could I be, demanding in my position. My role did not call for that. Therefore, I was an asset to Bob because I could get along with others who would confide in me, which was also helpful in a way to Bob.

The image of the Nixon administration being presented to the outside world was that of a smoothly running engine. People may have disagreed with our policy positions, but they believed we had successfully made the transition to an efficient operation. In actuality, it had been difficult. Haldeman continued to struggle to get it under control. I'm sure every new administration goes through similar growing pains. We probably had it a little easier because there were several White House veterans on our staff.

My mistakes continued to drive Bob crazy. During another meeting, at which several other people were present, he attacked me again. I responded to him in writing: "To be yelled at, overly criticized and put down is something saved for dogs. Something I will not tolerate, need not tolerate." Something important was starting to happen with me, as exemplified by my pushing back. These were my first steps toward more independence from Bob, something that would unfold significantly in the months ahead. Yet, as fate would have it, that independence never got totally established during my White House years because of the nature of the men with whom I worked and my own reservations about breaking away.

My relationship with Bob sometimes seemed like the bouncing ball in a movie sing-along. One day he would be effusive in his praise of my work while reminding me how much he needed someone he could trust completely supporting him. On other days he would angrily and bitterly attack me. I didn't like it, but I understood it and learned to sing along.

As we reached the end of our hundred-day honeymoon, the media began making its judgments. I felt *Life* magazine's Hugh Sidey, more than anyone else, got most of it right. He wrote that President Nixon was like a corporate lawyer, an orderly man who carefully programs his day: "The president after all these years was still ill at ease in many public situations . . ." I would take issue with that particular characterization because to me the president was more relaxed now that he was in the White House than he had been in public when he was campaigning. Sidey continued: "With the press he had been very cool and proper." Mostly. Though—and this was the result of the president's view of his presidency according to Sidey—"His presidency is one of the lowered voice. He believes that . . . the country reflects the personality of the president. It is the tone of the administration to keep it low . . . consolidate, pause, make sense of where it's going." That, to me, was the key: to "make sense of where [the nation was] going."

The president had his own thoughts about the press. "The honeymoon is over," he said, "but the marriage must go on for better or for worse." And he urged everyone to work together, so that "maybe it will be for the best."

History tells us how that turned out.

$$\star \quad 7 \quad \star$$

ACCOMPLISHMENTS BUILT AROUND THE PRESIDENT'S STYLE

Richard Nixon was already one of the best-known men in the world when, on January 20, 1969, he raised his right hand and took the oath of office as the President of the United States. He had been in the headlines for two decades, but no one knew how he was going to shape his presidency. Having spent so much time with him, I had seen firsthand his strengths and weaknesses. He was extremely smart, knowledgeable, determined, and decent, but there is no experience, no previous job, that can prepare a person for the presidency. Yes, he had served as vice president with President Dwight Eisenhower, from 1953 to 1961, but the only job the vice presidency prepares one for is the vice presidency. Until a person sits in the Oval Office, there's no way of knowing what issues he will confront or how he will respond to them. Until a person has in his grasp that incredible power, there is no way of knowing how he will use it. Having spent months and even years working with him, I had come to know Richard Nixon. I was confident that he could fulfill the promises he had made during the campaign. I was confident he was capable of doing great things for our country.

My confidence certainly was reinforced when, among the first decisions he made as president-elect, he appointed Bob Haldeman as Chief of Staff. The Chief of Staff essentially runs the White House. However, the job is actually whatever the president wants it to be. His predecessor, President Lyndon B. Johnson, hadn't bothered to appoint an official

Chief of Staff. Haldeman was working with a blank slate, and he designed every detail of the position to which he had been appointed. The model he created was adopted by most of the administrations that followed. Academic studies have analyzed the "Haldeman model" of management of the White House. When President Ford abandoned it for the "spokes of a wheel" approach, he quickly learned his spokes system didn't work efficiently. Even Jimmy Carter reverted to the Haldeman model.

Over the years I have discussed the process and management operations that Bob put in place with six former Chiefs of Staff: Jim Baker, Al Haig, Dick Cheney, Don Rumsfeld, Sam Skinner, and Ken Duberstein. All six men gave Bob tremendous credit for the contributions he made in establishing the job description of the Chief of Staff as integral to the efficient and effective operation of the office of the president.

Bob served as a buffer between the president and his staff. He managed the president's time and established the decision-making structure. The president wanted Haldeman to put in place a system that maximized the efficient exchange of ideas; put a focus on providing the information necessary for informed and wise decision making; and provided for the discipline necessary to make it all work. Bob created just what the president wanted. Many people didn't like the structure he established, which set controls on individuals' access to the president. They would have preferred that the president have a free-wheeling, open-door policy, whereby they could meander in and out of the Oval Office, not needing to be specific in presenting their ideas, let alone be accountable in implementing anything. Therefore, the type of organized meeting process that Bob created at the president's request was not popular with a lot of the staff. However, popularity was never an expectation or requirement for Bob's job. As he once described his role: "Every administration needs a son of a bitch. And I am Nixon's." Maybe he felt that way, but I didn't. Bob Haldeman was a fair broker, faithfully and honestly acting, always, in the best interests of the president and the country he served. However, I think the characterization does accurately underscore his no-BS attitude.

Haldeman had one client and only one, the president. He did not view his position as Chief of Staff, as would many of his successors in later administrations, as playing a public role or appearing on television or in the press on behalf of the administration. He did not leak information to the media and never served as a news source. The leaking now considered normal was not condoned without presidential approval in the Nixon administration.

Just as the president had challenged his cabinet to act quickly to take control of their departments, he also had to quickly practice what he preached and establish control over his administration. In the first days of the Nixon White House, with Nixon's backing, Haldeman sought out General Andrew Goodpaster to discuss the management of the executive branch. General Goodpaster was a West Point graduate. He had been assigned to work with General Marshall to rebuild Europe after World War II. Then the very distinguished and competent General Goodpaster had served as White House Staff Secretary during Eisenhower's presidency. President Nixon knew Goodpaster well and as vice president had witnessed how efficiently the Eisenhower White House had been managed.

Considering the large amounts of significant information that needed to move expeditiously from one place to another, Haldeman understood he needed an efficient system. It was absolutely necessary because we didn't have the luxury of time. A four-year term goes quickly. General Goodpaster was the perfect advisor in that regard. Few, including the press, ever knew of Goodpaster's contribution to what Nixon knew he needed and Haldeman put in place.

Haldeman set up a system, administered by the Office of the Staff Secretary, that provided the president the information he wanted to have, and needed to have, in order to make his decisions. While many individuals had important ideas to share with the president, Bob recognized that there wasn't time for each of them to individually convey his thoughts. The system he established provided that virtually all ideas to be conveyed to the president would be sent in the form of a written memorandum. An exception to that would be, for example, an "Eyes Only" memo that Henry Kissinger might personally carry into the Oval Office.

A typical "Memorandum for the President" arriving at the White House would first go to the Office of the Staff Secretary. That office would consider the subject of the memo and, before sending it on to the president, "staff it out" to whomever else might have relevant input. For example, a memo having to do with a domestic issue would be sent to John Ehrlichman or the appropriate member of his staff; a memo from the Pentagon having to do with foreign affairs would be staffed through Henry Kissinger's office; a memo from a member of Congress would first go to Bryce Harlow. Each of those people would review the incoming memo, being certain to consider who else might have important input on the subject at hand. After all relevant input had been collected, the original memo, along with a cover memo including whatever additional information had been deemed to be important, would be sent to the president. These memos or briefing books might include tabs, attaching views from appropriate staff members. All views, pro and con, were always provided to the president. These memos would typically end with options, such as:

The President Approves _____

The President Disapproves _____

More Information Requested_____

Set a Meeting to Discuss_____

After the president had reviewed these briefing and decision documents, they would be returned to the Office of the Staff Secretary, which would then send them on to the original person with whatever follow-up instructions the president had indicated. More often than not, the briefing documents would contain numerous presidential notes or comments. If further action was required from the original sender, that person would be given a date by which the president expected a response. A very efficient system had been established.

Some colleagues thought the operations were becoming too bureaucratic and structured to the point of isolating the president, which they felt wasn't conducive to the exchange of ideas. Compared to where people may have previously worked or the level of management they had experienced, their criticism could be understood. But, bottom line, Haldeman was putting in place the system the president wanted. Actually, Bob was putting in place not only what Nixon wanted but also what Nixon needed in order to handle the complexities of the many issues for which he was responsible.

The system worked perfectly for the president because, instead of having to sit in meetings with myriad people, he was able to receive their thoughts in memos. Nixon worked as a nonstop machine. Work was his hobby. But Haldeman knew Nixon needed lots of downtime and it couldn't be identified as such. Nixon insisted that our message always must be that "the president is working." That is why our "thinking time" scheduling option was used. Nixon imagined himself as an entirely rational and objective decision-maker. Haldeman knew the reality and had to construct an operation that honored Nixon's ideas but worked around them to achieve the desired efficiency. The reality was that Nixon didn't want to work with many people or see many people, and he didn't want people to know that. Also, he had no use or time for the cabinet system and all its inefficiencies. And, of course, he couldn't, he wouldn't, and he shouldn't admit to these views in public. So Haldeman had to work around all of this thinking, as did I, as implementer of the president's scheduling operation. The bottom line is that Nixon was most comfortable concentrating power in the West Wing, where his closest and most trusted advisors were located, and he preferred to interact with the fewest number of people possible.

The president's decision-making style changed once he was in the

White House. During the campaign, he made snap decisions because he had to. Issues presented themselves quickly, requiring an immediate response; and, while significant to the campaign, they paled in comparison to the issues he would be dealing with as president. As president, he had more complex and important issues to consider, and he necessarily became more reflective. He would think things through, consider the alternatives, weigh all the pros and cons. He could be swayed with facts and logic by those people he trusted in his inner circle. The administration included many smart people holding competing ideas, who were able to articulate their points of view logically and forcefully. That's where the system Haldeman set up served his interests by easily providing him with a wide range of thoughts. He didn't like meetings—abhorred them—and much preferred to have advisors submit memos that he could read and consider. We always said the president's comfort zone could best be labeled "aloneness."

The president would often work late into the night, reading briefing books in the Lincoln Sitting Room in the Residence, the living quarters of the White House. Or he might go to his EOB office and use some of his time alone to digest all of the sometimes conflicting opinions. He loved that "thinking time," loved it. I used to say that if Richard Nixon had his fountain pen, a supply of yellow legal pads, a comfortable chair with an ottoman for his feet, his natural leather Brooks Brothers briefcase on his lap, and a cup of hot coffee, all we had to do was stick the temple of his glasses in his mouth, clear everyone else from the room—and he would be in heaven. Oh, and a phone. He was a phone-aholic.

On a typical workday he would leave the Oval Office around noon and go over to his far more private and personalized presidential office in Room 180 of the EOB to spend the rest of the afternoon. First he would have lunch, usually cottage cheese, ketchup, maybe a pineapple ring, and a cup of tea or coffee, prepared by a navy steward. The cottage cheese would have been purchased and flown in from his friends the Knudsens, who owned a dairy company in California. After lunch, he often would take a twenty-minute nap. Then he was ready to sit by himself and focus on the problems he faced in achieving his administration's objectives. The more complex problems became, the more time we carved out for his "thinking," which eventually filled up most of the afternoons.

Only a small group of people—Haldeman, Kissinger, Ehrlichman, and to a lesser degree Special Counsel Chuck Colson—were ever invited on a regular basis to join him in his private EOB office. It was never used for official events. If he was preparing to make a speech, and his speechwriters were involved, he'd often see them there too. The vice president's office in that building was directly above the president's. I do not remember a single time that the vice president was invited down. The president met Agnew only in the Oval Office or the Cabinet Room.

Staff invited into the private office were not listed on the official schedule. The president would simply pick up his phone and invite them himself or ask the White House operator to find the person and send them in. Usually he had something on his mind to discuss or sometimes it might be for a robust discussion of ideas. Often the invitee would end up just listening to the president ruminate. I know Bob often thought that time was unproductive as far as getting his own work done, but it was necessary to the president as it was how he processed his thoughts. He would review options incessantly, looping back over subjects previously covered, until in his mind he had finally reached a decision or point of view with which he was comfortable.

In comparison, I've been told that President Johnson typically made decisions quickly and decisively, sticking with his first reaction. I never saw Nixon's more tempered process as a detriment. If a decision had to be made quickly, he could make it quickly. When Israel was under attack by the Arab states in 1973, for example, he told Kissinger immediately, "Goddamn it, use everyone we have. Tell them to send everything that can fly." But that was not his normal process.

Probably more than anything else, the president's contemplative, seemingly endless rehashing pattern would drive Haldeman semi-crazy. Bob would sit with him in his office, at times for hours, listening to him ruminate about the issues he was facing. Bob would walk out of that office, often mentally fatigued, with literally fifteen pages of legal pad filled with notes. Then we'd get in the car, the phone would ring, literally seconds later, and the president would say, "You know, Bob, I've been thinking about what we were talking about . . ."

Those ultra-long afternoon EOB "thinking time" sessions for Haldeman were frustrating because his management style was action-oriented. The difference between Nixon and Haldeman, we used to joke, was that Nixon was the ultimate decision-maker and strategist-in-chief par excellence, but when it came down to it, he couldn't execute a one-car motorcade. He would know a one-car motorcade was needed. He would know where it should be waiting, when it should depart, the speed it should go and the turns it would make, but he couldn't make it happen. Order it, yes. Do it, no.

Haldeman was the chief operating officer of the administration. He would put the right driver behind the wheel, make sure watches were synced, and launch the motorcade at the exact planned second. He would execute whatever Nixon wanted. The motorcade would follow the route he had laid out and arrive at the destination exactly on time.

Bob was a take-charge kind of guy, working in a subservient position. Yes, it was an exalted subservient position, but still one in which he was not the ultimate decision-maker. His philosophy was simple. He set as his goal, when the administration began, that he was "determined that we are going to do things right—the big things always and the little things as often as possible." And that is exactly what he expected from me.

What some historians have overlooked about Nixon is that he was a human being, subject to the same passions and shortcomings as the rest of us. Sometimes out of anger or his own frustration or whatever the emotion, he just spouted off. He would say things he might not really mean. Years later, listening to the secretly made Oval Office tapes in which the president at times made unpleasantly controversial remarks, I remembered this. It's not an excuse. It's an explanation. Haldeman's job was to filter out those rash comments and decisions while instituting administration policy. A lot of people say things they wouldn't want to leave on tape for posterity to remember. Unfortunately, for President Nixon, those things were left.

Bob's assignment, he believed, was to work to the best of his ability for the President of the United States—and to make sure that everyone else also was working to that level. This meant on all things, big and little.

Haldeman was never interested in influencing policy. That was not his role, he would tell me. He always was careful to not let his personal opinions affect Nixon's thinking. But if Nixon asked Haldeman for an opinion, Bob would give it. He never doubted Nixon's sincere desire to do what was best for the country—and he was able to separate that from his personal beliefs.

"There are some things about the guy I just don't like," he once told me. Those things had nothing to do with Nixon's performance in office. Rather, they were personality quirks. Bob was a very moral and ethical Christian Scientist. There was little flexibility in his values or beliefs. Nixon was a politician. By definition, a politician, if he wants to get results, has to be willing to compromise on some of his principles. Haldeman, being more rigid, was less open to the concept of compromise.

Haldeman was, by nature, more fair. Nixon could be less than direct, not always as tough when he needed to be. Trust was also an issue for the president. He was inherently suspicious. That suspicion made for a jadedness that can come from years of living in the political bubble. It repelled Bob. Nixon's use of foul language was also a turnoff for Bob. No one would call Bob a prude. He used objectionable language too, but rarely.

I have no idea how Nixon felt personally about Haldeman, but I do know that he loved Bob's managerial capabilities. Haldeman made it easy for Nixon to focus on being president. but accomplishing that made it difficult on the rest of us—especially me, because of our friend-ship. As Haldeman wrote to me after one verbal lashing, "I am con-cerned by the dispirited tone of your voice, and I know I've helped cause it by a relentless riding of your tail the last two days. I am sorry, but my tail gets ridden too, so you get some of the fringe benefits."

At times, admittedly, I deserved it, but very slowly he became abu-sive toward me. "There is a problem," he wrote to me, "in establishing and maintaining a viable business relationship when it is so strongly over-ridden personally and emotionally . . ." This was becoming a highly charged relationship crisis that was not healthy for either of us.

But even the changing nature of our friendship did not slow down the onslaughts of criticism: "You have a job that requires flawlessness in every phase of it—especially the pre-planning and the details . . ." and at times I was "as sloppy as hell" and my work was "incomplete, inaccurate and unpresidential." I once got a memo from him criticizing me for the poor quality of a memo I had sent to him, with a suggestion I clean the copy machine.

The structure that Haldeman created was built to satisfy his one cli-ent, the president, and that it did. Haldeman's structure generally func-tioned effectively for the day-to-day operations of the White House. We got things done. We operated smoothly and efficiently, but at times as I have said, it seemed like an emotional roller coaster for me.

From a memo I wrote six weeks after we'd moved into the West Wing: "[The president] has also asked that the number of meetings and ceremonial duties over the next two weeks be greatly reduced. He is concerned about the number of major decisions coming up. Needs to take time to think them through." In those first weeks, we were react-ing to, and accepting, virtually all requests for presidential participa-tion. As we got our footing, and as Haldeman got procedures in place, we took control of the schedule and we ran it versus it running us.

One of those initial policy decisions the president wanted time to think about concerned building a highly controversial anti-ballistic missile (ABM) system known as Safeguard. Believing it could protect

America from Russian and Chinese missiles, the administration's first major foreign policy initiative was to get Congress to pass and fund Safeguard. It was expensive and unproven; and a majority of the members of Congress thought it was unnecessary. They believed we already had a significant military advantage over the Communist world, but the president considered it essential as a bargaining chip. Nixon wanted to call the Soviet bluff, not because of any belief in its efficacy or even its wisdom. There were many who feared it would instigate another nuclear arms race, while others believed it would protect the country against nuclear attack. This was our first major public relations initiative. We needed to convince the American public that this system was absolutely necessary.

Nixon chose to surround himself with intelligent people who he knew wouldn't necessarily agree with him on everything. He wanted to work with people who would challenge him intellectually. As a result, there was a lot of debate about the ABM system within the administration. There were a number of people who argued vehemently against his position. President Eisenhower was literally on his deathbed when Bryce Harlow went to see him at Walter Reed about the issue. Eisenhower asked Bryce to deliver a strong message to President Nixon to not go ahead with the system. When Nixon read Eisenhower's comments he shook his head and said, "The bastards got to him."

Conversely, Counsellor to the President Arthur Burns, who eventually was named Chairman of the Federal Reserve, sent the president an encouraging note. "Once you make your decision," he wrote, "forget what the writers and politicians think." This was long-range policy, and Nixon worked at it for several years until he finally signed an agreement with the Soviet Union in 1972, permitting each country to employ two ABM systems consisting of no more than a hundred missiles. ABM survived into the SALT agreement largely because Nixon's bluff strategy worked, and the Soviets believed he was really serious about it. The far more important parts of the SALT agreement were the limitations on the number of offensive missiles each side would have.

"The presidency has many problems," Nixon said once, "but boredom is not one of them." The first real crisis we had to deal with took place on April 15, 1969, when two North Korean MiG-21s shot down one of our spy planes, an unarmed navy reconnaissance craft, over the Sea of Japan. Thirty-one Americans were killed. Every new administration is typically tested early on by a foreign adversary in order for them to find out how it will react. The attack by North Korea, a Soviet client-state, created an extraordinarily difficult situation. Fortunately, the Russians made it clear they did not approve of this attack by immediately sending two destroyers into the area to assist in recovery operations. The nation had elected Nixon to end the Vietnam War, not start another war. However, we had to make some kind of response to this aggressive action.

In January of 1968, only fourteen months earlier and also in the Sea of Japan, the North Koreans had fired on and captured the navy intelligence ship USS *Pueblo* and its crew of eighty-three. The ship had been patrolling in international waters, and North Korea released photographs of the bound and blindfolded sailors. The crisis had dominated the news for most of the year before it was finally settled late in December with the return of the crew (except for one who had been killed in the attack). It had made LBJ appear weak, and Nixon was very aware of the ramifications of Johnson's mishandling of the *Pueblo* incident.

In addition, every decision we made about every foreign policy issue was made against the subtext of Vietnam. How do we get out of there with honor? How do we project strength while leaving without a clear-cut victory? How we reacted to this murderous attack by North Korea was going to be interpreted as a signal, a hint of how tough, or weak, the Nixon administration was going to be. It was very important and one of the major factors in Nixon's thinking that had little to do with Vietnam directly. It was the impact on current and potential allies if we were to let an old ally down. However imperfect the South Vietnamese regime may have been, and it was far more perfect than some of our other allies in the region, it had been loyal and depended on our bona fides. For Nixon to back down to a tin-pot Communist regime like North Korea would have sent disastrously negative signals about American military strength and moral integrity across Asia and the Pacific, not least to China at the start of his concerted effort to woo the People's Republic of China. The president's response to this deadly provocation would set the tone for the next four years. Kissinger understood that, which is why he advocated that we hit them back hard. But it was a complicated military situation. Strategically, this was a difficult battlefield on which to fight. It wasn't possible to simply knock out North Korea with one attack because that country had the military capability of attacking South Korea by land or air, starting another cycle of war.

The National Security Council (NSC) met the next day and offered an array of options. The atmosphere in the White House was tense. People were in and out of the Oval Office all day. Kissinger continued to advocate a powerful military reprisal, which he believed would send a strong message to the Communists about Nixon's willingness to use force. He also thought it might help significantly in Vietnam.

The following morning Haldeman buzzed me into his office. A decision had been made, he told me. President Nixon had decided to bomb North Korea. He offered no details, other than that the NSC discussions had been centered on bombing airfields and strictly military targets.

Like many Americans I vividly remembered the 1962 Cuban Missile Crisis. I was twenty-two years old that October, right ahead of Nixon's defeat in his race for governor of California. President Kennedy had yanked Nixon's opponent, the incumbent Governor Pat Brown, from the campaign trail and flown him by a government fighter jet to Washington to be briefed. A picture of Governor Brown boarding the jet appeared on the front page of the *Los Angeles Times*. This was purely a political stunt by the Democratic president to help the Democratic candidate in the closing weeks of a close race. And it worked. There was absolutely no reason, other than positioning Brown politically, for President Kennedy to brief Governor Brown. But it did help Brown win, by a narrow

5 percent margin. Nixon thought the briefing helped push Brown to victory. I remember being aware that Russian ships carrying missiles were sailing directly into our blockade of Cuba. In addition, I remember waiting anxiously, along with the rest of the country, to see whether it would be President Kennedy or USSR Premier Nikita Khrushchev who would back down from the confrontation. Khrushchev blinked, relieving our entire nation and perhaps preventing nuclear war.

In that context, it was not at all unreasonable to believe that North Korea's attack had put us in a similarly precarious situation. North Korea was a closed society. We didn't have great intelligence about their activities. We knew surprisingly little about its Glorious Leader, Premier Kim Il-sung, who had been a founder of that country and had led it through the Korean War. We also didn't know about the disposition of his army or navy or arsenal. So there was no way of knowing how North Korea would react to an attack. If, in retaliation to such an attack, he invaded or launched missiles against South Korea, we could not stop him from killing tens of thousands of people and possibly drawing Russia or China into the conflict.

In addition to Kissinger, there were a lot of political hawks pushing the president into this action, among them the powerful Democratic Chairman of the House Armed Services Committee, Mendel Rivers. Even Haldeman was for it. He could always be counted on as a hardliner on national security issues. The question arose: How would we respond if North Korea counterattacked? Plans were drawn up to cover all possibilities.

Kissinger spoke with several top administration officials to determine what their reaction would be to such an attack. John Ehrlichman was the leader of a group strongly against it. The president was hoping to find consensus on some action he could take. Publicly he projected calm and strength, while privately he was keeping his own counsel, continuing to weigh all options.

The only people who knew about the president's decision to attack were Haldeman, Ehrlichman, and Kissinger. Because of the schedule implications and the need to put a media plan in place, I also knew. Bob stressed the need to continue functioning normally. We were going to stick to our regular schedule as much as possible. But if we attacked, and news broke of it during the day, we would abandon the schedule and the president would go on national TV to announce it. This was not the first or last time we would have to put on one face for the public and press, and another face for what was actually going on inside the White House. All modern presidencies are confronted with the difficult choice of when to withhold, for national security reasons, precise information from the press and public. It is always, appropriately, a controversial decision in a free society.

When I was informed the president would be holding a press conference to announce his decision, I figured the bombing was canceled, or at least postponed. Kissinger had strongly advised him against the press conference, but he went ahead with it. Reconnaissance flights over the Sea of Japan would be continuing, he announced, which was interpreted to mean there would be no reprisals. He also announced that we were sending a task force including four aircraft carriers into the region. Eventually that show of strength grew to become the largest display of military might in that area since the Korean War.

The world was watching, and so was everyone inside the administration. The weekend after that press conference, the president invited his closest advisors to join him at Camp David. Bob called me and told me Nixon would be meeting with Secretary of Defense Mel Laird, Kissinger, Secretary of State Rogers, and others, so perhaps he was still contemplating taking some military action. There was a lot of bluster, threats, and warnings, but no action was taken. Kissinger would go on to win a lot of battles inside the administration, but this was not one of them.

As it turned out, not taking military action against North Korea may have been the best decision. Many people applauded the president for his restraint, claiming he had taken a peaceful approach and saved lives by not making a face-saving, essentially meaningless, military strike. But to demonstrate to any country that might have interpreted this decision as a sign of American weakness, he ordered a show of force with regard to Vietnam. He decided to resume the bombing of Cambodia within two weeks. In an interview with historian Frank Gannon in 1983, Nixon was to say that not bombing North Korea was the biggest mistake of his presidency because, early on, it demonstrated a weak response to unjustified provocation and sent a wrong signal.

There are few decisions that impact the country in profound and lasting ways more than selecting a judge to be elevated to the Supreme Court. Nixon's remarkable Supreme Court nominations were for a Chief Justice plus three associate justices. And in terms of their rulings and their times, his appointments were very consequential.

Justice Abe Fortas resigned in the spring of 1969. Nixon tried twice to replace him and failed. Nixon had earlier run into serious problems when the first two of his nominees to fill Fortas's seat, Clement Haynsworth and G. Harrold Carswell, were voted down by the Senate. His trusted friend Attorney General John Mitchell had recommended both of those nominees. The Haynsworth nomination was defeated by the Democratic-led Senate for his record on civil rights and labor. Carswell's nomination sank when it was revealed that he had supported segregationist policies earlier in his life. In truth, he should never have been nominated. The big issue for both Haynsworth and Carswell was that they were southerners and Nixon was determined to place a southerner on the high court. Opponents claimed it was a part of his "southern strategy" and a dog whistle to racist voters. Nixon's third nominee, Harry Blackmun, was widely respected and easily confirmed, in May 1970.

In late summer 1971, Justice Hugo Black retired due to health issues. Around the same time, Justice John Marshall Harlan also retired. At that point in history only eleven presidential Supreme Court nominations had ever been defeated by the Senate. Two of them were Nixon's. There was pressure on the president to appoint the first woman, which he was prepared to nominate, but his choice of California appeals court judge Mildred Lillie was not supported by the American Bar Association. The ABA called her "unqualified," though this was partly politics and largely sexism. Mrs. Nixon rarely got involved in this kind of decision, but I do know she was strongly advocating for a woman. There was tremendous pressure on the president from competing constituencies. There didn't seem to be a perfect candidate.

In a national television presentation on October 21, 1971, President Nixon announced his two picks for the Court. First was Lewis Powell, a Virginia attorney and former president of the American Bar Association. At the outset, Powell was reluctant, due to his age and his eyesight. He was losing his vision and told Nixon he was afraid he wouldn't be able to keep up with the job because he couldn't keep up with the reading required. He was sixty-four at the time and felt Nixon should pick a younger man. Nixon telephoned him and personally persuaded Powell to take the office.

Then it was my good friend Dick Moore, the special counsel, who suggested to the president he consider Assistant Attorney General William Rehnquist for the other vacancy. As Nixon detailed in his memoirs, Moore sold Nixon on Rehnquist by pointing out that he was currently his lawyer (acting on Nixon's behalf at the Justice Department); had been first in his class at Stanford Law School; was from the west; and had served as a clerk to Supreme Court Justice Robert Jackson, who was Nixon's all-time favorite justice. The last selling point Moore used was Rehnquist's age: He was only forty-seven and was therefore likely to serve on the Court for many years. Attorney General John Mitchell weighed in, agreeing with Moore, and the deal to pick Rehnquist was sealed.

Senator Howard Baker, who had been recommended for the vacancy by Len Garment of the White House staff, had been under consideration and was highly respected by members of both political parties. Although feelers had gone out to Baker, he failed to respond until it was too late, and Rehnquist's stock was rising. Once Nixon's attention was on Rehnquist, Baker's chances faded. Baker remained in the Senate and later served as the ranking Republican on the Ervin committee investigating the Watergate break-in.

Although Nixon had suffered political abuse for over thirty years in the public arena, he had endured. It started in the later 1940s and became particularly fierce as Nixon flushed out Communists in the government during the Alger Hiss/Whittaker Chambers hearings in 1948. Eisenhower viewed himself to be above political machinations, so it was his vice president, Richard Nixon, who for the eight years of the Eisenhower presidency carried the political water for the GOP. Ike used Nixon to go after Joe McCarthy, despite it not being in Nixon's best political interests. Nixon was a good soldier. He made the powerful, nationally televised "shooting rats in a barrel" speech in 1954, sinking McCarthy. Political satirists mocked his partisan efforts with vicious cartoons. For the partisan activity he undertook on behalf of the Republican Party, he paid a price. And, of course, it was Richard Nixon who fought and lost to the Democrat John F. Kennedy for the office of president in 1960. Then in 1962 he lost the gubernatorial race in California to Pat Brown. Those two losses gave him the reputation of being a "loser." It was layer upon layer of vicious political abuse that tainted Richard Nixon prior to the emergence of the "New Nixon" in 1968. But all that prejudice against him really never disappeared. The antiwar movement, the national media, political cartoonists and the always anti-Nixon Democrats were soon to return with vengeance to confront the Nixon presidency. The greater the success of the Nixon administration, the louder the outrage of the Democratic opposition and the press, his enemies.

While his enemies remembered, with vitriol, how much they disliked Richard Nixon, the president also remembered how much he disliked them. His decades-long battles with the media and others had prepared him to anticipate immediate criticism. In anticipating continual attacks from the press, he had become defensively guarded, somewhat "paranoid," a word his enemies loved to use to describe him. I thought his defensiveness was understandable. But it didn't help him. In later years, he would write about those feelings. He came to understand them as his "Achilles heel," and he was even able to talk philosophically about it.

The president had mastered the art of politics, but he had not been able to overcome that deeply ingrained belief that this mean-spirited opposition existed mostly to destroy him at any cost. Concerning many reporters and institutions, he was absolutely right: There was a group that hated him. So it was only human nature to try to avoid them as much as possible. But I think his anticipation of the continual negative attacks by the press became too ingrained in his psyche and created complicated and unnecessary mental roadblocks for him. However, that's easy for me to say—because I had not suffered the abuse he had.

The president loved to exchange ideas while engaging in stimulating discourse. It was one of his great attributes. He would often ask that opinions be solicited on a range of subjects.

When creating policy, often there was no right or wrong answer. Rather, it was the ramifications of doing this as opposed to the ramifications of doing that. Deciding wasn't as simple as "taking a best guess." There were real-life consequences to these decisions, such as what might have happened if we had bombed North Korea. The consequence could have been anything as desirable as causing North Korea to back off on their aggressive stance to, worst case, starting World War III.

What Nixon did so well, usually, was move people toward a consensus. This was great when there was no time pressure. He was a very perceptive man and had the ability to get things done. He recognized the abilities of the people he brought into his administration, and he understood how best to utilize them. He would also know exactly where a staff person might stand on a given policy issue. His staff had policy experts with different ideological points of view. When necessary, he would pit those people against each other, in an intellectually competitive way, using them as a way to forge a solution.

As a direct result of the system created and managed by Haldeman, the administration was able to accomplish far more than history gives Nixon credit for. When we moved into the White House, the schools in seven states in the Deep South were still almost 70 percent segregated. When Nixon resigned, that number was under 8 percent. It was an amazing accomplishment for which Nixon deserves considerable credit. The real "southern strategy" that Nixon espoused was the need to recognize that the South had changed. While there were still pockets of unmovable racism, there were now many southerners who either supported civil rights as the right thing to do or were prepared to acquiesce to the shift of national sentiment. He was really reaching out to these more enlightened, or at least more realistic, southerners as part of his attempt to bring the South back into the nation. He was also appalled by the hypocrisy of northern Democrats, particularly from states like Illinois and Massachusetts, bemoaning southern segregation while their schools and neighborhoods were every bit as segregated, or worse.

The president, George Shultz, and John Mitchell worked out a scenario to desegregate the schools in the seven most segregated southern states. It was a well-planned and carefully executed strategy spearheaded by Shultz. He took an extensive number of trips visiting the offending states and major cities, explaining that the president was prepared to send in federal troops to enforce the law unless the states worked out arrangements on their own. He would persuasively inform and make clear there was no option—segregation was over. With Attorney General Mitchell's Department of Justice represented at the meetings, the picture became clear. As the states and cities acquiesced, the leaders were invited to Washington to meet in the Roosevelt Room at the White House. The determination of the administration led the states to set up committees of black and white leaders to meet and discuss the situation and somehow arrive at a unified front. They did not want Nixon and the administration to pull the trigger and send in the federal authorities. These meetings were remarkable, unprecedented, and a major part of the accomplishment. There Shultz, with Attorney General Mitchell, would motivate and then congratulate the officials for working together to reach a local solution and form a common front. The president would get reports on the progress in the Roosevelt Room meetings, help shape answers to questions and then "spontaneously" join the group, letting them know they were doing the right and just thing.

When the state of Louisiana proved recalcitrant, Nixon decided to go to New Orleans to try and broker an agreement. It was a courageous political act. Had he not succeeded, it would have been a major embarrassment and serious blow to his efforts. The president deserves credit for taking the risk and for the success he achieved.

★ **8** ★

APPOINTMENTS SECRETARY

When I was eight or nine years old, living in Wichita, Kansas, the brand new Crest Theatre opened three blocks from my house. It was a spectacular opening. Surplus war searchlights lit and crisscrossed the sky, exciting the whole neighborhood. The great singer Nat King Cole was invited to be the celebrity star for the opening. I remember standing in the large crowd, waiting for him to arrive. A car pulled up. He got out and waved to the crowd; then went inside. It was no more than a minute or two, but I was thrilled. I had seen a real celebrity, a man I had seen on television, in person.

The first celebrity I ever spoke with, a bit later, was Milburn Stone, "Doc" on *Gunsmoke*. Kathleen Hite, a woman who created that show, was a family friend and she came with Stone to our house in California one day. I was in awe. What impressed me most was his ability to entertain us with wacky sounds. He could cluck like a duck and impersonate Woody Woodpecker, Bugs Bunny, and Tweety Bird.

As I got older, my awe of celebrities was tempered by access and experience, but I never lost my appreciation for famous and accomplished people. Sitting in the West Wing gave me access to almost anyone in the world.

While the media painted a picture of the Nixon White House as a dark and suspicious place, with somber, buttoned-down people walking around looking over their shoulders, answering to the highly regimented Haldeman, in fact it was a great place to work. There were wonderful, smart people with great senses of humor. We laughed a lot. Bob laughed too. We were thrilled to be part of something in which we believed.

My official very formal title at the outset of the administration was Special Assistant to the President of the United States of America. In September 1970 I was elevated to the position of, and commissioned as, Deputy Assistant to the President of the United States of America. More commonly around the White House, I was known as the president's "appointments secretary." My job expanded to be whatever Haldeman asked me to do. I was accountable for the president's daily and long-range schedules, White House advance operations, and our television office. In the first nine months, before the job was taken over by someone else, I also scheduled the swimming pool and the tennis court, tasks that took a minuscule amount of my time. As the months went by, I was given responsibility for what we referred to as "game planning," maximizing the political impact of the president's activities and adding creative input when appropriate. To some extent, my job description was whatever came up that day. As Haldeman wrote in a note, "I'll keep pushing for increased opportunities . . ." But then, typically Bob, he continued: "but I'll also keep pushing for better performance . . . I'm going to keep riding you . . . because I've got an obligation to the president to keep grinding to make things work better . . ." Haldeman's drumbeat for excellence never let up.

Nothing happened in the White House without a specific purpose. The president always wanted to know why he was doing certain events or meeting various people, and he also wanted to be sure every event had "a tail," which meant extending the life of the event as long as possible. He was obsessed with events making an impact. The rule was simple: We didn't do events just for that day. There had to be follow-up op-ed pieces, magazine stories, and articles. If the president of the United States was going to take the time to do something, we needed to figure out how to maximize its impact. How do we keep the story alive for two or three days, let alone one or two news cycles? He was adamant about this. After an appearance he might suggest, in admittedly a sarcastic tone, "I suppose everybody thinks we're done now. Maybe they shouldn't be sitting on their asses. They need to go out and tell people what the president has done." I received countless memorandums from Haldeman, driven relentlessly by the president, on this subject. The president's default position was concern that no one was following up and maximizing his initiatives, speeches, or meetings. Reading through my voluminous files, one could come to the conclusion that Nixon was an absolute tyrant on the subject. He demanded we fight for every inch of political and policy public relations ground, day in and day out. I always considered this another response to the years of attacks he'd endured. He assumed that no matter what he did, some members of the media were going to attack him. He wanted to get out in front of them.

President Nixon got the news every day from a comprehensive "News Summary" prepared by Mort Allin, who worked in Pat Buchanan's office. Mort's sole responsibility was the News Summary. Nixon responded to the tone of the stories. One of our first domestic trips, for example, was attending the North Carolina Azalea Festival in Wilmington, North Carolina. It was an image-shaping trip, with great PR, and it turned out to be a wonderful event. The president beamed as his daughter Tricia was crowned Queen of the Festival. But it wasn't without some drama, as Tricia didn't initially want to go and had to be talked into it. The president also met with Billy Graham on that trip, which resulted in positive press for us. "The president was pleased with the public response to his appearance at the Azalea Festival," Haldeman wrote, "and feels we should try to find a way every week or so to set up some kind of activity for him that will show people being friendly and responding enthusiastically. He emphasizes the necessity of picking the right ways and the right places, doing this unexpectedly from time to time rather than on a formally set-up basis. He asks that Chapin be constantly on alert for these possibilities . . ." Which, as you can imagine, is how my job continued to expand.

As appointments secretary I managed the president's schedule. I had outstanding assistance with a schedule operation overseen by my deputy, David Parker, who, like both Haldeman and Higby, was a terrific manager. We didn't decide whom the president would see, but we made sure he saw whomever he wanted to see. We were managing a very important commodity: the president's time. While many people thought they needed to see him, we had to determine whom it was necessary for him to see. As Haldeman said, if everybody who wanted to see the president were allowed to see the president, it would have been impossible to govern. There weren't the number of minutes in a four-year term to satisfy all those requests.

At some point the media created the concept of the president being surrounded by a "Berlin Wall," or a "Palace Guard," referring specifically to Haldeman and Ehrlichman, men with Germanic-sounding names who supposedly prevented people from getting into the Oval Office. These were media myths. Anyone who actually had a legitimate or necessary reason to see the president got in to see him. Regardless, the "Berlin Wall" characterization stuck. The media sold it to the public and historians picked it up.

When a senator, governor, or administration official asked for an appointment with the president, we asked that a memorandum be prepared stating the reason for the request, the issue for which the meeting was necessary, who would be participating in the meeting, and, most important, what the president was being asked to decide. As described before, the document had to be "staffed out." It was a managerial system that worked, and anyone who actually did need to see Nixon got in. Bob outlined the objective: "Schedule his appointments so that he can see the people he wants to see for the purposes he wants to carry out."

Bob had another deputy, Alexander P. Butterfield. Alex, a friend of Haldeman's and Ehrlichman's from UCLA, was a career air force man. While my operation took care of all in-person meetings and events with the president, Alex's responsibility was all the paper, documents, commissions, and printed material that flowed to and from the president. Alex's operation was incorporated into the operation that Bob had established within the Office of the Staff Secretary. All presidential briefing books, for example, flowed through Butterfield.

The system had Nixon's endorsement. As a result, meeting requests were carefully considered in advance. Briefing books were presented to the president in advance of each meeting. This organization protected the president from wasting his time unnecessarily. On the other hand, it was difficult for many people, including some cabinet officers, to accept. They were not accustomed to having to so thoroughly think through a meeting request in order to document it. Some considered it offensive. But the smarter folks accepted the procedure and worked with it, realizing it wasn't something Haldeman dreamed up. There was no "Palace Guard" or "Berlin Wall" stopping them. The system was set up, at the president's request, in order to maximize the use of his time.

At the beginning of the administration the president insisted that time be allowed on the schedule to see legislators from both parties on a reasonably regular basis. The House and Senate were controlled by the Democrats. He wanted to meet with bipartisan leadership every Thursday for an hour or so. Nixon knew it was important to maintain personal relationships with elected politicians. Nixon had grown up in Congress with Democrats like Mike Mansfield, Dick Russell and John Stennis. He respected and enjoyed a good friendship with many of them. It all started off well. However, as the administration became more bogged down with the Vietnam War and eventually Watergate, it ended up not working as smoothly. Fewer of his old congressional friends were able to schedule time with him.

An example of that was Republican Senator Chuck Percy. Nixon thought very highly of Percy at the outset. In fact, for a time in early 1968, Percy was among those being considered as a candidate for the vice presidency. But when Percy began shifting his opinion, and publicly criticizing our conduct of the war, their relationship soured, to the point that Percy was not welcome in the White House. That drove both Bryce Harlow and Bill Timmons, who succeeded Harlow in charge of congressional relations, crazy. They kept trying to get Percy into the office but the president was clear about it: He didn't want to see Chuck

Percy. The president didn't want Percy coming in and lecturing him on Vietnam. Nixon knew the arguments and respected many of them. He didn't want to waste time hearing them. That was the president's decision, and it was fine—until Watergate erupted. When the scandal was breaking, the president needed people the nation trusted, like Percy, to defend the administration, and Percy understandably had little interest in helping.

Nixon understood the power of his office and used it well. As the midyear elections approached in 1970, we were told by Haldeman, "As a matter of general scheduling policy remember that, from now through November, all appointments should be weighed on the basis of their political implications. The president's time should be used to the maximum extent possible to aid in picking up Senate seats. No appointment should be made that would hurt us politically . . . We have, for the last year and a half, overloaded schedule activity to blacks, youths, and Jews . . ." Rather than a racist connotation, he was referring to those groups as voting blocs. "The concentration is now to be on Italians, Poles, Mexicans, Rotarians, Elks, Middle Americans, Silent Americans, Catholics, etc." He added: "There are to be just enough blacks to show we care and they are to be establishment oriented blacks and not opposition-type militants." In today's world, obviously, this sounds racist. However, in 1970 these cultural divisions were a political reality. In order to accomplish what an administration needs to accomplish, it needs to remain in office—and each of these demographics had to be considered in terms of their interests and voting patterns. While certainly not acceptable in today's political climate, it was an acceptable part of political dialogue half a century ago.

A week later, though—literally one week later—I got another note from Bob informing me the president had changed his mind: "The president wants to meet with a black group of some kind about once a month, but they should always be favorably inclined blacks, not militants or opponents. He does want to bring in more union members." My job became to find those people.

There was a continuous thread of interesting and often famous people visiting the Oval Office. For me, the most exciting visitor was former presidential candidate Tom Dewey, who had gained national fame as New York's gangbusting D.A. during the 1930s. I had particularly admired him for much of my life. The first presidential election I can remember was 1948, when Harry Truman defeated the heavily favored Governor Tom Dewey. I was eight years old. My family was crushed. Dewey was established in my mind after that election not as the defeated candidate but as a hero. Nixon and Dewey had known each other for a long time. Dewey had helped Nixon's rise in the Republican ranks. He was the first party leader to tell Nixon in May of 1952 that he could be president one day. The president had considered Dewey for a Supreme Court seat. I'd heard him talking about Dewey with great praise. The opportunity to meet him, to shake his hand, was thrilling for me.

Ted Kennedy was always an interesting visitor. He was in the White House often for the president's frequent meetings with bipartisan congressional leadership. The political career of the Democrat's strongest personality, Teddy Kennedy, had been virtually destroyed in 1969 when he drove a car off a bridge in Chappaquiddick, a small island off of Martha's Vineyard, Massachusetts. Kennedy had been drinking, and rather than trying to save his passenger, Mary Jo Kopechne, he swam to safety and the young woman drowned. The Kennedy people were desperate to get beyond that, to rehabilitate his image and to make him a viable candidate again.

I witnessed Teddy Kennedy visiting Nixon in the Oval Office after Chappaquiddick. A bipartisan leadership briefing on the just concluded Apollo 11 goodwill trip had adjourned in the Cabinet Room. Walking past my desk into the Oval Office, Nixon said to me, "Senator Kennedy is coming in." Trailing the president was Kennedy, with his head hanging down in an uncharacteristically demoralized way. The president, as he wrote in his memoirs, "was shocked by how pale and shaken he looked."

Within five minutes Kennedy came out of the office, wiping away tears. I can imagine the president telling Kennedy to never give up, telling him that a great future lay ahead for him—or something like that. I know for certain Nixon would have been very kind to Senator Kennedy that morning. That was Nixon's true character coming through. Nixon characterized it this way in his memoirs: "I spoke to him in the Oval Office for several minutes afterward and tried to reassure him that he must resolve to overcome this tragedy and go on with his life. In politics it is possible to feel genuine personal concern for an opponent and still be coldly objective about his position as a competitor. Even as I felt real sympathy for Teddy Kennedy, I recognized, as he must have done, the far-reaching political implications of this personal tragedy." Even while consoling Kennedy, Nixon partisans directed from the White House were in Chappaquiddick gathering the sordid details of the entire affair for political use, if needed in the future. Such was the reality of politics.

Probably the most unlikely visitor we had in the White House was Elvis Presley. I liked Elvis, but he wasn't Tom Dewey. Elvis at that time was one of the biggest celebrities in the world, but admittedly it was a strange pairing: the button-downed Nixon and the unbuttoned Presley.

One morning in late December 1970, I had just settled into my office when my secretary, Nell, walked in, "Mr. Chapin, you're not going to believe this. Elvis Presley left a note for the president at the Northwest Gate." (During my entire time at the White House, Nell refused to call me anything other than "Mr. Chapin.") Henry Cashen, a member of Chuck Colson's White House team, had just dropped in, as was his morning ritual, for a cup of coffee. "So, the King's in town," Henry quipped.

It was hard to believe: Elvis Presley at the White House. Unlikely. The note had been written on American Airlines stationery. Elvis had apparently dropped it off earlier that morning. He was staying at the Washington Hotel and wanted to see the president to offer his help with our antidrug program.

The thought of the president meeting Elvis was fascinating, but, like everything else, it also could have political ramifications. I called

Bud Krogh, who was in charge of our antidrug initiative. "Bud," I said, "Elvis Presley wants to see the president. What do you think?"

Bud didn't believe me. Bud and I were charter members, along with Henry Cashen, of a group of close friends in the White House called "the Brotherhood." Bud was convinced this was a Brotherhood joke and responded with something like, "And I had dinner with Marilyn Monroe last night." When I finally was able to convince him that Elvis Presley had truly dropped the note off at the Northwest Gate, he thought about it and said, "I think he ought to come in." Bud meant "come in" so we could check him out, not necessarily to see the president.

I wrote a memorandum to Haldeman explaining the situation. I recommended we put this meeting together. We were constantly trying to get the president to interact with younger people, and this offered great potential. Haldeman wrote back: "You must be kidding." But he took my memorandum to Nixon. To everyone's surprise, Nixon thought it was a great idea. "Arrange for him to come in," Bob told me, "but have Bud check him out first."

Presley arrived at the Executive Office Building to meet with Bud. He brought a handgun, in a wooden box, with him. It was a beautiful pistol, a WWII Colt .45, silver-plated, that he wanted to give to the president. The Secret Service accepted the gun and held on to it. Bud met with Elvis to make certain his request to meet the president was legitimate. Finally, Bud called, told me that Elvis had checked out and that the meeting could take place. Bud and Jeff Donfeld, a staffer on Bud's team, put together the necessary briefing document for the president.

Elvis showed up for the meeting at the White House later that afternoon. He was wearing a purple velvet suit, a belt with a heavyweight championship-size buckle, a jacket draped over his shoulders, and amber sunglasses. Usually when visitors arrived to see the president, Steve Bull, the president's aide, would ask them to wait in the Roosevelt Room or Cabinet Room until the president was ready to see them. But not this time. This time Bud met Elvis and escorted him directly into the Oval Office. Elvis walked through my outer office. Nell met him but not me. I was busy with something else, so while a significant bit of Nixon history was transpiring, I missed it—and I always felt sorry I did.

As Bud reported, the meeting went quite well. It ended with Elvis spontaneously hugging the president, who directed Bud to get Elvis the DEA special agent badge he wanted. Elvis got his badge saying he was a "Federal Agent at Large," along with an identification card that identified him, ironically, as a "Special Agent" of the Bureau of Narcotics and Dangerous Drugs.

Nixon, early on, had chosen Ollie Atkins as his official photographer. Ollie was in charge of the White House photo office. He administered that office and managed the other two photographers who were on staff part-time. Nixon loved having Ollie around. Ollie was continually, yet inconspicuously, taking pictures. He would appear, and disappear, as events unfolded. However, on this day Nixon had him front and center with Elvis. In fact, Ollie's photo of the two men shaking hands is now available on everything from T shirts to snow globes. That image of "the King and the President" that Ollie took remains the most requested picture in the history of the National Archives.

As the Elvis episode demonstrated, it was not unusual to have someone show up unexpectedly at the White House, hoping to see the president. These were people who believed they were important enough to get in to see the president or who were a little on the nutty side. Most of the time they were politely sent away. Occasionally, though . . . Nixon was a big sports fan, especially football. Living in Washington had made him a Redskins fan. One Sunday the Redskins won a great game after an incredible comeback. Nixon was so excited he called the team's famous coach, George Allen, to congratulate him. "We've got to get together," the president said, ending the conversation with: "When it's convenient for you, drop by and we'll talk some football."

About three hours later my White House home phone rang. The operator told me, "Mr. Chapin, we have the Southwest Gate calling. George Allen is there. He's come by to say hello to the president." They put George Allen on the phone. He explained that the president had told him to drop by.

With the coach waiting, I called the president and told him that Coach Allen was at the Southwest Gate. After a brief pause to consider that, he asked, "Why?" I explained that apparently he'd asked him to drop by sometime. After another brief pause while that reality sunk in, he said, "Oh, good God. Okay, tell him to come in." Coach Allen was invited in and spent part of the evening talking football with President Nixon upstairs in the Residence.

All presidents receive countless requests for meetings that are ceremonial, some asking for a presidential "endorsement." While Nixon disliked most of these kinds of meetings, he understood the political and public relations value, so we set specific times on his calendar in order that certain groups of people could meet with him briefly. This type of meeting would be put on the president's calendar as a photo opportunity. The reality was that a photograph with the president had tremendous value. These were not official, substantive meetings. Some examples would be groups representing the March of Dimes or the Red Cross, the honoring of a police hero, shaking hands with a contributor to a favored senator or congressman, the Proclamation at Thanksgiving pardoning a turkey, and so on. In a four-year term, there are thousands of these kinds of requests. At the outset of the administration we would scatter these types of appointments into the schedule sparingly. But it irritated the president. He might be in the middle of a policy issue when suddenly time was up because "the Student of the Year" would be waiting for a picture. While the student was important, so was the policy meeting that was being interrupted.

Our solution for handling these less important events was the creation of the "Open Door Hour." Two days a week, maybe from eleven until noon, we would invite certain individuals or groups to meet with the president. This accommodated the large number of requests while, at the same time, consolidated them into a specific hour in order that the president's workday was not continually interrupted. Nixon, being the consummate politician, understood the value of a photograph to people for all sorts of reasons. It could be hanging in a congressman's local office, or a reliable contributor would appreciate hanging it in his office. So we'd take groups through, letting them stay just long enough to shake hands with the president, while Ollie Atkins would snap a picture. We could get eight or ten groups or individuals through the office in one Open Hour, sixteen to twenty such groups a week. For the president, it was another way to optimize his time. Very often, these sessions would last considerably longer than planned. As the president engaged with the variety of individuals coming for their short appointments, he could get involved in conversations with them. Often he would extend the amount of time we had allowed for the meeting and invite the guest to stay longer. It was his prerogative, and he exercised it.

Conversely, when the president wanted to see or speak with someone, my job was to make that happen. I was working with five of the most impressive words in the English language, "The White House is calling . . ." The White House switchboard was amazing. They were better than the FBI at finding people when the president wanted to talk with them.

One of the most entertaining and fun requests took place on New Year's Eve 1970. There was a massive snowstorm in Washington. Susie and I had taken Kim and Tracy to the home of Ron and Anne Walker to celebrate with their daughters, along with Dick and Marsha Howard. At about eleven twenty, we turned on the television in order to join most of America in watching the popular bandleader Guy Lombardo. Lombardo was conducting his Royal Canadians in the grand ballroom of the Waldorf Astoria. His nationally televised New Year's Eve show had been an American tradition for many years. Lombardo was known as "Mr. New Year's Eve." My White House pager went off and I called in. The president came on: "Dwight, when it turns midnight, I want to talk to Guy Lombardo."

"Let me work this out," I said, having no idea how I was going to work it out. I asked the White House operator to get the general manager of the Waldorf on the line. I said, "The president wants to speak to Guy Lombardo right after midnight. We need a phone number for the president to call." The general manager gave me the number of a phone just offstage. When I called the number, the man who answered said he was standing where he could look onto the stage and see Lombardo. I could hear the music in the background as I asked him to please stay right where he was and not to leave because the White House would be calling. I called back and explained to the White House operator she was to get Mr. Lombardo on the phone at 12:05 A.M. and then put the call through to the president.

It was all arranged. At the Walker house we were glued to the television—especially me. I was saying a silent prayer that it would all work out. At midnight the horns and buzzers went off and balloons were dropped from the Waldorf ceiling. In the middle of it all stood Guy Lombardo, waving his magic baton as his Royal Canadians played "Auld Lang Syne," welcoming all of America into the New Year. Suddenly a man walked across the stage, tapped Lombardo on the shoulder, then whispered something in his ear. Lombardo nodded and handed his baton to the lead violinist, who got up and took the podium as Lombardo walked off.

I couldn't believe it. This was actually happening.

Lombardo returned a couple of minutes later. When the song was finished he said, "Ladies and gentlemen, I have just had the privilege of talking to the president of the United States, who wishes everyone a most Happy New Year."

Haldeman had once told me, while we still were at J. Walter Thompson, "Anything is possible, as long as you've got the money." Or, we now knew, that statement could be amended to "as long as you have the power of the presidency."

The only people who had immediate access to the president at any time were his family. No matter what the president was doing, when Mrs. Nixon or the girls came down, they had priority. It happened rarely, but when it did, the schedule stopped. I was the gatekeeper until Steve Bull took over. Steve and I both understood the president's feelings about that. I always wished people could see Nixon with his daughters, if only for a minute. Politically, there was "the old Nixon" and "the new Nixon," but personally there was a constant version of Nixon, the very present and attentive father. Tricia and Julie were young adults. They weren't the ages of the young Kennedy kids, who had been photographed crawling around the Oval Office floor in the John F. Kennedy days. We didn't have the opportunity for those very appealing kinds of pictures. But Nixon allowed that sensitive, emotional side of him, the part he kept so deeply hidden inside, to sneak out with his daughters.

While his family meant everything to him, there was one exception. There was one relative who had been hired by a shady businessman, Robert Vesco, who clearly believed he could gain access to the White House through that connection. The White House wanted to keep as much distance from Vesco as possible, which meant not having contact with this relative. I would get calls from this person and hear, "I want to talk to the president."

Per my instructions I would reply, "The president is at Camp David and I can't interrupt him."

The relative was not pleasant. "You can't keep me away from him."

"I'm sorry," I said, "but I can't put your call through."

The turndown was difficult because it involved family, even though it was extended family. Thankfully, there was never a ramification for the president over that issue.

Among the creative aspects of my job was spotting opportunities or suggesting events we could schedule. By early April of 1969, Haldeman was writing to me: "I want to move you out of the routine of running the schedule and get you more broadly involved in my whole area . . . areas such as the broader PR problem of the entire WH staff; and even broader PR issues of the presidency itself. Then there's the subject you raised of some really good planning for the president, a quarterly game plan . . . We are still letting the president's soft heart and his lack of self-discipline get in the way of doing the very best in the use of his time. We'll never get him to be perfect, but we can always improve."

Bob's April letter shows he had no illusions about—and understood the importance of—the role he played in protecting the president from himself. The president hated to be lobbied in person, partly because he did not like confrontation in case he had to refuse someone and partly because he realized, if only vaguely, that he was highly susceptible to personal pressure from others.

I would regularly send Bob suggestions: "Why don't we set a period once a week where we bring in one of the groups that serves the president so they feel they have contact with the man and what he needs . . . speechwriters one week, five people from the NSC . . ." I would make personnel suggestions: "Alex Butterfield has no continuing responsibilities . . . he must be given assignments and responsibility to justify it." And personally, I felt at ease giving Bob advice on how to handle his job: "As we enter into your next phase which will, I think, be the planning phase . . . map out the timetable for the president by quarters . . ."

And I was warning him: "You should be aware that there is a good deal of talk about you around the White House these days. I know you don't care and have enough to worry about just serving the president . . . This is something we should talk out for not only is it important to your effectiveness but also to the president."

The evolution was underway. My role had evolved from personal aide to management of the schedule and then to the actual planning of the presidential calendar. This planning responsibility was in addition to the management of the advance and television offices. I was replaced as the person who implemented the president's daily schedule and events by Steve Bull, a very responsible, buttoned-up former marine and an all-around great guy. (Nobody could play "Hail to the Chief" on a touchtone phone like Steve.) David Parker continued to keep us on track with his excellent management of schedule matters. Ron Walker was running the White House advance office. There was never anyone more competent or personally loyal to me and the president's efforts than Ron.

A favorite story about Walker centers around recruitment of some additional White House advance men for the 1972 presidential campaign. Fred Malek, who headed personnel, was charged with finding prospective candidates. Walker, a "diamond in the rough" kind of guy, was apprehensive and suspicious of the overly polished Ivy League candidates Malek was identifying. After Walker interviewed candidates, they would be sent to me. One of the men asked me, in the most quizzical way, "Mr. Chapin, may I ask you a question? Why did Mr. Walker ask me if I had ever pissed in an alley?" That was Ron. He had his way of testing. He wanted a corps of streetwise advance men and no prima donnas.

And a newcomer to the Nixon orbit, Mark Goode, a former producer of the Soupy Sales television show in Hollywood, ran our television office, which oversaw the management and execution of all the president's televised activity. Mark was brought in by Bill Carruthers, who had replaced Roger Ailes as our television consultant when Roger decided to solicit a larger client base. Carruthers was a star, a consultant who lived the Hollywood life and flew east to Washington as needed. The president loved Bill. We all did. Roger Ailes had been excellent at producing our TV segments. Carruthers was even better. Presidents Ford and Reagan would eventually utilize Bill's extraordinary communications skills in their administrations.

Mapping out presidential time and looking for opportunities to promote our agenda was a daily consideration. I was part of a team, including Bill Safire, Pat Buchanan, Herb Klein, Dick Moore, and Lyn Nofziger, who focused on "game planning." Chuck Colson, or one of his staff, would often join us, as would Deputy Press Secretary Jerry Warren. Our job was to match presidential initiatives and objectives with things the president or members of the administration might do. My responsibility was to set the agenda, focus our sessions, then take down the ideas and suggested activities, meld them into our ongoing schedule, and articulate them in the form of memorandums for presidential consideration. It was a difficult, sensitive, and stressful aspect of my job because it had the full attention of both Haldeman and the president. In fact, it was one of the most important of my responsibilities because it centered on how the presidency was to be utilized in order to communicate to the country and to the world. We had a major war underway and we were contending with a media that disliked the president. The press did everything possible to reinforce the negative image it had helped create, too often misrepresenting details and facts. This adversarial relationship with the media was a reality in our administration, and we were constantly considering it in our planning.

Our objective was to enhance and position the president's initiatives. I started to use the word "marketing" in terms of the initiatives. That word is too harsh, but we took it beyond "presenting." We sold. We marketed. It was necessary for Nixon's political survival. It is fair to say that Nixon was obsessed with his image, but only in small part for ego gratification. It was mostly defensive, and we all believed it was necessary if we were going to implement our agenda and survive.

Very confidentially we tracked the success of our White House game planning efforts on behalf of the administration. We had a 50 to 60 percent average success rate for getting a planned administration story for a given day on the evening network television news programs. It was not as difficult as it would later become, because we were dealing with only the three national networks (NBC, CBS, and ABC) at that time, plus local stations. There was no cable news and no talk radio. A significant amount of our effort went into planning events with real news value that would have to be covered on the nightly news broadcasts. We never talked about this success rate outside of the White House, knowing the networks would have changed their coverage procedures had they realized what we were doing. Our communications outreach efforts were groundbreaking and served as a model for later administrations, in particular Reagan's presidency. No White House before us had the success we did. When the Reagan administration arrived, Mike Deaver and their team got innovation and execution salutes from the media for things we had been doing years before. There always was, and still remains, negative bias against things "Nixon."

The White House received an endless flow of invitations to various and sundry events. Our rule was to initially turn every one of them down politely. But we didn't kill them all internally. Those with promise were put on our list of possibilities. We knew that if the president wanted to change his mind and accept an invitation we had previously turned down, the sponsors would welcome us. For example, our political operation might decide the president needed to be touching base in Arizona, in which case we would review the "possibility list" to see what event options were available there. If nothing acceptable was on the list, we would work with local people in order to create from scratch our own event.

You could say the operations of our White House were "political." Big news. All White House administrations are political operations, to their core. We looked at events that would resonate with large voting blocs. As Ehrlichman used to say, "It's much more effective to deal with a voting bloc where we can get a hundred thousand votes for the same expenditure of time and energy that we would put in to get ten votes." The consideration would be this: What is the political impact for the energy expended? Our goal was to always maximize the impact while spending the least amount of presidential time.

The president might also decide suddenly where he needed to go or with whom he needed to meet. No one in the administration had better political instincts than Richard Nixon. If he wanted to get out an economic message, I'd get a note telling me to "investigate opportunities" of the Detroit Economic Club or the New York Economic Club, some local appearance which would generate sufficient press coverage to get national attention.

We were always looking for opportunities to piggyback onto planned trips. If Nixon was going to spend a few days at his beautiful home in San Clemente, California, we would schedule events and have a daily work schedule at the Western White House. The Western White House right next to the Nixons' Casa Pacifica residence was a piece of federal property that served as a coast guard loran (radio navigation) system. The facility consisted of two prefabricated buildings with an office for the president and other offices for key aides, a conference room, and a galley. Next to the buildings was a helipad that was bult by the coast guard and was already in place when the Nixons purchased the Casa Pacifica property.

I'd put together a full preapproved schedule for our trips west and our time in San Clemente. But the schedule was very organic. It was constantly being revised. The president wanted to be seen as always working, regardless of where he was. It was not hard to prove he was busy because the press was kept as active as he was covering events and happenings.

We also responded to events. The war drove a lot of decisions. We knew, for example, when the antiwar demonstrations were scheduled, so we planned our own appearances in advance of those demonstrations. We got our story out early so it did not appear we were reacting to the antiwar protesters. We would think through where the president should be. Does the president stay in Washington or leave? Do we take a business trip somewhere or make damn certain the president is in the White House working during the large moratoriums? The answer was typically to stay in Washington and work. The demonstrators were not going to drive the president out of the White House. This was the president's strategic decision. This was the message he wanted to send to Americans.

We were always trying to come up with new ideas that would result in positive publicity. No one was better at doing that than Tex McCrary, a very skilled and famous public relations professional who served as a consultant. He was constantly sending me memos filled with ideas, some of them a little far-out. He used to refer to brainstorming sessions as "scrimmages," during which we would be "punting ideas around." To reinforce Presidential Counselor Pat Moynihan's efforts to revive the inner cities, for example, Tex suggested a real strange one: "With Agnew by his side—Agnew, the man who said 'After you've seen one slum you've seen them all'—the president will visit ten slums, winding up in Jersey City, one-time home of Boss Haig and a cradle of political corruption, now run by a mayor who is also a doctor and a Democrat . . . There in Jersey City the president [will] announce his homefront program."

While some of my ideas, or those from Tex and others, became reality, many more did not. That was the nature of the job, and the rejections didn't deter us. I just kept shoveling the ideas to Haldeman and the president. In the run-up to the 1972 election the president was going to be in Alabama for a Young Labor for Nixon event that promised to result in almost no press coverage. Someone suggested to me—and I agreed to forward the idea to Bob—that "the president pay a surprise visit . . . to George Wallace." Segregationist governor and former presidential candidate George Wallace had been shot and paralyzed from the waist down three months earlier. He was remarkably popular in the South. I thought a quick visit would serve as a message to those voters. "The president would just fly over and pay his respects to the governor," I wrote. "It is felt the political benefits from this would be significant." In huge, all capital letters, Haldeman responded in handwriting on my memo: "NO. NO. NO." That idea never got to the president.

At least that response was more positive than his reaction to my suggestion the previous September, that Nixon engage with college students. Because of the war, the majority of college students disliked him—"dislike" being a mild description. In a memo I suggested the president accept an invitation from Patrick Moynihan to go to Harvard and make a "spontaneous visit" to one of Pat's lecture classes, then answer questions. "It has the advantage of going to one of the most actively antiwar campuses in the country and would strike hard at the argument that the president can't go on a college campus," I suggested.

This time, in huge letters, Haldeman wrote across the memo "NEVER." He added: "You must be nuts." That idea also never got to the president.

I also suggested a Q&A session at Notre Dame. "I think that Father Hesburgh, the president of Notre Dame, and everyone else at Notre Dame would work hard to see that whatever program was put on had the dignity the president deserves and that undesirables would be controlled."

Haldeman's response: "Ridiculous."

Looking back, I was pushing against the natural political aversion that both Nixon and Haldeman had to risk taking. Undoubtedly, their politically safe approach was understandable. My instinct regarding the journey to see Wallace was undoubtedly wrong. However, the visits to Harvard and Notre Dame would have served to show people another side of Nixon. I still believe I was right-on with those ideas. Later he did make a spontaneous, unexpected visit to the Lincoln Memorial, which did serve to reveal that other side—but more on that later. President Nixon would have handled any of the visits I suggested beautifully, as he always did. In my view, they were among the dozens of opportunities missed.

I also was tasked with planning Mrs. Nixon's schedule for a short period, which brought with it a whole new set of headaches. She was particular about the events she would do. Once we had accepted an invitation for her to appear at a veterans hospital in Suffolk, Massachusetts, only to be told she wouldn't do it. I didn't know how to handle that, so I asked Bob, "Mrs. Nixon has said that she will definitely not do the veterans hospital. She flatly refuses. What do we do?"

Haldeman's written response: "Punt." That was helpful.

Any real estate expert will tell you the three most important factors when evaluating a property are location, location, location. My first White House office, located between the Oval Office and the Cabinet Room and just off the Rose Garden, put me in the very center of all the action. People were always just showing up. In a given day anyone from Vice President Agnew to Don Rumsfeld, Pat Moynihan, Bill Safire, Nelson Rockefeller (who never knew my name; I was "Hiya, fella"), or Henry Kissinger would be dropping by to ask if the president was available to talk.

It was July or August of 1969 when the president and Mrs. Nixon made a trip to San Francisco. *Air Force One* landed at San Francisco

International Airport. From there we took the president's helicopter, *Marine One,* to Crissy Airfield, located at the Presidio. *Marine One* had a large picture window, and the president and Mrs. Nixon were sitting facing each other. I was on the benchseat with Haldeman and a few others, sitting across from the Nixons. As the helicopter taxied up to the small terminal, there was a sizable welcoming crowd. I was just seeing the edge of the crowd. Mrs. Nixon could see more of it, and all of a sudden she said, "Dick, look at that sign for Dwight." "Oh, yes," the president responded. I had no idea what she was talking about. But when the plane turned, I saw a group of people holding a very large banner, at least twelve feet long, reading in huge letters: "Welcome Dwight Chapin." Then, in much smaller letters: "And President and Mrs. Nixon." My USC Baller friend Mike Woodson was the advance man at that stop, and he wanted to have some fun. Haldeman looked at me in the stern way only Haldeman could look and said, "I assume that sign will be gone." The Nixons knew I was horrified, but they actually thought it funny.

Throughout my childhood I'd made up for my academic struggles by being personable, so a strong social life was always important to me. The White House was a perfect place to form new and strong friendships. This was an amazing group of accomplished people brought together from across the country with a common purpose. In each segment of my life I've somehow been involved in putting together small private groups of close friends. In Birmingham High School we were the Studs. At USC it was the Ballers. In the White House we called ourselves the Brotherhood. And later in Chicago, with all our wives members of the Junior League, we called ourselves the Auxiliary.

There were nine of us in the White House Brotherhood. We had no rules and no officers, although Deputy Press Secretary Jerry Warren, the oldest of our group, was our chief justice. Whenever there was a dispute, such as whom we might add as a new member, the chief justice would rule and settle it. Our members were Ken Cole, John Ehrlichman's Domestic Affairs Deputy; Henry Cashen, Special Assistant to the President; Ed Morgan and John Evans from the Domestic Council;

Bud Krogh, who also worked with Ehrlichman; Pat Buchanan; and Ron Walker. It was a secret organization. We would meet at the call of Chief Justice Warren at one of the two or three bars we frequented. We'd pick places with discreet back rooms in order to be able to drink and have fun talking about what was going on in the White House.

A key element in all of those social gatherings was the consumption of alcohol. One thing about drinking: It makes more drinking easier. On Saturday mornings the car to the office arrived an hour later than it did during the week. I would be riding with Haldeman, sometimes praying that he was not going to ask me any questions because my head was throbbing from the night before. Occasionally, when I got to the White House, if I really felt horrible, I'd call the president's doctor, Walter Tkach, and ask for relief. He would send an ensign to my office to give me a B-12 shot. Looking back, there were clear signs that I was drinking too much. Well, it wasn't clear to me at that time. Except for the hangovers, it didn't seem to be affecting my work. The more I drank and continued to function, the more I believed I could drink without consequence.

I was wrong, as evidenced by this Christmas Eve 1970 story. Susie and I were giving Kim and Tracy a large tricycle. It arrived unassembled and must have had a thousand small parts. Okay, that's an exaggeration, but at the time, it looked that way. On Christmas Eve, after the girls were asleep, I had a few drinks as I proceeded to assemble it. Finally completing it, I dropped off to sleep.

I was in a deep sleep when our White House phone rang. "Mr. Chapin," said the operator, "we have Bob Hope and General Creighton Abrams on the line for the president." They were calling from Vietnam, where it was already Christmas Day. Bob Hope. I loved Bob Hope. One summer, when I was nine or ten years old, he had stopped in Wichita as part of his summer concert tour. My parents let me take a crosstown bus, with my friend Bruce Bumgardner, to see an early evening performance at our baseball park. Then, after we had moved to California, in high school, I worked in the auto service department for a Buick dealer, Bones Hamilton Buick, in Van Nuys. Buick sponsored

Hope's TV show and Hope had his car serviced at the Bones agency. After his car had been serviced, I would deliver it to his Toluca Lake home. So, as it happened, I had actually had opportunities to spend time in his presence. I got on the phone and explained, "Mr. Hope, Dwight Chapin. The president's at Camp David. Our instructions are not to put any calls through."

Hope understood. Then he put General Abrams on the phone. We all exchanged "Merry Christmas" wishes with each other, and I'm sure I must have told them I would relay their sentiments to the president. Then I went back to sleep. A week later I was riding with Haldeman into Palm Springs. We were staying with the president and Mrs. Nixon at Sunnylands, publisher Walter Annenberg's very large and beautiful estate. Annenberg had been appointed by Nixon as U.S. Ambassador to the United Kingdom. The main house was so big that when Ron Ziegler and I walked into the entry area for the first time, we joked with each other and wondered where the check-in desk was. The president and the First Lady had gone there for New Year's Eve. As Haldeman and I were being driven into town, Bob said, "The president had dinner last night with Bob and Dolores Hope." I was listening. Then he said, "Hope told the president that he enjoyed talking with you on Christmas Eve." Bells started going off. Haldeman had a certain acerbic tone in his voice when he was angry. He didn't raise his voice but continued: "Did it ever dawn on you that they weren't calling from Vietnam to talk with *you*?"

Remembering the call, I knew he was right. He continued: "This can never happen again. Never. The president was very upset that he didn't know about it."

I promised him nothing like that would ever happen again. It's an easy promise to make—when you're sober. But it wasn't funny, ever. As the years passed, my drinking became an issue that I eventually addressed by totally abstaining from alcohol.

★ 9 ★

PRESIDENT RICHARD NIXON

By this point I knew more about Richard Nixon's likes and dislikes, about his dreams and desires, about his personal habits and foibles, than anyone other than his family and a few other close friends and associates. I had spent several hundred days in numerous places at his side. I'd experienced his entire range of emotions.

He was a private man in a public business—that is, the business of leading our country. He had goals and dreams for our country that could only be implemented from a public position, though a public position was not his natural comfort zone.

He was an extraordinary man who could be vexed by what some would call petty concerns, such as his continuous struggle to deal with an unfriendly press. However, I challenge anyone to walk in the shoes of one who has an unfriendly (and, I would add, unfair) press nipping at his heels year after year, 24/7.

There is a story I like that might be applied to Richard Nixon. Supposedly it's a Cherokee legend. A young man told his wise grandfather he was confused about the battle between good and evil. His grandfather nodded in understanding. "There are two wolves battling inside me," he explained. "One is evil; he is anger, hatred, vengeance, resentment, inferiority, bitterness, revenge, misguided pride, envy, and ego. The other is good; he is peace, love, hope, decency, optimism, generosity, compassion, empathy, humility, and kindness. That same fight is going on inside all of us, including you."

The young man considered that silently, then finally asked, "Which one wins?"

His grandfather looked at him and said softly, "The one you feed."

There always were those two sides of Richard Nixon, the supposedly old Nixon versus the New Nixon, his light side versus his darker side. I think the wise Cherokee was right. Within ourselves we all have negative and positive urges. We try to control and downplay the negatives, and we show our more charming selves to society. Nixon was no different. Being human, he had his negative side, which was accentuated when it was fed by an incident such as criticism; or what he perceived to be unfairness; or when he had to deal with real, honest to goodness, by anyone's definition, "unfairness." At times, as so many other people have written, and as Haldeman had told me and as I had grown to know, the president could be his own worst enemy.

In the wake of Watergate, so much of what was actually accomplished by him and his administration has been forgotten or disregarded. For example, by any truthful measure, Nixon's domestic policy was brilliant and successful. Tom Wicker was a columnist at the *New York Times*. His "In the Nation" appeared on the op-ed page. He wrote a biography of Nixon, titled *One of Us: Richard Nixon and the American Dream*. Wicker concluded that Nixon's domestic accomplishments were more significant than his success in foreign policy.

The Council for Urban Affairs was created by Nixon with his first executive order, January 23, 1969. Nixon was chairman and Patrick Moynihan was executive secretary until succeeded by John Price. It included all the members of the domestic cabinet and Don Rumsfeld, the Director of the Office of Equal Opportunity. The president chaired twenty-three of the first twenty-five meetings. This was all prior to the Urban Affairs Council becoming the Domestic Council, headed by John Ehrlichman.

The ripples are still being felt today. With the extraordinary efforts of Ehrlichman's Domestic Council, Nixon's policies were way ahead of their time. Not only Democrats but most citizens today would be stunned to realize the initiatives and forward-thinking policies that came out of the administration. Among many other accomplishments, he founded the Environmental Protection Agency and instituted tougher standards for air and water quality. He signed Title IX legislation that banned gender discrimination in colleges, opening a path for female participation in intercollegiate sports. He launched the war on cancer by budgeting more than $100 million (in 1970 dollars), which led to the establishment of the National Cancer Institute. He advanced and supported the Twenty-sixth Amendment, which lowered the voting age from twenty-one to eighteen. He continued to support the civil rights movement by virtually eliminating segregated schools. He launched the first real attack by the federal government on organized crime. He gave birth to the first "affirmative action" programs by instituting George Shultz's plan to train and employ minorities to work on federally funded projects; he even added $2 billion to welfare reform programs and additional billions to LBJ's Food Stamp Act. He ended the draft with the all-volunteer army. He restored Native American rights to their lands and became almost a folk hero by returning their sacred Blue Lake to the Taos Pueblos. It's a long list of accomplishments. When I start enumerating it to people, their eyes open wide and they respond, "Nixon?"

Yes, Nixon. And, yes too, John Ehrlichman and his domestic affairs team of young men and women who would rotate in and out of government, business, and law, making contributions to other administrations for many years thereafter. The Nixon alumni group, for decades after Richard Nixon's presidency, has supplied Republican administrations with top-notch talent.

Few people remember that when the administration took office, it wasn't just the West Wing of the White House that was run-down. It was much of the entire District of Columbia. One afternoon early in our first year, Nixon and Pat Moynihan went for a ride in the presidential limousine, driving up and down Pennsylvania Avenue. I rode along with the president. Moynihan had had the idea and arranged the tour. He was very excited to get Nixon's undivided attention, and that's what he got. Moynihan had a dream of how he wanted President

With my mother, Betty June; father, Spencer; and sister, Linda, in 1954 on our Derby, Kansas, farm. That summer we moved to Brentwood in western Los Angeles.

With my quarter horse Pat. We won a white ribbon for barrel racing at the local rodeo.

The revived University of Southern California (USC) political party Trojans for Representative Government (TRG) wins the 1962 student body election.

We were married in the garden of Susie's family home in Hope Ranch, Santa Barbara, California, on August 18, 1963.

Celebrating Christmas 1967 in Cos Cob, Greenwich, Connecticut, and starting the 1968 presidential campaign year. Kimberly is two-and-a-half years old, and Tracy is six months.

Richard Nixon as the "Man in the Arena," an innovative format for political television. The University of Oklahoma's famous football coach Bud Wilkinson was the moderator. It was the first of what in later years would be called a "town hall."

Nixon comforts Martin Luther King Jr.'s widow, Coretta Scott King, during our private visit to the family home in Atlanta after the assassination.

With Pat Buchanan in his office during the 1968 Nixon for President campaign.

Working with Mrs. Pat Nixon aboard the campaign plane, the "Tricia."

Notes from my personal diary on November 6, 1968, in the early morning after election night while in the presidential suite at the Waldorf Astoria hotel in New York. You can find additional Election Day notes in Exhibit 6 of the Appendix.

4:00 AM
RN called Gov. Rockefeller—who was sound asleep—to thank him for effort—although didn't win N.Y—said looked like he would win.
C & H—[Chapin and Haldeman] suggest RN nap—said he couldn't would have to stay up till it was settled.

4:30
RN asked that any staff or friends who were still up be invited into the suite. Sort of an open house—those who came in—Price, Buchanan, Garment, Rose, Keyes, Harlow, Mitchell, Finch, Chotiner, H, C, these people passed in & out for the next two hours. RN had a beer which he nursed for at least an hour.

The Waldorf Astoria hotel, the morning after election night 1968. From *RN: The Memoirs of Richard Nixon:* "At 8:30 the door burst open and Dwight Chapin rushed in. 'ABC just declared you the winner!' he shouted. 'They've projected Illinois. You got it. You've won.'" I was the only person with a camera. In the photo, the new president-elect looks at the television in amazement. John Ehrlichman's arm goes up along with a shout of victory. The morning sun streams through the window. His long wait has ended.

President Johnson and President Elect Nixon talking in the Blue Room of the White House on the morning of January 20, 1969, before leaving for the inauguration at the Capitol. Standing a few feet away, I was witnessing this historic moment.

My White House credentials.

Ollie Atkins, President Nixon's official White House photographer, took this picture of me in the Rose Garden, spring 1969.

Boarding America's Cup racing yacht *Columbia* in Newport Beach, California, for an afternoon sail on the Pacific Ocean, September 1969.

President Nixon greets Henry Kissinger at the Western White House in San Clemente, California, upon Kissinger's return from his secret trip to China. The world learned of the trip that evening with Nixon's televised announcement.

With White House advance-team member Tim Elbourne (*left*) and my Chinese counterpart, Han Hsu (*center*).

On the Great Wall with Kissinger. I am in the middle of the third row.

This banquet photo ran in a news magazine that identified me as "Kissinger aide." Henry autographed the picture with the salutation *"To Dwight Chapin—the only aide who has ever survived. Highest Regards, Henry A. Kissinger."*

Reviewing plans with Bob Haldeman (*center*) and his assistant Larry Higby (*right*) aboard *Air Force One,* February 1972. Kissinger sits across the aisle (*far left*). Julie Pineau, one of Kissinger's secretaries, stands at the copier behind him, and standing at her right is Kissinger aide Commander Jonathan Howe. Winston Lord sits in the far back on the left, and Muriel Hartley, another Kissinger secretary, sits in the back on the right (between Haldeman and Higby).

President Nixon on *Air Force One,* studying briefing books on the way to China with Kissinger.

Tim Elbourne (Secret Service name "Snapshot") and Ron Walker (Secret Service name "Roadrunner") in the Forbidden City, Peking.

(*From left to right*) Military aide Lieutenant Colonel Jack Brennan; me; General Brent Scowcroft; General Al Redman; and my secretary, Nell Yates, in Hawaii, 1972.

The Arrival. Premier Chou En-lai greeting the president and Mrs. Nixon on February 21, 1972—the moment when *"the week that changed the world"* began.

On the first afternoon in Peking, the president meets Chairman Mao Tse-tung.

Meeting on *Air Force One* with Chinese officials.

A snowy Peking morning. Bill Livingood of the Secret Service (*left*), Ron Walker (*right*), and I (*center*) are leading the president, Mrs. Nixon, and their party on a tour of the Forbidden City.

Kissinger and Nixon toasting the signing of the Strategic Arms Limitation Treaty in Moscow. In the background is U.S. Secretary of State William Rogers (*center*) and USSR General Secretary Leonid Brezhnev (*left of Nixon*).

Mrs. Nixon and Kissinger watch the president address the people of the USSR on live television.

In the Oval Office with the president, Bob Haldeman (*left*), and John Ehrlichman (*center right*).

"The President and the King." This picture is the most requested in the history of the National Archives.

A 1972 GOP convention floor strategy meeting. (*From right to left*) Dick Moore, Terry O'Donnell (*back row*), Mark Goode, me, Bill Carruthers, Sandy Abbey, Mike Duval's back, and Ron Walker.

The 1972 GOP convention in Miami, Florida. (*From left to right*) Bill Carruthers, Roy Goodearle, Dick Howard, me, and Henry Cashen.

Appearing on the steps of the federal courthouse during my trial.

Don Segretti

I am demonstrating an interactive foreign-policy kiosk to Henry Kissinger at the Nixon Library in Yorba Linda, California, after the renovation of the exhibits in 2016.

With W. Clement Stone in his studio office at "The Villa."

(*From left to right*) Bart Leddel, Don Segretti, and me at our USC fiftieth class reunion.

With my family at Tod's Point in Greenwich, Connecticut. (*Back row, left to right*) Jack Burton, Kimberly, Dan Burton, Tracy, and Matthew Maher. (*Front row, left to right*) Terry, me, Emily Burton, Chase Maher, and Jeff Maher.

Nixon to change our nation's capital city. What we saw that day was a city in shambles. There were shanties, decrepit buildings. Everything looked dark and dirty. As we passed different areas, Moynihan would share with the president his vision of what was possible. We would stop at different intersections. Crowds gathered on street corners, watching as the president listened to Moynihan pointing and describing the possibilities with the public watching. Later, the two followed up with a helicopter ride over Washington, D.C. Nixon bought into Moynihan's plan completely. As a result of the tours and hearing of the potential, the president established the Pennsylvania Avenue Development Corporation and the city was gentrified. Washington, D.C., became more beautiful, one of the most beautiful cities in the world. Nixon?

Yes, it was Nixon, making Moynihan's vision a reality.

Pat Moynihan once described me to the *Washington Post* as "an unusually self-effacing man." Unlike Kenny O'Donnell, he said, who performed my appointments secretary job for President Kennedy and who was "very much a policy man in his own right, Chapin never aspired to that position. He was content to be a perfectly neutral executor." When Moynihan was asked by Dick Moore to write in support of my candidacy as one of the nation's Ten Outstanding Young Men, Moynihan wrote, "Dwight showers ideas." That comment from Pat Moynihan, his acknowledgment of my creative contribution to our game planning and scheduling, meant a great deal to me.

The plan for restoring Pennsylvania Avenue and the city of Washington, D.C., was inspired. It was "big thinking," a way of *dreaming and doing* that President Nixon loved. Unfortunately, the goodness and power of that kind of thinking and doing would be sabotaged by the president's own words, in the transcripts and tapes that would later be released of conversations in his office and on his phone.

The president had innocently—and in retrospect, for sure unwisely—installed a taping system to assist him in his post-presidency in writing the history of his administration. Instead, the tapes damaged him to the extent that he eventually had to leave office.

There is no way to undo the damage done by the tapes, which are not to be excused. But there is a perspective about the tapes of which most citizens may not be thinking. I found out by accident.

At lunch one day, a high official from the Reagan administration told me about taking his daughter to the National Archives in College Park, Maryland, to listen to the Oval Office tapes. When they entered, the host archivist asked, "Which section are you here to see? The 'general tape' section or the 'abuse of power' section?" Who could pass up that invitation? What the archivist didn't tell my friend and his daughter was that the "abuse" materials are a very small fraction of all the tapes from the period. The abuse tapes were the worst, most controversial tapes, and that was what they listened to: the abuse material with all the nastiness and profanity condensed into one startling stream of negativity. After hearing them my friend said, shaking his head, "I don't understand how you could have ever worked for that man."

I responded, "You're a smart guy. You listened to excerpts that have been edited into a concentrated collection of tapes. And then you passed instantaneous judgment on President Nixon. You ask how I could have worked for 'such a man'? You listened to only a tiny fraction of the tapes. What picture do you think listening to all the tapes might have painted?"

In 2014, in a conversation with Judy Woodruff of *PBS NewsHour*, historian Luke Nichter, possibly the premier expert on the Nixon tapes, said that the abuse of power tapes are 5 to 7 percent of the total. But he added, significantly, *they are almost 100 percent of what people know.* Let's use the 7 percent high number. The public, along with my Reagan friend and his daughter, have not listened to 93 percent of the tapes from that roughly three-year period. Give it a slightly different twist: How many people would want that grayer side of their illustrious lives measured by the 7 percent where they may have done or said inappropriate things? There is another point to consider. As Nichter wrote to me in June of 2021 as we worked on this book, "The Watergate transcripts are known to have a lot of errors, including serious ones like mixing up speakers during substantive portions of conversations. I estimated that I found something like ten thousand errors when I reviewed most of them for my book *The Nixon Tapes: 1973*."

Of course, the difference is that we are talking here about a president of the United States, and the words in those tapes are—or, better said, *they were*—measured on a different scale than the words of us everyday citizens might be. I believe President Nixon, with regard to the tapes, has been very misjudged.

Bottom line, the profanity was blown way, way out of proportion. The only times I heard Nixon swear were when he was angry about something or someone and wanted to underscore those feelings—which is when most people use questionable language. It bothered Haldeman, who did not use profanity aggressively, but I never had a problem with it. His usage of profanity was probably no more nor less than most of the staff, and I don't recall anyone being bothered by anyone else's language.

The difference, of course, was that we weren't being taped. It was hearing the tapes, seeing the words in black and white or seeing the word "Deleted'" spotlighted on television screens. All of that came together to accentuate the issue.

Another part of Nixon's historical image that I think has been distorted is the portrayal of him as an uptight, rigid man. Sometimes maybe he was, but that too was only partially true. The public Nixon was always rather shy, especially for a politician. He was by nature an introvert, but the private Nixon could relax. He loved sports, for example. Watching sports was a great relaxation for him. We would joke among the staff about his lack of coordination. We would say that there couldn't have been a taping device because he wouldn't have known how to operate it. In fact, he had been a decent athlete. He had played football at Whittier College. Although he didn't often get off the bench, on occasion he would talk about his coach, Chief Newman. In fact, at the 1968 Republican Convention, he said, "I learned more about life sitting on the bench with Chief Newman than I did by getting As in philosophy courses." As he got older, he became a decent golfer. But he was always a big sports fan. He read the baseball box scores and loved talking baseball for hours with Julie's husband, David Eisenhower. He knew the players and he understood strategy. Baseball and football were both part of his weekend relaxation, when he wasn't working. But his all-time favorite pastime was actually working. He was a workaholic.

Unlike many politicians, he attended sporting events, not for political posturing but because he loved the game, whatever game it was. The media tried to suggest his attendance at such events was merely to divert attention from the Vietnam War. No matter what he did, such as attending a sporting event for the pure pleasure of it, he was endlessly bumping up against a hostile press.

Admittedly we did use every opportunity possible to get out our story. We declared the week before a scheduled antiwar march in Washington as National Unity Week. Tex McCrary, a mentor of mine and our communications consultant, had suggested that "it could be celebrated with pro-administration propaganda" at football games. He added, "Perhaps all games could have a red, white, and blue theme or all halftimes begin with 'God Bless America' and end with 'This Land Is Your Land.'" That week Nixon became the first president to attend a regular season NFL game.

The reality is that Nixon loved going to sporting events. Maybe he loved it a little more when the crowd responded positively to his presence, but no matter what the media claimed, that was not why he went. He even went to Redskins practices on occasion, and there certainly was no political gain there. On at least two occasions he called NFL coaches to suggest plays—that failed. But certainly there were political benefits. Herb Klein, the White House Communications Director, urged him to attend the Super Bowl because "the president's association with athletics is a major asset in relating to sports fans as not only a strong leader, but a 'regular guy.'"

The president was a regular fan—a fanatic, actually. I went to several football games with him, both college and pro. I also went with him to a game at West Point, and to the National Championship showdown in Fayetteville, Arkansas, between the two top-rated college football teams in America at the time, Arkansas and Texas. This was in 1969, the hundredth anniversary of collegiate football. Someone in the administration came up with the clever idea of the president awarding a plaque to the winner, honoring them as the National Champion. It was a terrific idea, except for the fact that we received ninety thousand angry letters and telegrams from Penn State fans because their team had been undefeated for several seasons and had an equally strong argument for the top ranking. Penn State Coach Joe Paterno, during a commencement speech at Penn State in 1973, said about Nixon: "I've wondered how President Nixon could know so little about Watergate in 1973 and so much about college football in 1969."

Along with his intellectual brilliance, there were flaws. Listening to his Oval Office taped comments about Jewish people, for example, bothered me. The president I knew was not anti-Semitic, but some of his taped comments about Jews sure added fire to the charge by some that he was. In judging Nixon on Jewish matters, maybe the best way to do so is to measure the actions he took and to look at the number of highly intelligent people of the Jewish faith he brought to his White House team.

There were many Jews who worked closely with Nixon every day in the White House, among them Henry Kissinger, Bill Safire, Alan Greenspan, Herb Stein, and Bruce Herschensohn, all of whom he relied on and trusted. Nixon also brought in Democrats, such as Jerome Jaffe to run the antidrug program; and Len Garment, a trusted advisor from his law firm days. There were also younger staff members such as Bobbie Greene and Bill Kilberg. In addition, several of his major supporters, men like Max Fisher, a businessman from Detroit; Bunny Lasker, a New York investment banker; and Taft Schreiber, one of the top talent agents in the world, were Jewish. It's impossible to convince me that men and women of their caliber would have continued working for Nixon if he was that person who so hated Jewish people, as he has been sometimes portrayed.

Two other White House men who are my friends, and happen to be Jewish, are the writer and comedian Ben Stein, who was a speechwriter; and Jeff Donfeld, a lawyer who worked with Bud Krogh on the Domestic Council and was instrumental in formulating the Nixon administration's non–law enforcement (treatment) drug abuse policies. I have heard Ben at public talks extolling the virtues of Richard Nixon and his policies toward Israel, and he would flatly say, with absolutely no equivocations, "There is not an anti-Semitic bone in Richard Nixon's body."

Jeff Donfeld recalls a telling personal experience with the Nixons. In the summer of 1967, Jeff worked at Nixon's law firm in New York as an intern, where he met Tricia Nixon. They stayed in touch when Jeff returned to law school that winter, and Tricia invited Jeff to escort her to the International Debutante Ball the winter of 1967. Jeff was operating on a law student's frugal budget and lived in California. A New York hotel was out of the question. He was invited by the Nixons to stay in the guest room of their Fifth Avenue apartment. Next, it turned out Jeff needed formal wear. He had none, nor the means to rent everything needed. Jeff, with a little laugh tied to the memory, tells of Richard Nixon getting his tails, black tie, shirt, and dress shoes out of the closet and outfitting him perfectly for the ball. As Jeff says, "It was hardly the actions of someone harboring anti-Semitic feelings, inviting me to stay in their apartment, eat at their dinner table, and lending me his own clothes."

On a recent phone call Donfeld said to me, "I wish all presidents were as anti-Semitic as Nixon. Look at how he saved Israel in the Yom Kippur War."

While it is clear that he had issues with some individual Jews, I believe this posture and the negative things it led him to say in exasperation or frustration were primarily political.

Politicians, Nixon included, tend to see the nation as large voting blocs. Nixon believed, for example, that Billy Graham could deliver the Baptist vote with the push of a button. Ehrlichman described Jews as "a mobilized political force . . . all out of relationship to their number because they have political impact." It frustrated Nixon terribly that he couldn't win the Jewish vote. He could never understand why, and he resented the Jewish bloc as a result.

Nixon was always a very strong supporter of Israel. His foreign policy was clearly aligned with Israel, and he resented the fact that he never received acknowledgment of that, nor support from the wider Jewish community. I remember receiving a request from the office of Senator Jacob Javits, a New York liberal Republican, to meet with the president the week before Israeli Prime Minister Golda Meir was scheduled to visit. Nixon instead wanted Javits to meet with Kissinger, complaining, "When is one Jew—just one—going to thank me for the Phantom jets" he had sent to Israel.

There was that kind of schoolyard they-don't-like-me-so-I-don't-like-them attitude. I agree it was not attractive. But he knew the Jewish vote was strongly Democratic. He was angry at those people who would come into the office and ask for whatever it was they wanted for Israel—to "suck up to me," as he said—and then cream him in the media. I watched him lose his temper as he talked about it. "Goddamnit. I'm supposed to sit here and do favors for these people and then they're walking out of the office and telling people how terrible I am."

While hearing some of the language Nixon used when discussing Jews was difficult for me, it is important to keep in mind the long, widespread antipathy Nixon experienced from the Jewish community.

"The Jews are all over government," he complained to Haldeman. "Most Jews are disloyal," he said, meaning they supported his policies toward Israel, yet still voted against him. "But Bob," he is heard saying on the tapes, "generally speaking you can't trust the bastards. They turn on you. Am I right or wrong?"

On the tapes Haldeman can be heard agreeing with the president. I knew exactly what Haldeman was doing. He was humoring the president, going along to move the meeting along. As wrong as all this sounds then and now, I can say, based on the many thousands of hours we spent together, that Bob Haldeman was not an anti-Semite either, not in the slightest. It just wasn't who he was as a human being.

But the Berlin Wall impression, created by the media and reinforced by the release of the tapes, took hold and has become widely accepted. My friend and Brotherhood member Henry Cashen and I were having dinner at Elio's in New York two decades after leaving the White House. Our host was the investment banker Michael Saperstein, a good friend of Henry's. At one point Saperstein said he wanted to introduce the two of us to CBS Chairman Sumner Redstone and took us over to his table. Redstone was having dinner with Walter Cronkite. Saperstein introduced us, then said, "Henry and Dwight worked in the Nixon administration." Redstone looked at us and, in response to the introduction, said, "So, you guys are Nazis too?" A question? Lots of nervous laughter. It was a full-frontal, personal attack. Redstone wasn't joking. It was clear he meant it. That exchange was only one man's view of Nixon and those of us associated with him, but Redstone was a powerful member of the Jewish community and the owner of CBS. That illustrated, to me, a prejudicial attitude and animosity toward the entire Nixon administration.

The minute Nixon entered office he was confronted with a national crisis, the war in Vietnam. President Kennedy, followed by President Johnson, had committed the nation to the winning of the war. On January 20, 1969, when Nixon was inaugurated, 510,000 United States troops were in Vietnam. Nixon came into office despised by many ultra-left Americans because of his political history of fighting Communism. His flat refusal to end the war instantly gave those same people a cause around which to rally. As the months of the Nixon administration unfolded, nothing—no other issue, no problems—nothing sucked up as much air in the White House as the Vietnam War. It was there in the background of everything we did. While the left refused to believe it, rather than using the war for political gain, Richard Nixon did everything possible to end it as quickly and as honorably as possible. As a World War II veteran and as a student of American history, he was greatly frustrated by the viciousness and antipatriotic demonstrations of the opposition, and not least frustrated by their counterproductivity. Without the protestors knowing, they were reinforcing the enemy's determination not to end the war short of complete U.S. capitulation, and therefore prolonging it. North Vietnam premier Pham Van Dong's message of support to protestors before the October 15 moratorium was a nail in the coffin of Nixon's plan to end the war by the end of 1969.

When scheduling an event for the president, we always had to be aware of the antiwar protesters and take steps to make certain we were able, as best as possible, to avoid confrontation. But there was only so much we could do. They were always there when we traveled. Not thousands, but maybe one or two hundred, standing outside the hotel holding signs, banging drums. The president ignored them as much as possible. He didn't want them to think they were getting to him, but he always was aware of their presence. Nixon was both annoyed by them and obsessed with them. He did want to know about them. More than that, he actually wanted to understand what they were feeling. He felt they were wrong, that they didn't understand they were being used by America's Communist enemies as pawns. He knew this because there was evidence. They forced him to back off his threats to use force to end the war if North Vietnam wasn't a productive partner in negotiations. Their protests made his negotiations for a peaceful settlement more difficult to accomplish.

The demonstrators never gave him a chance. They were never willing to listen to him, to talk about policy. It was about a week after he was inaugurated that he and Mrs. Nixon went to Northampton, Massachusetts, to visit Julie and David Eisenhower who, recently married, had just rented their first apartment. Their intention was to have dinner with their daughter and new son-in-law. Demonstrators made the family dinner miserable. The local authorities completely mishandled it. The president, Mrs. Nixon, and everyone in the White House were furious. When we departed Northampton that evening, Julie was in tears. What was meant to be one of the most memorable dinners a young couple could possibly have, the first dinner they hosted in their small apartment for her parents, was ruined. This was how our first week began. While we certainly knew about the opposition to the war, while we understood and even appreciated the right to protest, I don't think any of us were really prepared for the unrelenting hatred we encountered everywhere we went. It became part of our lives. Nixon knew the war was dividing our country, and he wanted to end it, but it was becoming harder and harder to find a way out. And it affected the rest of the agenda he wanted to accomplish.

Later in this first year, David Broder of the *Washington Post* would write: "It is becoming more obvious with each passing day that the men and the movement that broke Lyndon Johnson's authority in 1968 are out to break Richard Nixon. The likelihood is great that they will succeed again."

At the outset we recognized the demonstrators were not all socially conscious students or citizens who opposed the war. In the White House we believed many of them were paid disruptors. Their disruptions were planned and organized. They had successfully taken down President Johnson, who chose to abandon the presidency rather than run for reelection. Their next objective was to take down President Nixon. The antiwar movement would increase in terms of the thousands and then tens of thousands who would march and voice their outrage against the war. It would eventually become the central issue in the 1972 campaign.

We had inherited a terrible policy. Six weeks after the January 1969 inauguration, I noted, "Vietnam is getting much worse." I also wrote that, although he wanted to wait to see Senator Eugene McCarthy's reaction to the proposed ABM system proposal, the president had agreed to meet with McCarthy, a leader of the antiwar movement. Many people forget, if they were ever aware, that from the beginning of the administration, Nixon was trying to find a way out of Vietnam. In early May, for example, Ambassador Henry Cabot Lodge, who was representing the United States at the Paris peace talks, issued an eight-point plan as a basis for ending the war. It proposed "phased mutual withdrawals of all outside forces, within a year, and international supervision of South Vietnamese elections." While the plan did have much in common with LBJ's proposals, it went further on some key points, so much so that Senator Mike Mansfield, a strong antiwar Democrat, told the *Times* he was impressed because the Nixon plan appeared to leave room for flexibility, compromise, and give and take.

However, American withdrawal could not be the starting point of discussions. To make it clear to the North Vietnamese that this was not the beginning of an American withdrawal, a week later we began bombing the North Vietnam forces who had been operating out of "neutral" Cambodia, from sanctuaries supplied by the Ho Chi Minh Trail. As explained previously, they had moved into Cambodia believing that, in making that move, they could escape U.S. actions against them.

As for me, thanks to exemptions offered by President Johnson, I had been deferred from being drafted—first because I was married, and then because I had children. But there were times I felt ashamed that I was not fighting in Vietnam, as if I had cheated because I had not served in the military. My cousin Ross Chapin, an American who was raised in Canada, had served in Vietnam. Tod Hullin, John Ehrlichman's assistant, had come directly to the White House from the army. Steve Bull had served as a marine in Vietnam as had Haldeman assistant Bruce Kehrli. Our military aides to the president, terrific men all, had served in Vietnam. Also I was meeting many young soldiers, returning from the war, who visited the White House on a regular basis. I admired them all and the cause for which they had served or fought. No wonder I had a "lesser than" feeling for not having joined them.

I was against the antiwar demonstrators because I believed then, and still do, as previously stated, that they were making it harder for President Nixon to end the war. At least at the beginning, I know the president believed the unfortunate result of the protests was that more of our military would be wounded or killed.

Rather than ending the war, the protesters were prolonging it. Would that war have ended sooner without the antiwar protesters? No one will ever know for certain, but we strongly believed the North Vietnamese leadership, the entire Communist bloc, knew all about them and were encouraged by them. It was hard to miss actress Jane Fonda sitting on an NVA anti-aircraft gun or Pham Dong's letter of support to the moratorium, the propaganda use of the POWs and other visits (besides Fonda's) to North Vietnam.

In fact, one day I got a memo from Haldeman telling me: "We need an immediate investigation of the demonstrators, a look into whether there is some external control in planning these demonstrations on the president's visits . . . Get something set up and going fast . . . get our intelligence people to start looking into these things ahead of time." I don't remember how we proceeded, but if there was an external control planning any of this, we never found it.

The president was being advised on the best way to end the war by three different groups. There was the State Department, headed by Secretary William Rogers; our intelligence agencies, like the Central Intelligence Agency (CIA) and the National Security Agency (NSA) with the Pentagon; and Henry Kissinger's National Security Council (NSC). It was a constant battle among the three of them, usually won by Kissinger. No surprise. After all, at the outset of the administration, the president had made it clear that policy would be run by him from the White House via Henry Kissinger and the NSC. The battle for decision-making power between Kissinger's NSC and Rogers's State Department was ongoing.

Henry had a habit: When it looked as if he wasn't going to get what he wanted, he would threaten to resign. Haldeman would then have to soothe his feelings. On a flight to China in 1972, I sat chatting with General Alexander Haig, Henry's top deputy. Al mentioned casually that Henry was more depressed than he had ever seen him and he hoped he was still a member of the White House staff when we got home. The reason for this, Haig speculated, was that Kissinger believed the president was playing him against Secretary of State Rogers to the benefit of Rogers. Haig told me, for the first time, he had heard Henry actually criticizing—and blaming—the president. Haig made the point to me that Kissinger was sick of the whole Rogers "syndrome" (the word he used). Haig also was extremely critical of Secretary Rogers, telling me that world leaders had little respect for him. He told a story about Rogers meeting Germany's foreign minister, who got so bored that he took out snapshots of his grandchildren and suggested, "Perhaps we should just start talking about our children."

Apparently Nixon knew about Kissinger's unhappiness and had urged him to speak with Rockefeller. According to Haig, Rocky's advice to Henry was to either get it straightened out with Rogers or leave. I was always attentively listening to the inside drama of this high-stakes White House political poker.

In recent years, I have learned that Al Haig was much more calculating and political than I had realized at that time. Looking back, I suspect Haig's confidential chat with me on our January 1972 flight to China might have been his attempt to pipe information to Haldeman. If that was the case, it failed: I kept the conversation confidential.

There were people in the State Department whom the president did trust. The advantage to his having been in government as long as he had was that he'd worked with many different people and had found a group of people on whom he could rely. Having had his range of experiences, Nixon knew what he wanted or needed to know, and he had a pretty good idea of where to get that information. So he would leapfrog the State Department's bureaucratic apparatus, those people taking weeks to prepare thick briefing books, and rely on the personal connections that he trusted. When career State Department personnel, particularly the nonpolitical ambassadors, came home on leave, the president would meet with them and pump them for their perspectives. These were ambassadors like Kenneth Rush, the ambassador to Germany; and Walter Stoessel, former ambassador to the Soviet Union and then currently in Poland. Foreign policy was Nixon's "A Game." He actually admired those State Department warhorses who, like him, were solid thinkers. It was the bureaucratic State Department, the known Democratic holdovers, he distrusted—for good reason.

There was no question the president very rapidly lost confidence in our intelligence agencies, not that he had much to begin with. I have no idea when Nixon realized how badly his predecessor, former President Johnson, had been misled by our intelligence network. Supposedly Johnson had warned him against accepting war intelligence as they rode up to the Capitol for the swearing-in. The president continually made jokes, with a tone of disgust, about the CIA's botched reports. Kissinger would walk into the president's office waving a folder, telling him, "We've got the new CIA report," to which the president might respond, "What did they do, Henry? Bomb the wrong target again?"

Nixon always seemed to have a cynical reaction to so-called "intelligence." In his perception they either were missing the right targets or bombing the wrong targets. This attitude most likely was the culmination of years spent receiving often inaccurate intelligence, which made him understandably become leery.

It also became obvious that he didn't trust his military brass. They would give him military intelligence one day, then retract it two days later. They continually provided enemy strength estimates and bombing reports that later proved wildly inaccurate. Nixon lost a lot of confidence in his congressional friend Mel Laird, his secretary of defense, whose reports too often obfuscated the mistakes made by the Defense Department.

Nixon felt the military command had been so compromised and neutered by LBJ's capricious and vindictive conduct that they had become undependable. He was also aware of the major debates over strategy within the ranks, which added additional levels of problems. As an example, the "Westies" who supported General Westmoreland opposed General Creighton Abrams.

Early in the administration, the president and Haldeman put the White House advance office, established by Ron Walker, under my jurisdiction. The consummate advance man himself, Ron was very buttoned up and an excellent administrator. The most difficult problem we faced in planning domestic trips was figuring out how to keep demonstrators far away from the president while still not interfering with their right to protest. It was a balancing act we had to deal with at every event. It wasn't just about protecting the president. My good friend and USC fraternity brother, Tim Elbourne, managed the press advance and worked with Walker and our advance teams on all travel. It was Tim's role to be thinking through how the media would cover the demonstrators and where camera and media would be placed to cover the events.

The president was frustrated by his inability to have any kind of meaningful communication with the antiwar movement. Deep inside, I still believe he felt that if they could only understand what he was trying to accomplish and would give him some breathing room, they might back off a little. Nixon believed that President Johnson had created a big problem for himself by not keeping the American people informed. So from the start, the president set out to correct that with a series of major speeches from the Oval Office. The first one, on May 14, 1969, set out in considerable and unprecedented detail American attempts to achieve peace and the North Vietnamese rebuffs. The president was determined to achieve peace in his first year—and his strategy was to offer conciliatory words and back them up with stern military measures if the North Vietnamese didn't react or tried to weasel out. The problem was that while the president was applying this strategy, the domestic peace movement was growing. The president had set a date of November 1 for the North Vietnamese to act, or else. However, because of the domestic antiwar movement, with large demonstrations scheduled to take place in Washington on October 15 and November 15, the president had to back away from his implied threat. It became increasingly clear to North Vietnam that all they had to do was wait for the U.S. antiwar movement to either drive the president to the negotiating table before 1972—or replace him in the '72 election.

The first march on Washington was held on October 15, 1969. More than two hundred thousand people participated in the march. Then on November 15, a month later, another demonstration brought half a million people to Washington. The plan was to hold mass demonstrations in Washington and cities all across the country on the fifteenth of every month until the war was ended. We didn't really know what to expect, so the White House was barricaded with D.C. Metro buses parked nose to tail. National Guard troops were stationed inside the Executive Office Building, just in case. If the White House grounds had been penetrated by the demonstrators, the National Guard was there to protect the president, his staff, and the buildings. It was never an actual threat, but having the National Guard stationed there was a reassuring security measure. The troops were sitting on floors through-out the EOB just waiting, in case they were needed. I went along with President Nixon as he strolled through the hallways of the EOB speaking to the troops, thanking them for their service. At some point I left the White House with several colleagues. We walked around the grounds outside the White House, trying to get a sense of the demonstrators and the feeling of the event, and reported back what we saw, our feelings, and impressions to the president and others.

Inside the White House we understood the passion of the protesters. The president wanted to end the war just as much as they did; the difference was how to end it in a way that did not damage America's security. Nixon's frustration caused by his inability to get that point across reached a climax on the night of May 9, 1970, five days after the Ohio National Guard shot and killed four students at Kent State University, when one of the most remarkable events of the administration took place. Nixon had ended a press conference about ten o'clock and finally got to sleep slightly after two. He woke up at four o'clock and, as he remembered it in his memoirs, he "went into the Lincoln Sitting Room and was listening to an Ormandy recording of Rachmaninoff." Manolo Sanchez, his valet, heard this and joined him. Nixon continued: "As I looked out the window and saw the small knots of students begin to gather on the grounds of the Washington Monument I asked him if he had ever been to the Lincoln Memorial at night . . .

"At approximately 4:35 A.M. we left the White House and drove to the Lincoln Memorial. I have never seen the Secret Service quite so petrified with apprehension. I insisted, however, that no press be informed and nobody in our office be informed."

That order was disobeyed, and Haldeman was informed. He then called and woke me around 4:40 A.M. to tell me he would be picking me up in fifteen minutes. We were both unaware that we were about to witness, over the next couple of hours, one of the more consequential events of the Nixon presidency.

In the meantime, the president, Manolo, staffer Bud Krogh who was on duty that night, and the Secret Service went first to the Lincoln Memorial.

> *I showed him* [Manolo] *the great inscription, "In this Temple as in the hearts of the people for whom he saved the Union the memory of Abraham Lincoln is enshrined forever," above the statue and told him that, along with the inscription over the Tomb of the Unknown Soldier, was, in my opinion, the most moving sight in Washington . . .*
>
> *By this time a few small groups of students had begun to congregate . . . I walked over to a group of them and shook hands . . .*

Just imagine what those young people must have been thinking as President Nixon—of all people, the man they had traveled miles (and so many miles in a lot of cases) to protest and was now right there in front of them—walked up to them and extended his hand. I wasn't there, but I had been with him often enough to imagine the absolutely sincere look on his face. And not just his face. He could exude sincerity via his demeanor—the way he listened, stood, looked right at you. Later, the president dictated his lengthy verbatim account of the morning and its impact. He did this because he was frustrated the story was not getting out. The press coverage seemed based on a few students saying he was clueless and talking about surfing and football, basically degrading the occasion.

"They were not unfriendly," the president recalled. After asking several get-acquainted questions, he welcomed them to the city and hoped they were enjoying their visit there, and "that I wanted them, of course, to attend the antiwar demonstration, to listen to all the speakers." Several of them told him they had not been able to hear his press conference, and he replied, "I said I was sorry they had missed it because I had tried to explain in the press conference that my goals in Vietnam were the same as theirs—to stop the killing and end the war to bring peace. Our goal was not to get into Cambodia by what we were doing but to get out of Vietnam.

"They did not respond and so I took it from there by saying that I realized that most of them would not agree with my position but I hoped they would not allow their disagreement to lead them to fail to give us a hearing on some other issues where we might agree. And also particularly I hoped that their hatred of the war, which I could well understand, would not turn into a bitter hatred of our whole system, our country and everything that it stood for. I said, I know that probably most of you think I'm an SOB but I want you to know I understand how you feel."

He continued talking about his own experiences leading up to WWII. As a Quaker, he said, "I was as close to being a pacifist as anybody could be in those times." He had supported England's Neville Chamberlain and his policy of appeasement. He had considered Chamberlain's meeting Hitler at Munich in 1938, in which Czechoslovakia was sacrificed to the Fuhrer's demands, a triumph for "peace in our time." He had thought Winston Churchill was a madman but, perhaps in his own defense, "I think now that Chamberlain was a good man but that Churchill was a wiser man" because Churchill "had the courage to carry out the policies that he believed were right even though there was a time both here and in England and all over the world he was extremely unpopular because of his 'anti-peace' stand."

The conversation continued for some time. Reading the long memo he had dictated the next morning, it was obvious how much he had enjoyed the opportunity to mix with those young people who cared so much about ending the war. After discussing the war he talked about his own youth and other pressing issues. "I knew that on their campuses the major subject of concern was the Negro problem. I said this was altogether as it should be because of the degradation of slavery that had been imposed upon the Negroes and it would be impossible for us to do everything we should do to right that wrong, but I pointed out that what we have done with the American Indians was in its way just as bad. We had taken a proud and independent race and virtually destroyed them."

He said that he considered the economic plight of Mexican Americans in California even worse than the plight of African Americans. He talked about the administration's environmental efforts, and then he took them on that tour-de-force world tour that had so often impressed me. He suggested they might consider a trip to India, which, although terribly poor, has a history and philosophical background and mystique that they should try to understand. When one of the students asked him to describe Russia, he thought for a moment before saying "gray." Then volunteered, if any of these students needed a visa, they should contact his office. "This seemed to get a little chuckle from them."

The group had continued to grow. Mostly they had been listening, but then one of them warned him, "I hope you realize that we are willing to die for what we believe in."

Nixon replied that he understood that, recalling, "When we were your age we were also willing to die for what we believed in and we're willing to do so today. The point is we're trying to build a world in which you will not have to die for what you believe in."

He told them that, to him, what mattered most was people, people all over the world.

I know that the great emphasis is currently being put on the environment, the necessity to have clean air, clean water, clean streets . . . We have a very bold program going further than any program has ever gone before to deal with some of these subjects . . . but cleaning [that up] is not going to solve the deepest problems that concern us all.

Those are material problems. They are very important. They must be solved . . . What we all must think about is why we're here. What are those elements of the spirit which really matter? And here again I returned to my theme of thinking about people rather than places or things.

By this time Haldeman and I were racing into the District. We didn't know what was going on or what to expect. We had never dealt with anything like this before. We knew sometimes the president would awaken early and take walks or dictate notes. Was this just a whimsy on a sleepless night? While the Secret Service was charged with physically protecting him, our job was to politically protect him.

As he stood there at the base of the Lincoln Memorial, the sun began to rise, and the Secret Service was getting very anxious, knowing that word was spreading and more militant demonstrators might be headed there for a confrontation. As Nixon finally walked to his car, he stopped to take a picture with "a bearded fellow from Detroit. As I left him I said . . . I knew that he and his colleagues were terribly frustrated and angry about our policy and opposed to it. I said, I just hope your opposition doesn't turn into blind hatred of the country. Remember, this is a great country with all its faults. If you have any doubt about it go down to the passport office and you won't see many people lining up to get out of the country."

Some of the students had slightly different memories of that conversation, but the gist of it was similar. Clearly he was reaching out, trying to find some common ground.

From the Lincoln Memorial, the president took Manolo to the Capitol. That's where we caught up with them. He gave Manolo the complete tour of the House and the Senate. In the House, Manolo had been permitted to sit in the Speaker's chair, and Nixon joked and told him to give a speech. "What citizenship means to me" was Manolo's topic. We intercepted them in the Senate chamber. We stood in the gallery because we weren't allowed on the floor. I guess Manolo was permitted there because of his guide. The president was showing Manolo the Senate desk he used to occupy. The president met three of the African American cleaning women he had known while serving there, and he signed the Bible one lady had with her. We watched, silently standing back, giving the president lots of space.

After that, he wanted to visit an old haunt and have breakfast at the Mayflower Hotel. He sat in the same small area where, as he told us, he and J. Edgar Hoover had always had lunch over the years. I rarely saw him as comfortable as he was that morning. This was the first time in five years he'd had corned beef hash and a poached egg.

When we were finished eating breakfast, he decided he was going to walk from the Mayflower back to the White House. By then it was almost seven o'clock and the District was coming alive. The Secret Service told him flatly that he couldn't take that walk. The president of the United States was not going to take an impromptu morning stroll on the streets of Washington, particularly not with so many demonstrators in town.

I had seen that desire of his to be better understood, maybe to be liked, many times before. I'd seen it at Ohio State, for example, when we were campaigning. I'd seen him suddenly walk over to a crowd and start talking to people. He liked to spontaneously engage with people. That certainly was one of the contradictions in his personality. It's been described as his being an introvert in an extrovert's business.

The morning after this long-night's-journey-into-day excursion I got a memorandum from Haldeman. The president had been musing about it, and he told Bob he knew this conversation would have generated more news coverage if he had engaged the students "with a spirited dialogue about why we were in Cambodia, why we haven't ended the war sooner, the morality of the war." Instead he realized this might be the only time these kids would ever talk to a president, so he was "trying to get something across in terms of what a president should mean to the people—not in terms of news gimmicks."

Bob continued: "He realizes all of the gimmicky stuff with full

202 ★ DWIGHT CHAPIN

television coverage is big stuff and makes big news. He then says, 'I really wonder in the long run if this is all the legacy we want to leave?'" If that was it, he said, then perhaps government should be left to the true materialists, who "'rule ruthlessly without any regard to the individual considerations, the respect for personality that I tried to emphasize in my dialogues with the students.'"

That was Richard Nixon. The exceptionally sensitive side of Richard Nixon. But there was also the other side, the political side. And that's where my story becomes more complicated.

$\star$ **10** $\star$

A MORE CREATIVE ROLE

In August 1969 Hurricane Camille devastated the Mississippi Gulf Coast. It was one of the most destructive storms in American history. We were at the Western White House in San Clemente, California, and were set to return to Washington. It was decided that the president would visit Gulfport, Mississippi, on the way back to reassure those people that the government would be sending them as much aid as possible. As we flew over the area on *Air Force One,* we saw hundreds and hundreds of miles of flattened forests and destroyed homes.

We landed in Mississippi. The crowd was huge and charged up. As we started moving toward the platform set up for the president to make his remarks, the crowd began pushing in on him. There were no rope or sawhorse barriers to define the space and hold the crowd at bay. I was next to the president. The Secret Service was surrounding us. The local people loved Nixon and were pushing aggressively to get closer to him. I started pushing back, and I must have pushed back harder than normal. Whatever it was, the president noticed it. I had been walking through crowds with him for several years, but this time he either felt or maybe saw something different, something that didn't sit well about my actions.

At this time, with all the new and different pressures around my expanding role, I was feeling less enthusiastic by the day with my "personal aide" role. Being as perceptive as he was, I believe the president sensed the falloff in my previous enthusiasm. My guess is that he had talked to Haldeman about it. It explained why they asked me to train Steve Bull as my backup.

The following day Haldeman called me into his office. "The president was very upset about how you handled that crowd situation yesterday," he told me—maybe "scolded" me is more accurate. "We're going to have to make some changes." But he told me, "There is an upside."

I had been managing the president's appointments and serving as Nixon's personal aide since 1967. As I have alluded, while my job was exciting, the routine personal aide aspects of it, the moving of people into and out of the Oval Office and on the road, were starting to feel like interruptions to my other work. Haldeman and I were continually butting heads on the routine aspects of my job. While I was actually moving upward in my White House career to ever more challenging assignments, Bob expected me to also carry out my aide duties. I just was not minding the store at the level required by Bob. The president must have sensed it too, and he wanted a change.

The "upside" of my move was very significant and positive. Within a month I was replaced as the president's personal aide by Steve Bull. Bull took over the implementation of the president's daily calendar, managing guests and administration members in and out of the Oval Office. There could have been no better choice as my replacement. Steve also took over my prime office space. So I moved down the hall. As part of the West Wing renovation by the historic Williamsburg team of designers, an interior office was designated for my use. It was on the first floor of the West Wing, next to the Roosevelt Room and across the hall from the offices of Haldeman and Rose Woods. It was immediately off a larger room where my secretary, Nell Yates sat, along with Alex Butterfield's secretary, Toni Sidley; and Kathy Bachman, one of Haldeman's secretaries. In April 1971 Terry Decker moved from the Office of the Staff Secretary to my staff. She worked with Nell as my second secretary, and eventually she joined the trio outside my office.

In my new, albeit smaller, West Wing office, I was still sitting at the center of the West Wing world.

While I continued to oversee the advance and television offices, my daily responsibilities shifted and my creative opportunities expanded. Along with creating and organizing the president's calendar, I was assigned more long-term communications planning for administration policies. The move definitely turned out to be beneficial, as it expanded my responsibilities and gave me the ability to make more of a contribution to the presidency. President Nixon never said a word to me about the move. And, more important, it got Haldeman off my back bigtime. Much of the daily pressure I had been feeling simply dissipated with the move.

In my expanded role I became more involved in our efforts to sway public opinion about the administration's Vietnam policy. The war was tearing the country apart. Without question it was getting worse, not better. The nation was exhausted and wanted it to end. Initially the protesters had been mostly young people, but gradually their parents were joining the movement. The left had been using the war as a sledgehammer to bludgeon the administration for political gain. We fought back. An important part of my new job was to help develop strategies to get out our message about how we were working diligently to end the war. Many of the White House staff were submitting and articulating communication strategies for the president's consideration. Now I had been invited to weigh in too. It had been only a couple of years earlier, in March of 1967, that I had begun as Nixon's personal aide at the law firm. Now, two and a half years later, I had been given the opportunity to weigh in on sensitive public perception issues at the White House. Many others in the White House were sending in their strategy suggestions too. Part of my role was to assess and organize the thoughts and recommendations.

I wrote a long memo to Haldeman urging that the administration "isolate" and "expose" the radical leadership of the left, the "hippies" and the "yippies," to bring middle-class America "into the fold of national

206 ★   DWIGHT CHAPIN

consciousness." I suggested how we might counter the antiwar move-ment by, for example, inundating the White House, Congress, and the media with phone calls, letters, and telegrams. It was time for the "Silent Majority" to speak up loudly. I used that term, "Silent Majority." Who actually coined that expression, I don't recall, but Nixon popularized it.

On November 3, 1969, in one of the most memorable addresses of his presidency on national television, Nixon reached out for support from "You, the great Silent Majority." Millions of Americans identified with that description.

The Democrats were the antiwar party and intended to run in the 1970 midterm elections on that issue. The more radical elements had taken over the party's ground game. They were supported by the me-dia and the academic establishment. The radicals were for immediate action, including unilateral withdrawal, if that is what it took to bring U.S. troops home and end the war. They thought we should pack our bags and simply withdraw from North Vietnam. However, it wasn't that simple. The war had begun a decade earlier, during the Kennedy administration, and immediate withdrawal was neither the president's position nor what the public expected. Our strategy was to wind down our involvement, bringing about peace with honor. We wanted the country to see how we, the party of law and order, were different from our opposition, the Democrats and the violent radicals. Richard Nixon had been the law-and-order candidate in 1968. We wanted to make the country aware of what we were up against with the protesters. These were no longer "peaceful protests." They had become violent. The demonstrators were now determined to occupy roads and bridges in order to shut down Washington, D.C. As the anger on the left grew, their demonstrations were getting out of control. We decided to use their violent protests to our advantage.

In May 1971, antiwar demonstrators staged a three-day protest in Washington that erupted into violence. As the *New York Times* re-ported, "The protesters . . . did succeed in disrupting the city's normal functioning . . . using as weapons trash, tree limbs, stones, bottles, bricks, lumber, nails, tires, rubbish bins, and parked cars . . . At the height of the disturbances, tear gas fumes filled the air over some of the city's most famous monuments, streets, and grassy flowered parks. Garbage cans, trash, abandoned automobiles, and other obstacles littered some chief arteries."

More than eight thousand people were arrested and held in JFK Stadium. This is when, as can be heard on the tapes, the combative side of Nixon emerged. Haldeman told the president, "They're gonna stir up some of this Vietcong flag business as Colson's gonna do it through hard hats and legionnaires . . . do it with the Teamsters."

"They've got guys who'll go in and knock their heads off?" the president asked.

"Sure," Bob responded. "Murderers."

"Guys that really . . . that's what they do . . . It's the regular strikebuster types . . . and then they're gonna beat the shit out of some of these people . . . smash some noses . . ."

Thugs? Beating people up? Those words from the tapes sound frightening, bizarre. But they were said in the context of a very frustrated president, trying to end a war and continually feeling his efforts being thwarted by the antiwar demonstrations. This was the first demonstration in which peaceful protests, like sit-ins, had been replaced by a proactive strategy aimed at provoking a confrontation. There had been more than two thousand domestic bombings since 1969, and it was feared this kind of violence was now going to be expanded in the nation's capital. There had been a Capitol bombing at the start of 1971, which was why the newly formed May Day protests were considered to be so dangerous.

Those kinds of exchanges that you can hear on the tapes were not the president and Haldeman planning an attack. Rather, they were expressing frustration and tossing thoughts around about the types of Americans who supported us and shared our anger in having to endlessly deal with the protesters and its casual acceptance by media and academe. These were people such as the hard hats, the take-no-prisoners construction and building trade union guys, the Teamsters. These were men who flew the American flag on their cranes at job sites, who wore the American flag on their hard hats and put it on the side of their trucks. There were Americans who backed the president and the country, and had little regard for the punks in the antiwar movement, who were making it more and more difficult for us to negotiate a settlement in Vietnam. The president appreciated the support of these people. If the demonstrators wanted to play tough, so could we. So, in the tapes, you can hear the president talking one way before shifting gears—as he so often did. In that same conversation with Haldeman, he went on to wonder about "thugs," and "Why doesn't someone introduce a resolution . . ." or "circularize a letter supporting the president on the handling of the demonstrations? . . . praising the chief of police or praising the attorney general?" And then, moving 180 degrees from that thought, he immediately contemplates: "Maybe it isn't worth the bother."

That's the thing about the infamous Oval Office tapes. When specific segments are taken out of context, it's hard to get a clear picture of what was being discussed and understand that often Nixon, and sometimes Haldeman, were musing out loud. Maybe we should do this. Maybe we should do that. Then, seconds later, you can hear them changing their minds. A lot of what they were saying was simply the two of them venting their frustrations. That's why sometimes when Haldeman got an instructive memo from the president, he would wait a day or so before taking action, knowing there was a high probability that the president was going to change his mind. One also should take into account this was well before the politically correct times of today, and represents the jargon of the times and a choice of colorful words. Take "thug," for example. "Labor thugs" had been widely used to describe union "enforcers" who worked picket lines and dealt with union dissidents. So "thug" had a context then that it doesn't have today.

The Democrats, with the growing help of the media, were doing everything possible to convince Americans that Nixon, Kissinger, and the entire administration were murderous warmongers. In response, we wanted the country to know that the opposition was violent and out of control. We believed they were anti-American. The great American middle class was going to have to choose a side in the election. *Time* magazine described the strategy, writing: "Throughout the [1970 midyear] campaign Nixon . . . has tried to win Republican votes through popular resentment against extremist—and sometimes not so extremist—dissidents. At times, small groups of hecklers were deliberately allowed into his audiences, just numerous and noisy enough to enable Nixon to score points . . ."

The week before the election the president, along with Governor Ronald Reagan and another former actor, California Senator George Murphy, spoke at a rally at the San Jose Civic Auditorium, in California. We had been campaigning relentlessly, hitting twenty-two states in three weeks. When we landed at the airport, our lead advance man, Ron Walker, was very concerned. Ron informed me there were several hundred demonstrators outside the center, and they appeared to be much more violent than we had seen previously. Prior to arriving there, as *Time* magazine had reported accurately, I had issued instructions that a small number of protesters were to be admitted to the rally. The idea was that allowing the news cameras to capture them screaming at us and threatening us would make effective news footage. However, when we got to the site, it looked far more dangerous than I had anticipated. The president didn't help matters. He was angry and wanted to stand up to his detractors. As he got out of the limo, he turned and faced the protesters, who were behind barricades about forty yards away. He raised both arms in that classic Nixon pose, waved to them, and gave a big V for Victory sign with his arms and fingers. They responded, as I'm sure he knew they would, by getting louder and angrier.

Once the president was safely inside, I stood alone outside the hall. The demonstrators saw me and started toward me, screaming obscenities. I went inside the hall behind the locked doors. The demonstrators pushed up against the windowed doors; they began smashing some of the windows. Instead of feeling anxious, I saw this as an opportunity for the television cameras to capture the violence. Understanding what I was trying to accomplish, Haldeman approved the idea. However, Ziegler pushed back, worrying mainly about how the press would report it. There was an argument among the three of us about what we should do. Ziegler's concerns were legitimate, but we opted for letting a possible incident occur.

The police and some volunteer ushers were using ropes to hold the doors closed. Demonstrators kicked in some of the wooden door panels and sprayed mace at the police officers. As we moved around the concourse, a rock about the size of a golfball shattered a window. Meanwhile, the president had begun speaking in the hall. His remarks were being well received. As he was wrapping up his talk and we were getting ready to leave, I think it was Ron Walker who suggested moving the overflow crowd into the area between the presidential limo and the protesters. That would put friendly supporters closest to the president. As we walked to the limo I told the president, "Mr. President, when you get outside, pause at the rear of the car with Senator Murphy and Governor Reagan. There are quite a number of demonstrators outside, who will start screaming at us, which will give the press a chance to record it all."

He understood what I meant. In fact, he understood it even more than I did. He raised his arms and gave his signature V sign as the crowd got louder. He told me that he wanted to approach the group.

Our head Secret Service agent, Bob Taylor, said flatly, "No, sir, you can't go over there. It's dangerous."

In response, the president nimbly jumped on the hood of his car. I was so taken by surprise that I didn't respond. I should have grabbed his coat and stopped him, but his move was so unexpected, so out of character, that I just stood there. The Secret Service was surprised too. They surrounded the hood of the car and moved to help him down, or catch him should he fall. This was a dangerous security breach. The president, standing on the hood of the presidential limousine, threw up his arms. I heard him say, "This is what they hate to see!" as he one more time gave them his signature V. There could be no mistaking his meaning. He stood there defiantly for about thirty seconds. As he climbed down, an object whizzed past his ear. He later said he thought it was an egg. Bob Taylor thought it was a small rock. Several more eggs were thrown at him. One reporter was hit. The press got it all on videotape. Now all we had to do was get out of there safely.

The president got into his limo and I walked to the lead car. As I did so, more eggs and sticks landed nearby. I got into my car and signaled the motorcade to get going. The police had cleared a path through the demonstrators. As we left, they began throwing more eggs and rocks. I could see the projectiles bouncing off the president's armored Lincoln Continental. The car in which Haldeman was riding was hit by a large rock. When the driver of Haldeman's car stopped suddenly, several cars behind his bumped into each other. I was worried about the safety of the Secret Service agents and journalists who were riding with tops down in convertibles.

We certainly had gotten the political mileage we wanted. Haldeman later wrote, "We wanted confrontation," but it had been a dangerous situation that came close to getting out of our control. The president was furious at the demonstrators. Rose Woods, who was with us on this trip, compared it to the attack on his car during a visit to Caracas, Venezuela, when he was vice president. While we were flying back to Washington, Ron Ziegler drafted a statement for the president: "This was the action of an unruly mob that represented the worst of America."

Upon arriving back at the White House after our San Jose encounter, I realized that, in our response to the demonstrators, we had crossed over that fine line from "acceptable" to "unacceptable." I dictated a set of notes on the event. It was my thinking immediately after the event that I had, that we all had, let things go too far and had put the president in real danger. Also, I believed the president had gone too far. He should never have jumped on the hood of the limousine. It had been a split-second decision that inflamed the demonstrators and stoked their hatred of him. It could have had catastrophic results. After that experience, we purposefully decided to de-escalate the intensity of our interactions with protesters. We wanted no more over-the-line moments like we'd experienced in San Jose. And we had none.

When demonstrators did get too close, Haldeman was all over me. The angriest exchange he and I had came after a presidential trip in August of 1971. The president had gone to New York for a dinner at the Waldorf Astoria. Demonstrators managed to get within a block of the hotel. While the decision of how close to us the demonstrators could approach had been made by the New York City Police Department in consultation with the Secret Service, Haldeman thought they were too close and blamed me. Our relationship at that point was particularly strained. I had become tired of his continual criticism. I preempted the attack I expected from him in a note that began: "Prior to your writing some well-articulated and degrading note to me . . . Plans were laid to handle the demonstrators and keep them a block from the hotel. The plan didn't work . . . for you to make fun of an advance man, lose your cool and worry about justifying yourself to the president may be a problem . . . the main problem here is you . . . We want to do a good job for you and the president. We will not be cowards and take shit we don't deserve or tolerate treatment unworthy of someone who works for the president." We all were feeling the growing pressure and beginning to respond by lashing out at people we cared about. As I read these notes so many years later, I cannot believe how defensive I sound and how uptight I must have been to address Bob that way.

Obviously, this was a difficult time for me. I had idolized Bob Haldeman. But our relationship was changing, and maybe my spine was stiffening. Among those few people who were aware of this changing dynamic, and to whom I will be forever grateful, was Dick Moore. Dick had come to the White House in 1970, after serving at the Justice Department as a special assistant to his close friend Attorney General John Mitchell. Dick served the president in a public relations role. (Almost two decades later, George Bush would appoint him U.S. Ambassador to Ireland.) Dick and I worked together every day. Gradually he became my friend and mentor. He was a great guy, funny and very smart, with terrific communications instincts. He was always pushing me, probing, suggesting, inspiring, editing, and, when necessary, offering protection. I shared much of my internal correspondence and orders with him. Sometimes Dick would read a directive I had received from the president or from Haldeman with which he didn't fully agree. His typical diplomatic response would be, "Well, we have to think about that."

On many occasions Dick would react with horror to Haldeman's reprimands and demands of me. For example, I had sent Bob a memorandum suggesting a simple change in the way our staff was using our initials in order to communicate internally. There had been confusion in an exchange of information, and I thought my suggestion would allay that confusion. Bob responded angrily: "This bunch of crap makes my points . . . far more effectively than anything I could say. I wonder if it really makes you proud and self-satisfied. If so, God help you . . . Obviously you could care less about doing things right," he continued, "but someday you will have to learn to."

For some reason I still felt it necessary to accept Haldeman's attacks, typically saying to Dick Moore, "Bob's right." Dick would tell me, either speaking it directly or through his body language, that he disagreed with me; he *really* disagreed. While it wasn't enjoyable for me to recognize that Bob was less than perfect, slowly but surely I was beginning to see he wasn't necessarily the infallible man I had grown to believe him to be. In retrospect, as I have said, Steve Bull taking over my duties as personal aide was one of the best things that could have happened. In the end, it probably saved my relationship with Bob by giving us each some space.

Maybe even more distressing, I was also learning that President Nixon himself didn't always handle things perfectly. At the beginning of the administration, he welcomed—even solicited—ideas from all corners of his advisory world. Over time, while those ideas were still being solicited, he didn't seem to take as much interest in hearing them. Nor

214 ★   DWIGHT CHAPIN

did they seem to affect internal debate as much as they had previously. The president was becoming increasingly isolated. By the third year of his administration we were reserving for him larger and larger chunks of "thinking time," time that he spent alone. The president would go over to Room 180 in the EOB around noon and work there until late in the afternoon or early evening. The joke among the staff was that "He is working on a Vietnam speech." Actually, that remark originated from Haldeman or maybe the president himself, but not as a joke. Looking for an excuse, one of the two men had said, "Tell them he is [I am] working on a Vietnam speech. No one can argue with that!"

Very early in the administration, Nixon had a meeting that led to the creation of something known as the Huston Plan. While it was never put into effect, it did presage the calamitous events that would change American history. It began because the president believed the potential for violent acts being taken against the government was real. Leading the effort for the administration was Tom Huston, a political operative about my age who was working for Pat Buchanan. Tom attended a meeting with the Director of Central Intelligence, Richard Helms, and FBI Director J. Edgar Hoover, as well as the heads of the National Security Agency and the Defense Intelligence Agency. The goal was to learn more about the dangerous radical groups who comprised the militant branch of the antiwar movement, in the hope of finding a way to deal with them. These groups posed a serious threat to public safety. They were making bombs. They were robbing banks. The public was being endangered. Innocent people were being killed. We had no intention of trying to shut down peaceful protests, but we did want to stop the violence.

The essence of the Huston Plan was to bring together all the domestic intelligence agencies under a central umbrella. It would supposedly eliminate duplication of efforts and streamline intelligence gathering. It was a very aggressive plan that included "black bag operations" (illegal break-ins) and domestic wiretaps. It certainly would have trampled on basic civil rights, but there were people who believed that taking the steps presented in the Huston Plan was necessary to defend the country against domestic terrorism. In fact, it is important to note that black bag operations had been executed in previous administrations and were approved by, even run by, the FBI. But this time, J. Edgar Hoover was strongly against it, probably because the times were changing, and he told Attorney General Mitchell that he didn't think the FBI should be involved. Mitchell agreed with Hoover and advised Nixon, "Mr. President, this can't go forward. It's illegal. It'll cause you more headaches than you can imagine." The president accepted the counsel of Mitchell and Hoover. The Huston Plan was deep-sixed before it began, but a seed of thought had been planted.

A few months later, in June 1971, the *New York Times* began publishing a series of articles with information from the Pentagon Papers. The Pentagon Papers was a Defense Department study assessing its decision-making regarding the Vietnam War. It covered the period from 1945 through the Johnson administration, but not the Nixon years. Daniel Ellsberg, one of the authors of the report, had leaked the study to the *Times*. At the urging of President Nixon and Kissinger, the Department of Justice got a temporary restraining order against further publication of the material, arguing that it was detrimental to U.S. national security. To find out who had leaked this information, and if further damaging materials existed, a unit that became known as "the Plumbers" was formed within the White House. The Plumbers' job was to plug leaks.

The White House Plumbers unit is worthy of a book itself. Basically, it was established in order to plug the leaking of documents from the executive branch. It was clearly believed by both Bud Krogh and David Young, the White House staffers assigned to administer the Plumbers operation, that they were operating in the interests of national security. They reported directly to Ehrlichman, who also believed he was acting on presidential orders and directly in the interests of national security. In past administrations it was the FBI that conducted black bag operations under the cover of national interests. It was the Nixon White House that brought these operations in-house in order to find and plug leaks.

It had been agents working for the Plumbers who broke into the office of Dr. Lewis Fielding, the psychiatrist of Daniel Ellsberg, to find documents that would help discredit Ellsberg. Some of those who planned and participated in the Plumbers' break-in would eventually play roles in the break-in at the Democratic headquarters in the Watergate Hotel. At the time I knew nothing about the Huston Plan or the Plumbers.

On a bright sunny spring day in 1971, I was working in my office when Steve Bull called: "The president would like to see you." Walking into the Oval Office, I found the president very relaxed with his feet up on his desk, the temple of his glasses hanging from his mouth. Bob Haldeman was sitting in one of the side chairs by the president's desk. Bob began: "We are talking about the campaign." I knew he meant the upcoming 1972 presidential campaign. "We've been talking about having our own Dick Tuck type of guy. We're wondering if you might know of someone."

"Think you know of anyone?" the president chimed in.

"I'll have to think about it," I responded. That was it. It was a simple request. I knew exactly what they meant. Their question didn't trigger in my gut any moral or ethical alarms. There was nothing sinister about it. However, it was one of those moments that contained life-changing consequences—not just for me, but for the future of the presidency.

Many of us knew Dick Tuck. He was definitely one of a kind. He was a nice, affable guy, with bushy hair and a rather impish look. Tuck was friendly, never vindictive or politically abusive. As previously described, Tuck's political "pranks" weren't intended to inflict damage or harm; they were aimed at causing the other side embarrassment or making them the butt of laughter and derision.

When Tuck and I ran into each other from time to time, we would joke and poke fun at each other. I remember running into Tuck on the floor of the 1988 Republican National Convention in New Orleans. He had "full access" credentials hanging from his neck. How he had obtained those credentials, I had no idea—but the fact that he had acquired them was a tribute to his cleverness. The ultimate tribute to Dick Tuck had to be that Nixon and Haldeman wanted me to find someone who could play his role for us. The *New York Times* obituary of May 29, 2018, called Tuck the "Democrats' Prankster-in-Chief," and described him as the "Prankster-at-Large" and a "king gremlin of political shenanigans." So, there was clearly a double standard at work regarding "dirty tricks."

As I thought about their Tuck request, the first and only person who came to mind was Don Segretti. Don was a core member of our USC Ballers group. He had arrived at USC from San Marino, California. We met as sophomores and hit it off immediately, even becoming roommates for one semester. Don was one of my closest friends. I knew him to be trustworthy, discreet, and loyal. Also, Don was an unassuming guy, a person who could easily blend into a crowd. He was also imaginative—and he was a lawyer. He would understand the legal boundaries within which to play his pranks. Don was perfect, in my opinion, for the Dick Tuck role. After graduating from USC, he'd received his law degree from Berkeley and was serving in the army's Judge Advocate Corps. Also, the timing seemed to be perfect, as he was preparing to leave the military and, as far as I knew, had no definite plans.

Gordon Strachan, a mutual friend of Don's and mine, was working in the White House on Bob Haldeman's staff, handling a range of assignments. Gordon had also been in our USC Ballers group and had been a fraternity brother of Segretti's. Upon graduating USC, Gordon went to law school, then joined Nixon's law firm in New York. I had played a role in suggesting that Gordon move from New York to work with us in the White House. Gordon and I were good friends.

It was around this time that Strachan was taking on a responsibility within the Haldeman staff to coordinate with the Committee to Re-elect the President, which was setting up shop a block away from the White House. Gordon was to be assigned as the liaison between the Haldeman operation and Jeb Magruder, the deputy campaign manager. Later, Gordon would take on campaign intelligence responsibilities, coordinating between the campaign operation and White House Counsel John Dean.

I explained to Gordon the assignment I had in mind for Don: that we hire him to be our Tuck. Gordon bought in, thinking it was a good idea. In fact, as I remember, he agreed with me that Don would be perfect. It was Gordon who then made the arrangements for Don to be paid.

As incredible as it may seem, I never once mentioned Segretti's name to President Nixon or Haldeman. I never told either man I had found, and hired, our own Dick Tuck. It never entered my mind that I needed an official sign-off from either of them. The request to find a Tuck had come from the two men, the president and Haldeman, sitting together in the Oval Office. That meant to me that I had an assignment—get going, get it done.

A few weeks later I invited Don to Washington. Gordon Strachan joined us for lunch. I explained to Segretti what we wanted him to do—"explain" being a very general term, as we offered no specifics. We didn't know exactly what he would be doing. But at that meeting, as Don later testified to a grand jury, "When Dwight hired me, he said he was doing so because I was a lawyer and I would know what was right and what was wrong." We decided I would be Don's contact while Gordon would arrange all the financial aspects of his work.

During this lunch I reiterated the necessity of making absolutely sure that it could not be known the White House was connected to anything Don did. As far as I was concerned, he was on his own, an independent operator. Any mail he might send was to go to my home address. I don't recall telling him, "Should you be caught . . . the White House will disavow any knowledge of your actions," but that was, no doubt, the message I gave him. I do remember spending considerable time telling him about all of the pranks I knew Dick Tuck had pulled over the years.

I have seen documents showing that I encouraged him to recruit volunteers to work with him. While I don't remember doing that, obviously I did. We discussed political strategy. The election was more than a year away. We believed the strongest of the Democratic candidates would be Senator Ed Muskie, and the weakest would be Senator George McGovern. Therefore we were, of course, hoping that McGovern would get the Democratic nomination. Segretti and I talked about how we could sow seeds of dissension among the various Democratic contenders to make it more difficult for them to unify later.

None of us—Segretti, Strachan, nor I—*none of us* could have imagined the incredible consequences of what seemed like a routine political prankster assignment. Eventually it would all backfire spectacularly and cause enormous personal pain and destruction to Don, as well as to me. I long ago accepted full responsibility for this horrible mistake and have apologized to Don many, many times. He was, and is, a great friend whose life was turned upside down by what was to come. Truthfully, though, at the time, I was blind to the possible consequences. It simply seemed like a good idea—and it was what was asked of me.

Fighting the war as well as the antiwar movement affected all of our lives, but especially the president's and Henry Kissinger's. I watched with fascination as the Harvard University professor I had located for the president only months earlier rose in importance within the White House and morphed into an instantly recognizable national figure.

At the beginning of the administration, Henry might well have been the least likely choice among the entire staff to become a rock star. During those first days, when my office was next to the president's, I saw him every day, sometimes several times a day. Even after I had moved to an office just down the hall from the president's, Henry always found time to stop and talk with me, though I think he sometimes was more interested in talking with the secretaries outside my office than he was with me. That was Henry being Henry.

He had a wonderful sense of humor and a well-known appreciation for the ladies. One day he had just left the Oval Office, papers under his arm, and was headed back to his office. He approached one of our secretaries in the hall. Keep in mind, this was the era of miniskirts. It was also before political correctness took root so that any kind of flirtatious remark or gesture could be taken as a personal assault. While today it would be considered unacceptable, as Kissinger approached her, he grinned and asked, "Are you growing—or is your skirt shrinking?" The ladies in the office roared with laughter when they heard the story.

The war put Henry in America's headlines. And Henry loved being in the headlines. In a White House full of very intelligent high achievers, Henry was the leader of the pack. And he knew it. He had a huge ego. He liked being Henry Kissinger. And he liked the praise he received from the "inside-the-Beltway" Washington crowd. The president understood this and seemed amused by it at times. Haldeman, too, loved to razz Henry about the social circles in which he moved. During the dark days of Watergate, some Nixon loyalists questioned Henry's loyalty, wondering if he was trying to keep all his elitist connections at the expense of Nixon. Some hard-core Nixon loyalists still harbor negative feelings about Henry's loyalty from the post-Nixon White House years.

It was always Nixon/Kissinger, never Kissinger/Nixon. Richard Nixon was an extremely competitive man, and to some degree, I know he was irritated, perhaps even somewhat jealous, of Kissinger's ascent. He knew Henry was making a valuable contribution. He knew how intelligent and well informed Henry was, but he wanted it understood, although he didn't say it, that he, Richard Nixon, was the president. Henry was phenomenally important, and he knew it. There was no question about that, but Nixon was the leader in the room and Henry was his brightest student. The two of them had tremendous chemistry. Both were extremely smart, knowledgeable, and creative. They were both strategic thinkers. They fed off each other's minds. They were able to talk to each other on a very sophisticated level. Nixon would develop his strategy and Henry would get on an airplane and fly off to negotiate. I have always described their relationship as Nixon being the architect and Henry being the builder. That certainly was true where Vietnam was concerned.

With regard to the Vietnam War, there was no right strategy. The North Vietnamese were willing to continue fighting in the belief that eventually the president, having to deal with so much national dissension, would be worn down in his determination to end the war with honor. The North Vietnamese were depending on the antiwar movement to fuel the opposition in America. In addition, we were in the middle of a larger Cold War against Communism. History provided no guidance. The Korean War had "ended" with a ceasefire more than fifteen years earlier, but there had never been an official end to that war; nor was there any kind of peace agreement.

When we moved into the White House, Henry's office was in what was known as "the basement" of the West Wing, though actually "lower level" would be more descriptive. When the West Wing was remodeled, Henry moved up to the main floor, into the front office. Thanks to Henry, that first-floor front office became the National Security Advisor's office, and I believe it has remained the office for the Director of the National Security Council in all subsequent administrations.

In order to maintain his power position, Henry was willing to confront any obstacles. When he had something to say, he said it. That resulted in difficult relationships, but he and Haldeman respected each other and found a way of working productively together.

Whenever Henry threatened to quit, it was always Haldeman who talked him off the ledge. In recent times, a friend of mine met with Kissinger in his Manhattan office. Henry told my friend that he didn't think Bob Haldeman had received enough credit for his contributions to the Nixon White House. I pointed out to my friend that I thought Henry was singing Bob's praises, in part, because it was Bob Haldeman who made it possible for Henry Kissinger to become the World's Most Important Diplomat. If Haldeman had not continually kept him from resigning, Henry would have never become U.S. Secretary of State, let alone the prominent world figure he has become—and no one knows the truth of that fact more than Henry.

No one in the White House worked harder than Kissinger, who expected the same level of commitment from his staff. He was very demanding of his highly talented and capable staff, and he was not easy to work for. Larry Eagleburger, who eventually had a distinguished career that led to his becoming U.S. Secretary of State under George H. W. Bush, was one of Henry's young aides. Maybe six months after we'd moved into the White House, Eagleburger had been working incredibly long hours, day and night, until he passed out cold in front of the door into Henry's National Security Council office. Henry came walking out of his office carrying some papers, stepped right over Eagleburger, handed the papers to a staff assistant, then turned around, and, without a word, stepped back over Eagleburger. He then closed his office door. Fortunately, Eagleburger recovered.

Just like the president, Henry would change his mind often, then change it back again and again. It used to drive Al Haig, Kissinger's deputy, crazy. When we were preparing for the China trip, I put together a rough schedule and logistics plan. Haig was very disappointed with it, telling me it didn't feel like it contained the information Henry had requested. Al and I ended up almost shouting at each other, at which point Haig backed off and said maybe I could tell, by his agitation, how difficult it was working for "this madman" (meaning Henry) for three years. "I'm about to go out of my mind, and I'm not about to do it much longer." The problem, he explained, was that we'd had five different descriptions of what Henry wanted in the plan that I was responsible for preparing. Al's problem, I believed, was that he simply went along with every change Henry wanted, rather than pushing back and convincing Henry to accept what was being presented.

Henry and I worked together on several projects, but most significant were our trips to China. After returning from China in October 1971, there was a photograph in *Time* magazine of Chinese Premier Chou En-lai, Henry, and I having dinner in Peking. Premier Chou and Henry were identified by name. I was incorrectly labeled a "Kissinger Aide." Henry gave me a signed copy of the photograph that said, "To Dwight Chapin, the only aide who ever survived, Warmest Regards, Henry Kissinger."

Henry always knew exactly who he was, and how to use the power of his position. Bill Safire liked to tell a story about going to a Washington

Redskins football game with him. At one point Henry turned to him and said, "You know how we could empty this place in a minute? We could have the announcer say over the loudspeaker, 'Dr. Kissinger, you need to call your office immediately.'"

Later at that same game, Henry told Safire that Washington's quarterback, Sonny Jurgensen, was going to pass. When Bill asked Henry how he knew that, Henry explained, "Oh, he passes on third down in this situation. Deep in his own territory, he won't pass on first down. The other side knows that and anticipates no pass on first down, and that's why he's getting killed."

Safire asked him what he would do in that situation. "Obviously, the next time he has the ball in his territory on first down he should cross them up and throw a pass." Sure enough, Safire said, in the next quarter the Redskins got the ball on their own 20-yard line. On first down, Jurgensen threw a pass, just as Henry had suggested. It was intercepted and run into the end zone for a touchdown. "There's a great lesson in this," Henry pointed out to Safire. "Never listen to the experts on the sidelines."

Henry understood the use of prestige and power, both when dealing with world leaders and in attracting beautiful women. Henry loved beautiful women, and a large number of them loved him back. He entered the White House as U.S. National Security Advisor and morphed quickly, as described by the Washington, D.C., press because of the number of great-looking women he dated, into "the Secret Swinger." His success with women was real. I remember being in San Clemente and hearing Henry would be taking a helicopter to Los Angeles for a dinner date. My parents lived in Encino, in the San Fernando Valley. I thought if I could take the helicopter with Henry, I could meet my parents for dinner. When I asked Henry if I could fly with him, he agreed. As the chopper landed at the Santa Monica Airport, a convertible, driven by the absolutely beautiful actress Jill St. John, pulled up. After Henry bade me farewell, he hopped into the car with her, and off they drove. My mother and father were watching this, as if it were a scene from a movie. My parents and I went off to dinner in Santa

Monica, and three hours later, I was waiting by the helicopter when Ms. St. John returned Henry to his chopper for our return to the Western White House.

The oddest thing about Henry was how incredibly insecure he could seem to be. Even at the height of his White House power, when he was on the front pages of newspapers daily, he remained overly sensitive. Someone could make the most insignificant remark that he would twist in his mind until it seemed to him like a criticism. He hated it when someone contradicted him or did not agree with him.

In Haldeman's diary he noted in January 1971 that the president "also raised the K [Kissinger] problem again. Apparently Henry had talked with E [Ehrlichman] this morning about the question of whether he should go back to Harvard or not and all of his problems with Rogers . . . The P [president] makes the point that Henry craves the ego satisfaction of raising these questions and having people reassure him that he's in good shape and all. He also makes the point that he'd be a damn fool not to stay on." Henry Kissinger was never a damn fool.

Regarding the efforts of the president and Kissinger to end the war, even all these years later, what remains very frustrating to me is the realization that there are people who believe that Richard Nixon and his administration did not want the Vietnam War to end; that the president kept it going because it was politically useful. I was there and I can tell you that President Nixon wanted to end the war. His countless hours spent working to bring it to an honorable end prevented the administration from accomplishing many of its other goals.

In fact, among the administration's greatest successes, the opening of Communist China to the West, took place at least in part because the president believed he could convince the People's Republic of China (and later the Kremlin) to put pressure on North Vietnam to find a workable peace solution.

It was a daring, complex strategy, but illustrative of Nixon's creative foreign policy thinking and action. He was, ultimately, a statesman to his core.

THE SEEDS ARE SOWN FOR THE HISTORIC CHINESE CONNECTION

One afternoon in 1970 I received a call from a man named Jim Jones. Jim had been a top advisor to LBJ in the Johnson White House and, a few years later in the Clinton administration, would become our ambassador to Mexico. "Dwight," he said, "I'm going to nominate you to be one of the Jaycees' Ten Outstanding Young Men."

I hadn't solicited this, so it came as a complete, and very flattering, surprise. I could just imagine how proud my parents and family would be if I were to be selected. I thanked Jim and told him I'd have to discuss it with Bob Haldeman. Knowing that, several years before, Bob had been nominated for the same recognition, I expected him to be happy to hear my news. However, instead of congratulating me, he said, "We can't do that. It has to be Ron [Ziegler]. Call Jim back and say that you'd be honored to accept the nomination some other time, but ask if he could nominate Ron instead of you." Rather than protesting or asking Bob why I should be giving up the honor, I did exactly as ordered.

I'd known Ron Ziegler since our Sigma Chi fraternity days at USC. After college we had both worked for Bob at J. Walter Thompson. Ziegler had a mixed reputation there because of the way he treated people. His style carried over into the White House. He had hired our fraternity brother Tim Elbourne to work for him, handling press advance and logistics; he then proceeded to treat Tim shabbily. He was often unnecessarily curt with me. He simply had personality issues. At the White House he was having a rough time as press secretary, especially in an administration that believed the press was the enemy. At the outset the president didn't even want to call him "press secretary" but rather something like "press assistant." What we did not understand at the time was that Ron had an addictive personality, which eventually led to his having to deal with alcohol issues.

Ron's work ethic was outstanding, which was why Haldeman hired him at J. Walter Thompson and brought him into the White House. You could count on him to do a great job, always, and he was up against the anti-Nixon press, not an easy place to be. Why Haldeman really wanted the nomination to be given to Ron, I don't know. My guess is that Bob thought it would help Ron's ego, give him a boost. Plus, Bob knew how emotional Ron could get about things and understood he could become unglued if I received the honor and he didn't. Bob also knew I was the guy he could count on to fall in line. My response to Bob was: "That's great. Ron's a deserving guy." Truthfully, though, I probably didn't really feel that way. I was just doing my duty. It didn't occur to me to ask, "Why?" or say, "No," to Bob's request. Ron ended up receiving the honor and never knew the whole story. Afterward Bob sent me a note: "Let me reiterate my high esteem for the selfless action on your part in taking yourself out of consideration . . . I firmly believe you did the right thing for the administration . . . I appreciate your loyalty and so does the president."

Two years later, primarily for the work I did on President Nixon's groundbreaking trip to the People's Republic of China, I ultimately received the same recognition from the Jaycees as one of the Ten Outstanding Young Men. On January 20, 1973, Richard Nixon was inaugurated for a second term. On that same day Susie and I were at the Mormon Tabernacle in Salt Lake City for the presentation of my award. Chet Huntley, the well-known NBC news anchor, presented the award at the memorable event, but my heart that evening was with my friends back in Washington.

In seven years I had traveled a long distance from advancing my first rally in Panorama City. Among my first significant responsibilities in the White House was planning and executing our around-the-world goodwill trip in celebration of the landing of the Apollo 11 astronauts on the moon in July 1969. Our lead advance man was John Whitaker, the Cabinet Secretary. Acting as John's deputy, I learned a lot about running sophisticated foreign trips. The advance work for that type of trip was far more detailed than any trip we had done domestically. Over the years, Whitaker had given me advice and guidance. A seasoned Nixon man and a veteran of the 1960 campaign, John was the most selfless man I have ever met, not typically the type one finds in the political world.

Nixon made his first overseas trip in February 1969, to visit our European allies. While I didn't make that trip, I did participate in the planning. John Ehrlichman was in charge of the advance team. One day, I remember, Ehrlichman took over the White House Situation Room in the National Security Council office for a "full debriefing" conference call. He talked with the advance people in every country from eight in the morning until around nine at night. It was a thirteen-hour call, during which he expected all the advance men scattered around Europe to participate and be present on the phone. At one point Ehrlichman asked Henry Cashen, who was advancing in Rome, "How many steps is it from the car to the entrance into the Vatican?"

There was a long pause, then Henry asked, "How many steps?" John repeated the question, then Henry asked, "Why do you need to know?"

"Don't argue with me," Ehrlichman snapped. "I want to know for the schedule exactly how far it is from the car to the doors of the Vatican!" Then he wanted to know how many steps from the entrance to the reception area. It was the kind of attention to detail I'd never experienced. Maybe it was John's way of letting everyone know who was in charge. I know from my later international advance work that the information John was demanding was not necessary.

Roy Goodearle was the advance man in Berlin. Ehrlichman was

scheduled to speak with him about two hours later. When Roy heard the question being asked of Cashen, he put his phone on hold, got in his embassy car, and raced to all the scheduled stops. So later in the call, when Ehrlichman asked him, "How many steps are there from the car to the entrance to the Berlin Wall platform?" Roy was prepared and replied instantly, "One thousand two hundred and thirty-eight!" Everyone on the call roared with laughter.

I was involved, one way or another, in almost all the president's trips and kept learning from each of them. Among the many complexities of foreign trips is knowing and respecting local protocol. Sometimes customs we have in this country are considered insults in other countries. For example, as I learned on the around-the-world goodwill trip, it is very important to the Vatican that Italy and Vatican City be treated as two completely different countries because they are—even though Vatican City is in the middle of Rome. A person is not permitted to visit the head of the Italian government in Rome, then go directly to Vatican City to meet the Pope.

Paying respects to the Pope is extremely important. The Catholics in America are a significant voting bloc, and no American politician can venture into that part of Europe without visiting the Vatican. We went there in late September 1970, in order that the president could meet Pope Paul VI.

The entire official party, plus some other staff and aides, walked through the Sistine Chapel into a chamber, where we lined up and were invited forward to meet the Pope, one by one. The president introduced each of us. "Your Holiness, this is Dwight Chapin." I shook hands with the Pope, who handed me a red leather box containing a bronze papal medal. It was quite a moment!

I was impressed with the president's thoughtfulness on this occasion. He could have limited our delegation to a few members, maybe just certain members of our staff who were Catholic, such as Rose Woods and Air Force General Don Hughes, head of the military aides office, but he included us all. In addition, he asked his military aide Vern

Coffey to check *Air Force One* to find out who among the crew might be Catholic. One of the Philippine-American stewards who stepped forward as a Catholic was invited to join us. I saw the tears in his eyes as he shook the hand of the Pope.

At dusk that day we motorcaded from our Rome hotel to St. Peter's Square in the Vatican. *Marine One,* the presidential helicopter, was in the middle of the square, waiting to carry the president from Vatican City to the United States Navy's Sixth Fleet in the Mediterranean. The president was going to spend the night aboard the aircraft carrier *Saratoga*. As we walked a short distance from the car to *Marine One,* Bill Duncan, head of our Secret Service detail, tapped me on the shoulder. Pointing toward a Vatican balcony, he said, "Look over there." Turning, I saw the Pope standing on his famous balcony where we have all seen him appear to bless large crowds. It was now dark. The balcony was lit, and the pontiff was dressed in white. He had come out to watch the president's departure.

Over the whirring sound of the chopper engine, "Sir," I had to yell at the president, "turn and look." The president turned, saw the Pope, and smiled. There were certain moments that were perfunctory. Nixon performed his duties as expected, but there were others that really struck a chord with him. This was one of those moments. Knowing him as well as I did, I could feel his appreciation for that incredible moment in time. I felt it too.

Nixon started up the steps of the helicopter; then turned and waved to the Pope. The Pope returned the wave. Then the president boarded his helicopter and sat by the window. The sounds of the chopper got louder as the blades started slowly turning. Looking one way, I could see the president. Looking the other, I could see the Pope. They waved to each other once again. Then, as *Marine One* started lifting off the ground, the Pope made the sign of the cross, blessing the scene before him. I am not a Catholic, but I have never forgotten that truly inspirational moment.

All of the foreign trips we had made could not have begun to prepare us for Richard Nixon's historic visit to the People's Republic of China in February 1972. At that time Communist China was a closed society, a brutal dictatorship run by Chairman Mao Tse-tung and Premier Chou En-lai. Westerners were not welcomed. It had been two decades since the last official American delegation had set foot on Chinese soil. Little was known about the country, its culture, and its government. Richard Nixon had earned a well-deserved reputation as a staunch anti-Communist. No one could ever have accused him of being "soft" on Communism, nor naive about the intentions of a Communist dictatorship. Eventually historians would generally agree that the attempt to establish a relationship with Communist China could only have been accepted by American citizens under the leadership of someone who had strong anti-Communist credentials, such as Richard Nixon.

Nixon recognized the importance of opening China to the rest of the world. In 1967 he had written: "We simply cannot afford to leave China forever outside the family of nations." He had begun laying the groundwork for his approach to China even before his election, writing in *Foreign Affairs* a year earlier: "There is no place on this small planet for a billion of its potentially most able people to live in angry isolation." The stakes were high. This trip, he believed, would change the geopolitical balance of the world. The last thing the Russians wanted was to see the United States open a dialogue with China. The Russians and Chinese had a precarious relationship, verging on war. By 1969 they were on the verge of nuclear war.

An opportunity to take a step toward opening a relationship between the two countries began during the 1971 World Table Tennis Championships in Japan, when America's Glenn Cowan formed an unlikely friendship with a member of the Chinese team, Chuang Tse-tung.

When Chinese leader Mao Tse-tung saw a televised report in which Cowan responded to a Japanese journalist's question by saying he would very much like to visit China, the chairman decided to extend an invitation to the American team. The United States government was taken by surprise. Chou En-lai described this visit as "a new chapter in the relations of the American and Chinese people." Nixon responded to this "ping-pong diplomacy" by easing our existing trade embargos and travel ban. It was after these steps were taken that secret negotiations began.

Very few people knew we were talking to the Chinese government. The president and Henry Kissinger kept their plans and strategies to themselves. There was no discussion with the Department of State, the Defense Department, the Central Intelligence Agency, or any other Washington entity. All the moves were carefully orchestrated by the president, with Kissinger acting as his agent. Henry participated in the strategy, but this was Nixon's doing, *his idea*.

In today's world, the relationship between the United States and China is taken for granted, but back in 1970–1971 the idea of opening China was shocking. President Nixon's vision and moves were courageous, considering the risks both abroad and at home. In this new way of looking at the world, the president was playing the highest level of three-dimensional chess. Among the other benefits of reopening a diplomatic relationship with Communist China, it would exacerbate the already strained ties between China and the Soviet Union. In mid-July 1971, we were in San Clemente at the Western White House when I sensed something big was happening. I knew that Henry Kissinger had been in Pakistan. We were told he had contracted a bad case of stomach flu, which forced him to spend several days recuperating at a "private guesthouse" provided by the Pakistani government and far away from the media. What I didn't know was that Henry was using the cover of stomach flu to "disappear" for a few days. With the full cooperation and knowledge of the Pakistanis, Henry, along with a couple of aides, flew secretly from Pakistan to Peking to meet with the Chinese. The president was acting excited, kind of hyper-restless (at least for him), in the sense that he kept inquiring about Henry and his travels. Both Haldeman and Al Haig, Kissinger's deputy, knew what was actually happening. For security reasons there had been virtually no normal communications between the White House and Kissinger in Pakistan or China, although a code message had been received indicating that the trip was successful. Yet nobody really knew what "successful" meant, so the president was eagerly awaiting Henry's return home.

Kissinger would usually arrive at the Western White House by helicopter, landing at a helipad a couple of miles away. From there he would be driven over by car. However, that morning, July 15, 1971, he landed on the president's helipad right next to our offices in San Clemente. Nixon left his office in his golf cart to pick up Henry at the helipad. From there the two men headed for breakfast at the Nixons' residence, which was a short golf cart ride away. I knew that whatever was happening had to be important. The whole flow of the morning was different from that of our normal days. As I recall, we suspected their meeting had to do with the Vietnam War.

It was midmorning when Haldeman told Ziegler to contact the news networks to inform them that the president intended to make an important foreign policy announcement to the nation that evening. Meanwhile, most of the staff still didn't know what was transpiring. Late in the afternoon we boarded helicopters and flew to NBC's Burbank studio to be present for the president's announcement. He went on the air with a written statement telling the nation of Henry's secret trip and that he, as president, had accepted an invitation from Chairman Mao Tse-tung to visit the People's Republic of China. At precisely the same time, the Foreign Ministry in Peking was making a similar announcement to the Chinese people. In terms of foreign policy, the impact of the announcement was seismic. The entire world was stunned by the news.

The announcement was such a surprise, beyond what most people could imagine, that they didn't know how to react. Politically it was complicated. The island of Taiwan had been established as an independent Chinese nation by Chiang Kai-shek when his independent forces were driven out of mainland China by the victorious Communists in 1949. It existed as an anti-Communist bastion. The conservative wing of the Republican Party, feeling protective of Taiwan, was in no way pleased to hear the president's announcement. They believed it was a betrayal of Taiwan, a staunch American ally. Even inside our administration several conservatives were not in favor of the president making the trip. I think a primary reason Pat Buchanan, one of our steadfast conservatives, was eventually included in our delegation to visit China was to help mollify his branch of the party. It may have also been to keep Pat from publicly expressing his disapproval of the trip.

The world had to catch its breath. Media around the world, caught up in the drama that Richard Nixon was going to China, were in disbelief. The move by the president was so significant and so consequential that over the many years since and right up to today, when something unexpected and surprising is announced, it is often called a "Nixon to China Moment."

This China moment was testimony, like no other single event, to Richard Nixon's strategic vision and foreign policy acumen. Nixon said at the time, *"We are going to China because in fifty years we will be adversaries and we must be able to talk to one another."* Taking into account the current state of United States–China relations, it is interesting to note that Nixon said that, prophetically, in 1972, exactly fifty years ago!

There was a lot of confusion and competition in the White House about how this trip would be planned and who would be traveling with the president. John Ehrlichman was, by this time, the president's Domestic Affairs Advisor. He had done the advance work for the president's first European trip. Initially it was generally assumed that he would plan the trip and manage the logistics. The anticipated trip to China was, and still is, indisputably one of the most dramatic, unprecedented, unchartered, risky, consequential diplomatic missions ever conceived and/or undertaken, and John was making a play for the assignment.

Everyone in the White House wanted a role in the drama, which naturally included Ehrlichman, who was, undoubtedly, the most qualified person to partner with Henry. But Kissinger and Ehrlichman were competitive with each other, and Kissinger did not want Ehrlichman on the trip. He surely didn't want a partnership. There probably were a number of reasons for Henry's reluctance to go with John, but among them may have been that John had a solid, personal relationship with Nixon, and Henry might have been concerned John would go over Henry's head and interfere with his leadership. Whatever Henry's reasons, he articulated them to the president, who accepted them. I imagine the president, knowing what an important trip this would be, recognized how Kissinger's partly real and partly imagined rivalry with Secretary Rogers had impacted and impeded his performance to date. Nixon wanted Kissinger to be free of concern, void of interpersonal issues—and able to devote his full attention to the actual substance of the trip.

As an alternative to Ehrlichman, Haldeman suggested "Chapin" to Henry. Henry agreed. My going also served to put Haldeman in an oversight capacity because of our relationship. In an Oval Office meeting, the president gave me the assignment. That first meeting consisted of the president, Bob, and me; Henry joined later. My job, Haldeman explained later, was to work with the highest levels of the government in Peking (as Beijing was then known) to plan where President Nixon would go, with whom he would meet, and for how long and, in part, for what purpose. In brief, my job was to organize the president's schedule in order to make the visit successful. Haldeman's characterization of my role was from a traditional advance viewpoint. However, China ended up being a nontraditional advance.

In addition to heading the logistics team, I was designated Acting Chief of Protocol. The White House and State Department Chief of Protocol was Bus Mosbacher. However, Nixon did not want him on the trip. Mosbacher was furious, but there was nothing he could do about it. Henry pushed for him to be part of the delegation, warning the president that Mosbacher might resign if he couldn't go. The president and Haldeman agreed: "That might be perfect. Let him resign." The excuse we gave was that this was to be a working trip, and the president did not want it to have a lot of official and formal diplomatic requirements. This ended up being nonsense, as it was to become one of the most historic and protocol-conscious diplomatic trips in history.

Initially there was only supposed to be a small contingent of staff traveling. In that first meeting the president even said he didn't want to use *Air Force One*. He said instead he would travel on one of the presidential JetStars, a plane a fraction of the size of *Air Force One*. He saw the presidential traveling party consisting of himself, Kissinger, Haldeman, a couple of Secret Service agents, and five or six press people. Secretary of State Rogers was not mentioned. As I listened, it sounded as if I might be in China advancing but not traveling with them. Mrs. Nixon would not be going because it was to be "all business." The objective was clear. The focus of this first trip was going to be on opening China for an initial dialogue, a beginning. High-level White House people would be the only ones traveling with the president.

The Chinese seemed to be thinking the same thing. We were informed initially they would permit just two journalists to accompany the delegation. However, because of the historical importance of the trip, they decided to allow us to bring four. All of this at-the-outset thinking was in late July and August. After the surprise announcement of the pending journey, all focus turned to who would go, how it would be covered, how best to serve both nations. There was a transformation underway. The issues moved from we have an invitation, we will keep it small; to how many staff and journalists can we take? As we set up communications and started exchanging cables with the Chinese, we realized they wanted worldwide media coverage. This was to be their coming-out party and it appeared they wanted to invite the world.

I became consumed by my responsibilities with the planning of the logistics and leading our White House team. Therefore, I was relieved of my normal day-to-day responsibilities, which were reassigned to my deputies. I kept my West Wing office and took over additional space in the conference room in the bomb shelter under the Residence. Nell Yates and I worked there along with our team: Ron Walker, advance office director; Tim Elbourne, Ziegler's press representative; Bob Taylor of the Secret Service; and General Don Hughes, the air force general who headed the military aides office. Other White House travel and support people, along with advance personnel, attended our meetings as the planning and preparation required. The bunker bomb shelter we were using had been built during the Truman administration. It contained all the communications equipment we needed and plenty of space, plus there was a perfect conference room for our countless meetings. Ironically, the shelter built to protect the president from a nuclear attack was being used to plan the first peaceful excursion to the People's Republic of China.

Any possibility that this was going to be a small, contained group limited to top administration officials evaporated within a few short weeks. We were inundated with media requests. The networks, the major local stations, newspapers, and magazines all wanted to send a correspondent. We had literally two thousand requests. The weight of the worldwide interest in the trip and the historical significance of what was unfolding changed everything. The heads of news organizations and their top executives all wanted to be on the trip, to the point they were bouncing their own correspondents off the trip manifest so management could go.

One of the first major decisions made was that Kissinger would have to go back to Peking to negotiate arrangements, and that I would go with him. The trip eventually was planned for October. I was expected to put together a rough logistics plan for Henry's approval that we would present to the Chinese. The president still insisted at this point that it was going to be a working trip and wanted the sightseeing and traveling limited as much as possible. He specified that if he had to go outside Peking, it would be a day trip only, not an overnight. Also, if possible, the visit would be shortened from a week to four or five days. Then he decided to further cut it to three days. This was typical Nixon. He made a decision, then changed his mind, then changed it again a third time, then a fourth time, until it was settled.

At our first meeting, the president was not focused on television. As I recall, he never mentioned it. As time went by and our plans started to take shape, we all came to realize the important role that television could play. Haldeman kept pushing me to always have television in mind as we solidified our schedule. It wasn't long before the president was understanding the significance of live coverage of his trip being streamed home to the United States from China.

The role television would end up playing in the trip was evolutionary. Its importance grew week by week, as the networks focused on what they thought was the skeleton schedule for the trip. They began to envision stratospheric ratings. They wanted Americans to see China, the mysterious kingdom. With the twelve-hour time difference, they foresaw multiple hours of both morning and evening programming. Again, it evolved into extended television coverage. It was not long before we wanted television coverage at every opportunity. Sure, the president wanted to be seen by the Chinese people, but more important, he wanted to be seen by the people at home. In truth, we had no leverage over what the Chinese government would show their citizens. The president thought it would send an important and significant message if he were to be the first American president to be greeted by millions of Chinese people. He understood the power of pictures. Even so, all of us underestimated the actual impact television would have on the trip. As it turned out, the president did not go alone to China. The whole nation, indeed the whole world, went with him. The impact was phenomenal. And remember, because Nixon and the rest of us all did, it was an election year.

Henry and I started to work on a proposed plan to take to China on our upcoming October trip. During the planning process, issue after issue surfaced, each one needing discussion, agreement, and, of course, eventual implementation. Communication was basic to everything being considered. China was then a developing nation. It lacked a modern communications infrastructure. For the president's security, for instant communications, and for the media, we had to build a satellite ground station. We came up with the unique idea of turning a Boeing 747 into a broadcast center, with television and radio studios. We would build it in America and then fly it to Peking for the visit. I believe it was Tim Elbourne's ingenious idea. It was an exciting concept, but Henry warned us right away that the Chinese might not agree to it. "TV in the U.S. makes no difference to them," he said. Henry was right and wrong. Eventually the Chinese wanted the television coverage as much as we did. What they didn't want was a Boeing 747 from the United States flying to the rescue, equipped with television and radio broadcasting capability and all the necessary satellite equipment. They did not want to give the impression that they lacked the ability to provide the facility for us. It was important to them that they provide what we needed. It was a face-saving issue.

Planning this trip was daunting. I knew nothing about China. I could find it on a map, but that was about it. We started receiving dozens of documents and briefing books from various agencies, all of them wanting a piece of the trip. Everybody had an agenda. We were all quickly becoming "experts," reading "Confidential" and "Eyes Only" reports describing the Chinese leaders. The problem was that our government had very poor intelligence on the country, let alone the leaders. Most of the biographical information was decades old.

I had only one client, the president, but I was actually working for three people: the president, Kissinger, and Haldeman. I talked to the president on occasion but received most of my instructions from him through either Bob or Henry or, of course, on paper. His primary objective, he made clear, was to reset global relationships and perhaps even make inroads toward ending the Vietnam War. Very gradually, the outlines of the trip began to take shape.

Kissinger had his own point of view, telling me, "Everything we are doing with Moscow to end the Vietnam War hinges on this trip."

We quickly learned, as we started our work, that the normal way we planned and executed presidential travel was not going to be the way the China journey would unfold. From the very start, everything was different. What an understatement. We were geared to always having a prepared agenda for every meeting the president had and for every trip the president undertook. The Chinese didn't operate like that. Getting specific answers from them on any details of the trip—things as simple

as where, when, and with whom the president would be meeting—
was extremely difficult. It proved impossible to make any firm plans in
advance of our trip. None of our plans could be solidified until I was
actually there with Kissinger—and even then, everything was planned
a day at a time. One thing became crystal clear quickly: This was going
to be a major undertaking. The original plan of one Jetstar and a small
staff traveling with the president was not going to be happening.

A small advance party accompanying Dr. Kissinger left on October
10, 1971. "Once again," Haldeman wrote to me, "a bright young man
sets out on a great adventure . . . You undertake an extremely delicate
and unbelievably important mission . . . You have the full confidence of
the president, Henry Kissinger, and, for what it's worth, me. I'm proud
of you, and of the fact it is you who will be leading this mission . . . I
would be less than candid not to admit to a touch of envy—I wish I
was going with you."

I suppose I should have been anxious about my ability to handle all
of the upcoming details for which I would be responsible—and sometimes it did seem a little overwhelming. But mostly I was excited. This
was unlike any experience I'd ever had. It felt as if I was working every
minute of every day. Yet I found enough time to enjoy and appreciate the experience. Kissinger himself, because of the respectful way he
treated me, allowed me to have an "I can do this" attitude.

On board the plane on our way to China, Kissinger gave me his best
advice for dealing with the Chinese. I was to hear these things repeated
many times:

First, try to anticipate their objective. Then figure our course and try
to move their objective toward ours. Eventually offer them something near their objective that also satisfies our needs.

Never raise anything that would cause them to risk losing face.

Never raise anything with a sly angle because it borders on trickery.

They move at their own pace and may take a day to make a simple decision. The example he gave was twin beds. They probably haven't thought about that, he said. They may want to put people together that way—two per room. Americans usually put one person per room, but they will take a day to consider it before returning with a solution.

Henry was a wonderful teacher.

If we are offered Western food, it would be better not to accept. Accept their offer of Chinese food. "It's much better," he said. (I had second thoughts on that advice when I was told one course was "sea slugs" and another was deep-fried "baby sparrows.")

Don't ask about shopping until we'd been there a few days.

Most important with the Chinese is to understand that they have tremendous pride. Don't badger them. They approach everything carefully. He had been dealing with the Chinese for more than two months and noticed that when they turned down our proposal, they would always come back with a counterproposal that either was close to our request or something that made more sense.

He warned us that we ran the risk of looking like a bunch of clowns and that:

Everything we do depends upon their trusting us. If they decide we're lightweights, they will kill us. (I assumed he meant it figuratively.)

It was important that we exaggerate the amount of opposition the president was meeting at home because of his new China policy. Let them know that he is being attacked from both the right and the left.

As for what not to say:

Don't mention Vietnam. If they bring it up, tell them we will "master that war. If they don't get it settled, we will, and we won't be responsible for the consequences."

Say nothing about the Soviets. Do not mention Mao. Don't ask about Chinese domestic politics.

Be positive: Nixon is going to be reelected.

It was interesting to witness Henry's obvious admiration of Chou En-lai. He called him a man of "great moral quality . . . one of the two or three outstanding men" he had ever met.

Henry also was furious about what he considered to be Secretary of State Rogers's attempts to ruin the trip. While we were en route to China, Secretary Rogers was in New York at the United Nations, fighting harder than he ever had, to be certain that Taiwan remained in the UN as an independent country and also to be certain that Communist China was not invited to be a member.

On our trip in October, we stopped in Hawaii on the way and stayed at the beautiful Mauna Kea Beach Hotel on the Big Island, where we were treated like kings. In addition to Henry, his top aide Winston Lord, Tim Elbourne, and some support staff traveled with us. After we all swam with Kissinger in the ocean, he hosted us for dinner. We enjoyed the rest stop for two nights, the purpose being to let our body clocks adjust. We were also testing out the timetable we would recommend to the president. As it turned out, for the president's trip we not only included a two-night stop in Hawaii but added one night in Guam, to give his body clock even more time to adjust.

We landed in Shanghai to pick up Chinese navigators, a People's Republic of China (PRC) requirement for our flight over Chinese territory. We were greeted there by a small delegation of Chinese, but otherwise the airport was completely deserted. Everything had a cold, unfriendly feeling. The propaganda banners with quotations from Chairman Mao in Chinese and English were hanging from the exterior of the terminal building. "Running Dogs of Capitalism," one sign proclaimed. Kissinger said they had been put there for our benefit. Everywhere we went there would be these inflammatory billboards and sayings. Of course, it was a propaganda-dominated society, where slogans of all kinds told the people what they were supposed to be thinking and feeling. I learned at our first meal that if we appreciated something we were eating, they would instantly bring an additional helping. I remember Tim Elbourne, our press office representative, joking that we would have to be careful or they would kill us with courtesy.

When we checked into our very well-appointed assigned rooms in the state guesthouse in Peking, we found booklets quoting Mao and exhorting the people of the world to "unite against Fascist Pigs." That was us. Henry was not happy about those booklets being placed in our rooms and had them all collected and returned to our hosts, telling them, "There must be some mistake." That was his way of establishing our boundaries. I came to learn that in China everything was significant, and little happened by chance.

I met Chou En-lai on our first working day in the Great Hall of the People meeting room where we all gathered. In my notes I wrote, "The Prime Minister can put things into such gracious, simple terms." I added he was "a slim yet magnetic type figure . . . almost poetic at times . . ." Although he spoke and understood English, we mostly communicated through his translator. At one point he asked me, "How old are you?" I told him I was thirty. He replied, "I'm very impressed your president would send such a young man." In Chinese culture, age advantage and respect are centered on the older person. Therefore, my age got disproportionate attention.

It was fascinating to watch Henry and Chou work together. I was witnessing two extraordinary diplomats who, working together, were about to change the world. At one point Chou complimented Henry for keeping this trip a great secret, comparing it to the secrecy surrounding the dropping of the atomic bomb on Hiroshima. Henry responded, "Yes, but this secret is much more constructive."

In addition to the political goals, which were basically (1) how do we go about seeking normalization and discussion of matters of common interest and (2) the question of Indochina (Vietnam), the primary issues we discussed on this trip were communications and security. During his previous visit, Henry told Chou he had recommended that ten journalists accompany the president on his trip. He continued: "But when I asked our press secretary what the absolute minimum would be that we could bring, he proposed 250 . . . We've reduced that figure from 250 to 150 but now he isn't talking to me anymore."

Chou responded, with a smile, "That also is a great disaster." He got a big, knowing laugh.

There were hundreds of requests from the press to get their reporters on the trip roster. The president handed them all off to Ron Ziegler. Ron had never had such power—or so many problems.

At the first welcoming banquet in the Great Hall of the People, I was seated to Chou's left. Henry was in the seat of honor, on his right. They served chicken, shrimp, and duck. I had had limited experience with chopsticks, but I learned from a real expert when Chou taught me how to use them more effectively. While I did fumble around using the chopsticks, I kept on trying and improved quickly. Chou complimented me on getting more adept. We discussed my schooling and how I got into government service. He seemed very interested in my background.

We did a little sightseeing on that trip, including trips to the Forbidden City, the Great Wall, the Ming tombs, the Emperor's summer palace, and the ballet, where we watched a propaganda ballet called *The Red Detachment of Women*. The ballet glorified the role of women in the Communist takeover of China. We even visited a new, massive petroleum installation. We drove by several communes and discussed farming techniques. When we talked about pig farming, I was able to talk about my experiences on Granddad Chapin's hog farm in Kansas. At the opera we unknowingly committed a cultural faux pas. We received polite applause when we walked in. Only later did we learn that, if we had returned the applause, the welcome they gave us would have been warmer. I was wondering at the opera what I was smelling. It turns out that while we in America might eat popcorn, the Chinese like to chew raw garlic.

Regarding my planning responsibilities, I insisted to our Chinese counterparts that we had to take back to the president some type of tentative outline of our program. We got into a long discussion about our need to have a phone nearby wherever we were. As an example, I used the possibility of an earthquake leveling New York City, in which case the president would have to be notified immediately so he could take action. In response I was asked by one of the Chinese if it would be possible to plan those emergencies in advance. Sometimes things were lost in translation.

We found ways to compromise. The Chinese agreed that we would be permitted to build a communications station, which they would buy, then lease back to us for the president's trip. It would be built adjacent to the Peking airport and allow us to upload directly to a satellite for worldwide transmission. At first, we didn't know why they wanted to do it that way. Then we realized one reason was that they wanted to get their hands on all our high-tech equipment and intended to steal our technology. There also was the "saving face issue." They did not want us to bring and control all the uplinking, a sign they were not capable of doing it.

Kissinger and Chou got along well. If not a friendship, they had certainly established a respectful understanding with each other. At the final dinner, again I was seated to Chou's left, which allowed me to listen to the conversation between Henry and him. Henry got Chou to discuss how Mao's Communists had defeated Chiang Kai-shek. It was very important, Chou explained, to not worry about the cities but rather maintain control over what they had as the enemy overextended themselves in the countryside. Listening to that explanation, it was impossible to not compare it to the North Vietnamese strategy of getting the South Vietnamese to make precisely the same mistake. At our banquet table were other ranking Chinese officials and ranking military brass. Because interpreters were utilized, most conversations were between two people, and in my case, three people—Kissinger, Chou and me.

We didn't have an opportunity to get a feel for the people. We weren't there long enough. Also, we were not allowed to explore beyond the guesthouse where we were staying, which was in a private garden area of Peking. We basically had no access to the average Chinese person. The atmosphere was bleak and gray, and the people we saw from our cars looked somber, though they appeared to be somewhat curious. Before our trip I had tried to imagine, as one of the first Americans to visit their country, what questions I might be asked. I didn't need to have spent any time pondering that because it was clear that no average citizen would be allowed to speak with us. Everything was tightly controlled.

On our final afternoon in Peking, we went to see a demonstration of a Chinese medical procedure called acupuncture. Keep in mind this was in 1971. Few people in America knew anything about acupuncture. "It is," I wrote, "the process of anesthesia by needle." We watched as they stuck needles in a completely conscious man and removed a tumor from under his lung. Then we watched as they twirled needles at approximately four hundred revolutions per minute and slit open a woman's stomach in order to remove a cyst. As soon as her cyst had been removed and her incision had been sutured, she spoke with us briefly through an interpreter and then walked out of the operating room. "It is an amazing process," I wrote, "and one which Americans are going to have to study." I was thinking that a lot of people at home weren't going to believe me when I shared these stories with them.

My Chinese counterpart, Han Hsu, accompanied us on our flight back to Shanghai. By now we both understood we would be counterparts for this historic visit. Han's title, too, was Acting Chief of Protocol.

While we were cordial with each other initially, it was the beginning of what would become an important, years-long friendship.

On the flight back home, Henry mentioned there would be a second advance trip sometime in December.

A lot of the satisfaction we were all feeling about the success of the current journey dissipated when we learned that the United Nations had voted to expel Nationalist China (Taiwan) from the organization and voted to replace it with the People's Republic of China, which was a loss for the United States. Henry was concerned he would be blamed for the vote and that people would associate the upcoming trip to China with this outcome.

Upon our return home, Henry asked—rather, he *demanded* that we not speak to the press. But he didn't say anything about talking with friends and family. As one of the first Americans to have visited China, and one among an even smaller number who had met Chou En-lai, I was a bit of a celebrity with our friends and even some White House colleagues. I had taken my Super 8 movie camera on the trip. When I got home, Susie and I invited friends for movie parties. It was a big deal. I had gone to China with Dr. Kissinger. Not only did I have stories, I also had pictures to go with them. In addition to sharing my movies and pictures with our friends, the CIA requested a copy of all my footage and still photographs.

That first visit (my first; Henry's second) had set the stage. The problem was that we still weren't certain what was going to take place on that stage. The Chinese were wonderful hosts, but they were masterful at avoiding commitments. No matter how hard we tried, they just wouldn't be pinned down about specific arrangements, which made planning a nightmare. The president liked to get involved in planning the events he would attend. He liked to have a specific schedule and to know what to expect. Recall my comments about the early days working at the New York law firm and Nixon wanting to know all the details of his schedule. He couldn't understand, nor could Haldeman, why I was unable to get a draft schedule from the Chinese. "Where is it? Get it!" was a constant refrain. The closest we had managed to establish was a suggested schedule. This *might* happen on this day. This *could* happen here. The trip would last seven days. Or maybe six. It was very frustrating. In an attempt to nail down details, a second advance trip was scheduled. I would go back to China with a group headed by Al Haig. The size of the presidential delegation continued to be a topic of endless discussion. Ziegler continued to plead for more slots for media, while the president and Henry wanted fewer people.

On December 30, 1971, I left Andrews Air Base with the Haig advance group for a two-night stay in Honolulu, planning to arrive in Peking on January 2. Ron Ziegler was on the trip in order to focus on the media setup. Ron Walker joined us, along with representatives of the White House Communications Agency, military aide Vern Coffey, and Bob Taylor from the Secret Service. A major goal of the Haig trip was to try to reach agreement on the final communique that would be issued at the end of the president's journey. Other objectives were to confirm arrangements and try to agree to the ever-changing schedule. The president, specifically, was interested in when he would meet Chairman Mao. We never did get an answer to that question until just before he met with Mao. I am talking fifteen minutes before.

Throughout the entire trip we tried to see it through a Chinese filter, hoping to understand what they were really saying to us. When we increased the bombing campaign in North Vietnam, for example, the Chinese statement about it was less tough than we were anticipating. Therefore, we decided, they must not be as angry about the bombing as we thought they were, or perhaps the president's trip was so important to them that they modified their reaction. Everything depended on how one wanted to interpret events at that particular moment, and a lot of people spent a lot of time trying to read the Chinese tea leaves.

Peking was cold and covered with snow when we landed that January. Among the people who greeted us was Han Hsu, who rode with me to our hotel and stayed by my side throughout the entire second trip. The hotel was in central Peking, walking distance to Tiananmen

Square and the Forbidden City. The hotel was several years old but nice, and it had a large dining room and clean, private one-person rooms. Han and I spent a lot of time together, both of us following diplomatic formalities but gradually establishing a personal relationship.

I offered to pay our bills for the hotel. Han said he had to formally turn down that offer. I responded that I had to formally make the offer and thank him for their hospitality. Then I told him, informally, that I assumed that was going to be the case, but we wanted them to know we were willing to pay. We were carefully handling all matters with sensitivity at the outset of our relationship.

The Chinese continued to be very hospitable. I learned a little Chinese, in particular the phrase *gan bei,* which translates to mean "bottoms up!" We did a lot of *gan bei*-ing on that trip.

On every issue where a decision needed to be made, we had to continually deal with the Chinese response of "maybe." It got to Ziegler more than anyone. Ron demanded answers, and he wanted them now. Ron and I ended up yelling at each other. Then he had another argument with Tim Elbourne. I wrote in my notes, "The emotions are close to the surface and people are fairly uptight about things." Part of the irritability people feel on foreign trips is how tired they become with the time changes and lack of sleep.

Ziegler's desire for immediate answers eventually reached Haig, who was furious with him. He believed Ziegler was not being candid with the networks about personnel, that he "had been playing games and now the chickens had come home to roost." It was true that when it came to network requests, Ziegler would often equivocate when the correct answer should have been a firm "No." But in Ron's defense, he was in a no-win situation with all the media demands, most of which were impossible to meet. And saying "No" wasn't easy.

In his own meetings, as Al shared with me, he made it clear to the Chinese that Vietnam remained a real barrier to improved relations between our two countries. He laid out precisely every step we had taken in terms of trying to end the war and get our prisoners back, and what we had tried to get the North Vietnamese government to do. The Chinese government, he told me, was startled when they learned from him all that had been attempted. They were surprised they had not known the truth from Hanoi.

We visited most of the same tourist sites on this trip that we had visited on our previous trip in October. Ron Walker was making notes of every site and every detail. After a day of touring, we would review everything. When necessary we would include Han Hsu to make sure we were understanding things correctly. As our lead advance man, Ron would be returning with his team in about ten days and would stay through the president's trip. Ron would become my on-the-ground contact in Peking with Han Hsu. Ron and I would communicate between Washington and Peking twice a day via a "suitcase satellite," which was sitting on the balcony of the advance team's hotel. We would be solidifying all the arrangements for the trip and solving any issues that presented themselves. Today satellite communications are everywhere. In 1972 this was state-of-the-art technology that amazed us all.

On this trip we once again observed acupuncture. At a local hospital we watched three needles being placed on points in a man's skull to treat nearsightedness. In addition, we were invited to tour a commune, including its machine shop and cabbage storage facilities, and the one-room homes of the workers. From there we visited a school. It was there that we saw in spades the regimented China we had expected to see. The young students sat at desks like robots. They didn't smile. They chanted their lessons loudly, in unison. The teacher stood in front of them, instructing. There didn't appear to be a place for individual personalities to emerge or express themselves. We saw the same thing in Shanghai when we visited the Children's Palace, a facility for children in which every person we saw, young and old, seemed programmed to perform a task, which they would repeat over and over, as we stood watching. The government had put on its best face for us. However, we believed the commune, the schoolroom, and even the playground had been staged as examples of authentic, everyday life in China. None of us believed it was actually authentic. It would be staged and repeated, once again, for the president and Mrs. Nixon when they visited.

During the trip we spent considerable time working out media logistics. At no place was the difference between our two cultures more evident than in discussions about the media ground station. During our October 1971 advance trip, my first advance trip, we had left them with a schematic overview of the Boeing 747–based broadcast facility. In the three months since our previous visit, the Chinese had almost completed building the ground station. It was remarkable to see how perfectly they had replicated our design. Han told me the replica had cost them $610,000 but they would charge us $650,000 in order to cover additional costs such as food and transportation. Several hours later he came back to say the government would be charging us only $610,000 [$4 million in 2020 dollars]. He explained they had lowered the cost so that it didn't appear they would be making a profit. As I wrote at the time, "The one thing they are scared to death of is making any kind of profit. With them it's a matter of principle and they are in no frame of mind to accept a profit."

Han explained that this was a principle of sovereignty, that by losing money and absorbing the costs they would be demonstrating their independence. Finally, to satisfy the convoluted thinking of the Chinese, Ziegler offered to give Han a flat guarantee that the People's Republic of China would lose money with regard to the communications facility they were building for us. This would assure them, in a roundabout way, that we would help make sure there was no profit.

As a diplomat, General Haig lacked the smoothness and patience of Kissinger. There was one somewhat awkward moment during a banquet in Shanghai. Al Haig did not respond in kind to a toast that was offered to him. Han asked me, confidentially, if his nonresponse was considered appropriate. The Chinese had interpreted Haig's failure to return the toast to mean he was unhappy about something. I told Han that I was sure no insult had been intended. Later, when Ziegler and I talked about it, he suggested that Haig had enjoyed too many *gan bei*s.

As we later discovered, Haig had actually been upset about the way he had been treated when meeting with Chou En-lai. Also, he was not happy with their public criticism of the president. Bottom line: His "rude" toast had been intentional. I made a note to myself to make sure the president was not put in that same position. Regarding toasts, he would match them toast for toast. I was learning that in China, everything mattered. Everything.

We toured. We visited. We saw. We went everywhere the president and Mrs. Nixon might go. We walked through magnificent parks. We were brought to beautiful ancient pagodas with carved Buddhas. We rode across a lake on a glass-bottomed boat. We ate in the same banquet halls in which the president would be eating. And, finally, we agreed on details.

Our delegation would include 375 people, quite an increase from the president's first thought of getting everyone on a Jetstar. We had at least a basic understanding of points of interest that the president and First Lady would visit. We also had a general idea of the time slots for the official meetings with Premier Chou. Han told me that Mao would probably meet with President Nixon twice. This was a bit complicated. It was my understanding that, because Chou En-lai would be present during the meetings with Chairman Mao, Kissinger would accompany the president to the meetings. On the other hand, Haig told me the president did not want Henry with him during those meetings. That was not my understanding. I was never told the president didn't want Kissinger attending official meetings.

There was an embarrassing moment at our final dinner with the Chinese. A member of our delegation who was seated with Al Haig and me said to our hosts, "There are many Chinese in America. Most of them are in the laundry business." Al's look could have killed when he heard those words. Feeling too embarrassed to look around, I just stared down at my plate. Our hosts nodded politely and were kind enough to ignore the comment. In a parting toast the next day, our host pointed out that some irritating comments had been made during the week, but "these should be forgotten because they will go away" and should not be allowed to disrupt the work.

Vice Minister Yu, one of the senior Chinese officials to host us, also complimented us, saying "there has been a spirit of frankness, cooperation, and friendship, and these are the hallmarks for a successful visit." In our final meeting Han toasted my family, an unusually personal gesture, and I reciprocated by toasting his.

This was a beginning. Al Haig had not succeeded in getting agreement on the final communique, but the preparations had been laid for the president's visit. It was clear to us that the Chinese were ready to rejoin the world. In our one meeting with Chou En-lai during that trip, Chou asked Ron Ziegler to tell the president that the Chinese Table Tennis Association "would like to pay a return visit [to America] next spring when the blossoms are in full bloom."

★ **12** ★

THIS WAS THE WEEK THAT CHANGED THE WORLD.
—President Richard Nixon

A SINGLE SPARK CAN START A PRAIRIE FIRE.
—Chairman Mao Tse-tung

It was snowing lightly in Washington on the morning of February 17, 1972, when President Nixon's plane took off for the People's Republic of China.

That's a sentence that few could have imagined would ever be written. This trip, I believe, had captured the president's full attention and interest more than anything else he had done. For years people had been referring to him as a foreign policy expert, a diplomat, an exceptional strategist. Here was his greatest opportunity to demonstrate it. He loved planning this trip. Loved it. At that time China had the largest population on earth. Yet it had no personal relationships, no business relationships, no diplomatic contact—that is, no communication whatsoever with the United States. Here was Richard Nixon, the leader of the free world, marching off to the darkest, and most mysterious, part of the Communist empire.

It had been Nixon's dream. At one point early in the first term, Kissinger was with the president in the Oval Office finishing up his daily briefing. As Kissinger emerged, he declared to all those around, "You won't believe this—he must be crazy—he says he's going to go to China."

But even as we departed Washington, we still didn't have a firm schedule. Several aspects were agreed to only a day or two before the trip. We finally had a vaguely defined framework, but it remained subject to change on the whim of the Chinese. The president and Haldeman understood the need to be flexible, that we were going to have to take things on a day-by-day basis. They didn't like it, but that was just the way it was.

We had come a long way in our planning. Ultimately 385 Americans made the trip, among them Secretary of State William Rogers; journalists, including Theodore White, Dan Rather of CBS, Tom Brokaw of NBC, William F. Buckley from *National Review,* Barbara Walters of ABC, and Max Frankel of the *New York Times*. In addition, countless other journalists from around the world had been invited by the Chinese. Initially the Chinese made it clear they did not expect, nor necessarily want, Mrs. Nixon to come. The problem, we knew, was that Chou En-lai's wife was never seen and Jiang Qing, "Madame Mao," was a virulent anti-American who had been a leader of the Cultural Revolution and in fact had her own faction that was actively plotting for power. The president wanted Mrs. Nixon to be there with him, and she wanted to be there; she was actually insistent on it.

Kissinger broached the subject with Chou, pointing out that America's First Lady would be accompanying the president on his trip to Russia later that year—and agreeing that other wives would not be making this trip. The Chinese finally agreed. What had started as a "working trip," an opportunity to establish an initial relationship, had become something much larger and more significant. It didn't appear to be what the Chinese had in mind when we started, but the Chinese government ultimately embraced the situation. By the time we finished negotiating, Mrs. Nixon had a full schedule and her presence became a very important part of the entire trip.

Air Force One was carrying an extra-heavy load of passengers and baggage. I was sitting with Kissinger and Haldeman at our staff tables, watching our takeoff on a small color television. Because of the weight of the plane, we made our way down the runway at an uncomfortably slow speed. Henry sat there, watching the TV in front of him, saying that he had never watched himself crash before. As the plane's landing gear left the runway, we all cheered. We were on our way to China. We would make two rest stops on the way to let our body clocks catch up with the twelve-hour time difference between Washington and Peking. Our first stop was Hawaii; the second was the U.S. territory of Guam.

The president was ebullient on the flight. He and Mrs. Nixon spent most of their time in the presidential cabin area. The president was wearing a shirt and tie with a powder blue jacket. Occasionally he would take a walk through the plane for exercise. Otherwise, he pored over several briefing books and met with Kissinger, Rogers, and Haldeman. Rogers was on the trip because it was important the State Department be represented, and not taking him would have had huge ramifications.

Nixon spent much of the final leg of the flight, from Guam to Shanghai, engrossed in the briefing books we had prepared. When we arrived in Peking, he was greeted on the tarmac by Chinese Premier Chou En-lai. The two men shook hands, which was of symbolic importance. In the 1950s Secretary of State John Foster Dulles had deliberately slighted Chou by not shaking his hand, which was a great public embarrassment to Chou. Nixon knew that. He had written in his notes, as a reminder to himself, of the importance of that first handshake. While most Americans watching probably had no idea of its significance, what mattered most was that Nixon and Chou knew. That handshake alone set the visit on the right track from the first minute.

Being present for that first meeting between Nixon and Chou was very satisfying and somewhat emotional for me. We all gathered in a large reception room, then were seated and served green tea. I had spent the last eight months of my life thinking about this, planning it, worrying about it. There had been so many obstacles and an infinite number of problems. At times we doubted this trip would ever happen. Yet there I was, looking around at the official parties of both the United States and the People's Republic of China, all sitting and talking with each other. The president was in great spirits, even telling a humorous story about traveling with Mrs. Nixon in Africa where she demonstrated the strength of Irish- and German-blooded people. He then joked he couldn't tell that story in the United States because it might cost him Italian and Polish votes. The feeling, from the very first meeting, was one of warmth and calm, and a knowledge that all would be well.

I was in a meeting early that first afternoon when one of our Secret Service agents found me and said that Han Hsu had arrived back at our guesthouse and wanted to see me. As I walked to the front entrance, I found Premier Chou standing with him. Han said, "We are going to see the Chairman," meaning Chairman Mao Tse-tung. "Please get the president." This meeting request was completely unexpected and a very big deal. Apparently, right before seeing me, Chou and Han had also told Henry that Chairman Mao wanted to meet with the president immediately.

Henry had scurried off to get Winston Lord, his deputy. I went to the president's suite. He was seated in a large overstuffed chair with his suit jacket off and his trusted legal pad. I told him Chairman Mao wanted to see him. The president was surprised. I don't think he had anticipated it happening so soon after our arriving. I know I didn't. Nixon said something like, "Only Henry, you know," which meant he didn't want to include Secretary of State Rogers. While the president put on his suit coat, I rushed to see Haldeman, who was in his room meeting with Ziegler. I literally burst in to tell them, "The president is leaving for his meeting with Mao." The three of us watched as the president walked from the guesthouse with Premier Chou, Kissinger, Winston Lord, and Han Hsu. Bob Taylor, the president's lead agent, was also allowed to go. They were off to see the Chairman. We had no idea where they were going or what to expect of the meeting. At home tens of millions of dollars are spent to ensure the safety of our presidents. We always know exactly where a president is and what he's doing at every moment. But that wasn't to be the case in China.

The first reports on the president's meeting with Mao were that Mao's mind was very sharp. While he had trouble walking, he registered a good sense of humor, and overall the president felt it was a good session. According to Bob's report in *The Haldeman Diaries,* the president was impressed that, at one point while talking, Mao reached over and grabbed the president's hand. The president found this to be significant. For me the significance of all this was how every little nuance was being interpreted and analyzed. We had found that to be true from the outset of our relationship with the Chinese. Now we were seeing it in how the president described his very first meeting with Mao.

Haldeman was not happy about how the Mao meeting had unfolded—not because he wasn't included, but because he didn't believe the President of the United States should be summoned to a surprise meeting with the leader of another country. He felt it put the president in a subsidiary role. He was right: It did.

Ron Ziegler did not inform the media about the meeting until the president had returned, and even then he was vague in giving them the details of what had transpired. We didn't want the first stories about the trip to report that the president had been escorted off to some unknown destination for a meeting that no one had known anything about in advance. It turned out the meeting took place at Mao's home, which was extremely unusual. It was considered a great compliment to the president. The fact that the meeting took place and took place so early was both an enormous relief to the president and a signal of the level of commitment by Mao.

That night the Chinese hosted a formal banquet in the Great Hall of the People, which was huge and could seat five thousand people for dinner. The Chinese honored us with an incredible feast, which included several courses and warm toasts by both the Chinese leaders and our U.S. delegation. A lingering memory for me was the Chinese orchestra working their way through an elaborate arrangement of "Home on the Range" and "Sweet Georgia Brown."

Afterward I met with Han Hsu to discuss the dinner the president was planning to host at the end of the week. Han told me that we had made a terrible mistake. The State Department had inscribed the invitations for our reciprocal banquet using old Chinese characters rather than the newer, Mao-approved characters. We had not called on the State Department to do many things with regard to the trip, but the invitations were their assignment. It was another one of those cultural faux pas we had no idea we were making. Han accepted my apology and allowed us to proceed. Having no fast or simple way to correct our error, we went ahead and sent out the invitations in the old calligraphy.

There were other cultural divides between our two nations. Diane Sawyer, later to become a nationally known television personality, was on the trip as part of Ron Ziegler's press office. After a long day in Peking she tossed her used pantyhose, which had a run in them, into a wastebasket. The next day she found them washed and wrapped neatly in paper on her bed. So she tried to get rid of them once again. She wrapped them in her own paper and threw them away a second time. The next day they were back on her bed, washed and neatly folded. Finally, before leaving Peking, she threw them away one last time. We left the hotel for the airport, in order to fly to Hangzhou and, as we started up the stairs into the plane, Diane's pantyhose were returned to her. The philosophy of the Chinese of that era was that nothing should be wasted.

Early in our visit the Chinese announced that, in celebration of this monumental meeting of President Nixon and Chairman Mao, they would be giving two pandas as their gift to the United States. The pandas would prove to be very popular with millions of Americans. The original giant pandas, Ling-Ling and Hsing-Hsing, would be welcomed to America by the First Lady. They lived for many years at the National Zoo in Washington. In Julie Nixon Eisenhower's book about her mother, *Pat*, she tells the panda story. The First Lady was sitting next to Premier Chou at a dinner and referring to a cylindrical tin of Panda brand cigarettes on the table in front of them. She said she loved them. Chou said, "I'll give you some." She said, "Cigarettes?" And he said, "No, pandas." And that's how history gets made.

President Nixon loved Boehm porcelain bird sculptures and kept several on the shelves in the Oval Office. Among our gifts to the Chinese government leaders were beautiful Boehm porcelain birds, among them a mute swan, which the president dubbed "the Peace Swan." To the people of China we were giving two musk oxen. We also sent redwood trees from California's redwood forest to the city of Hangzhou. Unfortunately, the first trees we sent died. When we sent replacement trees, we also sent an expert from the Department of the Interior to make sure they were planted properly and in the right soil.

I was spending most of my time on the trip with Han Hsu and working out logistics details with Haldeman and the president. Kissinger spent time with Nixon at official meetings, as well as meeting with him between sessions. All of us assumed there were listening devices, so conversations were discreet.

Ron Walker had arranged for one or two advance men to be present in each city. In Peking Ron served as lead advance man. He was constantly advising me on changing plans and arrangements. Mrs. Nixon had her own schedule during the day and would accompany the president for evening events. My role was to manage the continually changing schedule with the president, Haldeman, and Kissinger. I worked with Walker in making decisions to keep things flowing smoothly.

I would meet with Haldeman to go over our schedule-of-the-moment. Then Han would tell me about changes they insisted had to be integrated into the plan. Nothing was firm until it was actually happening. One evening, for example, we were all set to go to a gymnastics event but instead we ended up at the ballet to see *The Red Detachment of Women,* where we were unexpectedly welcomed by Chou En-lai, his wife, and Madame Mao. The essence of the ballet was the liberation of a peasant girl and her rise in the Chinese Communist Party. The president and Mrs. Nixon were seated with Chou and Madame Mao. I was seated directly behind the Nixons. The ballet went on and on for what seemed like hours. I recall us all being restless, particularly me, as this was my second time sitting through it. There was nothing I could do but pray the end was coming soon.

The continual changes in the daily calendars became problematic. Haldeman and Kissinger at times had competing agendas and ideas, or they were receiving information from different sources. I was caught in the middle of it, trying to satisfy everyone. Ron Walker might tell me that Han Hsu had arranged for us to go to the Great Wall the next morning. So I would tell Haldeman, who would pass on the plan to the president. Meanwhile, Premier Chou might have mentioned to Kissinger that we would go to the Great Wall the next afternoon. The president didn't know what to believe. Bob gave me heat for not staying abreast of the changes. I was trying to keep it all straight while juggling the complex set of arrangements between the Chinese, our own advance team, and Haldeman. Besides all that, I had to focus on Henry's schedule too. When you're the guy responsible for running a trip, you own all changes and mix-ups.

In the midst of it all, the president was sending memos to each of us. As he did whenever we traveled, he focused on the present while also planning for the future. He sent a note to Secretary of State Rogers, reminding him that the current regime would one day be gone, so it was important while we were there to try to identify the "comers." If possible, "we should establish some kind of rapport and contact with those who we think are comers." That was a tough order. He hardly knew the current officials, let alone those up-and-coming. To me, the note demonstrated the president's optimism about the possibility of a future relationship with China. After reading the note Haldeman said to me, "Well, you've got to admit, he's always thinking." Thinking ahead was pure Nixon. On all foreign trips, including later private trips when he was out of office, he would have Ray Price, his son-in-law Ed Cox, or others traveling with him identifying the up-and-comers in every country. Then, if his schedule allowed, he would always meet with them. He was continually building relationships with a view to the future.

On our third day in Peking it snowed. All was covered in white, which was a wonderful backdrop for Mrs. Nixon in the red coat she wore throughout the journey. It was Tex McCrary, our communications and public relations consulting guru, who had suggested the First Lady wear a red coat. Considerations of who would wear what may not sound important on a relative scale. But Tex had had a wonderful idea. The People's Republic of China was a drab, colorless society. By contrast, the red coat worn by our First Lady was a symbolic contrast of our two societies. In China, colors are considered very important and significant. Red is the traditional color of luck and success. Plus, for all the pictures, and especially for television, Mrs. Nixon, who was a standout to begin with, was easily identified as she appeared on television screens around the world.

The banquets kept coming. At each banquet there were toasts and more toasts and toasts of the toasts. Between banquets there were meetings and tours. Six months earlier I had known nothing about the Forbidden City. At this point, if it had been necessary, I could have conducted a tour myself.

We were happy about this trip, telling ourselves once again, "Another historic first." We were making history and changing the political dynamics of the world. We had limited free time to ourselves to be able to enjoy it. We were working hard, with never enough sleep and running on adrenaline. The excitement, through all the days we were in China, didn't taper off for a second for any of us.

For me, this was the culmination of the years I'd been with Richard Nixon, beginning in that small office in his law firm: his "political wilderness years" as people called them. During that period it seemed that only a small group of loyal supporters recognized him as a very special man, a man with a destiny. Rose Mary Woods knew it. Mrs. Nixon and his daughters felt it. Pat Buchanan, along with Ray Price, saw it.

Now here he was in China, changing the world. This was Richard Nixon's moment. He knew it and he was living it.

The China journey was changing the president's image, moving him to the highest status of world statesman. You could see and feel it happening. It was incredibly satisfying to watch his transformation. He looked healthy and tanned, relaxed, energized, and fully engaged. He was every bit the intellectual equal of Mao Tse-tung and Chou En-lai, a brilliant negotiator and dealmaker. More than at any other time in his presidency, a majority of Americans were united behind his leadership.

This trip was his finest moment, his and that of the entire administration. The glow engulfed us all.

Throughout the week, the president and Kissinger mainly, and to a much lesser degree Secretary Rogers and several others, were working with Chou En-lai and other PRC officials on the final words of the joint communique that was to be issued at the end of the trip. It turned out to be a lot more complicated than anyone had imagined. Every time I asked Henry how it was going, he would confide, "There's just one sentence holding us up." It must have been a difficult sentence, as they worked on it steadily for several of the seven days we were there. The main problem was how to address the status of Taiwan. The Chinese continued to insist that Taiwan was not an independent nation, while we insisted on recognizing it as such. There was a lot of infighting within our delegation, essentially Kissinger versus Rogers's State Department. Haldeman knew exactly what was going on and told me, at one point, that his respect for Henry "had gone up 300 percent." Bob said that State Department people were trying to undermine what the president was doing, and Kissinger was protecting him. The communique was the battlefield. I was awakened a couple of times in the middle of the night to deal with issues. I'm not sure Haldeman ever got to sleep.

The Chinese had insisted that all of our flights within their country be on Chinese aircraft, piloted by their own Chinese pilots. To my knowledge, an American president while in office has never flown on another country's aircraft. Our Secret Service was vehemently opposed to that plan. The issue ascended to the top echelon of the Secret Service. The Secret Service made its case, with pleas that the president only fly on *Air Force One*. The president understood it was a face-saving issue for the Chinese and overrode everyone. Understanding that it was a major point of pride with the Chinese, he agreed to use their planes and pilots. Chou En-lai flew with all of us in the official party to Hangzhou on their plane. He sat at a table with the president. It was very cold on the prop-driven plane, and the steam from their covered tea cups added a mysterious, movie-like overtone to the scene. On the flight they continued working on the final language for the communique. It was a far more difficult problem for the president than for the Chinese. The conservative wing of the Republican party was already spreading rumors that Nixon was going to sell out the Taiwanese Nationalists, which would be a serious political problem at home. The Chinese leaders didn't have those same kinds of concerns, since they were a dictatorship and they had no upcoming elections to be concerned about. Some people believed it might be better to just forget about a joint communique and let each side issue its own optimistic statement.

I was exhausted. We were approaching the end of my third trip to China in only a few months. I had been consumed by the planning for these trips. I was probably too tired to appreciate everything that was happening at this point or to reach any conclusions about the merits of the draft communique.

I had spent a few hours with Chou En-lai, who remains one of the most fascinating, complex people I have ever known. I sat in the meeting when we first met in October. In addition, we sat together, or near each other, at six or seven official dinners. As Henry had told us, Chou was an impressive man. He was smart and engaging, with a surprising sense of humor. While I abhorred the Communist system he represented, it was impossible to not appreciate and even like him. At times it was even possible to forget that he and Chairman Mao were responsible for the deaths of literally millions of their fellow countrymen in order to establish their Communist rule.

At the first banquet we had attended on our October trip, Henry and I sat at a round table on either side of Premier Chou. Peking duck was served, the entire Peking duck. The head had been split in half, exposing the duck's brain. In China this was considered a delicacy, so sharing it was a gesture of friendship and respect. Chou put the right side of the split head on Henry's plate and the left side on my plate. I stared at it, trying to figure out how to avoid eating it without insulting our host. There are psychologists who will tell you people can blank out when faced with a stressful situation. That's the only excuse I have for not remembering what I did. I literally have never been able to remember how I got out of that situation without embarrassing anyone. I may have eaten the duck brain. I don't know. Nor do I know how Henry survived it.

Chou En-lai was fascinated with America. It was surprising. I was sitting with a powerful world leader who was asking me questions. He did not hesitate to admit that America was far ahead of China in many areas, including technology and aerospace. China was such a young country, he said, obviously measuring time from the beginning of the Cultural Revolution. I had the impression that no matter what he was saying, he was really thinking, "But we will catch up to you."

We got into a discussion about America's focus on health. He asked me if it was true that there was a label on cigarettes warning that they caused heart attacks and cancer. "That is true," I said. He then asked me, if that was true, why didn't Americans put warning labels on butter, which also causes physical problems. The Chinese don't eat butter; and this was his attempt to make an ironic joke. We both laughed.

Chou seemed to be continually fascinated by America's young people. It amazed him that the president was willing to hand such enormous responsibility to a young man. He asked me all kinds of questions, some of which he had asked me previously during our October trip, about my age and my parents and where I'd gone to school. He was extremely interested in the role young people were playing in America. "Mr. Chapin," he said to me at one point, "you seem quite young."

"I'm thirty years old," I told him once again. My age as a subject came up with him on at least three occasions.

He considered that, then said to me, "So I admire you greatly. In this aspect we Chinese still have to catch up with you Americans because you dare to use young people."

At another dinner he offered a toast. Looking at me, he said, "I am the oldest, to the youngest: Bottoms up." And later he spoke in glowing terms to both the president and Kissinger about my work, for which I was most appreciative—proud, actually. I felt a connection with Premier Chou, one of those things you can't really explain but just feel.

In his book *Making It Perfectly Clear*, White House Communications Director Herb Klein wrote about the young staff at the White House and Chou's impression of me: "Haldeman's major mistake in forming this early staff was in bringing in too many young people in their twenties and giving them responsibility beyond their years . . . One major exception was Dwight Chapin, who had worked as a young assistant, first to Haldeman and then to Nixon, and who had a coolness of judgment which caught even the interest of Chou En-lai as Chapin met and dined with the Chinese leader while advancing the Nixon trip to Peking. Chou later told [Klein] that he moved in his government to upgrade more young people after watching Chapin in action."

I got to know Henry Kissinger much better on this journey. As it was for the president, this trip was the crowning achievement of his career—although his was still in its ascendancy—and he was determined to squeeze as much benefit out of it as possible. Henry saw the world as a chessboard, on which he enjoyed moving the pieces. For him there was a logic to global politics. Being able to play that game with men like the president and Premier Chou was his greatest delight.

Henry interjected humor when possible. There was a joke that I heard him tell our Chinese hosts several times. It was a calculated joke, told at the expense of the Russians: A Czechoslovakian was asked if he could have one wish, what would it be. He replied, "In six months the Chinese would invade Czechoslovakia." Well, if you had a second wish, what would that be? He said, "Six months after that the Czechs would be invaded by the Chinese again." When asked what his third wish would be, he said, "That the following year Czechoslovakia would be invaded by the Chinese once more." The questioner then threw up his hands and said, "But all of your wishes have been the same." And the Czech said, "Yes, but can you imagine the Chinese crossing Russia three times in two years?"

When he repeated it to Chou En-lai, the premier broke out in laughter. I noticed that even when telling a joke, Henry was the perfect diplomat. He told the joke and waited for the interpreter to repeat it. Then when his listener started laughing, Henry would laugh with him.

During the October trip, Chou En-lai would call Kissinger over to meet during the late evening hours. That was Chou's working pattern. A couple of times Henry woke me up at three thirty in the morning, after spending the night meeting with Chou, to tell me bits and pieces of what had taken place. I think he was so wound up that he just needed a safe release valve, so that he could settle down and get back to sleep. Thankfully, Chou met with Nixon during normal hours and did not expect him to meet at unusually late night hours.

At other times, again in October, when Henry was having an issue with Secretary Rogers or with Haldeman, or when he was upset about negotiations or the cables going back and forth to Washington, he used me as his shock absorber. I would sit quietly as he spoke his thoughts out loud. Maybe speaking aloud his own thoughts helped him reach some conclusions.

Another with whom I established a lasting relationship was my Chinese counterpart, Han Hsu. We had one very important thing in common: We were both representing powerful leaders. We knew the headaches. We were the point men for our delegations. When an issue came up on our side, I would talk to Han. Conversely, if his side had any problems, he would come to me. We were together in the morning, reviewing the schedule for the day; and again at night, going over plans and changes for the next day. We were together in hundreds of photographs and film footage taken during those trips, only because we were never apart.

Han eventually became head of the first Chinese Liaison Office to America and then the first Chinese ambassador to the United States. And he remained a solid friend. Han quoted, on occasion, a Chinese proverb to me: "Those who take the first steps together, walk the farthest distance." We spent considerable time together on these trips and got to know each other very well. Like me, he was married, with children, although his wife also worked in the government.

There was one moment that came several years later for which I will be forever grateful. After serving my nine-month sentence at the federal correctional institute in Lompoc, California, I finally returned home from prison. It was a joyous time. The day after I was released I was at home, in our backyard, playing with Kim and Tracy, when Susie called out that I had a call. "You won't believe who is on the phone," she said. It was Han. It was an incredibly decent and supportive gesture. The purpose of his call, he said, was to "welcome you home" and invite me to join him for a Peking duck lunch in Washington "so we could celebrate and continue our friendship." The next week I flew to Washington to join him for that special lunch at the Chinese embassy.

When we were in Hangzhou, on our last afternoon before going to Shanghai, Ron Ziegler suggested to the president that an official picture be taken with the press from all over the world who had covered the China trip. As the press grouped themselves, the president played the role of director and choreographer, as he personally placed the taller folks in the rear, the shorter people up front, and the women in the first row. He then stepped into the center of the group, and a picture that would be placed in news bureaus and press offices around the world was taken. For a media that generally had not been friendly to Nixon over the years, this was a moment when ideology gave way to the recognition of a President of the United States who had just accomplished a feat few ever thought possible. And they, like the president himself, wished to memorialize this moment in history to show they were part of it.

The last thing we did in China was release the Shanghai communique. By that time the language was still a major issue. Basically what the communique said, in diplomatic language, was that we had reached an agreement that we didn't agree on the issue of Nationalist China (Taiwan). As Premier Chou accurately stated, we were agreeing to disagree. It concluded that we would continue communicating with each other. In other words, the issue of Taiwan was not going to be a deal-breaker, but it was also not going away. That was a significant step back for the Chinese government, which previously had refused to even discuss the subject. As far as the People's Republic of China was concerned, there was only one China, and only one legitimate Chinese government. The communique was carefully worded so as to actually say as little as possible in the most serious way.

When I saw Henry Kissinger I asked how he felt it had gone. He seemed to think it was acceptable, but he told me he couldn't come down as hard as he wanted to, or would have, if he had been in Washington.

However, even that mild language wasn't enough for the conservative wing of the Republican Party. When Pat Buchanan learned the details of the communique, he was apoplectic. Later that night we were gathering at the motorcade to go to yet another banquet. Rose Woods had not come down, so I called her room. Pat answered. He had gone to her room to discuss the document with her. I told them to hurry. A few minutes later the president came down and got into his car. We were getting ready to leave when I saw Rose coming. I opened the door for her and she warned me coldly, "Don't rush me."

Okay.

She was furious. As she walked outside she snapped, "As long as we've sold out to these bastards, it doesn't make any difference."

I mentioned this to Haldeman as we rode to the banquet. He shook his head and said her reaction was simply reflecting Buchanan's.

My own feelings about the communique were mixed. I didn't think there was much to it, but whatever was in it, after all that time we had spent in China, I found myself admitting I didn't trust the Chinese government. I wasn't thinking of Han Hsu when I felt that distrust. What I felt was a distrust of the broader Chinese government. I believed that while we, representing the United States, would take an agreement like this seriously, I didn't believe it mattered to the Chinese.

At the banquet in Shanghai the following night, the president offered a toast he had scribbled on one of his yellow legal-size tablets in his suite. Little did he know at the time, his words would become the description of the trip that remains, and is used, to this day. He said: *"This trip was the week that changed the world."* Then he added, "Our two people tonight hold the future of the world in our hands." When I heard those words I immediately wondered how the Russians would react. They wouldn't like it, that was certain—which was interesting, considering it appeared that my next assignment was going to be planning the upcoming trip to Russia.

In retrospect, yes, it was "the week that changed the world," but as Chairman Mao had proclaimed, *"A single spark can start a prairie fire."* What a prairie fire of aggressiveness, influence, and trade, reaching around the world, was ignited by that week fifty years ago. Looking back I have a special appreciation for Nixon's prophetic prediction that "Within fifty years, the United States and China will be adversaries, and we need to be able to talk with one another."

The communique continued to be an issue on the flight home. Bob told me that Mrs. Nixon was questioning whether we had made a mistake. Haldeman's thought was that Rose was pushing her to discuss it with the president. Pat Buchanan also wouldn't let it go. His reaction upset the president, who believed the conservatives simply weren't dealing with reality. As Haldeman explained to me, the president believed we could no longer ignore 800 million people. Seeing the conflicting and hypercharged emotional reactions to the communique—in fact the reaction to the entire trip—reinforced the political and historical belief that only a pragmatic conservative like Richard Nixon could have opened our country's relationship with China.

Also, during the flight home, Bob told me the president had called Billy Graham, the evangelist, and Paul Keyes, the producer of the popular comedy show *Laugh-In,* from Shanghai. I joked that this was the last of our "historic firsts" on this amazing journey. It was the first time Paul Keyes had received a collect phone call from China.

An important recognition, to me, for my role in working on the China trip came from Haldeman. Our relationship for several months had been bouncing from high-highs to low-lows and back again, so I appreciated his words: "I know you are tired at this point—but you have in your mind, your memory, your movies, and your scrapbook the evidence of your participation—and in many ways your creation—of one of the greatest events of contemporary history. All of your efforts, worries, tensions, and concerns were totally worthwhile. The trip could not have been better planned or executed by anyone . . . It is the greatest satisfaction and pleasure I could ask for to see you come through in such great style. I'm proud of you as a friend and an associate."

That mattered. Coming from Bob Haldeman, it mattered a lot. I had been part of a talented team that turned a great challenge into a historic success. It was a large step forward in my life, and I assumed it meant I would be getting more such assignments as we moved into our second term following the 1972 election.

In the end, the entire traveling party, official and unofficial, totaled 391 people! We all became charter members in a unique association that President Nixon proclaimed "The Order of New China Hands." The symbol on our membership certificate, signed by the president, was a close-up picture of the president and Premier Chou's handshake at the welcoming ceremony.

There is a virtually unknown story that centers around the president's and Kissinger's secret planning of the China trip, and the fact that it was solely conducted from the White House. The previous December, between the Kissinger October 1971 trip to Peking and the Haig January 1972 trip, we made a brief trip to the Azores, Portuguese islands off the coast of Spain. While there, the president met with French President Georges Pompidou to discuss economic conditions. During the flight Haldeman, his face unusually taut, took me aside. This was the super-serious Bob. "I have a secret to tell you," he said. I was to tell no one about it. No one. I listened in stunned silence: "The military have been spying on the president and Kissinger." It took a few seconds for that information to register. It made no sense. There was a spy ring in the White House? He was talking about potential treason.

As I learned, the discovery of its existence had begun when *Washington Post* op-ed syndicated columnist Jack Anderson filed a story titled "U.S. Tilts Towards Pakistan." The gist of the article was that the president had decided to support Pakistan in its war against India because Pakistan had an ongoing relationship with China, and Nixon and Kissinger believed that might be helpful in their efforts to open China. But it wasn't so much the information in the story that was upsetting, because the story was accurate. What was disturbing was the fact that Anderson had obtained a verbatim account of Henry Kissinger's remarks at a meeting of the Washington Special Action Group. It was classified "Top Secret," supposedly known to no one outside the White House. Henry's remarks had been anti-India, and this disclosure was very embarrassing—as well as evidence Anderson had copies of the minutes of this secret meeting.

At the same time Haldeman was giving me this information, while we were in midair headed to the Azores, an internal investigation had begun at home. The mission was to find out who had leaked that information, and, more important, how the press had gotten hold of it. The Azores trip itself was a success—although Nixon caught a serious case of plane-envy. Pompidou had flown to this meeting in France's supersonic Concorde. The president traveled in our less sophisticated Boeing VC-137C SAM 26000, known as *Air Force One*. Looking at the two planes sitting near each other on the same tarmac, it looked like our past was being introduced to their future. The president had supported funding for the SST, the American supersonic jet effort to compete with the Concorde. Nixon was not happy that Congress had just voted it down.

As we got ready to board *Air Force One* and return home, the president signaled to me. "I want to go over and get on that plane," he said. It was parked about half a mile away. The Secret Service did not have an issue with that request because it had been guarded by French security. I called the motorcade back and off we went to board the Concorde. The president was really excited. He bounded up the steep stairs and we went inside. The plane was sleek and narrow. He walked all the way down the aisle, then back. He talked briefly to the French pilots and admired the design of the plane.

It turned out his quick visit to the Concorde wasn't simply a sightseeing trip. Some members of the press were waiting at the bottom of the steps as he left the plane. He told the reporters how beautiful the Concorde was and expressed his disappointment that our country, which had always been an aerospace leader, did not have the will to build our own SST. The next day the papers in the United States were filled with the president's comments about the congressional lack of will to fund the SST.

While we were in the Azores, an investigation led by John Ehrlichman and Kissinger assistant David Young had broken open the spy ring. Ironically, Young and Bud Krogh were the original Plumbers, and Bud and David had been tasked by Ehrlichman to find the leaker. The ring went right to the top at the Pentagon. The military leaders had been upset that they were being left out of the thinking, planning, and decisions being made by the president and Kissinger. The Chairman of the Joint Chiefs of Staff, Admiral Thomas Moorer, and others at the Pentagon were desperate to know what the president and Kissinger intended to do on policy concerning China and Russia. Using the Pentagon liaison office in the National Security Council as a conduit, a spy channel had been established. The head of the liaison office to begin with was Admiral Rembrandt Robinson, followed by Admiral Robert O. Welander. Both admirals used as their primary agent a young navy enlisted man who was assigned to them as a military stenographer, Yeoman Charles Radford. Yeoman Radford copied documents directly from Kissinger's briefcase. He also took contents from high-security burn bags.

According to David Young, it was Admiral Elmo Zumwalt, Chief of Naval Operations, and General Haig who worked together with Robinson and Welander to set up the spying operation. The objective was for Haig to pass information to the Pentagon without anyone knowing where it came from. As Kissinger's military assistant and later deputy, Haig needed to stay above and separate from the operation. Young confirmed this information to me in the spring of 2021.

It seems to have begun in the summer of 1970. Yeoman Radford was a trusted secretarial support person to Kissinger and Haig. He made six overseas trips with them, all the while secretly passing classified documents and information to Robinson and then Welander for the Joint Chiefs. Radford estimated that he passed more than five thousand documents to the Joint Chiefs. That was how the military first learned of the trip to China, what progress was being made at the Paris peace talks, the status of the arms limitation negotiations with the Soviets, our Vietnam strategy, and other "Eyes Only" information. The military's rationale, when caught, was that, from their point of view, Nixon and Kissinger were not working in the best interests of the United States. When caught, Radford admitted, "I took so much stuff that I can't remember everything I took."

In their book *Silent Coup,* Len Colodny and Robert Gettlin wrote that the Joint Chiefs grew "increasingly desperate through the first years of the Nixon administration, believing that the political side of the United States governing elite was undermining the military's legitimate efforts to conduct a war and to keep the country safe from external threats of harm."

From the president's point of view, of course, any bureaucratic involvement, and/or resistance, from the Department of Defense or the

Department of State would slow progress to a turtle's pace. He had a four-year term within which to accomplish his various goals and had no intention of being weighed down by the bureaucracy. An additional issue was confidentiality. He wanted to avoid press leaks designed to undermine the administration. Nixon knew that at the State Department, and at every cabinet department and government agency, leaking was a flourishing and long-established cottage industry. Whether the leaks were for spite, for ideology, for personal gain, and/or because people like to talk and inflate their own sense of importance, the result was the same. Nixon knew that 99 percent of his proposals and policies would die the death of a thousand leaks unless he kept them confidentially close.

Uncovering this spy ring inside the White House was like peeling an onion. As the investigation continued, it became clear that more and more people were involved. Starting with the Joint Chiefs of Staff, eventually the list included Secretary of Defense Mel Laird. Nixon was furious, calling it "a federal offense of the highest order." Nixon told Ehrlichman, "I want the hard proof," and Ehrlichman's Plumbers got it. According to John Mitchell biographer James Rosen, "Nixon wanted to prosecute Moorer for espionage but was convinced by Attorney General John N. Mitchell that the ensuing controversy would imperil all of Nixon's secret foreign policy initiatives and do grave damage to the armed forces." The president, taking Mitchell's advice, decided it would serve no purpose to go public with this revelation. In fact, the president thought it might negatively affect both the China and Russia trips. In addition, the fact that his own military thought it was necessary to spy on the President of the United States could only have complex and negative consequences. In his own memoirs, Nixon spends less than one page on this important episode, which is a clue that he didn't want to give it much historical attention.

Shortly thereafter, Yeoman Radford was transferred to some faraway post. Nixon and Mitchell decided the attorney general would invite Mitchell's old friend Admiral Moorer to his apartment in the Watergate for drinks. During that meeting Mitchell told Moorer, essentially, "Tom, the president asked me to talk with you. He knows about the spying, about what's going on. It is to be stopped immediately. Understood? Let's get on with the business of the nation."

The next morning the attorney general paid a visit to the Oval Office and informed the president: "Tom got your message." When John Ehrlichman learned about this meeting he responded confidently, "Now he is our admiral," meaning that in the high-stakes game of political intrigue, the president "owned" Admiral Moorer.

However, as it turned out, Nixon probably was not aware of everyone who was involved in the spying. For a moment he suspected that General Haig, Kissinger's deputy, could be part of the ring. However, Ehrlichman convinced him that Haig was not—even though David Young says he was insisting Haig was not just a participant but the key figure in the White House. In his handwritten notes from December 23, 1971, Ehrlichman reports meeting with the president and Haldeman. His last notation was probably a comment from Nixon: "Don't let K [Kissinger] blame Haig."

Ehrlichman's conclusion appears not to have been accurate. The bottom line, I've come to believe, is that Al Haig did his best to bury his own connection to the spy ring. As recently as 2021 David Young confirmed to me his belief that Haig and Admiral Zumwalt had helped set it all up. The truth of this was not verified for years, but the historic evidence seems to substantiate the facts of Haig's complicity. Haig was an ambitious guy. He saw a big political future for himself. He was going to be president, or head of the Joint Chiefs, or secretary of state, and he couldn't allow this to interfere with his career. Ultimately he did become secretary of state in the Reagan administration. Beyond that I was a guest at a fundraiser luncheon for him in 1987 as he explored the idea of running for the presidency.

When I did find out about Al's involvement from tapes released years later, it began to make sense. Haig was as political as anyone in the White House. He would come into my office two or three times a week when he was really angry. "Henry and the president are nuts," he'd say. "They're getting ready to . . ." then fill in the blank. I guess he thought it was safe to blow off steam with me, or perhaps he thought I might make a good ally. It was interesting, too, to recall the confidential talks we had on the January 1972 China trip. I listened. I smiled. But I never responded. In retrospect, I never understood the depth of the palace intrigue taking place right in front of me. Amazingly, it seems that the president was also unaware.

Had the president pursued the spy matter to the very end, I believe he would have discovered Al Haig's involvement. Then, rather than bringing Haig in as Chief of Staff to replace Haldeman, when the president had to eventually fire Haldeman in the heat of Watergate, Haig would have been fired earlier. My belief is that Haig, as Chief of Staff, did not serve the president well in the months before the president decided to resign.

The discovery of the spy ring was one of my greatest shocks and disappointments while working in the White House. However, within weeks it had been almost forgotten in the euphoria that followed the China trip.

For me, events were moving so fast I couldn't stand still and enjoy the acknowledgment and praise I was receiving for my work on the China trip. I was back in the basement bunker, already deeply involved in planning the president's trip into the heart of the Union of Soviet Socialist Republics.

13

NEXT STOP: THE KREMLIN

While the historic nature of the trip to China dominated the headlines, the trip to Russia was also historic and more immediately productive in the president's attempt to end the Cold War. President Franklin Roosevelt had visited Russia, but no American president had ever been to Moscow. Richard Nixon was going to the Kremlin to sign the Strategic Arms Limitation Treaty, known as SALT, that for the first time would slow the nuclear arms race and perhaps lead to additional agreements that might prevent the Cold War from heating up. While the Shanghai communique, the document signed in China, said basically, "We'll agree to disagree on what we disagree on and then move ahead on the things we agree on," the SALT agreement was perceived to be a tenuous first step toward mutual disarmament.

Begun in late 1969, negotiations had been going on for almost three years. This was a second major foreign policy achievement for both President Nixon and Kissinger. Like the China initiative, it was very controversial, especially among the conservative wing of the Republican Party. There was incredible distrust within the United States among conservatives and also on the other side in the Soviet Union. Making progress required someone like Nixon, who long before had established his political bona fides to turn disarmament into reality. I was assigned to lead the advance party to Russia with Air Force General Brent Scowcroft, Deputy Assistant to the President for National Security Affairs, who was Henry's assistant on the National Security Council.

The two trips, to China and Russia, were as different from each other as the Chinese were from the Russians. The Chinese were well mannered, intelligent, and curious. The Russians we dealt with were basically thugs, according to Kissinger, "who will plug away to try to pick up pennies whereas the Chinese take a long-range historical perspective." It was always difficult to get the Chinese to commit to scheduling an event, but when they did, the event would unfold as we had agreed, or they would tell me in advance about any changes they wanted to make. On the other hand, the Russians would agree to something that either would never happen or, if it did happen, would bear little resemblance to what we had agreed. And in Russia, interactions between our delegation and the Russians actually got physical.

From the very beginning the Russia trip lacked the excitement of the trip to China. Maybe that was because the Chinese were still a mysterious unknown entity while the Russians were a fairly well-known adversary. Maybe the fact that an American president was going to Moscow for the first time simply didn't generate the excitement or the curiosity of a visit to . . . the Forbidden City! Also, the Russia trip was the second of the two. It was more of a working trip than the dramatic trip that had initiated the United States' diplomatic relationship with the People's Republic of China.

One of the first things we were told on the airplane was to be very careful about using the "back channel," our clandestine CIA agent in Russia. Apparently he worked in the decoding room in our embassy in Moscow and no one was sure that even our ambassador, Jacob Beam, knew his identify. At Henry's direction, much of what we did in Russia was to be kept secret from Ambassador Beam. This had to do with the inability of the State Department to maintain confidentiality. Both the president and Henry wanted to minimize the probability of leaks. In China we had neither an embassy nor State Department employees. In Moscow we had an established embassy with a large number of bureaucrats, and that increased the possibility of leaked information making its way back to the State Department in Washington. Nixon and Kissinger didn't want us to get bogged down in any part of that bureaucratic web and were fixated on keeping all arrangements and knowledge as confidential as possible.

We also were warned that the Russians might try to seduce us with vodka and women. We were told that when we met an attractive woman in a public space, we should assume she was working as a spy for the government. As I wrote in my notes, "All of our guys are red-blooded men and they may succumb to the treatment they're likely to confront." The good news is that no one succumbed, but the Russians did try.

The president was going to spend the first night of the trip in Salzburg, Austria. We stopped there to inspect the residence—actually a palace—where he would be staying. We were not impressed when they proudly informed us that Hitler had stayed there when visiting Austria.

The security on this trip was far more extensive than it had been during the China trip. When we got to the American Embassy we were first taken to a room on the top floor, where we stepped into a plastic cube, which was supposed to be completely soundproof and bugproof. The Russians were known to bombard our embassy with listening devices, so this was considered the most secure place to talk. Most major U.S. embassies around the world have these secure rooms.

A lot of the scheduling for the president's foreign trips was routine. But a problem arose when the Russians insisted that the president use a Russian aircraft when flying inside the country. We had caved to the Chinese on this issue so there was no way we could make a credible stand against it with the Russians. Though nobody, particularly the Secret Service, was really comfortable with this, we finally agreed to fly on their planes.

There were other issues. The president wanted to address the Russian people on live television. However, the Russians wanted to tape it, telling us they intended to play it the day we left the USSR. We didn't like that. There was no guarantee they would ever play it—or that they would play it unedited. The Russians were aware that Nixon had made a very effective televised address to the Russian people on his trip in 1959.

Reading my notes from this trip, I noted how beautiful the ambassador's private residence was, then added with an eye toward the future: "Maybe I wouldn't mind being an ambassador at a post such as this." At that time this kind of pipe dream was not just plausible, it was possible. I was thirty-two years old and was already an experienced White House veteran. I had made important and powerful friends and acquaintances in the years I'd worked with Mr. Nixon, and I felt I had earned a reputation as a hardworking, competent young man on the way up. And, like almost everyone else in the administration, I was ambitious. I had plans, even if I didn't know exactly what form they might take. However, a world of possibilities had opened for me. Absolutely anything seemed possible.

The city of Moscow was quite a contrast with Peking. We had been warned the city was stark. However, unlike Peking, it felt vibrant and alive. It was brightly lit. There were people on the streets. There was traffic, and I noted that there were men and women walking hand in hand. That show of affection was something I had not seen in Peking.

The Russians with whom we met to plan the president's itinerary generally were serious and somber. At a luncheon a senior member of their delegation offered a toast. "A head of state was visiting Georgia," he began. "At a dinner during that trip a Georgian, who obviously had had too much to drink, stood up to offer the toast. 'To the head of state's coffin!'" he said. When we heard the translation, we were startled. This was not something we expected to hear in Russia. But then the man continued: "'May your coffin be the most beautiful coffin in the world. May it be made out of hundred-year-old oak." Everyone thought he was out of his mind. And then he finished: "And may that oak tree be planted today." The laughter was as much in relief as in response to the story. Who knew Russians had a sense of humor?

As usual when advancing a trip, we toured all the sites the president would visit. Whatever my expectations had been about the Kremlin, the reality exceeded them. As beautiful as the Vatican was, it paled in comparison to the Kremlin. St. George's Hall inside the Kremlin was astonishingly beautiful, the most spectacular large space I had ever seen. There was nothing in Washington to compare with it. We shopped at GUM, the largest, mostly empty department store in the world, and we were treated to a performance of *Swan Lake* at the Bolshoi Ballet.

With the experience of China behind us I was feeling quite confident, and I had no problem standing up to the Russians. When we were in Leningrad (now known as Saint Petersburg), I raised several points, causing their Deputy Chief of Protocol to warn me, "You raise questions and cause problems now, but we will cause problems later."

I understood the threat. It was important to stand up to these people, to set the tone. "Sir," I told him, "if you already have the intent to cause problems then you are not the kind of people we wish to work with."

Attempting to negotiate world peace was not always easy. While it seemed the natural stance for me to take at that moment, I became aware I was feeling a new level of self-confidence.

An essential aspect of Communism is the elimination of religion, Marx's "opiate of the people." Toward that end, the Communist regime confiscated church property, ridiculed religion, harassed believers, and propagated atheism in the schools. Actions toward particular religions, however, were determined by state interests, and most organized religions were never officially outlawed.

On Sunday in Leningrad, in order to make a point about the importance of religion in our lives in America, we asked to go to church. The Russians at first pushed back and then eventually agreed to take us to a very old Christian church. The church was virtually empty, without a single pew. Everyone was standing. In attendance were only a couple of dozen old women, all dressed in black. The women were Christian widows of soldiers who had died in WWII, or so we were told. The bleakness and sadness of it all left a lasting impression.

On this first trip we managed to get a sense of Russian history. We were taken to the graveyard where hundreds of thousands of people who died in the siege of Leningrad against Hitler had been buried. We also went to the Hermitage, one of the largest and most impressive museums in the world. We were given special treatment at the Hermitage with a visit to the private, nonpublic archives where some of the most valuable national treasures are on display.

There was an odd occurrence toward the end of the trip. We had scheduled a meeting with Ambassador Beam. The meeting was to have included the top officer of the KGB, the thuggish Committee for State Security of the Soviet Union. However, the KGB officer was strangely absent from the meeting. Not until two days later, in Iran, did we learn from the newspapers what had happened. At the same time we were in Moscow advancing the president's upcoming trip, Henry Kissinger had also been there, secretly meeting with Soviet General Secretary Leonid Brezhnev. Ambassador Beam, who was with us, had no idea that Kissinger was in town. However, the KGB officer clearly knew. It turned out that on the day we left Washington, the president had ordered the military to resume bombing the North Vietnamese cities of Hanoi and Haiphong. Kissinger was in Russia to determine whether or not the president's trip would be canceled as a result of the bombing. We knew nothing about any of this while we were there. It was impossible to know if the Russians with whom we were meeting were aware of it. All we did know was that key people were missing from our meetings without any explanation.

When we got back to Washington, Henry told me that he had met with Brezhnev and, while the Russians were upset about the timing of the bombing, the trip probably was still going to happen. The Soviets had been embarrassed by the worldwide recognition and consequences of the China trip and had, in fact, tried to maneuver to have the Russian trip come first. Despite the provocation of the Vietnam bombing, it would have been doubly humiliating for the Russians to have their summit canceled.

From Leningrad we went to Kiev in Ukraine. In the Russian tradition, vodka was served, toasts were made, and more vodka was served. One of the most difficult aspects of this entire advance trip was saying, "No thank you" to the next vodka, and meaning it. No glass remained empty for long. As I wrote in my notes about our banquet: "We had, besides the vodka, red and white wine and champagne. Everybody drank. Personally, I only had about three glasses of vodka and some champagne and was feeling no pain."

After leaving Leningrad, on our way home, we stopped in Tehran. Iran, at that time, was governed by the Shah, Mohammad Reza Pahlavi. Under his leadership, Iran was moving slowly and deliberately into the Western world. It was a loud, bustling city, complete with American-style traffic jams and crazy, wild drivers. We were told about the number of pedestrians who were killed each year, hit by vehicles on the streets of Tehran. It was a staggering number, very high. I noted that everywhere we went we saw pictures of the Shah, the empress, and the royal family, all to make us and the population believe, "They are obviously very beloved people." I continued, there seems to be a . . . "very sincere warmth of the people toward Americans and the United States."

The final stop on the president's trip was Warsaw, Poland. The government had proposed a very full schedule. The president knew that toward the end of a long international trip he would be ready to wrap it up and head home. It became my job to pare down the Warsaw visit to the minimum without letting anyone know I was doing so at the president's request. I knew the president so well by this point that it was easy for me to determine what he would want to do or not do, when he wanted to do it, even with whom he would do it. Having Mrs. Nixon along on the trip made arrangements slightly more complicated, as we also had to figure out a schedule for her.

However, I was making good progress when Haldeman told me the SALT summit was in jeopardy. It appeared the Russians had over-promised what they would actually be capable of delivering, and the president was contemplating canceling the trip. Kissinger had made another secret one-night trip to Paris for a meeting that apparently had not gone well.

My job had now morphed into having to continue to plan a trip that Haldeman was telling me would most likely be canceled. Nothing could feel more tedious than planning a complex trip that is likely not going to happen. We never ran out of details to deal with, such as how many people would be going, where we would be staying, when and what we would be visiting, and how every hour would be filled. I didn't make decisions so much as recommendations to Bob as to what was possible and desirable. The size of our delegation kept shifting. The Secret Service, in particular, requested a large number of slots, claiming security needs in Russia were significantly higher than they had been in China. In reality, as I learned much later from Bob Taylor, a great number of those people actually were intelligence operatives and espionage experts who intended to use the trip as cover for other assignments.

Less than a week before we were scheduled to depart, our communications consultant Tex McCrary had drafted a statement we could issue in case the summit was canceled. We knew the Democrats would use the cancelation of the trip to attack the president, so we wanted to get ahead of their attacks and make certain it was clear that the Russians were the ones responsible. Tex suggested: "The succession of efforts by six Presidents of the United States to achieve lasting peace on earth and goodwill among all nations has once more been cut down from Moscow . . . Once more, rejection, while Moscow through Hanoi holds hostage American prisoners and the American electorate."

In fact, until *Air Force One* took off from Andrews Air Force Base on May 20, 1972, we were never certain this trip was actually going to happen. We were all completely worn out from the planning. Kissinger said he was as tired when we departed as he was when he finished the China trip. I knew exactly how he felt.

We stayed in a veritable palace in Salzburg. It was gorgeous but could house only a portion of our official party. I made the mistake of placing myself there instead of Rose Woods. She was not happy about that and did not hesitate to complain to the president. Rose and Mrs. Nixon were very close, so I'm sure the president took it seriously when Rose also expressed her anger to Mrs. Nixon. However, I needed to stay in the palace because I was running the trip and that's where the president and Haldeman were staying. The fact that there was limited room didn't soothe Rose's feeling of being shunted aside. I had always had a wonderful relationship with her, so knowing she was upset on the first overnight stop of our Russia trip was not a great start to the trip for me.

As usual, I spent considerable time with Kissinger on this trip. As we took a walk one afternoon, he told me he was going to return to China in early summer, which he thought would be a good follow-up to this trip. It seemed to me he was trying to balance these two trips. As he had liked and respected Chou En-lai, he felt similarly about the Soviet Minister of Foreign Affairs, Andrei Gromyko. He was an excellent man, Henry told me, very knowledgeable, very astute, and then he compared Gromyko to Secretary of State Rogers, who he believed was miscast in his role. In fact, Henry told me the president was going to tell Rogers some of what was planned for the trip to Russia—but he was not going to give him the entire working scenario. The administration's distrust of the State Department bureaucracy went very deep. Kissinger was concerned about the president's desire to discuss Russia plans with Rogers, fearing Nixon would tell him too much. The president liked Rogers personally and therefore, to compensate for not including him in important diplomatic plans, he might begin offering him some plums of rather inconsequential summit information. As I listened, I was thinking of how, at times, the intrigues of world politics can have petty, high school overtones.

Part of my assignment on this trip was to brief the president on the ceremonial details of our arrival. Once when I opened the door to the president's cabin I was surprised to hear him reading aloud the toast he was to give at that evening's dinner. In all the years I had been with him, in all the hotel rooms, on all the flights, I had never seen him rehearsing a toast aloud before.

We had all been briefed by the Secret Service on what to expect. They warned us that our hotel rooms undoubtedly would be bugged and secretly monitored. They went so far as to suggest that the women traveling with us, in order to ensure their privacy, might want to change clothes under a sheet. We were all given little soundboxes that played a recording of people talking with loud music in the background. When we were going to have an important conversation, we were advised to put the device between us and turn it on, then lean close and speak softly to each other, in order that the Russians couldn't eavesdrop.

Our first afternoon, once again—as happened in China—the president "disappeared." He was taken by the Russians to meet secretly with General Secretary Leonid Brezhnev. With no regard whatsoever for our meticulous planning, the Russians had absconded with the president. I had no idea where they went.

By the next afternoon it was clear to me the president was upset about something. As he went through the scheduled activities, he seemed fine enough and gracious, but I could discern there was a problem, a certain uptightness. I guessed he may have been feeling that he was being pushed around, and he had no intention of letting the Russians take advantage of him. Only later did I learn they were still negotiating provisions of the arms agreement and it was not going well. In addition to the SALT agreement, he was going to sign several other documents, including an environmental pact. During that ceremony Nixon was testy. After the document was signed, champagne was served. The president quickly took one sip for the cameras, then put down his glass. He made it very clear he had no intention of clanking glasses or drinking champagne with the Russians.

Whatever was going on, I was not privy to it. Bob told me later that that morning at four thirty the president had gotten up, gotten dressed, and simply walked around the Kremlin grounds for about an hour. This was not unusual. He often was up very early in the morning, and, considering the difficulty we all were having in adapting to the time change, it made sense. But still, there was something almost poetic about the thought of staunch anti-Communist Richard Nixon exploring the Kremlin very early in the dark morning.

The president would have made a great tour guide. Nell Yates was with him at one point when he suddenly started talking about Napoleon's attempt to capture Moscow. I had seen that before. We would be somewhere and he would start talking extemporaneously about a site, describing great events that had occurred there, almost as if he was playing a recording of the past in his mind.

What bothered me most about this trip was how little control we had of events. Here we were again, experiencing the same kind of continual schedule changes we had experienced in China. Every day the schedule changed at the whim of the Russians. There were days we would get started in the morning with no idea of what would be happening that afternoon. This was not only true of the president's schedule, it also was true of Kissinger's, Rogers's, and just about everyone else's. The second morning, for example, the president was scheduled to lay a wreath on Russia's Tomb of the Unknown Soldier. A high-ranking Soviet military officer was going to accompany us, so I agreed we would use a Russian car. But the Russians refused to allow a Secret Service agent to ride with the president in the car, which clearly wasn't acceptable. To solve the issue the Secret Service placed one of our cars directly in front of the entrance to the Kremlin. The Russians were furious when the president walked out of his residence and went directly into our car. One of their KGB agents went to Ron Walker's nearby hotel room and raised hell. He was so angry he could barely talk. I had the impression he was worried, literally, that his throat was going to be slit. Ron and I were just as angry, although happily we had no fear of facing a possible life-threatening consequence.

The entire world was watching in awe as the leaders of the two great superpowers took a first tentative step toward disarmament. Meanwhile, the problems we were really wrestling with, such as whose car we were going to use, were far more mundane. These types of issues became significant as they pitted our Secret Service against the Soviet's KGB. At the conclusion of one meeting the president had with Brezhnev, the KGB directed him and the Soviet leaders through a back part of the Kremlin and put them all into a Russian limo. This was done without informing our Secret Service, although in that instance Bill

Duncan, the head of our security detail on the trip, rode with him. The two leaders, the president and Brezhnev, were driven to a boat and taken to a dacha to have dinner with Brezhnev, Soviet Premier Alexei Kosygin, and Nikolai Podgorny, the Chairman of the Presidium of the Supreme Soviet.

Meanwhile, I was dealing with my own problems. Brezhnev had requested we officially gift him with a Cadillac. He was a "car guy" and wanted—expected—a new car at each USA and USSR summit. That was not the type of gift that would fit into our State Department's "gifting to heads of state" protocol. It was on the extravagant side, to put it mildly. So we had to figure out how to disguise the gift of the Cadillac as something other than what it was, but Brezhnev got his Cadillac.

It was impossible to not continually compare the Russians with the Chinese. In just about every way the Chinese seemed more refined, more sophisticated, and more mindful of the purpose of our meetings. I remember watching as Brezhnev was walking with the president. In order to point something out to the president, Brezhnev grabbed him by the lapels of his jacket. There was no finesse in his gesture. It was commandeering. I knew how much Nixon hated—hated!—being grabbed like that.

Conversely, nothing we saw in China compared to the unique physical beauty of the Kremlin and Red Square.

We had arrived on Monday, May 22, 1972. The initial plan had been to sign the SALT agreement sometime Friday, but on Friday negotiations were still taking place. Things changed hourly. The SALT signing was going to be postponed until Sunday. Then it was going to take place Friday evening. Then it wasn't going to happen at all.

Our reciprocal dinner was scheduled for that Friday night. It was held at Spaso House, in Moscow, the beautiful residence of our American ambassador. The performance by American pianist Van Cliburn, whose legendary career had begun in 1958, when he won the inaugural International Tchaikovsky Competition in Moscow, was a highlight of the evening. He began by playing both the American and Russian national anthems, which was a highly emotional moment. I literally had tears in my eyes. For those few minutes I forgot all the hassles, all the frustrations, all the anger, and I could actually believe we were there to accomplish something very important for the world.

The signing ceremony was finally scheduled that evening for eleven o'clock. It was to take place in the Great Hall, officially St. Vladimir's Hall, inside the Kremlin. Mrs. Nixon wanted to go with the president to witness this historic event, but Nixon felt he couldn't take her because the other leaders were not bringing their wives.

There were still some small technical disagreements in the document when it was signed, but both sides decided to overlook them. Mrs. Nixon actually came into the room with the president, then stepped behind a column to watch the official signing. I thought it was such a special moment. I took pictures of her kind of peeking out from behind the white marble pillar. She stood there throughout the entire ceremony.

A great cheer burst out when the president and General Secretary Brezhnev signed the SALT agreement. Then they stood together and shook hands for the cameras. "We want to be remembered by our deeds," the president said, "not by the fact we brought war to the world but by the fact that we made the world a more peaceful one for all peoples of the world."

Premier Alexei Kosygin responded, "This is a great victory for the Soviet and American peoples in the matter of easing international tension. This is a victory for all peace-loving people, because security and peace is a common goal."

It was difficult to reconcile the reality that some Americans considered the president to be a warmonger while he had just negotiated and signed what some experts consider to be the most important arms limitation agreement in history.

When the signing ended, Mrs. Nixon was waiting for the president in the hallway. Then they returned together, hand in hand, to their residence in the Kremlin.

The next day there was a large celebratory reception. The celebration was overflowing with champagne, vodka, and caviar. Diplomats from most of the nations that had established relationships with the Russians had been invited. They attended in uniforms and national costumes. Arabs were dressed in robes. Dictatorships were in sharp uniforms. I hadn't seen anything like it since being with the president at a reception following Charles de Gaulle's funeral in Paris. And in the middle of it all, a satisfied smile on his face, responding to the toasts, stood Richard Nixon.

This wasn't one of those "pinch me, I can't believe I'm here" moments. I felt that I had earned the right to be there. Having been handed the assignment of putting the trip together, I had done it. Earlier I might have felt like an intruder, but not then. I was proud of what I had accomplished, and I was looking forward to eventually sitting down with Bob Haldeman to talk about possibilities regarding my post–White House plans.

We flew to Leningrad the following morning on a Russian airplane. It actually was quite impressive: quiet, fast, and comfortable. Aboard the plane I learned there had been a real dust-up after the SALT signing. Apparently Gerry Smith, who was a key arms control negotiator from the State Department, had taken Kissinger's place at a press conference and essentially bungled his responses. He was neither upbeat nor positive, and he gave no credit to the president for his role in making the SALT agreement a reality. Gerard Smith was a very clever career bureaucrat who understood how to play the State Department game. At one point during the preliminary negotiations he gave an aide two telegrams to be sent to Secretary of State Rogers. The first one outlined the point he wanted to make. The second one, which he ordered sent half an hour after the first one, instructed the recipients to ignore the first one and destroy all copies, claiming it had been sent without his authorization. His reasoning was that the first telegram probably would be overlooked in the flood of cables, but the second telegram would pique their interest in the first one. They would dig it out and read it.

That was typical State Department reasoning and behavior. The

Smith situation was a perfect example of why the president and Kissinger never trusted the State Department and didn't want the bungling bureaucrats involved in any of their efforts. Henry was irate that Smith was denigrating the president and that inaccurate information was being given to the press. Actually, he was beyond irate. When the president learned what had happened, he ordered Gerard Smith to be fired. As he thought about it, and became even angrier, he ordered that Secretary Rogers also be fired. Then, typical Nixon, he calmed down and managed to calm Henry down. The media never heard a word about the fact that the president almost fired the U.S. Secretary of State and one of the agreement's principal negotiators on the night of the triumphant signing of the Strategic Arms Limitation Treaty.

I was pleased to have only learned about it later, as I had slept through the whole mess.

We spent a pleasant next day in Leningrad. The president placed a wreath at a cemetery, smiled throughout a luncheon, toured the Summer Palace, and read his prepared remarks. It felt almost like a campaign stop of a decade earlier. It all felt rote to the point that I was wondering if the president was even thinking about where he was.

We returned to Moscow for the Sunday night speech the president was going to make to the people of the Soviet Union. His speech would focus on a little Russian girl by the name of Tanya. He had read about Tanya and her family on his trip to the Leningrad war cemetery earlier that day and personally written her story into his remarks. This would be another of our "historic firsts," addressing the Soviet nation live. He had addressed the Russian people in a taped broadcast in August of 1959, when he was vice president and had visited Russia for nine days. But here he was eleven years later and this night, due to our negotiations, his address would be live.

The speech was scheduled for 8:30 P.M. At 8:00 P.M., I received a call that I needed to get over to the makeshift press studio, which had been set up for the president's address. KGB goons were playing hardball with our American press contingent. There were some minor confrontations, pushing and shoving, and some insults were being flung at our press. Fortunately it was kept under control by our Secret Service and some KGB agents. The president gave a wonderful speech, telling the Soviet citizens that we now had a real opportunity to work together for the good of the world.

Following the speech we had arranged a photo opportunity for both the American and Soviet press to capture the spirit of the event. Unfortunately, the tensions that had been building all night in the press area finally erupted into a brawl. White House photographer Ollie Atkins was taking photos when Soviet thugs, "KGB security," grabbed hold of him and started pulling him out of the room. Ollie fought back. One of the Russian agents put him in a stranglehold. I grabbed that guy and pushed him against the wall. Haldeman rushed in and pushed another Russian aside. A fight had broken out at a peace conference. The KGB types were shoving, grabbing, knocking people to the ground. The Russians seemed to be enjoying this. The whole thing lasted less than a minute, but it was stunningly inappropriate. Brawling was probably not the best way to form lasting friendships.

Our final day in Moscow was mostly ceremonial. Nixon met with the troika of Soviet leaders: Brezhnev, Kosygin, and Podgorny, as well as several Russian cosmonauts. Kosygin and Podgorny came to the airport for one final display of friendship. After the traditional handshakes, we piled into the Soviet plane, somewhat relieved that this part of the trip was over. Our departure was being televised back in the United States. Bob Haldeman was actually on the phone with his wife, Jo. She told him that she was at that very moment watching our departure on NBC's *Today Show*. The stairway was pulled away from the plane and we waited for the engines to roar to life. Finally they started, but then they stopped. It's never a good sign when you're expecting to take off and the pilot turns off the engines. We waited. I looked out the window. Podgorny and Kosygin were standing there, looking at the plane. After a few minutes someone approached them and spoke. Podgorny started waving his arms, and the stairway was reattached to the side of the plane.

The door opened and Podgorny, Kosygin, and two other men walked down the aisle, directly to the president. Podgorny had a very stern look on his face. Through the interpreter he told the president, "I'm sorry. There is a problem with this airplane. We are going to have to change airplanes." After all the negotiations that had resulted in our being on this plane, this was a major embarrassment for the Russians.

The president handled it easily. "We'll work it out," he said.

Podgorny pointed to the man standing next to him. "This is the Director of Civil Aviation. This is his responsibility, and he is at fault," he said. "We will do anything to him you tell us to do." It was very funny, but not really. I had little doubt that if Nixon had said, "Assassinate him," Podgorny would have had someone pull out a gun and kill him right there on the spot. However, Nixon did not suggest that. Instead he said, "Oh, it's not his fault. I've been on many airplanes in different countries, and mechanical problems happen." In fact, he added that the man probably should be promoted because he found the problem before anyone was endangered. We all got off the plane and climbed into the backup plane, sitting and waiting to take off as all the food and baggage was transferred. Meanwhile, the Russians had shut down the satellite feed, cutting off the broadcast. Jo Haldeman had watched us board the plane—and then the connection was cut. As we were sitting on the backup plane waiting to take off, Bob got a call through the White House signal operator from Jo, wondering if everything was okay. She was worried because the *Today Show* had pulled the plug on the live feed. We laughed about it then, but we laughed about it a lot harder once we were safely on the ground in Ukraine.

The president's schedule in Kiev consisted of more ceremonies; more toasts, and more sometimes forced smiles.

I think we were all very happy to be leaving the Soviet Union the following afternoon. While the country was beautiful, the people we had to deal with were difficult. I might have felt differently if we had been allowed to meet the Russian people, but we weren't. Everywhere we went, barriers were set up to prevent us from having an opportunity to talk to real people. On some roads, buses and trucks were lined up nose to nose or back to back, and crowds were kept back by soldiers. As we moved from place to place in our motorcade, we could see people on balconies waving to us, but other than the workers in hotels, the only people we met were government officials, designated drivers, and translators.

As we left I wrote, "I have become even more anti-Soviet or anti-Communist in terms of the system. I have a great hatred for these people and the way they handle other people. Maybe I'm just too much of a romanticist . . . it burns me to the bone to see their attitude."

From Moscow we flew to Iran, an oil-rich country moving into the Western sphere. Everything in Iran was lavish, big, and beautiful. As it turned out, though, visiting Iran and meeting the Shah at that moment was the equivalent of meeting Czar Nicholas a few years prior to the Russian Revolution.

In Tehran we all moved along the protocol line and met the Shah, his wife, Farah Pahlavi, and their family. SAVAK, the secret police that the Shah and our CIA had established for the protection of his dynasty, did an excellent job in discreetly keeping their distance the first day we were there. They were exercising complete control over the population in order to protect both the Shah's family and our American delegation from the militant mullahs who were threatening the Shah's rule. The Shah's ironclad control preexisted and continued after the Nixon visit until 1979 when the Shah was forced to leave the country.

The following morning, as our motorcade prepared to depart for a sightseeing outing, we were informed that there had been a terrorist bombing during the night. We were told that Ray Price had been in a car that was hit by a bomb and that both his legs were broken. Ray Price was the president's chief speechwriter on this trip. It was stunning news, disastrous and difficult to believe. I immediately contacted Ron Walker so he could let all the members of our contingent know they were not to go out among the public. It seemed obvious the attack was connected to the president's visit. This trip was developing into the Secret Service's worst nightmare.

General Brent Scowcroft, serving as Kissinger's deputy, was on the trip. When I saw him, I asked about Ray Price's condition. "You mean General Price?" he asked. As it turned out, the Ray Price who had been injured was General Ray Price, a person assigned to our embassy in Tehran. We were obviously disturbed to learn of General Price's condition, but at the same time, it was a relief to us all that it wasn't the Ray Price we knew so well from the White House.

The president came downstairs in the guesthouse with Haldeman a little after eight thirty on the morning he was planning to lay a wreath at the Rey mausoleum. The mausoleum was revered by the Shah. He had had it built for his father, Iran's previous leader, who was buried there. I was informed that a bomb had gone off there ten minutes earlier. This was particularly bad news because we had believed the mausoleum was a secure site. Bob Taylor explained that a timing device had detonated the bomb and that there might be additional bombs hidden in the area. Both our Secret Service and the Iranians subtly suggested that the president cancel the event.

The president decided to leave it up to the Iranians. If the Shah wanted him to attend the ceremony, he would go, even against the recommendation of his Secret Service detail.

I contacted the Iranian Chief of Protocol. He told me the Shah wanted the president to do what he thought was best. He said if our security advised against it perhaps he shouldn't go, but he left it as the president's decision. I responded that the president wanted to do whatever His Majesty felt was best. This back and forth went on for forty-five minutes. It could have gone on all afternoon. Finally the president said he would prefer to go ahead with the laying of the wreath. The Shah's representative responded that the Shah would prefer that too. That settled it. We were all feeling very tense as we drove to the city of Rey.

In contrast to the way we were feeling, cheering crowds lined our route. After the absence of cheering crowds in China and Russia, this was very welcome. The president quickly laid the wreath at the mausoleum without incident. As we were getting back into our cars, I was informed that another bomb had been exploded in a car about two blocks away. We did our best to move quickly, without it appearing that we were in semi-panic mode to get out of there as fast as possible. The motorcade raced back into Tehran at high speed.

Our last morning in Tehran, we were driven to the airport in a limo that the Iranian government provided for us. The motorcade raced past large crowds waiting for us. I knew that racing past the crowds infuriated the president. If people had spent the time coming out to greet the President of the United States, he believed those people should be acknowledged. Speeding past them as if they weren't there was not the way he wanted to leave the country. He felt if we had been in our own cars, we could have set the pace of the motorcade and spent some time greeting the Iranian people who had come out to honor him. When we got back to Washington, he told Haldeman he would never again take a trip without using our aircraft and our cars.

We left Tehran and flew to our final stop, Warsaw, in Poland. Large groups of people strained to see the president everywhere we went. Polish soldiers struggled to hold them back. This was the kind of reception the president loved. He participated in the official ceremonies because they were required, but what he sincerely enjoyed was meeting the people. In Warsaw, for example, as we drove back into the city after laying the wreath at their Tomb of the Unknown Soldier, we stopped the motorcade, as planned. The president got out and started shaking hands. "The incredible thing," I wrote, "was that the crowd acted like a magnet and the president . . . was drawn to them . . . They chanted 'Nixon, Nixon,' 'Long Live Nixon' . . . on and on . . . As he worked the crowd, our Secret Service went out of their minds."

The president worked one side of the street, then crossed and walked down the other side. The crowd was starting to push through the barriers and engulf our cars. There was some shoving by the Secret Service to hold them back. Children were there, who were also being shoved. It was a spectacular event, reminiscent of the height of the presidential campaigns. For the president, it was déjà vu because a similar situation had taken place on his 1959 trip to Poland. This was Nixon at his political best, clearly enjoying the direct connection he could make with the people. But as the crowds pushed harder to be close to him, it was starting to feel dangerous. As we continued to fight the crowd, we got the president back into his car. The motorcade began moving through the crowd. Bob Taylor and I were in the control car, from which Bob could issue orders. When our driver had to slam on his brakes, Bob went flying into the security partition but fortunately wasn't seriously hurt.

We had yet another banquet in Warsaw. The Polish food was actually better than the food in Tehran. In retrospect, as I think of our trip from Austria to the Soviet Union to Iran to Poland, I can't imagine how I ate so many different foods without getting sick. I had become adept at moving things around on my plate to make it appear as if I had eaten more than I actually had. However, there was no culinary challenge on this trip that came close to having to deal with the brains of the Peking Duck on our China trip. When you hear that it takes a strong stomach to be in politics, it can be taken quite literally.

We had talked the president into addressing the nation when we returned from Poland. Believing there was little more for him to say, he was initially against it. However, it was too good a political opportunity to forgo. The plan was for the president to take *Marine One* to Capitol Hill, making for a dramatic return to Washington, which was Tex McCrary's idea. The next day's *New York Times* had a front-page story of the president's return and address to Congress, with a picture of *Marine One* descending onto the Capitol grounds in the dusk of evening and the Capitol in the background. Tex taught us something he had learned from his own successful years of PR experience, which was that the formula for getting great print press coverage was by linking HPS: Headline, Picture, and Story. Tex later modified his HPS strategy to HPSC, adding the C to include the Caption on a story.

I flew on *Marine One* with the presidential party. It was among the most memorable times of my life with Richard Nixon. Few cities are more beautiful at night than Washington, D.C. We circled over the White House, passing over the Washington Monument and the Lincoln Memorial. *Marine One* set down between the Capitol and the Supreme Court Building. The president was reviewing his speech as we landed.

We were greeted by both of the president's daughters, Julie and Tricia; Tricia's husband, Ed Cox; and the leaders of Congress. David Eisenhower, Julie's husband, was not there because he was on active duty as a naval officer. We were taking, in essence, a victory lap.

I got home late that night exhausted. The next day, as usual, I made my personal notes, then wrote a memo to Haldeman. "And so another chapter comes to a close," I began. "The trip went better than I had ever dreamed it would. My hope is you feel the same. A couple of incidents marred moments . . . Over the next few days I plan on spending some time looking at what I can do here in the next few months. At some point . . . this is something I think we should talk about. At the expense of being called a traitor, under no circumstances am I convinced that to remain here is best."

It had been an amazing year. The world had opened for me, both literally and figuratively. However, as I glanced into the future, I could not possibly have imagined what was about to happen.

14

WATERGATE

June 15, 1972, was a fun and relaxing day. It was our daughter Tracy's fifth birthday. As always, Susie had invited some little ones to celebrate with Tracy. It was a festive affair, and, for a change, I actually was home for it. After months of travel and intense, nonstop work, it was really nice to be home, sharing this with Susie and the girls. All the kids playing and having fun gave a sense of normalcy to our lives. As the president was away in Florida, Susie and I were even planning to go off for the weekend with friends.

Saturday evening, June 17, had been wonderful. It was a hot, humid, rainy spring evening. Gerard Smith, the same man who had led our delegation in the SALT talks—until he was fired by Kissinger—was hosting a thirtieth birthday party for his daughter, Shelia Griffin, at his magnificent estate on Maryland's eastern shore. We had so much to celebrate. We were young, successful, and at the very center of power.

Susie and I attended the party with Henry and Leslie Cashen. Hank, a great friend and member of the Brotherhood, served as the White House liaison for special interest groups, and, as he himself was Catholic, he was also our in-house expert on Catholics. The Cashens and Susie and I were all staying at an inn in Easton, near the Smith's estate.

It was late that night, close to two in the morning, when we got back to the inn. As the four of us walked in, laughing, the desk clerk said to me, "Mr. Chapin, you've got to call the White House immediately. Mr. Haldeman has been trying to reach you."

That didn't exactly sober me up, but it definitely got my attention. I had no idea what it was about but, given that we had been partying all night, I wasn't looking forward to calling Bob. I said to Cashen, "Hank, can you stay here with me?" I called the White House and was patched through to Bob, who was in Key Biscayne. Bob asked me, "Do you know anything about a break-in at the Democratic headquarters?" I don't think he identified the location as the Watergate.

"No," I told him.

He went on: "Has Colson or anybody else spoken to you about something like that?"

I repeated, "Bob, I have no idea what you're talking about."

Again he asked, "You know nothing about any kind of plan that would involve breaking into the Democrat headquarters?"

"No," I repeated once again.

"Okay," he said. "Good night."

We hung up and went to bed. Whatever was going on, it didn't strike me as any more important than the other countless issues we dealt with every day in the White House.

Obviously, Bob had had no advance knowledge of the break-in or he wouldn't have been asking me about it. Also, when he asked me if I had heard anything about Chuck Colson being involved, it told me that Chuck was his first thought. There was a pattern of Chuck having things going on that we didn't know about, and we never knew precisely what he was up to. If Colson was involved, he knew the White House was involved.

Later I learned what had prompted Bob's call.

While the president was on Walker's Cay, in the Bahamas that Saturday morning, Bob Haldeman and his assistant Larry Higby had been working on the beach in Key Biscayne, Florida. Ron Ziegler joined the two of them with a wire report about the arrest of five men who had broken into the Democratic campaign headquarters, which was located in D.C. in the Watergate Hotel. When they first heard the story, Higby laughed and suggested, in jest, that it could be "Colson's boys." None of them were seriously considering that the White House could actually have been involved. Other than making a couple of calls, including the one to me later that evening, Bob didn't do anything more about checking out the story. In his memoir Bob says he wasn't concerned, because he knew that Ehrlichman was in Washington. If there was anything he needed to know, John would have been in touch with him.

Bob had it right. In fact, in his book, Ehrlichman said he did try to call Bob, but he wasn't able to reach him because Haldeman and his wife, Jo, were having dinner with Larry Higby. Unable to reach Haldeman, Ehrlichman next called Ron Ziegler.

Ehrlichman had heard of the break-in, thirteen hours after it transpired, from a Secret Service agent. The agent had called him because of a police report alleging that one of the burglars who was arrested was carrying a check with Howard Hunt's name and the White House phone number on it. Hunt had apparently asked the burglar to take the check home to mail from Florida to pay the dues at a club to which Hunt belonged (to maintain the fiction of his nonresident status).

When Ehrlichman heard Howard Hunt's name, he called Chuck Colson. He wanted to find out if Hunt, who had been one of the Plumbers hired to investigate leaks, was still on the White House staff and to learn why he would be walking around with the White House phone number. Colson told Ehrlichman that he knew absolutely nothing about a planned break-in.

On Sunday, Ehrlichman tried to reach Haldeman again. They had a "brief phone conversation," during which Ehrlichman expressed to Haldeman his concern that Colson, even though Chuck had said he knew nothing about it, could possibly be involved. John wrote in his book: "We agreed I'd turn the question over to our counsel, John Dean, the next day."

Undoubtedly, Ehrlichman and Haldeman, both with excellent political antennae, knew they needed to determine who had knowledge of the break-in and find out what the facts were. This was logical staff work, set in motion by the president's top two advisors. They had decided that John Dean, the White House Counsel, was the man who could sort out what had happened.

While Susie and I had been partying with friends on the Eastern Shore, the president had been relaxing that weekend with his two good friends, Bebe Rebozo and Bob Abplanalp, and getting some sun in the Bahamas. They were on Abplanalp's private island, with miles of sandy beaches to walk on and warm turquoise water to swim in. It was one of Nixon's favorite spots. It wasn't until Sunday, after the president had returned to Key Biscayne and gone to the kitchen to get his morning coffee, that he read a small story on the front page of the *Miami Herald* about the Democratic headquarters break-in. He ridiculed its stupidity. "Why would anyone break into a party headquarters? Anything worthwhile would be in a candidate's headquarters," he said in a phone call to Haldeman.

Watergate is now becoming ancient history. Most Americans are curious as to what it was about, but their eyes glaze over when anyone starts to talk about the details of the story. It is very complicated and there are dozens of side stories that add intrigue to the core events of the break-in and the subsequent cover-up. I won't attempt to retell the entire Watergate story here. Rather, I will explain how I experienced what was going on around me at the time and how my life was affected as a result.

For starters, I was the first person to go to trial in the aftermath of the Watergate break-in. However, I had nothing at all to do with the break-in or cover-up. As I mentioned in a previous chapter, I had hired my good friend Don Segretti to implement Dick Tuck campaign work. Don's work attracted the attention of the press. Once the press learned of Segretti's work, they tied him to me. Given that I was working in the West Wing, the press had successfully "entered the White House" and were then steps away from the president. The president was the ultimate target of the Democrats and the liberal media. Don and I were important for only two reasons: to move the scandal into the White House and to tie it directly to President Nixon.

While I had been working hard in the bomb shelter, planning the China and the Russia trips, the 1972 presidential campaign apparatus was being put into place. Jeb Magruder, a deputy to Herb Klein, the White House Communications Director, had been dispatched to manage the start-up of the Committee to Reelect the President (CRP), which was being set up in office space on Pennsylvania Avenue down the street from the White House. Jeb arrived first and was named the deputy campaign manager.

John Mitchell, Nixon's attorney general, was scheduled to resign from the Department of Justice and become chairman of CRP in the early spring of 1972. However, while Mitchell was still attorney general, meetings were held with him at the Justice Department in which campaign intelligence activity directed at Democratic opposition candidates was discussed.

It was John Dean, the White House Counsel, who recruited and then took G. Gordon Liddy, a former FBI agent, to Mitchell's office and introduced him as the one at CRP who would be responsible for campaign intelligence. Liddy had been recommended to Dean by Bud Krogh and had been one of the White House Plumbers working under Krogh. It was, according to Liddy's account, at the end of that introductory meeting with Mitchell that Dean specifically told Liddy to prepare an intelligence plan.

As requested by Dean, Liddy drew up a proposed plan, called "Gemstone." Reading Liddy's description of Gemstone today is like reading a second-rate spy thriller. The plan that Gordon Liddy proposed was startling. It included things such as using prostitutes, breaking into opposition offices, and dozens of other highly improper activities.

At a subsequent meeting, while still attorney general, John Mitchell listened as Liddy proposed a revised political intelligence-gathering operation that was still clearly illegal. According to Mitchell, he did not approve the plan. In fact, Mitchell said he assumed he had completely shut it down. Liddy had revised Gemstone, scaling it down at the urging of both John Dean and Jeb Magruder. John Mitchell maintained he never approved any of the revised versions. Later, in testimony during the Watergate hearings, and in the autobiographical books that would be written by Dean, Magruder, and Liddy, it is clear that the men saw and heard things differently. Liddy never testified at any concurrent legal proceedings (except in a later libel suit by Ida Wells following publication of Len Colodny's book *Silent Coup*). Yet Magruder told him Mitchell had approved his plan. Jeb Magruder testified—and then recounted in his book—that he had received Mitchell's approval to proceed, which he passed along to Gordon Liddy. Magruder and Liddy said they believed they had been given the go-ahead to plant listening devices in the Democratic headquarters at the Watergate Hotel—and that called for breaking-in.

It was G. Gordon Liddy and Howard Hunt, a retired career CIA Agent, who put together the break-in team, which included additional former CIA officers and assets. They broke into the Watergate originally in May 1972 to plant the listening devices, or "bugs." So if the bugs had already been planted in May, why did someone order the second break-in for June 17, the night they were caught? According to several Watergate books, the listening devices installed in May were not as "productive" as they had hoped. Thus the second break-in was planned to install better devices and, according to some accounts, to find compromising information on a possible call-girl service being used by Democratic officials. So on June 17, they went back in. That was when the five burglars were caught, and the story we know as Watergate, and its cover-up, began.

Both Liddy and Hunt had worked with the White House Plumbers unit and had been involved in the break-in at Dr. Fielding's office with regard to Daniel Ellsberg and the Pentagon Papers. The men had then moved from the White House to work for CRP. However, it would be discovered later that Howard Hunt still had an office in the EOB.

Nixon, Haldeman, and Ehrlichman knew nothing about either the

May or June Watergate break-ins. That is indisputable. However, clearly, there were people who did know. We know at CRP that G. Gordon Liddy and Howard Hunt knew, along with CRP's security director, James McCord, an ex-CIA official who had been caught as part of the break-in team. After the arrests had taken place at around two o'clock, it was Liddy who later that Saturday morning called Jeb Magruder in California to inform him. John Mitchell was also in California, on the same reelection campaign trip with Magruder. By then Mitchell had resigned as attorney general and had officially become chairman of CRP. That same morning Mitchell learned about the break-in from Magruder.

Though this was disputed by both Magruder and John Dean, Mitchell always claimed he knew nothing about the planned break-in or the arrests until Magruder informed him. We know that by the late morning of June 17, the highest levels of the campaign management, John Mitchell and Jeb Magruder—those two men at least—knew. Mitchell made no attempt to call the president, Haldeman, nor Ehrlichman to inform them. That would have been John Mitchell's first opportunity to keep events from unfolding as they did.

John Dean was serving as White House Counsel, having replaced John Ehrlichman in the oversight of political intelligence matters. Dean was acquainted with (1) the Huston Plan that had been vetoed by J. Edgar Hoover and John Mitchell; (2) the White House Plumbers activities, which included the Dr. Fielding break-in; and (3) the military spy ring on the president. He was also aware of all activities directed at controlling the antiwar demonstrations against the president. Dean knew that both the president and Haldeman welcomed intelligence information, particularly political intelligence. Dean made sure he was in the middle of all intelligence reports from the Department of Justice in order to be the key person providing that kind of information to his superiors. It followed that he made certain he was the designated man for similar intelligence information flowing to and from CRP. Dean reported to Haldeman, and it was Haldeman who had delegated to Dean the intelligence oversight responsibility with CRP. At this point, the coming presidential campaign was the biggest game in town. I remember Haldeman making the point to Higby and me that he needed "to get more things off my plate," meaning he needed to delegate more to his immediate staff. Delegating intelligence oversight to Dean, whom Bob trusted, was an easy decision.

It was Gordon Strachan with whom I had discussed hiring Segretti. Segretti had not only been a member of our Ballers group at USC, but he and Strachan had also been fraternity brothers. When I hired Segretti, Strachan agreed it was a good idea and then arranged for his compensation.

As the reelection campaign began to take shape, Haldeman assigned Gordon Strachan to work as the coordinator between his office and CRP. More specifically, Strachan was assigned to work with Jeb Magruder. As a result, Strachan was in the thick of anything political taking place between the White House and CRP. This would include all the polling activity and political intelligence matters. In practice, anything Magruder wanted reported to Haldeman would have to go through Strachan. One of the key responsibilities Strachan had was the coordination of intelligence information and materials. In that regard, a memorandum from Haldeman directed Strachan to work with, and report to, John Dean on all campaign intelligence matters. Strachan was young, smart, and savvy. He served his masters, Haldeman and Dean, well by always making sure he knew what was going on at CRP.

On the evening of the break-in John Dean was in the Philippines, in Manila. Upon receiving an urgent call from Jeb Magruder, he immediately flew back to Washington, arriving late Sunday, June 18. The following day, June 19, among the first people Dean called was Gordon Liddy, the man he had recruited to prepare the campaign intelligence plan. Dean chose to take a walk with Liddy in Lafayette Park, directly across the street from the White House. Dean's explanation for the park meeting with Liddy was to get to the bottom of the break-in. We know from Dean's testimony before the Senate Watergate Committee that he asked Liddy, "Who at the White House knew in advance of the Watergate break-in?" Why would he have asked him that question? Was it to get the information because Dean didn't know? That seems unlikely, since John Dean and Gordon Strachan were the White House staff in charge of coordinating intelligence information with CRP. Dean already knew that he and Gordon Strachan were the White House contacts with CRP regarding intelligence information. It seems more likely that Dean asked Liddy that question to see what Liddy's response would be, and to see if Liddy's response would incriminate him, John Dean. In his testimony to the Senate, Dean does not answer truthfully what he knew: that there was a member of the White House staff who did know in advance of the break-in. He also doesn't report that information to the president. Instead, speaking of the break-in, he continually tells the president that "no one in the White House knew in advance." It wasn't until nine months later, on March 13, 1973, that Dean changed what he was telling the president from "no one on the White House staff knew" to "Gordon Strachan [on the White House staff] knew." (See Exhibits 4A and 4C in the Appendix on pages 430 and 439.)

Gordon Strachan said he learned of the break-in and the arrests on his car radio on Saturday, June 17. He said he tried to reach Magruder, who wouldn't take his call. Magruder testified he wouldn't respond to the calls because he thought Strachan was calling at Haldeman's behest and he didn't want to have to answer Haldeman-style questions. Gordon, in his Watergate testimony, said he sweated bullets all weekend.

The president and Bob were flying back to Washington from Key Biscayne on Monday, June 19. Meanwhile, Ehrlichman, the former White House Counsel, took steps that day to learn the truth about the break-in. His were the very first steps. He met with John Dean and "asked him to find out how the break-in had occurred." Ehrlichman then met with Dick Kleindienst, who had replaced Mitchell as U.S. Attorney General, and asked to be kept abreast of the investigation.

Later that Monday afternoon Ehrlichman met with John Dean and Chuck Colson. Bruce Kehrli, a young Haldeman assistant, also attended that meeting. One of the facts that emerged was that Howard Hunt, then under arrest as one of the break-in burglars, still had an office in the Executive Office Building across the street from the West Wing. In Hunt's office was a safe. Kehrli was tasked by Ehrlichman with getting the safe opened and inventorying the contents before delivering them to Dean's office.

Inside the safe was Hunt's address book. In that book was the name Don Segretti and his phone number. When the contents of the safe, including the address book, were later turned over to the FBI, the FBI ended up on Segretti's doorstep. That address book was Segretti's tie to CRP. Howard Hunt had apparently entered Segretti's number when he and Liddy met with Segretti in Florida in late spring of 1972.

The week following the break-in, there was a going-away party for the president's army aide, a terrific man named Vern Coffey. The party was on a rented yacht docked in a marina on the Potomac River. It was very humid that night. Many of the young staff from the White House were there. Colonel Jack Brennan, the U.S. Marine Corps aide to the president, had organized the event and ably served as master of ceremonies. Everyone was in great spirits.

I was inside the cabin of the yacht when Hugh Sloan approached me. A year earlier, before he had been reassigned to work for Maurice Stans and Herb Kalmbach as CRP treasurer, Hugh had been working in our appointments office, handling invitations and helping with the president's calendar. Hugh ordinarily was a very proper guy, but he'd had a couple of beers and was really cranked up. "We have to talk," he told me. "Dwight, you wouldn't believe what's going on over at CRP. There's money everywhere." He started talking about the whole operation and how out of control it was. The news reports of the break-in had set Hugh on edge. "There's going to be more serious trouble," he said. We were having this conversation in the middle of a boisterous party, so I suggested we continue the following day.

We met for coffee the next morning. "Things are way out of control at CRP," he told me. He was very disturbed and told me that someone had to take control there or that things were going to get worse. "You have to tell Bob."

After talking with Hugh I was concerned. He was very persuasive, and I sensed he had important information to pass along to Haldeman. It was eight thirty in the morning and the location indicator light on my phone told me that Haldeman was with the president, so I called Ehrlichman. "John, Hugh Sloan is here," I told him. "He's telling me about some things that are going on over at CRP. I think you ought to talk to him."

Hugh left my office and went directly upstairs to Ehrlichman's office. According to Hugh, Ehrlichman told him he did not want the president involved in anything they were doing at CRP, but if Hugh felt he needed some legal advice, John would be happy to arrange it. That was the end of that—unfortunately. If only Hugh had been heard. Ehrlichman, as smart as he was, seemed to have determined that the best way to handle the chaos at CRP was to distance the White House from CRP's activities. I can imagine the frustration Hugh must have felt as he walked away from that meeting.

Later that summer, I was out of the bomb shelter and working on several projects, including the Republican National Convention, scheduled for the third week of August in Miami Beach, Florida; and the fall campaign, which would culminate in the election on November 7. While I had hinted at leaving the White House at some indeterminate time in the future, in fact I was really looking forward to the next four years. There couldn't possibly have been a better job, even with the constant headaches. The truth is that even while I talked about leaving, I was apprehensive about the loss of the prestige that comes with giving up a West Wing office. Plus, my relationship to Haldeman seemed to be back on a more positive and productive footing. I was being given considerably more independence.

Planning for the convention was exciting because we were preparing to present President Richard Nixon to the nation and to make the case for why he should be reelected. As with the China trip, the focus was on how we could get out our message centered around television. I was now swamped, once again, heading a committee dealing with the television aspects of the convention. Bill Timmons was our convention chairman. Working under his direction, we were planning what would transpire on the large convention screens, what videos we needed to produce (using footage from both our China and Russia trips), and, most important, what we would attempt to get the television networks to carry on the air. That was the "big enchilada" of that era of conventions—getting as much of the convention coverage onto live network television as possible.

In those days, all three networks, plus the large independent networks, carried gavel-to-gavel convention coverage. They would often interrupt our official convention program for coverage of their commentators, delivered from the large studios they had built in the convention hall. That was our challenge. We were using the game planning skills that we had honed during our daily meetings in the Roosevelt Room to keep the network cameras focused just on our convention program. Our television producers, consultant Bill Carruthers and White House television office producer Mark Goode, plus Dick Moore, Tex McCrary, and, at times, Bill Safire, were all part of our planning group.

While at the convention, Susie and I learned one of my two beloved grandfathers, Dwight Chapin, had passed away. When the convention ended, Susie and I flew to Wichita, Kansas, for his funeral. The president flew from the convention to Hawaii to meet with Kakuei Tanaka, the Prime Minister of Japan.

After the funeral Susie and I returned to Washington. I was home for only one day when I met for the first time with agents from the FBI. Having found Don Segretti's address in Howard Hunt's safe, the FBI had met with Don twice in Los Angeles. Don was preparing to appear before a grand jury, and now the FBI wanted to meet with Gordon Strachan and me. Gordon and I met with them in John Dean's EOB office. I answered all the FBI's questions truthfully. I said I had no knowledge of anything going on at CRP. An important and startling

THE PRESIDENT'S MAN ★ 311

aspect of the interview was my mentioning that Segretti was paid by Herb Kalmbach. When I said that, John Dean, who was present, "interjected that Kombach [*sic*] is a very close personal friend of the president's." (See Exhibit 5 in the Appendix on page 446.) That statement escalated the importance of everything with the FBI. While true, it was beyond belief that the White House Counsel would disclose, on a voluntary basis, the president's relationship to Herb Kalmbach during the interview. In hindsight, I've wondered if Dean mentioned this to deflect attention from his own role.

After being interrogated by the FBI, I remember thinking about the conversations I'd had with Hugh Sloan a couple of months earlier. If only we had listened to what Hugh had been saying and had started conducting our own investigation.

The next day I left for Palm Springs. One of our wealthy supporters had loaned me a house there for a few days, and I stayed there as I waited for the president and his staff to return from Hawaii. For me it was a short recovery "vacation." I was sitting by the pool in the California sunshine, working through a pitcher of vodka gimlets and feeling very good about life, loving the hot August desert sun. Early in the afternoon an aide to Vice President Agnew stopped at the house. The vice president happened to be in town and was staying at Frank Sinatra's home. Sinatra was having a dinner party that night—and I was invited.

Dinner at Frank's? You bet. I drank what seemed like two pots of coffee, trying to get myself in shape to be there at six thirty. The house was beautiful. There was a big picket fence around the property. It was a compound with a large rambling one-story main ranch house; a couple of small guesthouses, one of which the Agnews were occupying; and a large clubhouse with a theater and a helipad. I said hello to a couple of the Secret Service agents I knew from the vice president's detail and rang the bell.

Frank Sinatra answered the door. In the background his rendition of "Fly Me to the Moon" was playing on the sound system. It was surreal.

I had met Frank at the convention and had spent a little time there with his group. "Come on in, Dwight," he said. "Let me show you around." I took one step inside and sank into a thick white carpet.

He walked me through the house, then offered, "Let me buy you a drink." As we stood at his bar, the vice president and Mrs. Agnew arrived. Then other guests began showing up, among them Jack Benny and the actor Rory Calhoun. While I felt a little outside my comfort zone, I was having a good time.

By the time we sat down for dinner, although I was focused on watching how much I drank, I'd had more than my share of cocktails. There were two large round tables. Sinatra sat with the vice president's wife, Judy Agnew. I was sitting with Frank's wife, Barbara, and the vice president. Several wines were served. During the dinner we got into a discussion about the convention. That was when I told Vice President Agnew that he and his coterie of Secret Service protectors, who would typically accompany him wearing dark glasses, "looked like a bunch of thugs walking around the convention." After I had expressed that thought, everyone at the table grew very quiet.

The vice president didn't respond. Most likely he was wondering if my views reflected the president's.

After dinner we went to Frank's large clubhouse theater for a show-ing of the Charlie Chaplin movie *City Lights*. I'd had way too much to drink and was feeling light-headed by this time, so I thanked Frank for the evening and headed home.

I woke up the next morning hungover and horrified at the thought of what I had said to the vice president the night before. My words couldn't have been more inappropriate. I knew I had overstepped my bounds. I felt so bad that I packed and left Palm Springs a day early for the Western White House in San Clemente. The presidential party was due back from Hawaii the next day, so I went there to hook up with them.

A few days later I was back in my office when Nell Yates said, "Mr. Chapin, the vice president is calling." I was not looking forward to picking up the phone.

"Dwight," he said, "remember when we were at Frank's, you said you could prove to me how bad it looked at the Convention, me walking around with—I think you used the term 'thugs.' I'd like you to put that footage together for me."

I called Mark Goode, who ran the television office, and told him what had happened. I asked him to put together a videotape to send to the vice president. To Agnew's credit, after watching the footage, he called me back and told me I was right, saying, "We're going to change some things." He expressed appreciation for what I had said. I thanked him. In retrospect, if I could do it over, I would have apologized for having spoken out in front of the other guests.

During September 1972 there were numerous press stories on Watergate-related news as the media started sorting out fact from fiction. The Republican and Democratic campaigns were underway. The Democrats were flinging Watergate charges our way. However, the idea of the break-in at the Watergate being a major scandal had not taken hold of the public at large. Or so it seemed.

As the election of 1972 approached, the media grabbed hold of Watergate big time and wouldn't let go. And the Nixon White House gave them plenty to grab hold of because the White House didn't come clean early. One of the reasons the White House response was lacking is that the president had no idea of exactly what had happened, or why it had happened. He was treating it like a public relations problem. He was listening to his White House Counsel, John Dean, and following Dean's advice, but he was not demanding the facts and details that constituted his usual approach to serious matters. So while the White House was not being forthright with the information that it was coming to understand, drip by drip, headline by headline, Watergate grew into a scandal.

Doggedly pursuing the Watergate story were two young *Washington Post* reporters, Bob Woodward and Carl Bernstein. They claimed to be receiving information from a source inside the White House. Much later, in their book, that mysterious source would become known as "Deep Throat."

Deep Throat, they claimed, was a source with insider knowledge of the investigation who was willing to share it with them. Actually, as I was to learn from a personal conversation with Deep Throat's family lawyer in 2020, Deep Throat found Woodward and Bernstein. One Saturday night in October, Deep Throat made a cold call to the *Washington Post* press room. Working late that evening was reporter Carl Bernstein. Apparently Deep Throat offered a tip to Bernstein that night that would lead Bernstein first to a former army buddy of Segretti and then directly to Don Segretti himself.

Decades later, in 2005, we learned that Deep Throat was FBI Deputy Director Mark Felt. Mark Felt, it turned out, was a very ambitious man. FBI Director Hoover, who had run the Bureau since its founding in the 1920s, had died on May 2, 1972. Two insiders were competing for his job, Associate Director Mark Felt and another official, Bill Sullivan. However, Nixon named Pat Gray, a Justice Department official, as Hoover's temporary replacement. Felt apparently was furious, believing he was entitled to that job. He decided he was going to show Nixon that Gray, an outsider with no FBI experience, was incompetent. So he started leaking information about the Watergate investigation to the *Washington Post*. He also leaked, I was told many years later, to *Time* magazine's Sandy Smith. His intent, I believe, was to show Nixon that the FBI was leaking like a sieve, infuriating Nixon, which would perhaps lead to Felt's appointment as director. In that way Deep Throat, the ultimate inside source, was born.

It is true that Deep Throat was not a name used for the confidential source during the actual reporting of events. It wasn't until Woodward and Bernstein's book about Watergate, *All the President's Men,* was published that a name was needed for the character who provided their information. That was when the code name was created. Many of us believe that Deep Throat was a cover for more sources than just Felt, including, most likely, Al Haig.

According to Mark Felt's family lawyer, with whom I spoke in 2020, the reason Felt called the press room that Saturday night was that he sensed a lapse or pullback on the intensity of the Watergate coverage. In his own paranoia, he was thinking not only that the White House might escape the scandal, but that the Watergate drama needed to intensify in order that the president might, in his disgust with the leaks coming from the FBI, consider replacing Gray as director. So the number-two FBI official leaked the information that led to Don Segretti. Confidential FBI information was being leaked by the number-two official at the FBI who had sworn an oath to protect the Constitution.

In retrospect, Watergate was like an eighteen-wheeler coming at us over the next hill. We never anticipated it. While the break-in was growing into a huge scandal, I was focused on the upcoming election. I wasn't concerned at all about Watergate. I had played no role in it, knew nothing about it, and had no reason to think the White House should be concerned about it.

If there were internal discussions about Watergate in the White House, I not only wasn't involved in them, I have no knowledge of them. And I do know for certain that I never heard Richard Nixon mention it. We were too busy preparing for the convention, and then the election, to worry about it. There certainly was no effort on anyone's part to protect the president because we didn't believe the president needed to be protected. He hadn't done anything wrong, as far as I knew. Besides, primary responsibility to get the facts on Watergate had been assigned to his counsel, John Dean.

While Watergate continued to be in the headlines, it was not affecting our campaign. Americans didn't seem to care about it. In the White House, we were looking ahead and making plans for our second term. However, Tex McCrary, older, more experienced, and wiser, realized there was a storm brewing on the horizon and suggested that we needed to prepare for it. Tex in his unique style warned us just before the election, "How far has he come from 'Tricky Dick' to 'Plucky Dick' to 'Lucky Dick' to 'Mr. President' to 'Thanks, Mr. President' to 'Thanks, President Nixon' to 'I like Dick.' The danger is that in the wake of Watergate, which isn't even a ripple in the polls, but it is a rip in many a gut . . . that the other side will turn 'Tricky Dick' into 'Dirty Dick.'"

Tex advised us: "Again I urge all of you to put down in very cold type, every detail . . . every shred of any story that God Almighty might find and twist and print in the *Washington Post*. And then seriously consider giving all the meat of that story to a single pencil, radio, or TV reporter in a one-to-one interview which would give you the high ground before the battle begins. The expendables would be quick casualties and that could include you, but the president would be safely beyond ambush and snipers for the next four years."

If only we could have truly heard what Tex was saying. What incredible insight he had. He was a straight shooter.

Watergate eventually became like a whirlpool, a vast black hole, sucking everything around it, including Don Segretti and me, into the abyss. Technically, over the months he worked for the campaign, Don was reporting to me. But truthfully he was working without very much supervision. I was so busy I had little or no contact with Don and wasn't aware of what he was doing. From time to time I did, however, make suggestions to him about things he might pursue. Periodically he would send so-called reports—letters, actually—to my home. I tossed most of them in a pile without even opening them. At times Don would call me at the White House. We would talk, although briefly. I had so many other responsibilities that his work just wasn't a priority for me. I knew he could handle his assignment and that he didn't need further direction from me. In fact, at some point Gordon Strachan told me to forget all about Segretti, that he would be working under the auspices of CRP. It was at this point that Gordon might have given me the information that evidently Haldeman had approved of Segretti's work being shifted under the guidance of Gordon Liddy. That was fine with me. I don't ever recall being told. It wasn't that I didn't care. It was simply that I was swamped with other responsibilities.

The summer of 1972 I was interviewed twice by the FBI about Segretti. The first interview was right after the convention and the next was a few weeks later. I told them that I had hired Segretti, but I emphasized that I did not know about anything he had done that was illegal. There were a couple of small "tricks" that might have been embarrassing if they had been made public, but to the best of my knowledge, he hadn't done anything illegal. According to the FBI report, "Chapin suggested to Segretti that he arrange for a group to picket with pro-Humphrey or pro-McGovern signs" at an Ed Muskie rally. "He told Segretti . . . he should focus on the senator's stand against the SST program and his statement that he would not consider a black running mate . . . [and] arrange for blacks to picket Senator Muskie's Washington residence." That was the level of the "dirty tricks" we were planning.

In early October 1972, Ziegler received a call from someone at the *Washington Post,* presumably Woodward or Bernstein, asking questions about Don and his connection to me. Ziegler called me to ask, "Who is this guy Segretti?" He did not know about Don's assignment. There was no reason he would. Other than Gordon Strachan and John Dean, as far as I knew, nobody in the White House had ever heard his name.

The night the *Washington Post* story was published, Susie and I and our daughters were at Dick Moore's house. Dick Moore, a White House aide, was my friend and mentor. About eleven o'clock Dick and I went out and got a copy of the early edition of the paper. Segretti's picture was on the front page. That's when it hit me for the first time that this was potentially a very serious matter. At that point I became aware that things were really heating up around him, and I was feeling a lot of concern for Don and about what was happening to him.

Ziegler suggested that the administration just ignore the Segretti story. In retrospect many wrong decisions were made. Don Segretti had nothing to do with either the break-in at the Watergate or the cover-up. He had no connection to Watergate, but the press portrayed him as an important figure. In October, right in the middle of the campaign, the *Washington Post* reported that Segretti had been hired by CRP to conduct "a massive campaign of political spying and sabotage." The press was inaccurately expanding and sensationalizing Don's role. The report could not have been less accurate, but they ran with it anyway. They were merging the two stories: Don Segretti's Dick Tuck work with the break-in at Democratic headquarters. Neither story had anything to do with the other. But in merging the two stories, Don Segretti was becoming a nationally known figure, who was being portrayed as a significant player in the Watergate break-in.

Two days after its first story, on Friday October 13, the *Post* followed up on its initial reporting of Segretti with a story that I had hired him. The deduction of the press was that Segretti worked for CRP, as did the Watergate burglars—and therefore Segretti had to be connected to the larger Watergate break-in. Once again, it wasn't accurate. Don Segretti wasn't connected to anything other than his Dick Tuck assignment. I was to later learn that Segretti had been put under Liddy in the spring, but he never carried out any Liddy assignments. The *Washington Post* story was very damaging. It connected Segretti to the White House as a result of Segretti's connection to me. Until that story, anything Watergate-related had been restricted to the reelection campaign. The president was very upset about this shift of focus from CRP to the White House. He saw what was happening. It was another here-the-press-comes-again moment for him. He suggested to Haldeman that Segretti should sue the *Washington Post* for libel.

On Sunday morning we met in the Roosevelt Room, directly across from the Oval Office, to try to figure out how to respond to these attacks by the *Washington Post*. Dick Moore was there. John Ehrlichman was there. John Dean was in and out. Ron Ziegler was in and out. I had never been the subject of such focus as I was that day—and the focus was not a good thing. Suddenly I was smack in the middle of something I knew virtually nothing about. What I didn't understand at that moment was that when you're working in the White House and you become the focus of a news story, your position becomes very precarious. This is a fundamental axiom of politics: "Stay on message. Focus on the points you want to make. Anything—or anyone—that distracts from that focus is disposable."

That night Susie and I once again had dinner at the Moores'. We got home about nine o'clock. We pulled into our driveway, and as we were walking to our front door, I heard someone trying to attract my attention. "Psst, psst. Dwight." We had a large tree in our front yard. A man came out from behind it. "Dwight, it's Bob Semple."

Bob Semple was a *New York Times* reporter and their White House correspondent. "Bob," I said, astonished, "what the hell are you doing in my front yard?" Bob and I had become friends, as he had covered Richard Nixon from the moment he announced his run for the presidency that long-ago January 1968 day in New Hampshire. Bob had traveled the same road to the White House as I had, only he was on the news side of the campaign. He was a great reporter, and he was sincerely embarrassed to be there that night.

"Believe me, I don't want to be here," he admitted. "My editors know I know you. They made me come."

I told him, "Bob, I can't talk to you."

"I told them that," he said, "but they made me come anyway."

That was the first indication I had that I was going to become far more important "in the telling" than I actually had been "in the doing." I was . . . confused. My initial response was to do exactly what Tex McCrary had suggested: to hold a press conference and tell the whole story. I had nothing to hide. I told John Dean I wanted to do that, but he was desperate that I avoid doing anything involving the media. He even suggested he could arrange for me to be checked into Walter Reed on some flimsy medical excuse so the press couldn't reach me. I thought it was laughable. Susie didn't think it was laughable at all. Dean's suggestion really upset her. I had just returned from Russia, where that was exactly the kind of thing they did when they wanted to put someone out of reach. A few decades later, after Susie and I had been divorced for many years, she happened to see John Dean on television talking about Watergate. Susie emailed me to say what was still on her mind: "Make sure you never forget that Dean wanted to keep you from telling the truth by sending you to Walter Reed."

Haldeman started digging deeper into the Segretti situation to see for himself what the issue was. After hearing the facts, he decided, as he wrote in his diary: "It turns out that we don't have any real problem,

I don't think, on it. Some of the actions were questionable but none of them were serious. And it's clear that [Segretti] was operating without direction, although he did maintain some contact with Chapin as he went along. But he did not have a direct reporting responsibility or relationship there."

Haldeman's conclusions were absolutely accurate. However, John Dean was on the verge of panic. He had been doing his best to control the Watergate story, coming up with all kinds of crazy ideas, without much success. Two days after the burglary, he had apparently told Howard Hunt that he wanted to get him out of the country. Dean said he received this instruction from John Ehrlichman. But both Ehrlichman and Chuck Colson, who were in attendance at the same meeting, denied it. Later Dean suggested to Haldeman that the CIA step in and tell the FBI to not interview two possible witnesses because it was a national security issue. Dean had told Haldeman the CIA idea had come from Mitchell. It hadn't. Mitchell denied giving Dean any such suggestion. Dean even told Segretti at one point he could get him a job in Montego Bay, to get him out of the country. We assumed that, as White House Counsel, Dean was doing all this to protect the president. I don't think it ever occurred to anyone that the person he was actually trying hardest to protect was himself.

Dean clearly was the person who could have stopped this from escalating into the maelstrom it became. At one point Dick Moore advised him to call everybody together, sit them down, and get all the facts. Circle the wagons and deal with it. That never happened, and only years later did we figure out why. My friend Bruce Herschensohn, who was a special assistant at the White House at the time, told me that it was the wise Dick Moore who told John Dean, "There is a cancer on the presidency." Unfortunately, Moore didn't know at the time that Dean was the cancer. According to Herschensohn, ten minutes after Dick Moore had uttered those words, Dean walked into the Oval Office and repeated them to the president.

On October 15, on the front page of the *Washington Post,* Woodward and Bernstein reported: "President Nixon's appointments secretary and an ex–White House aide indicted in the Watergate bugging case both served as 'contacts' in a spying and sabotage operation against the Democrats. The appointments secretary, Dwight L. Chapin, 31, meets almost daily with the president . . . Federal law enforcement officials have said much of this spying and sabotage is probably illegal, but that any unlawful activities connected to the undercover campaign would be difficult or impossible to prove in court."

This was the first major *Washington Post* story about me. On Tuesday I went to John Dean's office for another visit with the FBI. Dean introduced me to the agents and then left. His deputy Fred Fielding sat in on the meetings. The FBI agents asked me a series of additional questions about Segretti. I told them the entire story, everything that I could possibly think of that they might be interested in. The next morning what I had told the FBI, confidentially and under oath the day before, appeared on the front page of the *Washington Post*.

Two or three days later the two agents returned for some follow-up questions. They spent the first few minutes of that meeting apologizing to me, telling me they had no idea who had leaked their report. Even though in hindsight it couldn't have been more obvious, none of us considered that the leaks could be coming from the FBI, let alone someone as close to the top of the FBI as Mark Felt. It never occurred to us as being remotely possible. Although, the Bureau had a long and ugly history of leaking. That's an abuse of power I personally experienced that I found to be outrageous conduct.

"This is some very powerful information," said one federal official, "especially if it becomes known before November 7th." I read it and reread it and re-reread it. "Spying and sabotage?" That October 15 *Washington Post* story had absolutely no relationship to reality. It made Segretti's activities sound like the crimes of the century. But that quote about powerful information gave away the real purpose of the *Post*'s story, which was to damage the White House before the election on November 7.

Watergate did not have any serious impact on the election. The president defeated George McGovern by a historic margin, winning forty-nine of fifty states in the Electoral College, sweeping the entire once-Democratic South, and receiving over 60 percent of the popular vote. Nobody cared about the break-in. However, below the surface, it was less of a victory than was generally perceived. I remember there was a tension, a different feeling, that was not one of exuberance after the victory. The president had no coattails and Republicans remained a distinct minority in both houses of Congress. McGovern had been an unusually weak candidate. A majority of Americans still supported our policy, even with the antiwar movement, but we remained mired in Vietnam. And while Republican elected officials—senators, House members, governors—were supportive in public and loved being photographed with the president, there was a certain absence of enthusiasm. Political relationships had not been maintained properly between the 1970 off-year elections and the 1972 election. The president in that period was riding a personal popularity high from the opening of China, from the SALT agreement with Russia, and with the knowledge that he had a weak opponent in McGovern. So when things started getting rough in 1973 and 1974, elected GOP officials who might have earlier fought hard for the administration were few and far between.

The morning after the election, there was a large staff meeting in the Roosevelt Room. The president made a speech in which he quoted British Prime Minister Benjamin Disraeli, who said, "You behold a range of exhausted volcanoes. Not a flame flickers on a single pallid crest." His point was that he didn't want any spent volcanoes around in his next term. The administration was going to take on big issues and it needed people with great energy, dedication, and enthusiasm. The president went on and on—and then he left the room. Haldeman then asked everyone to submit his resignation. It was a very unsettling moment that no one was properly prepared for, a very dumb management move, especially with the juxtaposition of the reelection the night before. It was pro forma, I figured. Maybe I even felt a little sorry for

THE PRESIDENT'S MAN ★ 323

a few people whom I suspected were not going to be asked to stay on. But me? After what I had accomplished? The possibility that my resignation would be accepted never occurred to me.

A few days later Susie and I flew to Ireland for a long-planned vacation with our friends Ron and Anne Walker and Dick and Marsha Howard. We spent three weeks there. I don't remember what I was thinking about while we were there, but there was zero focus and attention on White House matters. I had worked incredibly hard to help with the president's reelection and felt I had proven my value. I was anticipating remaining as part of the White House staff going into the next four years. While my relationship with Haldeman was not what it had once been, we certainly were still close. And things had actually gotten better, easier. I had great respect for him and assumed he felt the same way about me.

I flew home from Ireland with Ron Walker and Dick Howard on December 3, on an air force general's plane, landing at Andrews Air Force Base on a dark Sunday afternoon. Susie was flying home with the other two wives commercially the next day. A White House car picked me up and drove me directly to the White House. I expected there would be a pile of work waiting and I wanted to get a head start. As the president was at Camp David, the White House was virtually empty. I turned on the lights and sat down at my desk. Seconds later—literally seconds later—the phone rang. John Dean was calling. He must have been notified when I arrived. "Welcome back," he said. "Did you have a good trip?" I told him that we had. He continued: "I'd like to come by in the morning and talk to you."

"Terrific," I said. "See you in the morning." His call, immediately upon my return from Ireland, seemed a little unusual, but I didn't think too much about it. Unusual was the norm in the White House. Adjustments were always being made, but it never occurred to me that I might be swept aside in a general post-election housecleaning of anyone whose name had come up in connection with Watergate.

About eight o'clock on Monday morning, December 4, John Dean walked into my office. I poured coffee. We sat across from each other for about a minute, talking mostly about the beauty of Ireland. Then he said to me, in a casual tone, "Have you given any thought to what you're going to do next?"

I had never been fired before, so I didn't grasp his meaning at first. Then I asked him, "John, what are you trying to tell me?"

He looked right at me. "Well, I think you need to be giving some thought to what you're going to do next."

Next? I had no idea how to react. "Does Bob know you're here saying this?"

He nodded. "Yeah, he does."

I hesitated a few seconds as I tried to control my anger. "Get the fuck out of my office," I told him.

When he was gone, I called Haldeman. The switchboard reached him at Camp David. He was there with the president. "Bob," I said, controlling my tone, "is there something you want to tell me?"

He didn't answer directly. "Why don't you come up here tomorrow."

Tomorrow? My heart was racing. Something crazy was taking place. Tomorrow?

"I can't do it today," he explained. "Come up tomorrow afternoon."

When we hung up, I sat there letting reality sink in. Was I being fired? Kicked out? I went across the street to Dick Moore's office in the EOB. I told him what had happened and asked him if he knew anything about it. "No," he lied. "No. No. This is horrible. I can't believe this." As I was to learn, Dick Moore knew everything. He had been in on the planning of it. Dick Moore had been my friend. Beginning with the 1968 campaign he had been my mentor. I was stunned to find out that he had been involved in deciding what I was to be told at Camp David, but he sat there with me for hours, literally for hours, commiserating with me. And incredible as it may seem, when I learned this many, many months later, we sat and discussed it, agreeing we had been entangled in something much larger than we were aware, and we did not let it destroy our friendship.

Meanwhile, Susie's plane was landing and I had to pick her up. I took her home and smiled and tried to act as if my heart wasn't breaking. I didn't tell her anything. I didn't want to tell her because I was holding out hope that, when I talked to Bob, we'd figure something out. There had to be some kind of misunderstanding, I told myself. It made no sense.

The next afternoon a White House car took me to the Pentagon helipad for the short flight to Camp David. The only other person on the helicopter was Gerry Ford, who at the time was the Minority Leader in the House of Representatives. We didn't say very much to each other. My mind was racing. My world was falling apart. My entire identity was tied up with Richard Nixon. I'd been unfailingly loyal every minute for almost a decade. I couldn't suddenly turn that off.

I had to keep reminding myself that I hadn't done anything wrong. I had hired Don Segretti because I had walked into the Oval Office one afternoon and the president and Bob Haldeman were sitting there and Bob looked up at me and asked, "Do you know anybody who can do Dick Tuck type stuff?" I never went back and told them, "Hey, I've thought of somebody." That's not the way our system worked. I didn't need a further stamp of approval from them. I was expected to do exactly what I'd done. What Segretti was doing was no different from what had been done in campaigns for generations. The only person I'd spoken with about this was Gordon Strachan, who, like me, knew Don from USC.

It was already dark when we landed at Camp David. We were met by staff driving two golf carts. One took the Minority Leader, Congressman Ford, off to meet with the president. The second one took me to Haldeman's cabin. Bob greeted me and we sat down. He looked really tired. Amazingly, I found myself sympathizing with him. "You know," he began, "while you were away we did a lot of looking into things, trying to figure out what happened and what your friend Segretti did. It's beginning to look like this guy Ervin [North Carolina Democratic Senator Sam Ervin] might go ahead and hold some hearings.

The president's thinking is that if we have you and Colson and [Attorney General Richard] Kleindienst leave, it might help us get past the situation."

My eyes welled with tears.

"Therefore, you're going to have to leave. We'll do everything we can to help you figure out what you're going to do next. We'll be supportive. You don't have to leave right away, but over the next couple of months. The inauguration's on the twentieth. Your job from now on is to figure out what you're going to do."

By the time he finished we were both crying.

"Bob," I said—maybe I pleaded—"this isn't fair."

"I know," he agreed, but he said there was nothing he could do about it. Years later Bob's wife, Jo, told me he had called her that night crushed that he'd had to let me go. "I hope I never have to go through an experience like that again," she said he told her. "It was horrible."

If it was horrible for him, just imagine what it was for me. I was reeling from the shock of what I had heard. What was happening didn't seem possible. It made no sense. I had been with Richard Nixon long enough to know that when losses needed to be cut, they were cut. Everyone was expendable. But me? Processing what I had been told was very painful. I was the person who had watched other people leave. Now I was having to go myself.

Before I got into the White House car to be driven home, I went into the men's room to wash away my tears. Dick Kleindienst was there, bawling like a baby. Obviously he had just been told he had to leave too. His meeting had been with Ehrlichman. Neither of us saw the president, who was—unbeknownst to any of us, including Nixon himself—meeting with the man who would be the next President of the United States.

It was two months later, February 28, 1973, when it was announced I had decided to leave the White House to pursue other business opportunities. By the time Nixon acted to save his presidency, it was too late. He too had been caught up in the swirl of events. He had committed his own cardinal sin: He had taken actions before he had sufficient information. In a televised speech to the nation on April 30, 1973, he announced, "There can be no whitewash at the White House," and he said he had accepted the resignations of Haldeman, Ehrlichman, and Kleindienst; and he had fired John Dean. Gordon Strachan also submitted his resignation, as had Chuck Colson and Jeb Magruder earlier.

For me, I believed it was over. I had paid a high price. A year earlier I'd been having dinner with two of the most powerful leaders in the world, Richard Nixon and Chou En-lai. Now I was out of the White House, jobless. The exalted status I had once enjoyed was gone.

But as I was about to find out, my most serious problems were about to begin.

★ 15 ★

WATERGATE—TRIAL

I didn't leave the White House without a fight. Well, at least without a memo. In December 1972, I wrote a carefully constructed note to Haldeman. "Upon returning from Ireland, I ventured to Camp David for what you must know was the most difficult talk ever. The conclusion was the slate should be wiped clean and to make that possible I should leave. Perhaps too much the loyalist, I agreed without further argument."

But, I continued: "No one buys the idea the Segretti thing was done on my own. They warn us to watch how the press will adopt me only, as we know, to tie into you or the president. We will find I am the nice guy while you men are the bastards who threw me to the wolves." (Note: I was not calling my good friend Bob and the president bastards. I was suggesting the media would portray them that way.) And then my plea: "I am most reluctant to move out as part of the housecleaning staff cuts. Although I realize that more has been received than contributed, my loyalty and efforts it would seem deserve more than a 'get out' at this awkward time . . . As well as most I understand the need to be politically expedient, but if it is at the expense of all, does it make sense? I am concerned that proper thought is not going into this problem."

Too late.

That period of my life remains one of the lowest points. I was dying about having to leave the White House. But having spent a decade with

Richard Nixon, I should have understood there was no going back. It might have taken him some time to make up his mind, but once he did, it was final. Nixon was a pragmatist. He was not a sentimental person. At least he wasn't sentimental about issues like this. It wasn't about me, I kept reminding myself. It was the situation. My feelings shouldn't be hurt. It was nothing personal, I rationalized. The fact that he never said a word about this to me was typical of him. He was never very good at saying his goodbyes.

As I packed my office in February, I still had difficulty accepting reality. "I thank you from the bottom of my heart," I wrote to Haldeman at the time. "If it ever becomes possible, I want to help out wherever I can—to stay in touch and continue to play a part on your team."

Once I regained a little of my equilibrium, I accepted reality and began trying to figure out how to move forward. I needed a paycheck, but more than that I needed a job that would challenge me. What do I want to do? I asked myself. Unfortunately, the answer always came back to the same place: I wanted to go back into the White House.

There were numerous opportunities. I had unique experience. I had a long list of powerful business contacts, as well as my political relationships. Potentially I was a valuable employee. I started my job search at the top. My interviews were with corporate presidents. I met the president of American Express in New York. I met with the head of Quaker Oats in Chicago. I had an offer in Washington, D.C., from Marriott's food service division.

Only one person mentioned the cloud hanging over my head. Lew Wasserman, the politically well-connected head of MCA/Universal, told me directly, "I have many friends in Washington. I want you to know that I think you have a very big problem." My heart sank. This Watergate thing was not going to disappear, he continued. The meeting lasted no longer than twenty minutes. Thank you very much, Mr. Wasserman. Next.

Herb Kalmbach arranged an interview for me with Justin Dart, who ran the conglomerate Dart Industries and was part of Ronald Reagan's

"Kitchen cabinet." Dart told me he was a member of the United Air-lines board of directors and that a McKinsey study the airline had just completed suggested that it needed "a good, solid marketing person." Minutes later he was on the phone with Eddie Carlson, United's chair-man of the board. "Eddie, I may have found our marketing guy. I have sitting across from me Dwight Chapin, who is leaving the White House."

Mr. Carlson asked me to meet him the next day at San Francisco Airport. By that time my picture had been all over the newspapers. As I walked into United's Red Carpet Room, people recognized me and literally started hissing. I ignored them. How do you respond to that? "Pay no attention to those folks," Carlson began. I saw a man at that moment who had more guts than most people I'd known. At his sug-gestion I flew to Chicago and was hired by Rob Mangold, vice presi-dent of marketing for United. The airline industry of that era intrigued me. I knew a lot of really bright people in that sector. It was growing rapidly and seemed to have a dynamic that might be exciting. Mangold was a rising star in that industry, a wonderful boss. He could not have been more supportive.

I started at United Airlines on April 1, 1973, slightly more than a week after John Dean had told the president there was "a cancer on the presidency." This was the same day that Dean's new criminal de-fense lawyer first approached prosecutors to begin Dean's surreptitious dance regarding plea negotiations. I was completely out of the loop and knew nothing about that. Nobody did. Our family was in the process of moving to Chicago, specifically to Winnetka. While I was sad and resentful about the way I had been treated, in retrospect accepting the job at United Airlines turned out to be an extremely fortunate decision.

The week before I officially started at United, Robert Stuart, the chairman of Quaker Oats, a Chicago company, and his wife held a dinner at their Lake Forest home to welcome Susie and me to Chicago. Stuart was a great friend of Dick Moore's. The Stuarts hosted quite an affair, a black-tie dinner. The guests included Mr. and Mrs. Eddie Carlson, Mr. Carlson being my new boss; Mr. Arthur Woods, the chairman of Sears, and his wife; Illinois Governor Ogilvie and his wife; and a few other couples. After dinner, as we were all having coffee in the living room, standing in front of the fireplace, Mr. Stuart invited me to give his guests my view of "What in the world is going on in Washington?" I did my awkward best answering their questions about Watergate and Governor Ogilvie's probing questions of concern about his "good friend John Mitchell."

As Watergate unfolded, Susie and I had a phenomenal group of supportive, enthusiastic friends in Chicago. They rallied around us and sustained us through a terrible time. While it had been painful to leave Washington, moving to Chicago was one of the best things that could have happened to us. It moved us out of the white-hot media intensity of Watergate in Washington, D.C.

Almost as soon as I had settled into my new office at United in April of 1973, John Dean began calling me, asking what I knew, keeping tabs on whether I had been contacted by the prosecutor's office. I thought John was concerned about me, maybe wanting to make sure I didn't let down the old team at the White House. I understand now that what was really going on was that Dean was gathering information to make the best deal possible for himself. He knew how little involvement I'd had with Segretti's actions and he also knew I had no involvement with the break-in or cover-up. (See Exhibit 4A in the Appendix on page 430.)

It was difficult settling into the job at United. After going to work every morning at the White House and focusing on issues that affected the entire world, or seeing ideas translated into strategy, or representing America in the distant places of the globe, planning seating capacity with Boeing or improving the service image of the airline didn't generate the same excitement. Having my picture or story on the front pages of the Chicago papers day after day created a very awkward ongoing public relations problem for the airline. But to his credit my immediate boss, Rob Mangold, like Mr. Carlson, never wavered in supporting me.

Others at the executive office of United—many who had opposed an outsider being brought in, let alone a Nixon Watergate guy—relished the adverse publicity I faced. Other than Mr. Carlson, I became the best known person at the airline, for a negative reason.

"The change to a new life has been tough at times," I wrote Haldeman. "But—all in all—[it] has gone very well. At times I feel that I belong there with you—and that is the hardest emotion to temper." I also said in this letter that I had recognized "something very important was missing from my life . . . Therefore I am making a real attempt at Christian Science . . . and I am off to a good start." I was seeking spiritual support to replace my loss.

More than once, as I adjusted back to real life, I remembered Bryce Harlow's advice at the very beginning of the administration: "Remember, this is temporary." As I was learning, hearing it and accepting it were two very different things.

Only a few years earlier Ian Fleming had introduced to the world James Bond, who was fighting the evil Spectre, a darkness that cast its shadow over everything. I had my own evil Spectre hanging over my head, the investigation that was continuing to grow. Reputations and careers were being made on the front pages of newspapers and the evening news. Every Democratic politician, every journalist, and every ambitious prosecutor wanted a piece of it. It was basically a franchise business. Watergate was its own profit center for the media. They made more money from Watergate and the sale of newspapers, television commercials, and eventually books than ever before. It was a financial bonanza so, as far as they were concerned, the longer it went on, the better.

A scandal like Watergate was a new thing. It had been many, many years since we'd seen any significant Washington scandal of Watergate's magnitude. So it was exotic as well as exciting. Today's scandals have become commonplace and the public has become more inured. "Ordinary" scandals today involve things that make Watergate at its worst pale in comparison. So the whole genre of modern politics, the present-day scandal culture, was being born on our backs, my back. It was new, and there were no rules. Wildly inaccurate things were written and reported. In many cases, reporters were used as dupes to make points or settle scores. In other cases, reporters juiced up stories to be more interesting and therefore more competitive.

Two weeks after starting at United, I was subpoenaed to testify in front of the Watergate grand jury that was investigating dirty tricks. I had no understanding of what that meant. I didn't understand the mechanics of a grand jury. Haldeman knew about it, and he gave me advice: "Go in there and tell the truth." My intention was to do exactly that. I wasn't going to be gushingly forthright, but I wasn't going to try to hide anything either. The only thing I wanted to avoid admitting, because it was the only thing I could imagine that could possibly hurt them, was that Nixon and Haldeman had told me to hire a Dick Tuck type person. Two days before I was scheduled to testify, Mr. Carlson called me into his executive office and asked me, "Who's your lawyer?"

"John Dean," I said. That's how naive I was. I actually assumed Dean and I were still friends.

Carlson shook his head. "He's the president's lawyer," he said. "He can't be your lawyer. We'll get you a new lawyer." Mr. Carlson was a very savvy, smart guy. He realized I was clueless about legal matters, that I had no idea of what I was going up against. "Dwight, you're a political football. You're in the middle of this thing because you worked for Richard Nixon."

My new lawyer was a solo practitioner who had done work for United Airlines. We met at his Washington, D.C., office. I remember two things. First, it was late in the afternoon and I could smell liquor on his breath. Second, he explained that he would not be allowed in the hearing room but that he would be sitting outside to answer any questions.

The grand jury was a collection of Washington, D.C., citizens who met in a large room. I sat behind a table. There were chairs all around. The grand jurors were reading newspapers or books. As the prosecutor started asking me questions, many of the grand jurors were paying no attention. The prosecutor asked me questions about my relationship to Don Segretti and his activities. Did I know what he was doing? Did I know he was distributing campaign literature? Which candidates did he distribute literature about? My mistake was trying to avoid answering directly. Rather than a simple "Yes" or "No," I would respond, "Not that I recall," or "Not that I remember." I was trying to keep it general, I guess. At the end, when they finally asked me specific questions, I admitted the president and Haldeman had told me to hire someone to do Dick Tuck stuff. When I walked out of the room my attorney asked me how it went. "Fine," I said, and I believed it.

I had no idea how prosecutors work. I was so trappable; it was unbelievable.

I was right about my testimony having been "fine," at least for a little while. I learned much later that following that hearing one of the prosecutors had written a memo saying that I was "unindictable." The reason for that, he wrote, was that when Segretti appeared before his grand jury he had testified, "When Dwight hired me, he told me one of the reasons he was hiring me was that I was a lawyer. I would know what was right and what was wrong. I would know the legal ramifications." In the opinion of that prosecutor, Segretti's testimony made it nearly impossible to indict me for anything Don did.

Meanwhile, back in Washington, every attempt the administration made to contain Watergate had failed. The drip had become a flood, and as incredible as it seemed to all of us, Nixon's presidency was appearing to be in jeopardy. It was impossible to believe that less than a year earlier we had been celebrating extraordinary successes. Now it was all falling apart. I was out of it, I believed, but I really wanted to be there with Bob defending the fort. I wrote him several letters suggesting different strategies. "He [Nixon] must really hack up the fellows who have left or are about to—the blame must be fixed beyond too much speculation . . .

"I would argue one thing to get out soon . . . is the true Segretti story. It is small league, however, if the Senate moves against it for exploitation purposes; it can add to the cheers to knock off the big boys." My problem, the Segretti connection, was small but might be used as a handle to get to the president, which was exactly why my little problem became a big league problem.

There was no way to get ahead of it. By the time Nixon tried to contain it, it was too late. And the fact that John Dean was on the inside, working secretly with the prosecutors, made it even worse. In late April 1973 the president had to jettison his two closest advisors, Haldeman and Ehrlichman. "From reading the papers and listening to the news, one would think you are about to be tossed overboard," I wrote to Bob. His attitude, I'd been told, was "tremendous, and I am not in one least bit surprised. You were always made of something special."

Three days after I wrote that letter to Haldeman, the president fired him. None of this seemed possible. I wrote again: "Tomorrow will be a black day in presidential history . . . I am 'Joe Emotion' as you know. But I feel the president is probably doing what is necessary. Personally, I feel most or all of what has happened is his fault. But I also feel the critics have won this round. We must score later—and we will . . ."

"Bob, you have been and are my idol. I have misserved you so, at times in the past . . . Tonight I feel you have been hurt so very bad . . . Over a period of time we will register our side. That some of us—if it takes the rest of our lives—will see you clear of this mess . . . So our great adventure has taken a curve for a while. I can only think that in many ways it will make better men of us. And as my lawyer said, one thing we can rest assured of—'this too shall pass.'"

Well, that was optimistically hopeful. For me it didn't pass. It got progressively worse. In terms of being oblivious to what was going on, I wrote again to Bob in early May: "It is wrong from the standpoint of [Christian] Science, I guess, but I would prepare yourself for the worst on the prospect of indictment. You may be completely innocent in fact—but public opinion is going to strongly influence those grand jury members toward an indictment."

When I offered Bob that opinion, it never occurred to me that I was also writing about my own situation. Watergate had become a political feeding frenzy. In mid-May Harvard professor Archibald Cox was appointed the Watergate special prosecutor. Cox had served as U.S. Solicitor General in both the Kennedy and Johnson administrations so, public statements aside, it would be difficult to believe he was unbiased.

I still believed I was legally clear. However, after hearing the "dirty tricks" probing from Senator Ervin's Select Committee on Presidential Campaign Activities, Dick Moore and Henry Cashen told me I'd better get myself a real lawyer. At their recommendation I hired the politically astute and politically connected Jake Stein. Jake was the perfect Washington criminal defense lawyer. He looked and talked the part. But what he wasn't, it later became clear, was what I needed most: a tough son of a bitch. He was smooth and nonaggressive, a low-key problem solver. He agreed to represent me.

When we met in his office, Jake Stein asked me to "run through the story." When I was finished, he asked me to go through it again. And again. I said to him, "You mean I'm sitting here paying you to tell this story over and over?"

He smiled. "Tell me again." Eight times. Literally, eight times.

Senator Ervin's full Watergate committee never called me because they knew I intended to utilize my Fifth Amendment rights to not incriminate myself. It would be a waste of the committee's time. Jake made that clear. His advice was good: Keep your mouth shut. Do not put yourself in a position to perjure yourself. Instead I met with Connecticut Senator Lowell Weicker and several other people and, as I had said I would, refused to answer on the grounds that it might incriminate me.

You may be wondering why, if I was innocent, I wouldn't want to testify. Jake advised that going before the Watergate committee would be setting myself up for a perjury trap. When the government is after you, he told me, there's no way to win, and the perjury trap is always the easiest way for them to nail a person.

I was one of the few Nixon administration people who refused to testify in front of the Watergate committee. Other people were running for cover or making deals. In September Don Segretti agreed to plead guilty to three misdemeanor counts of campaign law violations for not placing "proper attribution on campaign literature" and to cooperate with the special prosecutor. I had absolutely no problem with his decision, and I continued to feel responsible for having put him in that position. Eventually he served four months in prison.

I don't remember when I first began hearing rumors that I myself might be indicted. Indicted? Indicted for what, I wondered. I hadn't done anything wrong.

Nixon had spent the summer fighting back. That was who he was. He had moved past the juncture when he could have solved the problem. He was in it now for his political life. During the summer Alexander Butterfield, a deputy assistant to the president, had announced at the Senate Watergate hearings that there was a taping system in the White House, which was recording the president's meetings and phone calls. I was stunned; I had no knowledge of the taping system.

In October Nixon made a momentous decision. After this revelation about the existence of the Oval Office recording system, he tried to negotiate a deal to limit access to the actual tapes. When Archibald Cox, the Watergate special prosecutor, refused to accept that deal, the president fired him. That same day both Elliot L. Richardson, who had replaced Kleindienst as U.S. Attorney General, and Deputy Attorney General William D. Ruckelshaus resigned. Nixon also tried to abolish the office of special prosecutor and ordered Cox to immediately cease any efforts to obtain additional documents or tapes. After what became known as the "Saturday Night Massacre," Nixon was forced to appoint a second special prosecutor. He chose Leon Jaworski, a distinguished Democratic lawyer from Houston.

Jaworski inherited the highly politicized team that Cox had assembled. Then he immediately expanded his investigative team partly in response to Cox being fired. Public sentiment was for action on the prosecutorial front. Jaworski's team needed a "public hanging," so to speak, a "we're taking action" statement, so they went after the most obvious target available: me. Talk about being in the wrong place at the wrong time. I used to joke that I was never closer to the president than during this period. Woodward and Bernstein mentioned the fact in their book that when they were reporting about me, one of their editors began adding material about my closeness to the president in every story.

I knew Don Segretti had testified, but I did not know what he'd told anyone. Whatever it was, it obviously concerned me because I was beginning to see that if what I told the prosecutors didn't match what Don told the prosecutors, I could be in real trouble. And, the truth was, I had very little idea of what Don's activities had been. Therefore, I wasn't in a position to be corroborating anything to which he had already testified. The prosecutor's office called Jake Stein and informed him I was a target. They wanted me to turn on the president. They started putting pressure on me to incriminate both the president and Haldeman. I was their connection into the White House. They were determined to get me to flip. This is a common tactic used by prosecutors: to "squeeze" someone in a lower position and make him testify against someone in a higher position, in order that the person in the lower position could save his own skin. In my case, there was nothing there to squeeze.

For starters, I would never have testified against the president or Haldeman. Even after the way I had been treated, I remained a staunch Richard Nixon loyalist. Second, and most important, I had absolutely nothing to tell them. They already knew everything from Segretti and from what I had told them. The prosecutors very simply would not, could not believe I didn't know more. They felt certain I was withholding information that would harm the president and/or Haldeman.

I still had no idea what crimes I had supposedly committed.

One cold, rainy Wednesday evening in late November 1973, Jake Stein called. "Dwight," he said, "I have some bad news. You're going to be indicted tomorrow unless you agree to cooperate with the prosecutors. If you'll agree to cooperate, we can work something out."

"Jake," I replied, "tell them to go fuck themselves."

I am certain it was a Wednesday because that was the night the Christian Science church had its meeting. During a Christian Science service, people will tell their stories and offer their personal testimonies. To maintain my own peace, I had turned more and more to Christian Science. My mother's side of the family were Christian Scientists, and during my childhood I'd gone to a Christian Science church, though I hadn't taken it very seriously. Through subsequent years I dabbled in a lot of other religions. Susie and I had wanted Kim and Tracy to experience the benefits of faith so we tried to get them to Sunday school when they were young. The fact that Haldeman was a practicing Christian Scientist had rekindled my interest and during this time it provided an absolutely necessary spiritual base for me.

After hanging up with Jake, I told Susie I was going to be indicted the next morning. By this time neither of us was surprised. It wasn't as if this was a flash of some very unexpected news. The two of us had been in the fight for months. Susie never wavered, not for an instant. We believed to our core that we were fighting the good fight. To her, as it was to me, this was a "political fight" we were in. We never viewed it any other way. To this day I still consider the entire saga a political attack.

After telling Susie the news, I called Mother and Dad. That was a different story. They were crushed. Worse, devastated. I asked them to call my sister, Linda, and her husband, David. Then I did the hardest thing. I called "Pop" and "Nano," my grandparents. I was their only grandson. I had introduced them to the president one spring morning at the mission in San Juan Capistrano, California. They were so proud: Their grandson worked for the president of the United States. I had to tell them that evening, "Tomorrow, I am going to be indicted, but don't worry, I am going to be okay. This is just a political thing." A week later my mother called to let me know that Pop had passed after suffering a heart attack. When I responded with, "I broke it!" Mother said, "Don't think that way." But to this day I think it was true.

I went by myself to the church that night. I just sat and listened. As I was leaving, an older man stopped me. "I'm Herm Stein," he said, offering me his hand. I introduced myself. We spoke for a few moments and then he said, warmly, "It's nice to have you here. If you ever want to get together, I'd love to talk to you."

"Mr. Stein," I said, and I don't know why, "are you available tomorrow morning?"

Winnetka is on Lake Michigan. At ten o'clock the next morning we were strolling on the beach. I told him, "Mr. Stein, I'm being indicted right now." I wanted to talk about it. I needed to talk to someone, and he was there. That marked the beginning of a close friendship. We got together every week for the next eight years when I was home.

Herm Stein, as I learned, had been the treasurer of the AC Nielsen corporation. His son had been the treasurer of Bell and Howell Corporation. Both companies were two of Chicago's greatest. What I eventually learned was that Herm's son, daughter-in-law, and one grandchild were flying in a small plane with the family dogs to their summer cabin in northern Michigan when the plane exploded, killing them all. I was younger than his son, but Herm's daughter told me that he liked being with me because I helped fill that void. But for me, the gifts that Herm gave me were priceless. Herm shared with me his wisdom, his common sense, and the depth of his Christian Science belief. Herm was another of the most important mentors in my life.

The day I was indicted, I walked the Winnetka beach with Herm. "Dwight," he said, "as you go through whatever is to unfold, remember you are God directed and God protected. No one can hurt you."

I was indicted on four counts of making false statements to the grand jury. The first count was my answer to their question: "To your knowledge, did Mr. Segretti ever distribute any statements of any kind, or any campaign literature of any kind?"

I replied, "Not that I am familiar with." Refreshing a defendant's recall is something commonly offered by the prosecution. However, they didn't show me anything that would have helped me remember, nor did they give me a clue to what they were referring.

A second count accused me of lying to the grand jury when I told them I didn't know "how much money Herb Kalmbach had paid Segretti." The judge dismissed that count after Kalmbach, the paymaster, testified that he himself didn't know how much he had paid Segretti.

A third count concerned my answer to the question: "What candidates do you recall receiving information about? Senator Muskie, was he one?"

I replied, "Yes. I think Muskie and Humphrey . . . virtually all of them." The truth is that I did not have information about Don working on a specific candidate or distributing materials. I had no specific recollection of receiving the information or what the information consisted of, and the prosecutors thought that was a lie.

And then, the fourth count: "Did you express any interest to him, or give him any directions or instructions with respect to any single or particular candidate?" Again, they only asked the question, offering nothing to refresh my memory. "Not that I recall," I honestly replied. They didn't believe me.

The prosecution was an attempt to entrap me, hoping that I would flip and provide evidence for more important prosecutions. I didn't realize that at that time. The problem with that attempt was that I had no knowledge about those other investigations.

While the questions may sound frivolous, there were serious penalties to be handed down if the jury didn't believe me. The maximum penalty for each guilty charge was five years in prison and a $10,000 fine. I knew that when I went into the grand jury. My intention was always to answer honestly. However, they didn't believe my answers to those four questions. I was being indicted. It didn't seem possible that I could be facing prison for the same kinds of political tricks Dick Tuck had been carrying out for years. When the indictments were announced, I stood on my front lawn and told a battalion of journalists that I wasn't guilty and that I intended to fight all charges.

Immediately upon being indicted, I was suspended from United

Airlines without pay. The airline really didn't have any choice. It was a publicly held company with a need to protect its reputation. Mr. Carlson, United's CEO, assured me my job would be waiting for me if I was acquitted. The prosecutors, with full cooperation from the media, had been very successful in confusing the public and making it appear that my indictment for "false and misleading statements" regarding Don Segretti's Dick Tuck work had something to do with the break-in at the Watergate. The media relentlessly tied the break-in with headlines and stories about "saboteurs," "dirty tricks," and "dozens of agents," creating the illusion it was all part of one big conspiracy. Nothing could have been farther from the truth. Each was distinctly different from the other.

Without an income we had to survive on our savings, which were not substantial. Looking for help to pay my legal bills, I wrote letters to friends proclaiming my innocence and asking for their assistance. They set up a defense fund. Over a hundred wonderful and supportive people eventually contributed. Bill Safire wrote about it in his *New York Times* column, announcing, "Today I sent in a check to Dwight Chapin's defense fund." Safire had been in the White House. He knew my prosecution was unfair. Jake Stein received every penny of the fund.

In preparation for my trial, Henry Kissinger had agreed to appear as a character witness for me. That made me feel very good. Henry and I had developed a warm relationship. But a couple of months before the trial began, Al Haig, his deputy, called and said, "Dwight, I have some bad news. Henry's come to the conclusion that if he testifies at your trial, he will have to do the same thing for Bob and maybe some others, and he just can't do it." That was devastating news to receive. It made me wonder if my relationship with Henry was as special as I had believed it to be. But then Haig added, "I'll testify for you." Okay, it wasn't Kissinger, but Haig still was an impressive man and would make a strong statement.

A month later Brent Scowcroft called to tell me, "Dwight, I'm sorry. Al just can't do it." I don't remember if there was a reason given, but the result was the same. Eventually Nell Yates, wonderful Nell Yates, was one of my character witnesses from the White House. The other was John Whitaker, who worked on John Ehrlichman's domestic affairs staff, a man whom I knew well from the White House. John and I had worked together over the years on several projects, including the Apollo 11 around-the world trip in 1969.

My trial began on April Fools Day, 1974. The news in Washington, D.C., was nothing but Watergate, 24/7. The *Washington Post* was banging away on the president and his men every day. I was one of the evil Nixon people. There was little chance I was going to get an unbiased jury. Jake Stein was a pragmatist. He told me that if the trial were held in D.C., we wouldn't win because of the deeply held prejudice against the president and his administration. "They will convict you," he told me, "simply because they hate Richard Nixon." So he requested a change of venue. The judge turned down the motion.

Jake Stein had expected that the change of venue would be denied. If we won, he explained, it probably was going to be on appeal. I was still so naive that I thought I would be fine. I thought telling the truth would be sufficient. As the *New York Times* reported, "The charges against Mr. Chapin did not involve the Watergate burglary or even political spying or sabotage, but simply whether he had told the truth when he testified under oath before a Grand Jury.

"Although the charges were relatively minor, the special prosecutor's office was especially interested in winning a conviction since it was the first of its cases to come to trial." The prosecutors had to win, in other words, in order to establish criminal intent in the minds of the public. My trial, being the first, was so important to the prosecution that Leon Jaworski, the Watergate special prosecutor, attended each of the five days in their entirety, which was a surprise to all of us.

Don Segretti was my first defense witness. He testified that he had sent samples of phony news releases, embarrassing questionnaires, and wrongly credited posters to my home. When questioned by Jake Stein, he admitted that he could not recall telling me that he, personally, had distributed any materials. Herb Kalmbach testified he wasn't sure what he had paid Segretti. John Dean testified that I was in charge of running Segretti and that he had told me several times that it was unlikely I had done anything illegal—and that I should rely on Dean for legal advice.

Ironically, while my trial was in progress, it was announced that Richard Nixon had agreed to pay almost half a million dollars in back taxes. His staff had not properly documented the donation of a portion of his papers to the National Archives, so his claimed charitable deduction was disallowed. Whatever one might believe about Nixon, the concept of his knowingly cheating on his taxes was beyond absurd. Bob Haldeman, who was speaking to reporters for the first time since leaving the White House, insisted that Nixon "didn't know a damned thing about Watergate" and that "he didn't know about a cover-up of Watergate." Asked what the president's greatest weakness was, Bob replied, "This is one you probably won't find credible, but I think his greatest weakness is his softheartedness at a personal level."

Bob continued: "He's a very tough guy in the abstract, but it is very hard for him to deal with personal problems. He has a very soft heart at the person-to-person, human relationship level. It's hard for him to fire people, to reprimand people . . . His chewing out was sometimes indirect and delicate, and sometimes that got in the way."

That was a pretty good description. It was a characterization of the president I knew to be true. In fact I understood it as a major reason I had not heard directly from the president after being let go from the White House.

On the third day of my trial I took the stand. To find me guilty, the jury had to believe I had not only lied to the grand jury, but that I did so intentionally. They also had to believe that I knew I was lying when I gave my answers in front of them. My defense was that, if I had made false statements to the grand jury, I had done so unintentionally because I didn't understand the deliberately broad questions, or specifically what they were asking. I also said there were some things I just didn't remember. After I testified that I had not told Don to focus on any particular Democratic candidate, for example, the prosecutor presented a note I'd written to Segretti telling him to focus on the front runner at the time, Senator Ed Muskie. It was embarrassing to me that the note was offered as evidence, because it had to appear to the jurors that I had been lying. However, the truth was that I had no memory of having written the note. None. I wrote dozens of notes and memos to dozens of people about dozens of subjects every single day. As I had honestly told the grand jury, I simply hadn't remembered writing it. In the middle of a five-day trial focusing on my relationship with Segretti, that memo became very important because it did look to the grand jury as if I was lying. It was my word, saying, "Not that I recall" versus an embarrassing memo in my handwriting that indicated the truth was something other than what I had testified.

I was on the stand for almost three hours. I acknowledged that I had received materials from Segretti but, I explained in all honesty, that I had quickly become "bored" with what appeared to me to be a "hodgepodge of junk" and I threw most of it away without even opening it. I admitted that Bob was aware that I had hired someone to do something, but he never asked about it. The main point we emphasized was that I was so busy. I had so many serious responsibilities—like advancing the president's trips to China and Russia—that I mostly left Segretti on his own. An assistant prosecutor asked me, "Weren't you interested in what Segretti was doing?"

"Not particularly, no," I responded. To the grand jury—none of whom had any experience in senior government positions—that answer was not believable.

I had one additional big problem. Seven of the twelve jurors were African American. One of the false press releases Segretti had issued claimed that Shirley Chisholm, the New Yorker who was the first black woman ever elected to Congress, had been committed to a home for the mentally ill and diagnosed as a schizophrenic. Admittedly it was highly inflammatory. Segretti testified that when he showed it to me, I had laughed. I didn't remember it, but I also didn't claim it hadn't happened. It had never come up in my FBI interviews, nor do I remember it from my grand jury testimony. Some of Segretti's material was nasty stuff. I hadn't suggested any of it, hadn't worked on any of it, and had no involvement in circulating it. But it was the product of an effort that I had initiated. The tenor of those materials certainly didn't make Jake Stein's job easier. Nor could I expect a black juror to view them favorably.

The jury deliberated for almost twelve hours. It was a Friday. Jake had told me they would reach a verdict that day because no jury wants to come back to court on a Monday. While we waited, Susie played gin rummy in a small room with some friends. I played backgammon with my parents. White House friends Ron Walker and Bruce Herschensohn stayed with me. Other friends who lived in Washington dropped by to visit and encourage me. Among them was my college roommate Mike Guhin, who worked for Kissinger in the National Security Council and had stood right next to me that November day twelve years earlier at Nixon's "last press conference." Of all the incredible and unexpected experiences we had shared, this one was beyond our understanding.

I was very optimistic. I thought we had done a good job at the trial. I also thought the fact that the jury was out so long was a good sign. Of course, I had also been certain Nixon was going to win the 1962 gubernatorial election.

I was stunned when I was found guilty on two counts. Susie was crying. My parents didn't know how to react. I went out to the front of the courthouse, with Susie next to me, faced the cameras, and told them I intended to appeal. At the same time, the president was returning from France, where he had attended the funeral of President Georges Pompidou. I was told that when word reached *Air Force One* that I had been convicted, it was greeted with a concerned silence. I suspect there were several people on that flight who were thinking of their own futures.

The special prosecutors had gotten the conviction they needed. Most Americans mistakenly believed that I was convicted due to my involvement in the Watergate break-in. A month later I was sentenced to a prison term of ten to thirty months on each of the two counts.

It was beyond surreal. There was nothing in my life that could have prepared me for that sentence. The unfairness of it felt overwhelming. Jake Stein filed two strong appeals, essentially claiming I had not purposefully lied, which was absolutely true, and that it was impossible for me to have gotten a fair trial in Washington because of the prejudice against not only Nixon, but his men, which also was true. I told reporters we intended to appeal to the Supreme Court, which we did. Both of our appeals were turned down.

I was going to prison.

$\star$ **16** $\star$

LET MY LIGHT SHINE

At eight o'clock on the evening of August 8, 1974, Susie and I were sitting in our den in Winnetka watching Richard Nixon resign from the presidency of the United States. The girls were in bed. I cried. We both cried. Neither of us had cried when I was indicted. We had not cried when I was put on trial. Susie had cried at the verdict, while I had not. But that night watching Nixon resign, and the following day, I cried.

I was overwhelmed by sadness and by what I considered the extraordinary unfairness that was taking place. This ridiculous, completely unnecessary burglary had changed American history. "These years have been a momentous time," Nixon said in his resignation speech. The evidence of my participation in that momentous time, in all of it, was hanging on the walls around us. Photographs, commissions, notes, mementos of my life with Richard Nixon. "We have ended America's longest war," he continued. "We have unlocked the doors that for a quarter of a century have stood between the U.S. and the People's Republic of China . . . In the Middle East 100 million people, many of whom have considered us their enemies for nearly twenty years, now consider us their friends . . . We have begun the crucial breakthroughs that have begun the process of limiting nuclear arms."

We just sat there surrounded by our past. So many memories. That bitter Richard Nixon, resigned-to-defeat, was not the man I was remembering. Rather, I was thinking of an early morning on our way to China.

We had stopped to spend a night in Honolulu to enable our body clocks to begin adjusting to the time change. I had gotten up at dawn, put on a swimsuit, and gone out to the beach. It was an absolutely gorgeous morning, not a cloud in the sky. I lay there on the sand, my eyes closed. The sun was creeping over the horizon. Maybe I fell asleep.

All of a sudden I heard a familiar booming voice: "Dwight!" I opened my eyes. Staring down at me was the president of the United States, who was out for an early morning walk on the beach with a team of Secret Service agents. He had a big broad smile on his face. "Are you getting your sun?" he asked.

"Yes, sir," I said. And he laughed as they went marching off down the beach.

That was the Richard Nixon I knew. He was on his way to one of the great diplomatic victories of his career. He wasn't the man whom I was watching on my television set, delivering this message of resignation.

I cried again the next day as I watched him leaving the White House for the final time. He made a farewell address to the White House staff. Many of our friends were there that day. Everyone was standing. Many of them were crying too. My heart was breaking, as was Susie's. I felt he was talking directly to me when he said, "No man or no woman came into this administration and left it with more of this world's goods than when he came in. No man or no woman ever profited at the public expense or the public till. That tells something about you. Mistakes, yes; but for personal gain, never. You did what you believed in. Sometimes right, sometimes wrong."

We did what we believed in. That was so true. I had no regrets about my actions. I was proud of the role I had played. I believed completely that we had left this country far better off than it had been when we'd moved into the White House.

I felt his pain as he paused and looked into his heart. "I remember my old man," he said. That was so unusual for him. Nixon was so guarded, so protective of his privacy. I remembered that late night plane ride so many years earlier when he suddenly started talking about his childhood, his parents. I hadn't realized at the time how rare those moments were. He talked about his father, "a common man," he called him, "but a great man because he did his job."

And then he started talking about his mother. I remembered being with her at those rallies in 1962. This was an incredibly difficult day for me too and, I was certain, for Bob, for all of us. Later in the afternoon I sat down and wrote a note to the suddenly former president. I wanted to send him just a few supportive words. It was almost two months later when he responded, apologizing for the length of time in doing so. "We have all gone through a terribly difficult time, but we must keep the faith and always remember that history will put the difficult events of the recent past in their true perspective. You played a very historic role . . . and I shall always be grateful for your loyal friendship and support."

When Nixon resigned there was quite a bit of speculation about what he might do. There were numerous options available to him. But not to me. I had no job and no income. It was not surprising that few employers were interested in hiring a guy whose conviction had been front-page news. Fighting to stay out of prison is an expensive way to not make a living. Susie and I were spending everything we had saved. We were feeling anxious about our future. Our lives had been turned upside down, inside out. I was trying to figure out how to pay our next month's mortgage.

What I did have, among those people who knew the facts, was my reputation. That had value. Herb Kalmbach, who had remained a friend and mentor since first hiring me in 1962, put me in touch with W. Clement Stone, a self-made man who had founded and built a billion-dollar insurance company. Mr. Stone was a strong believer in providing people with an opportunity to succeed. He wrote many bestselling motivational self-help books. He donated hundreds of thousands of copies of his books to prisons around the nation to help inmates. He was one of the largest contributors for years to the Boy's and Girl's Clubs of America. Thousands of charities across the country received contributions from the W. Clement Stone and Jessie V. Stone Foundation. The Stones gave their fortune away doing great things to help people. W. Clement Stone had been a major contributor to both Richard Nixon's 1968 and 1972 campaigns. Herb, thinking Mr. Stone might be able to help me, arranged an interview.

We met at the Stones' home. Home? Their massive house on Lake Michigan was so large it was known as "The Villa." Mr. Stone was warm and welcoming. He was well aware of my situation. This was a man who had spent considerable time and money helping others, and I needed help. I suggested I could write articles for *Success*, a small magazine he published, to generate some income. He asked me to come back the following day.

"The magazine is not where I can use you," he said. "I could use you at W. Clement Stone Enterprises. We own a variety of things and I think you could help me with the business side of it." He asked what I had been making at United and offered to pay me the same salary.

I don't know what I would have done without him and Mrs. Stone, Jessie. I was struggling at best. I had no idea what my new job would entail and, honestly, I didn't care. His "Enterprise" headquarters was in Chicago. Among those "things" his corporation owned was a Los Angeles company called Trans-American Video, the largest supplier of videotaping trucks and equipment in the country. The company also owned several soundstages. Basically, they provided the video equipment for televised events. If you were watching a football game on TV, it was because Trans-American Video was there with their live cameras. At that time the company had no president, so I filled the role while also running the search for a permanent head.

I loved it. I worked there until all my appeals had been rejected, slightly more than a year. When it appeared I would be going to prison, Mr. Stone and I worked out a unique arrangement. I wanted Susie and the girls to be able to stay in our home, with as much stability as possible. The opportunity that Mr. Stone offered me is that he would continue to pay my salary while I was in prison. In return, after I was released, I would work for him for five years at the same salary. He was offering security for me and my family. It was amazingly generous and very much appreciated.

After my final appeal to the Supreme Court had been rejected, I received a phone call, then a note from the former president. "I just want you to know that Mrs. Nixon and I deeply sympathize with you and Susie during this ordeal which has been imposed upon you . . . Remember too that as a young man you have many years ahead in which you will render great service to the Nation in one capacity or another. Time is a great healer and, while things may look pretty dark at the moment, just have faith that a new day will be coming . . . when your services to the administration and the nation . . . will far outweigh the charges which have plagued you."

Based on what I had been told by my lawyers, I anticipated spending four months "behind bars" . . . well, there were no bars. I was assigned to the Federal Correctional Institution, Lompoc, California, a minimum-security camp. I had requested Lompoc because it was about sixty miles from Santa Barbara, where Susie's parents lived. At that time, there were no walls or electrified fences at the low-security facility. But it was right next to the maximum-security prison at Lompoc. In the camp the inmates lived in dorms rather than cells. Admittedly the physical conditions were not harsh, but the mental toll was horrific. The loss of freedom, and the loss of the right to make any decisions about my life, was devastating.

I reported to prison on August 10, 1975. Susie brought Kim and Tracy to see me the second week I was there. We had a picnic lunch outside. The girls were very young—ten and eight—and couldn't have completely understood what was happening. We wanted them to actually see me so they would understand they didn't have to worry. We wanted them to understand that I was not in a dangerous situation. I was just in prison, and I was safe.

I do have one regret: I wish I had the knowledge I'd gained in prison before going to work in the White House. It was one of the most valuable learning experiences of my life. Being in prison, even just for several months (although there is no "just" when talking about being in prison), changed me. It exposed me to situations and people that otherwise would never have been part of my life. There are people who tell you they vowed this or that before going to prison. That wasn't me. The only objective I had when I walked through the gates was to walk out as soon as possible. I didn't expect to be a different or a better person.

On August 9, 1975, the day before I was to enter Lompoc, I flew to Los Angeles. Susie and I had decided that, in order to avoid the drama of my saying goodbye to the girls at the airport, it would be better for me to say goodbye to them at home. In Los Angeles I stayed with wonderful friends from USC, Dick and Marsha Howard. Marsha made a great Mexican dinner. Early the next morning, Dick drove me to Lompoc. On the way we stopped in Santa Barbara for pancakes.

I walked into prison with the clothes I was wearing, a kit with a razor and shaving cream, and a determination to tough it out. I had spent considerable time working with Herm Stein, my Christian Science mentor, and had found a peaceful place in my mind that I could turn to over the months, as necessary.

Before leaving Chicago, I visited with Herm. He offered assurances to me, in his warm supportive way, and then said something profound, "Just remember Dwight—prison can get the best of you, *or you can make the most of it.*" I heard him.

The prison officials were expecting me. Because of all the publicity surrounding me for the previous couple of years, I was classified as a high-profile inmate. They took my physical possessions and bagged them, then showed me where I would be sleeping. I was in a large bunk dorm room. I looked around and reality began to sink in. I was in prison. I had literally gone from the White House to the "Big House."

On the second day I got my work assignment. Because I had such high visibility, I was told they couldn't give me any type of special treatment. That was fine. I hadn't expected any. The work assignment they gave me was to put me on a tractor. My job was to plow a field, then run a disk over it to break up clods of dirt. They had no way of knowing that this was about the best possible job I could have been assigned. I couldn't believe it. I had learned how to drive a tractor as a twelve-year-old in Kansas. I was absolutely delighted with this job. It meant that I would be able to spend hassle-free days out in the field, on the tractor, all by myself.

Federal Correctional Institution, Lompoc, had previously been part of a military base. It was a pretty basic setting. There were three or four two-story cinder block buildings resembling barracks, our dormitories, surrounding a grass courtyard. The camp office was located on the ground floor of the main building. Any doubt I had that the inmates knew who I was evaporated by my second day there. As I walked across the courtyard, someone yelled out a window, "Hey! Nixon man! Nixon man!" I ignored him. I just kept walking.

There were an array of characters at Lompoc, ranging from older white men to "Señor Volkswagen," a very small Mexican who hurried along at high speed to keep up with his friends, usually carrying a radio, which was never on. Most of the Mexicans being held there would "escape" to go home at Christmas. After Christmas they would return to the United States to be captured. At Lompoc they worked in the furniture factory and were paid fifty cents an hour. A guaranteed job in America. They sent their earnings home to Mexico. The whole routine never made sense to me: escape for Christmas—return to the U.S. to be caught—escape again for Christmas—return to be caught . . .

After several weeks some of the younger African American inmates started harassing me. It wasn't that bad. They'd bump into me in the hallway, then give me a nasty look. It was more of a veiled threat than any kind of altercation. I mentioned it to one of the older inmates, who told me I'd better speak to a man I'll call "Big Mike Davis," although that was not his name. I went to his "house," his room, and knocked on the door. The door opened and the light disappeared as one of the largest men I had ever seen filled the doorway. "I'm looking for Mike Davis," I said—although one look at this man made it pretty obvious I had found him.

"I'm Mike."

"Well, my name is Dwight Chapin, and I've been told it would be smart for me to come over and talk to you."

"Come on in," he said, stepping aside. It was a "Let there be light" moment. I fully trusted Mike from the moment I set foot in his room. Having spent ten years in Soledad Prison for armed robbery, Mike knew the system. I told Big Mike my story over the next hour or so. It was a good move. We became good friends. I never had another problem on the inside. No one came near me. The word had gone out: "Leave Chapin alone."

It turned out Big Mike was very interested in politics. We would talk at length about my experiences. While I was at Lompoc, Pat Buchanan published a new book. I asked Pat to autograph a copy for Mike. I had never considered that I'd be asking Pat to autograph a copy of his book for a friend I'd made in prison. I taught Mike a lot about politics. Much more important, he enlightened me about racial issues in America. "Dwight, you have no idea what it's like to be standing on a corner when a car stops at a light. They see me standing there and I can hear them hit the automatic door locks. I'm black. I'm big and I scare them." He was right: I had no idea about any of that. But I learned. I learned a lot from Mike.

Eventually I was transferred from the tractor to a kitchen job, which essentially was a half-day every-other-day job. That gave me a lot of free time, which is not necessarily a good thing when you're incarcerated. I received a lot of support from my friends. It was fascinating to see how different people reacted to my situation. One of the very first letters I received was from Bryce Harlow. Bryce summed up the way we all felt: "There's a malignance, as well as a malevolence, in what has happened to so many of our friends . . . Everyone who knows you feels terrible that our process of justice could go so grotesquely awry."

Billy Graham wrote and suggested, "While there, it would be interesting for you to study in the Bible how many of God's greatest servants spent time in prison. Each one came out stronger for it . . . This experience will strengthen you in every way."

In her letter Nell Yates said, "I think of you every day . . . Of all the people I know you will be more able to see your present situation in the brightest light possible . . . I simply do not understand WHY you are there . . . I feel I know better than anyone that you are guilty of nothing. You and I were a good team and we made a big contribution not only to good government but hopefully to bring about a more orderly and peaceful world."

In those few words Nell summed up what those of us in the administration believed we had been doing. The fact that it had come down to Watergate was painful for all of us.

Bob Haldeman was busy fighting his own legal battles. Earlier in 1975 he had been convicted of conspiracy and obstruction of justice. That was just outrageous. He had been sentenced to as much as eight years in prison. In one of my early letters to him I suggested he visit Lompoc, if the court allowed, so he "might get a feel for what it is like here and see it."

Bob Haldeman and I had been exchanging notes and letters for more than a decade. And it had finally come down to this: I was suggesting he visit me in prison so he would have some sense of what to expect when he began serving his own sentence.

"You seem to be surviving your back to college experience," he wrote to me in September. Then he brought me up to date on his own situation. He mentioned that people we had worked with were lawyering up, fighting charges, preparing for trial.

It was so difficult to believe our lives were now all about lawyers and court hearings and, ironically, publishing deals. Americans were fascinated by Watergate. Woodward and Bernstein had become media superstars. Haldeman had been approached to write a book. Chuck Colson wrote to me in September to say that finishing his book was "comparable to giving birth to an elephant."

Chuck Colson had gone to prison before me. While there, he experienced a spiritual awakening that was to last the rest of his life. In the White House he had been known as a tough son of a bitch who said he would "walk over his grandmother" to get Richard Nixon reelected President of the United States. So when we first heard about his "enlightenment," many of us weren't sure what to make of it. His work with Prison Fellowship Ministries after his release certainly proved how sincerely he had found a new inspiration and a new calling. Among the thoughts he wrote to me: "It is utterly preposterous, as I reflect on it now, to think of what earthly good is being done just to cart Mr. Nixon's men off to prison." In another letter: "The important thing for you to remember is that the experience can either make or break you. Knowing you I am convinced it will make you a stronger person." Interestingly, "make or break you" was very close to the insight Herm Stein had offered.

The whole situation seemed out of control. John Dean wrote that Colson, Magruder, and Kalmbach were with him, all incarcerated together at Fort Holabird, a "safe house" facility in Maryland: "And we are enjoying visiting with each other. It helps." Looking back, I am cynical about the sincerity of the Dean letter. He must have really felt some guilt to have written. Interestingly, I received one "congratulatory" wire when I left prison. It was from John Dean and his wife, Mo. John Dean clearly knew how wrong my prosecution had been.

The hardest part of it all for me, other than being away from my family, was the knowledge that I didn't belong there. "This whole thing is a joke," I wrote to Bob, ". . . but I must accept the punishment and know that somewhere there is a reason and, with proper study, I'll come out a better person. Not because I served this time here but because of what I did with my time."

While I was serving my sentence at Lompoc, my family was home in Chicago. They were serving a sentence too. Little kids can be mean to other little kids. Kim and Tracy were young, in middle school and grade school. They were teased about their dad being in prison. I can imagine how difficult it must have been for them. Susie didn't share those kinds of stories with me at the time. I didn't learn of some of their trauma for years. Later in life, as grown women, through their tears they confirmed horrible memories of being bullied by their class-mates. Their teachers were outstanding and a big help. Susie was a hero, keeping our home together, helping the kids cope, and sending me care packages. The girls wrote, sending me letters, pictures, and handmade posters almost weekly.

I was fortunate in that I had a stream of visitors. In addition to Susie visiting every month or so, dozens of friends came to see me. As any-one who has been in that situation will confirm, visitors matter. They make a difference, especially those people like my wife and Haldeman, who brought McDonald's hamburgers and fries with them. It's amaz-ing what you miss. There was always a sadness as I watched a loved one or friend leave to return to his or her life. However, the feeling of being connected to the world that their presence brought really helped. Mostly it meant I was not being forgotten.

Tim Elbourne was among my most memorable visitors. Unbe-knownst to me, Tim had baked marijuana into the brownies he brought. When I commented about feeling lightheaded he started laughing. I had never had marijuana before. Other friends somehow pulled off the orange juice and vodka combination. While all this was appreciated, considering where I was, it was very risky.

Haldeman's visit was tough for both of us. We had gone to the mountaintop together and now I was telling Bob all about life at Lom-poc. He had many questions, as he foresaw the real possibility that Lompoc was going to be his home for several months. His visit had a very understandable awkwardness to it. I think both of us felt it.

My most memorable visitor was W. Clement Stone. Mr. Stone had often spoken in prisons, so I arranged with the warden, Chuck Turnbo, to have him speak to the inmates at Lompoc. When he arrived at the prison we met with the warden in his office. What a contrast: Mr. Stone in his powder blue three-piece, highly tailored suit, his painted-on signature hairline mustache, sparkling eyes, happy face, and wild-colored bow tie verses the drabness of the prison. He had brought a box of Cuban cigars as a gift for me. Because of the Cuban blockade, those cigars were considered contraband. Chuck Turnbo explained to him that he couldn't allow me to have them. Mr. Stone looked at him and suggested, "How about we all have one." The warden was a good man, but he followed the rules. That box was never opened.

After that, we went into the chapel for his address. Mr. Stone was an inspirational leader and speaker. He always started his speeches the same way, whether he was talking to salespeople or, as it turned out, prisoners. He would shout out to the audience, "How are you feeling today?"

In response, the audience was supposed to shout, "I feel healthy! I feel happy! I feel terrific!"

Then he would cup his ear and shout, "I can't hear you. Louder!"

"I feel healthy! I feel happy! I feel terrific!"

"Once more!" he would shout. "I can't hear you! Stand up! How do you feel today?"

Usually by this point, his audience would be on their feet screaming the answer. Usually.

It's one thing to do that in a sales meeting. There's a very different audience in a prison. Happy? Terrific? Those are not words I would use to describe the way most inmates feel. I was ready to be embarrassed for Mr. Stone, but he plowed right ahead. And his optimism was infectious. He started—and the prisoners responded. By the time he was done, they were all on their feet, shouting loudly.

I was laughing so hard that tears were rolling down my face.

"And so you are," he said to the group. "Sit down and let me talk to you." He went on to tell the prisoners they could change their lives. There was a future, and it was theirs to plan. That was Mr. Stone. He had an amazing ability to reach people. I knew many people looked at him as a salesman's salesman, some as a snake-oil salesman, but that was unfair. Mr. Stone was an incredible businessman, a booming success, and, yes, a character. God didn't make many W. Clement Stones. My fellow inmates thanked me for weeks afterward for arranging his visit.

Dick Howard, who had driven me to Lompoc the day I checked

in, was given a special assignment. He visited one day and brought an electric skillet. As one of my fellow inmates, a policeman from Chicago serving time for taking a bribe, walked along the dirt road bordering Lompoc, Dick's car approached. In a split second the skillet was under a blanket the excop was carrying. Thanks to Dick we were able to fry steaks in our room. The steaks were obtained by paying a guard with cigarettes under the table to import them from a butcher in town. The electric skillet was a real step up. Prior to obtaining it we used a light-bulb covered with aluminum foil to create the heat to cook the steaks. That process took forever.

I made my prison time pass as best I could. Every Sunday, just as I had when I was in the office next to the president of the United States, I would plan my week. But rather than scheduling meetings with senators and foreign leaders, I would plan my worktime, my reading time, my piano practice, my leatherworking. I learned how to make bookmarks and belts. My White House Brotherhood pal Henry Cashen was known for always having a cigar lit. The belt I made Henry had cigars all around it.

Reaching back to my meetings with Herm Stein, he inspired me with the idea that, even in prison, I could let my light shine. It was a spiritual thought that I've carried with me ever since. My translation was in the leather cover I made for my address book. On the cover I hand-carved a candle and a basket. The basket was leaning away from the candle. *The message was my reminder not to hide my light under a basket. I was free, in prison or anywhere, anytime, to let my inner light shine. That could not be taken from me.* Herm had undoubtedly referenced it from our earlier studies and Matthew 5:14–16, which in part states: "Let your light shine before others, so that they may see your good works and give glory to your Father who is in heaven." For me, it was a meaningful, guiding message to self.

I also set up an employment agency to assist some of the other inmates. People were leaving Lompoc with no job, no prospects. With the permission of my counselor, I literally set up an office. Men would come in and we would work on their résumés or send out job applications. Eventually I was relieved of my kitchen responsibilities so I could devote myself full-time to my employment agency. I couldn't help everybody, though. I remember asking one young man where he was going to go after he was released. "Back to L.A.," he told me. I asked him how much money he needed to live. "'Bout three or four hundred thousand dollars."

"What's your occupation?"

"Well," he admitted, "I was a drug pusher."

"What's your education?"

"I didn't quite finish high school," he said.

I was honest with him: "We're going to have trouble finding you something making that kind of money."

"Then I'm going back on the street," he said matter-of-factly.

I exercised every day. I walked around the track so many times that I lost twenty-five pounds. I came out of Lompoc weighing what I had weighed when I graduated from high school. Sometimes I would carry my portable cassette player and listen to music, mostly Neil Diamond, but just as often, I would repeat different mantras that I had memorized: "God protected and God directed." I had these good thoughts, positive thoughts that I would repeat as I walked around and around the track.

Overall, I was able to maintain a decent attitude. In one letter Colson suggested I should keep copies of the letters I was sending out. He had read a letter I sent to Kissinger and told me I had "the makings of the first humorous book to come out of Watergate." I have no memory today of what I said to Kissinger. But it was an interesting concept because there was nothing humorous about what had happened to all of us in our efforts to serve our country. Bryce Harlow was accurate in his description of what we faced: malignance and malevolence.

I experienced ups and downs throughout the nine months I spent at Lompoc. There were times when I felt heartsick. For sure I was often homesick. It was a crummy place to be. The loss of freedom to make any personal decisions at times seemed overwhelming. I kept going because I knew my stay there was temporary. I knew I would be going home. What I didn't know was how soon. The average time served for all the people in my category who went to prison—Dean, Magruder, Segretti, Ed Morgan—was about four months. Because I continued fighting to maintain my innocence, I served longer than any of them. Federal Judge Gerhard Gesell, a Democrat and Lyndon Johnson appointee, didn't like me. He was a staunch liberal who was characterized in his *New York Times* obituary as "impatient" and "quirky." The judge probably was anti-anyone Nixon. I felt it from the first moment I entered his courtroom. Because I fought, he was getting even. That is how it appeared to me. What was going on felt wrong. It didn't feel like justice. It felt like injustice. I was being punished for lying, but I had not lied. The system wanted me to show remorse, to admit my wrongs, and I just wouldn't do it. My lawyer, Jake Stein, and several other people continued telling me that I had to write a letter of contrition to the judge to be released. Jake could not have been any clearer: "If you don't," he said, "we probably can't get you out of there for another several months."

There was a principle involved. I refused to do it. I refused to . . . I refused . . . Time wore me down. I broke. "Dear Judge Gesell," I wrote in November, as Stein filed a motion for my release. "You may want to know that I have accepted your punishment with the keen awareness that I would not be here if, indeed, I had not done something wrong. If an acknowledgment of my wrongdoing is meaningful—be assured it is so offered." In addition to acknowledging my guilt, I had to show I was rehabilitated. "While blessed with some attributes there are, hopefully were, some critical flaws in my character . . . How does one rehabilitate his character? Slowly. I am working at the change."

I didn't believe a word of what I had written to Judge Gesell. In fact, the personal notes I wrote as I awaited my release date, probably as I struggled to decide what I would say to the media, more accurately reflected my beliefs. My honest thoughts were in my personal notes: "My indictment was political. I am a political prisoner. The prosecution was political and had many of us served a man named Kennedy [that is, a Democrat] instead of one named Nixon [a Republican], we would have never faced prison. Watergate and the subsequent revelations had been a circus of hypocrisy . . . I served six months because at a moment in time the privilege fell my way to serve a President of the United States. The shadows of Watergate are only a small part of the glorious adventures in which I was fortunate enough to have participated." (In the notes I wrote that I had been there for six months, which was what I anticipated the length of my sentence would be. However, it turned out to be nine months before I was released from Lompoc.)

In my mind, as I wrote those words, I was a free man. I was imagining myself reading my statement to the media, finally revealing how I felt. I sent a draft to Tex McCrary for his advice. His advice was, essentially, to keep my mouth shut. "I think," he wrote, "it would be remembered by politicians only as an irritant . . . I would caution a 'low profile' for you." Great advice. Tex was always influential because he cut to the truth of a situation. "Dwight—wrong time. No one wants to hear from you."

But the statement of contrition I had written to Judge Gesell, as hypocritical as it was, was both necessary and apparently effective. As a result he reduced my minimum sentence to six months. He recommended the parole board release me at the earliest possible date, which would have been the following February. (Nonetheless, because of bureaucratic screwups, I actually wasn't released until April 1, 1976, which was exactly two years from the day my trial had begun in 1974.) I also was approved for a Christmas furlough, a few days outside the grounds to spend with my family. Susie and I took Kimberly and Tracy to Santa Barbara for the holidays and had a wonderful reunion.

I heard from a lot of old White House friends. John Ehrlichman was "delighted to hear that Gesell did the right thing." Typically, John was working on an outline for his second book while waiting to hear from the court of appeals about his own case.

John Mitchell heard the news and said, "Perhaps some sanity is coming back to the country."

Haldeman, naturally, was happy for me. He told me during his visit that he was having difficulty finding the right collaborator for his book—but in the meantime he had "reacquired typing skills. I'm especially good at using the fantastic new erasing devices."

I was often asked if I intended to write my own book. People assumed that if you had worked for the president, you had to be writing a book. I understood why some people would do it. It was a quick way to harvest some desperately needed dollars from the notoriety of Watergate. My answer to those people who wondered about it was to point out that I really wasn't a writer—although, I added, that didn't seem to slow down several of my former colleagues. The truth is I didn't intend to write a Watergate book. In many ways I thought it was unseemly.

As the time came for the parole board to confirm my release date, it somehow was revealed that Mr. Stone had continued paying me while I was in prison. In the *Chicago Sun-Times* it was a front-page story. It was the salary we had agreed upon a year earlier, and in return for that I had agreed to work for him for five years at that same salary. No raises. But the parole board obviously gave it a very different meaning. The idea someone would be "paid" while in prison being punished did not sit well with them. It didn't happen, thankfully, but for a period of time I was led to believe they might extend my incarceration because of the story.

That one really would have hurt. Susie and I had been making plans for some fun things we wanted to do with the girls. When your freedom is close enough to almost touch it and then it is snatched away, you carry every minute of that additional time on your back. I was finally released on April 1, 1976, nine months after I had entered Lompoc. I had served my time. Any debt I owed because of Watergate had been paid.

My parents picked me up at five o'clock the morning I was released. The press was waiting for me, off the main road, near the entrance to

Lompoc. Dad knew that and had figured out a back exit we could take so that, as they whisked me away, we avoided the media. My loving, supportive, and relieved parents were there, overjoyed that they could drive me to the airport to fly home to Chicago.

I flew back to Chicago with Dick and Marsha Howard. They were coming for the "Welcome Home Dwight" party at our Winnetka home that evening. When the plane landed, Susie and the girls met me at the gate. It was jammed with arriving and departing passengers and an incredible number of reporters, including television cameras. For once, the questions were easy: "How does it feel to be home?"

It was wonderful to arrive back home on Ridge Road. That evening dozens of our Chicago friends and many from out of town gathered to celebrate my being home. Yet it was like experiencing shell shock to me. I remember the loudness, the music, the laughter—contrasted with, twenty-four hours before, the stillness and my anticipation there at Lompoc over what was to come when I got home.

All Susie and I wanted was to have normal lives again. Somehow, we managed to do that, picking up our individual routines pretty quickly. We didn't spend any time wallowing in what had happened.

The first letter I received at home was from Haldeman. It was a note from his heart, filled with biblical quotes, then a suggestion: "The real challenge does lie ahead and not behind; and you will gain immeasurably from what you have had to go through. I firmly believe that this will be the hardest test for you—and that you are well prepared to meet it and that you will do so with flying colors." For the first time he added to his P.S.: "and Love, Bob." For Bob P.S. stood for *perge superaque,* Latin for "onward and upward." That salutation was engraved on an ancient pewter mug that Bob had gifted me in 1963 or 1964. Over the years, almost every letter he wrote ended with the P.S. "Onward and upward."

I was asked many times why I wasn't angry that Richard Nixon didn't go to prison. People couldn't understand why, especially after so many members of the administration had had their lives disrupted and, in some cases, destroyed. My answer was that I didn't think any of us, other than the people who planned and carried out the burglaries, should have gone to prison. More than that, though, in my mind, I was still on the team. I was never off the team. All through prison I was still in the game.

The president had an attitude that I really liked. Always. In a four-part television and radio broadcast in 1977 with David Frost, he said there were people who believed they would be living the most wonderful life if they "could just not have to work every day, if they could just be out fishing, or hunting, or playing golf, or traveling."

> *That would be the most wonderful life in the world. But they don't know life. What makes life mean something is purpose, a goal, the battle, the struggle, even if you don't win it. I know a lot of people, and I can understand they say, gee whiz, it just isn't fair for an individual to get off with a pardon simply because he happens to have been president when another individual goes to trial and maybe has to serve a prison sentence for it. I can understand how they feel. I can only say that no one in the world, no one in our history, knows how I felt. No one could possibly know how it feels to resign the presidency of the United States. Is that punishment enough? No, probably not. Whether it is or it isn't . . . we have to live with not only the past but for the future . . . Whatever it brings, I'll still be fighting.*

I'll be fighting. That was the Richard Nixon that I knew.

17

HEALTHY, HAPPY, AND TERRIFIC

At times it seemed my life had been a series of unlikely adventures. I had come from the farmland of the Midwest to rise to the very top of American politics. I had gone to prison for crimes I believed I had not committed. And I was still in my midthirties.

The question for me, though, was what would be coming next. I remember being caught in a terrible traffic jam on the Edens Expressway, a major artery in Chicago, not long after I had been released from prison. I had a CB radio in the car, by which I learned we were waiting for President Carter's motorcade to pass. It was going to use an overpass so all traffic going both ways beneath it had been stopped by the Secret Service. The longer we sat there stalled, the more frustrated I became. I got on my CB radio and said, "That's it. I will never vote for this son of a bitch again." As I got them riled up, other people on the network agreed.

That might have been my last political trick. I certainly had not voted for Jimmy Carter.

But I certainly grasped the symbolism of the situation: I had gone from being in a car in the presidential motorcade to being just another guy inconvenienced by the presidential motorcade.

I took inventory of my situation. The types of skills I had mastered in the White House were unique. The president, Bob Haldeman, Dick Moore, Tex McCrary, Bill Safire—everyone had been my teacher, and

I was the beneficiary. I had learned in our game planning sessions how to communicate big ideas. From years of scheduling the president's time, I had learned how to set priorities, then hammer those priorities in order to get things accomplished. Generating creative ideas was a gift with which I had been born, but sorting out what ideas actually worked took it to another level. It had all been great practical experience. I had a significant number of friends and acquaintances with whom I had developed solid relationships during my Nixon years. And I still had my reputation.

Yes, my reputation. Those people who knew me, knew me. They knew the kind of loyal person I was and that, while I had done the time, I hadn't done the crime. My friends—our friends, our true friends—never stopped believing and supporting us.

I also had W. Clement Stone and a five-year commitment to work for him. My former job was gone. He had sold Trans-American Video. "but the magazine has not been doing well," he told me. "The magazine" was *Success*. "How would you like to run that?" he asked.

Success was a *Reader's Digest*–size magazine that essentially pitched how people could motivate themselves to succeed. It was the magazine for would-be Horatio Algers, people looking for guidance about how to transform their talents and their dreams into marketable success. It preached attitude as much as process, in part by telling the stories of how other people had become successful. The tagline under the logo was "The Magazine with a Positive Mental Attitude." One time Mr. Stone told me, "People think that having a positive mental attitude means running around saying, 'Whoopee!' No, a positive mental attitude means having the right attitude in a given situation."

Success had not been particularly well published. The advertisers were mostly companies selling self-help equipment or services. My challenge was to turn it into a financial success. It was the perfect place for me to land. While I was no longer working for Richard Nixon, I was still a part of the Nixon universe. Like any group of people who have shared a meaningful, life-altering experience, the Nixon team was bonded. Nixon himself and the Nixon years were the glue that held us together. Our Nixon alumni group was a fortress of solid, good people who believed in and supported one another. I began to put to use all the contacts I had made while working for Richard Nixon.

I also began by changing *Success* into a full-size magazine, which made it easier to attract national advertisers. I had friends at Leo Burnett, one of the leading advertising agencies in Chicago. We were able to attract Oldsmobile as an advertiser, thanks to my good friend Jim Oates. After that, a few more major companies followed. Americans were used to spending their entire careers working for one company that provided security. But the world of independent contractors, freelancers, and independent salespeople was just starting to grow.

We also started "Positive Mental Attitude" rallies. We would bring together the leading motivational speakers in the country and fill large venues with self-starters who were looking for motivational inspiration. We worked with insurance salesmen, Amway distributors, people whose incomes depended on their ability to self-start and connect. In addition to Mr. Stone himself, our speakers included people like radio personality Paul Harvey; the Reverend Robert Schuller, pastor of the all-glass Crystal Cathedral; Zig Ziglar; Cavett Robert: the leading motivational speakers of that time. We would draw as many as ten to fifteen thousand people to these events.

My friend Ron Walker, who had run the advance office in the White House, had started Ron Walker and Associates with his wife, Anne. The Walkers were among our best friends. I hired Ron's firm to advance these rallies. Together we hired several of the people who had done advance work for the administration. We were using the same techniques we had used to attract people to a political rally to bring them to our motivational events. They were hugely successful. In addition to presenting speakers, we would market products like audio programs and books authored by our speakers. We created a money machine.

When I was thirteen years old my grandmother Chapin gave me a copy of Dr. Norman Vincent Peale's classic book *The Power of Positive*

Thinking. I read it before I could understand it, but I frequently referred to it as I grew up. And here I was hiring and spending time with Dr. Peale. He was an extraordinary man. He spoke at many of our events. We'd pay him five thousand dollars for a speech, which was considerably less than what we paid other speakers. One morning at breakfast in San Diego before the big rally of the day, Dr. Peale asked me nicely what we paid the Reverend Schuller. I said, "Dr. Peale, before I tell you what Bob Schuller gets, I want you to know that we're happy to pay you a bigger fee, but every time I mention that to your secretary, she tells me you are happy with what we're paying you." I paused. "We pay Bob Schuller twenty-five thousand dollars for each appearance." Dr. Peale was stunned. He looked at me and asked, "Is that Christian?" Mr. Stone was at breakfast with us, and he and Dr. Peale's wife, Ruth, both roared with laughter. Even so, Dr. Peale would never accept a higher fee.

Creating these events was considerably easier for me than publishing the magazine. We could contract the speakers we needed and promote them into a successful rally. The crowd building was the harder part, but the advance experience we had gleaned from our Nixon days helped greatly. However, I knew nothing about magazine publishing. It was a never-ending cycle of marketing, building circulation, generating editorial content, creating layouts, and attracting advertising. I learned publishing and I loved it, just loved it. I had the responsibility of picking or approving whoever would be on our cover. Whoever I thought was exemplifying the type of entrepreneurship, leadership, and positive attitude that might inspire people got the cover. We hired great people. Mike Schrauth from the White House advance office joined the team. Chuck Weigold was CFO and guided me on the business side. Our editor, Bob Anderson, was excellent and brought in terrific young talent. And I had a succession of great personal assistants, among them Jann Mahan. Jann later married my White House advance-man friend, Mike Duval. She was so talented that she ended up in the Reagan White House working directly with President Reagan on his weekly radio address and television appearances.

Admittedly all the Nixon connections helped—significantly. For example, Diane Sawyer had worked for Ron Ziegler in the press office during the Nixon administration. When she was launching her career at CBS on a morning show with Bill Kurtis, we put them both on the cover. It wasn't all Nixon. In 1980 we put California Governor Ronald Reagan on the cover and distributed *Success* to every room of the GOP convention hotel in Detroit. We worked all of our political connections, and we were somewhat bipartisan. There were often stories on solid conservative Democrats.

Mr. Stone was the perfect boss, always practicing what he and all of us at *Success* were preaching. He called our house one Saturday morning and our daughter Tracy, nine years old at the time, answered the phone. "Hello," she said. Mr. Stone then responded, "How are you today?" Tracy replied, "I'm fine. Thank you." Then there was a click on the phone as he hung up.

The phone rang again. Again Tracy answered. "Hello!" Again Mr. Stone asked, "How are you today?" Again Tracy responded, "I'm fine. Thank you." Again there was a click as Mr. Stone hung up.

That sequence repeated one more time. "Is this Mr. Stone?" she asked. It was. "Why do you keep hanging up on me?" she asked. "Because you're not giving me the right answer," he told her. And he hung up again.

She was confused. "Daddy," she said, "it's Mr. Stone, but he keeps hanging up on me because I'm not giving him the right answer."

I asked her what he had said to her. "He asked me how I am today."

I laughed. That was Mr. Stone. "Sweetheart," I said, "don't you remember? The answer you're supposed to give is 'I feel healthy. I feel happy. I feel terrific.' He's going to keep hanging up until you give him that answer."

The next time the phone rang, she raced to pick it up. She couldn't wait to give him the right answer.

The relationships formed around Richard Nixon survived his presidency, survived Watergate, and, in most cases, survived prison. We all spoke Nixon. We understood each other. We trusted each other. When possible we continued to work together. Bob Haldeman, for example, faced an even more difficult readjustment than I had. He had a far higher profile in the administration and was actually charged in the Watergate cover-up. He served eighteen months at Lompoc. And when he was released, he wasn't certain what he wanted to pursue.

Although I hadn't gone to visit him at Lompoc, we had remained in close touch. He had this idea that we should go to China as private citizens and see if we could turn our contacts there into business opportunities. I had been there with Kissinger and Haig prior to the president's historic visit and knew more about it than he did at that point. We were talking about forming a company. The concept of working with Bob again excited me. I jumped onboard immediately. I had no idea what we were going to do, how we might do it, or with whom we could do whatever it turned out to be. But it looked to me like a fun, and potentially successful, opportunity.

Mr. Stone had no objection. He saw our vision as entrepreneurship at its best. Everyone agreed that the opening of China presented incredible business opportunities. Everybody agreed, but nobody seemed to be able to figure out how to take advantage of those opportunities. Eventually Bob, Dick Howard, and I spent a week together in the People's Republic of China.

The Chinese government was very cooperative. Former President Nixon remained well respected in China, and doors opened for us. We just didn't know which doors to walk through. We had numerous meetings with state-owned companies about potentially importing their products. I remember visiting a company that wanted us to import its fine china into the United States. As we were sitting there discussing possibilities, Bob turned over one of their dinner plates. The logo on the bottom read "J-U-N-K-O." Bob spent the next twenty minutes explaining to them why this label might not be a good idea. Another day we met with a company that wanted us to import pig hearts into this country. It turns out that a pig's heart is roughly the same size as a human heart. At that time our research labs were doing considerable experimentation to find out whether parts of a pig's heart might be used as replacement tissue in human hearts. It actually turned out that pigs' valves could be safely implanted in the human body. That was among the most boring meetings I have ever attended. We enjoyed terrific access, but nothing concrete came out of that trip. Bob eventually started working in various capacities for billionaire businessman David Murdock.

John Ehrlichman also approached me with a China business idea. He was involved with a treasure hunting venture in the South China Sea. The people with whom he was working needed the approval of the Chinese government, and he suspected I could help him get it. I helped him make contacts but that venture never materialized.

Don Rumsfeld, who headed the Office of Equal Opportunity for a year under Nixon and was a Nixon favorite, hired me in the early 1990s to be part of a group bringing digital high-definition television to America. Rumsfeld was the chairman of General Instrument and had given Bill Timmons, chairman of the lobbying group Timmons & Company and a former head of the Nixon White House congressional office, responsibility for running our "campaign." The challenge was how to get the president and Congress to agree to have the country move from traditional analog to high-definition broadcasting. Federal approval was necessary for the implementation of the new technology. Don, Timmons, Rumsfeld assistant Bernie Windon, and technical guru Bob Rast were our leaders at General Instrument. We approached the project aggressively, as if we were running a political campaign. The team, which consisted of an engineering side and a political/creative side, included several people who had worked together in the White House. I was on the political/creative side. Our problem was that we needed congressional approval to move forward, but to get it we had to demonstrate the value of the technology. It was a gigantic undertaking. We were setting out to disrupt the television industry. To demonstrate to Congress the value of high-definition television we actually made a half-hour HDTV tape, using rudimentary HD equipment held together by baling wire, masking tape, and anything else we could utilize. The tape was produced and directed by Mark Goode, the man who headed our White House television office back when it reported to me. When the taped show was finally edited, we got special FCC approval to close down NBC's Washington affiliate for thirty minutes and broadcast the program into the Capitol for the heads of the various committees related to the Federal Communications Commission to witness the future of television. We were the ones that brought HDTV to America—first! We took that process from an initial idea to what Americans actually see on their TV sets today.

Not every relationship forged during the Nixon years was positive. There were people who held grudges. It was around 1979 that I was at a hotel in Palm Springs with several friends from the Nixon years. We would get together regularly. It turned out former Vice President Spiro Agnew was living in that area. He had fallen off a bicycle and injured his ankle. Roy Goodearle, who had been his Chief of Staff, suggested the two of us visit him. We were sitting in the Agnews' living room, reminiscing. "Go down the hallway," he told us. "Go into the master bedroom and look at what's on my dresser. Then come back and tell me what you see."

We walked down the hall into the bedroom; and there, on top of a tall bureau, was a statue of a huge seated Buddha. Roy and I couldn't imagine what its significance could possibly be.

"What does that statue remind you of?" Agnew asked. When we couldn't answer, he explained, "That's that fat slob Ehrlichman. I have it on my bureau so when I get up every morning, I can look at it and remember how much I hate that son of a bitch!"

Agnew's view of his nemesis Ehrlichman was 180 degrees different from mine. As was true of Bob Haldeman, John Ehrlichman was a man of great integrity. I admired John and felt a kinship with him. We had first met in 1962 during the California governor's race, in which Nixon was defeated by Pat Brown. My desk in our '62 campaign office was six feet from John's office door, and we talked daily. In the White House, John always took time to probe about how my work under Bob was going. He knew that Bob and I were close, and he understood Bob was very tough on me. John saw it. Once he nicely asked me, "How do you take it?" I always felt—and in his fatherly way Ehrlichman made it seem to be the case—that if I ever decided to move out of the Haldeman orbit, perhaps I could work for him.

I also never lost my fascination for politics. I'd seen how one man can change the world, and elective politics can be the path to that. The campaign experience I had gained proved to be invaluable. All national politics at that point still reverberated with an echo of Nixon and Watergate. Whether politicians liked or hated Nixon, most admired his political genius. In fact, that remains true to this day. And they wanted to take advantage of whatever magic of his had rubbed off on us.

In 1980, for example, I flew to Houston to meet with John Connally, who was contemplating running for President of the United States. Connally was a former popular Democratic governor of Texas and was in the car and wounded when President Kennedy was assassinated in Dallas. Nixon loved Connally. If it had been possible, the president would have replaced Agnew with Connally as his vice presidential candidate on the 1972 ticket. Conservatives were leery of Democrat Connally, and a move by Nixon to switch from Agnew would have been seen as a little too clever on Nixon's part. But, Nixon felt, and it was true, that Connally had swagger. He was the political version of John Wayne: tall, handsome, and self-assured. He had great political instincts and good judgment. We had gotten to know each other when he was Nixon's Secretary of the Treasury. I remember he came to the White House once to talk with some of the young staffers. His theme was that one of the most important things you do in politics is pick your straw enemy. A straw enemy needs to be something big against which your constituents will rebel. Budget deficits that will bankrupt the country, billionaires getting more benefits than ordinary people, the Deep State—those are all examples of possible straw enemies.

I became peripherally involved in Connally's campaign. In May 1973 he switched party affiliation from Democrat to Republican. His run for the White House was a disaster. He was running against Ronald Reagan and George Herbert Walker Bush for the Republican nomination. His campaign spent $7 million and ended up winning one delegate. Connally appealed to many of us who knew him from the Nixon years, but he was not so popular outside of his home state of Texas.

The morning after John Connally dropped out of the race, I received a phone call from George H. W. Bush. "Now that John's out," he said, "will you come and help me?" My White House friend Dick Moore was very close to both George and Barbara Bush. My guess is that it was Dick who suggested to Bush that he call. Bush was running for the nomination against Reagan. I accepted his offer. As usual, Mr. Stone was supportive. Maybe secretly I thought it was possible that I might somehow make it back to the White House. Dick Moore, our Nixon White House television consultant; Bill Carruthers, who had worked on television in the Nixon White House; Jann Mahan, my assistant at *Success,* and I all joined the Bush team to work the television side of the campaign. We started with the 1980 Pennsylvania primary, putting on telethons for Bush, and worked through the June California primary. The real Bush strategy, which he had worked out with Jim Baker, was to run a campaign that would put him in the position that, if he didn't win the presidential nomination, he would be picked as Ronald Reagan's vice presidential running mate, which is precisely what happened.

Besides Bob Haldeman, the other person with whom I have shared just about my entire life in politics is Pat Buchanan. Pat was working in Richard Nixon's law office when I first started there. We went through two successful presidential campaigns together, which led us to our experiences working in the Nixon White House, which led us to life after Watergate together. Fortunately for Pat, he wasn't caught up in any of the Watergate drama and, therefore, wasn't among the group who went to prison. In the Nixon administration, Pat was our go-to conservative. Nixon took him to China with us to make sure that the conservative wing of the Republican Party was mollified. Keep Pat happy and we keep conservatives happy. Pat was that influential with conservatives at the time.

I had the pleasure of introducing Pat at the 2013 Nixon centennial birthday dinner at the Mayflower Hotel in Washington, D.C. My theme was: "Where's Buchanan? Get me Buchanan!" Those were the words I heard hundreds of times from Nixon. The president always held Pat in the highest regard.

Pat and I also became business partners years after Watergate. One night in the late 1980s I was watching him debate the liberal Michael Kinsley on the CNN program *Crossfire*. It occurred to me that he was a natural to publish a monthly newsletter. Roy Goodearle and I raised the money to start the newsletter, which we called *PJB from the Right*. It was very successful in terms of circulation and impact. Pat did all the writing, and I ran the backroom operations and marketing. We built the circulation to fifty thousand paid subscribers in a few short months. Until Rush Limbaugh began publishing his newsletter, Pat's was the largest political newsletter in America. When Pat decided to run for president, his newsletter circulation base provided him with an incredible fundraising list to launch his eventually unsuccessful campaign. As we were not able to return our investors' investment before ceasing publication, they sadly took a hit, which always bothered me.

No matter what I have done in my career; no matter which turns my life has taken, there has always been Watergate. Always. Those of us who went through that grinder came out changed forever. It affected each of our lives.

For a term project her junior year in high school, my daughter Kimberly contacted several veterans of the Nixon White House and asked whether there were lessons they had learned from their Watergate experience. Besides hearing from Bob Haldeman, she received letters from former Attorney General John Mitchell, former Domestic Affairs Advisor John Ehrlichman, and from former President Nixon himself. What becomes obvious from the responses is how differently Watergate had affected each of us.

"The public generally does not understand what Watergate was all about and never will," John Mitchell responded to Kimberly. John Mitchell, a good and decent man, eventually served nineteen months in prison for his part in the cover-up. "[Americans] believe that everything that happened during the pertinent time was wrong because [they were] told that such was the case and never thought it out." The result, he continued, was that "the country lost a very competent president during a time when it needed him, particularly in the field of foreign affairs."

John Ehrlichman tried to put it in perspective in his handwritten response: "Everything called 'Watergate' comprised a fraction of 1% of what was going on in these years by any given measurement . . . To me, it was tragic to see the loss of momentum that occurred as Richard Nixon became more and more diverted from the solution of the country's domestic and foreign problems to the issues of Watergate . . . As a result of that, for about seven years [through the Carter administration], the field lay unplowed, weeds grew, the well went brackish, and the coyotes trampled paths where once good crops grew."

Bob Haldeman's neatly typed letter was as direct as he always was: The main lesson to be learned from Watergate, he wrote, "would seem to be the basic point that any problem must be dealt with openly and realistically—not put aside or covered up . . . The actual break-in was the result of misguided efforts of lower level personnel to try to carry out what they believed—erroneously—to be the wishes of their superiors."

Typical of Bob, he believed the problem had been the result of poor management. He continued:

> This kind of thing can be cured by better administrative and managerial procedures and internal communication—being careful to assure that all understand clearly what is expected of them and what standards they must operate under . . .
>
> The greatest tragedy of Watergate was the collapse of the Nixon presidency just when it was poised to make some very real and very major contributions to world peace . . .

Of course, the more personal and more painful tragedies of Watergate were in the disrupted and in some cases partially destroyed lives of those who were caught up in it . . .

Another misconception is the popular view that Watergate was a totally new and unheard-of kind of thing that had never happened before in our history—and that somehow exposed villains with unprecedented evil plans and programs. That also is totally untrue . . .

The misconception arising from Watergate that bothers me most is that I was lacking in integrity and honor.

That last sentence was pure Bob. I can hear him saying this. This is what mattered: "Because I was convicted of perjury, I am recorded in history as a liar—yet the strongest motivation I have always had is for truthfulness. I understand the reasons for the perjury charges—but feel they were completely without merit."

Richard Nixon also replied to Kimberly, prescient as usual, and I could feel his sadness as he wrote: "Among the greatest tragedies of Watergate has been the legacy of cynicism with which so many people now tend to view even the most conscientious government leaders . . . This greatly increases the difficulty an administration faces in trying to awaken the American people to the real dangers we face and to the difficult steps that we have to take in order to meet those dangers."

I had written my own explanation of those events to my daughters as I prepared to leave prison in 1976: "For six months I have been away from home because our government felt that I had broken our laws."

One day, my daughter Tracy asked, "Daddy, how did Watergate happen?" I said to her, "It is a complicated subject, and many wise people are still trying to sort out what went wrong."

And I said to my daughter Kimberly at the time, "Kim, you'll recall when I told you that although I was still going to appeal to the Supreme Court, I was going to begin serving my time. You said, 'But then you're admitting you're lying.' . . . Yes, going to prison hurt because I knew I was going for the wrong thing. You see, the law is not always perfect, just like us. I hired an old friend to play what were called 'dirty tricks' on Democrats in the 1972 election. The government's lawyers could not tie me to Segretti's acts so they took my testimony before a grand jury and developed what they considered a perjury case against me. Yes, I fought, lost, and served my time. But because I went to prison doesn't mean Daddy lied."

I continued: "You would be interested in knowing that my attorney was approached by the government lawyers and they implied they would 'go easy on me' if I would help them in providing information on President Nixon and Mr. Haldeman. They took my lack of assistance to imply that I was uncooperative. You see, I didn't even know anything they had done wrong."

My real guilt, I later wrote to the girls, was that "I did an injustice to our system of government. Not only did I interfere with the free elective process, worse yet, through that act I added to the cynical attitude many Americans have toward politics . . . Watergate came about not because of Richard Nixon or Richard Nixon's men . . . No, Watergate was inevitable." By writing "I did an injustice," I was acknowledging that our Dick Tuck activity, as innocent as I thought it to be, did interfere in a negative way with the process. That was not our intent, but it ended up being interpreted that way.

The real problem with the political process, as I wrote then—and my thinking has not changed in all these decades—is money: millions and millions of dollars. There is too much money coming into the elective process in the wrong way.

Kimberly's thoughts were certainly influenced by her access to those people at the heart of Watergate—as well as her own experiences and point of view. This is part of the conclusion she expressed in her paper: "Certain tragedies came out of Watergate that continue to have an effect upon those directly involved and on the nation as a whole. The personal lives . . . were jeopardized by their severe exploitation by the press . . . Life became a struggle between family life and a series of court dates."

I do know that my involvement in this scandal caused great distress to those I love, my family. My parents, who had been so proud of me, who had visited me in Washington, who had been introduced to the President of the United States by their son, could never quite figure it out. I probably didn't realize how deeply it had affected my father until he was on his deathbed. He thought the process had been completely unfair. The Segretti thing, as he referred to it, "was a pimple on an elephant." He was furious that our Dick Tuck pranks had ended up being intermingled with the Watergate break-in and cover-up. Having the family name cleared meant something to him. "Son," he said, "promise me you'll try to get a pardon."

I promised. At that moment it became a goal for me. It made no difference in my life, but it was the last promise I'd made to my father. So when George W. Bush was in office, I decided it was perhaps the right time to make an application, for I knew a lot of people working in the White House and I believed there was a good shot of its being granted. But granting presidential pardons can also have political consequences. Bush was in his first term and would be running for reelection. It looked to me to be questionable that he would want to offer a pardon to a so-called Watergate figure. I understood that political thinking, and there was no way I wanted to cause problems for President Bush.

My talented friend, Jack Carley, another Nixon alumnus whom I'd met during the 1962 gubernatorial campaign in California, had helped me with legal matters for years. Jack gathered all the pardon documents and information I needed. The application for a pardon was at least four inches thick. I had to document everything I'd done since being incarcerated. It was going to be a complex, time-consuming, and expensive process.

After Jack showed me the application, I told him I wanted to think about it. I called my daughters. I told them that just before their grandfather died, he made me promise I would try to get a pardon. The reason I was doing this would be to honor his request and to restore our good family name and my reputation.

Neither Kim nor Tracy thought it was necessary. They told me that it would make no difference whatsoever to them or, in their opinions, to the people who love me. They were in agreement on that.

I dropped it. I had been carrying Watergate on my shoulders for a long time without even realizing it. It actually was liberating to realize how little it meant in my day-to-day life.

It was fascinating to me to watch Richard Nixon transitioning from the flesh-and-blood man I knew and had worked for, with all of his quirks, into an authentic historical figure. Understanding Richard Nixon became its own industry. After leaving the White House, the former president first moved back to San Clemente; then to Manhattan for a while; and from there to Upper Saddle River, New Jersey. His was a rehabilitation process in which he had to recover from both health issues and public perceptions. But the former president was no longer a political threat, so the magnetic nature of his personality, wisdom, and political acumen drew people of influence, as well as the general public, back to him. It was, and even continues to be, an amazing process to watch the continual reevaluation and understanding of our beleaguered former president.

Over the years, I would see him a couple of times a year, mostly at events. He was always cordial and friendly. His heart was always in the game. He never hesitated to pick up the phone to contact people to give advice, whether it was a world leader or a pro football coach. He also continued writing. He published eleven books in his lifetime, nine after he left the presidency. In addition to his books, he wrote many op-eds, articles, and long essays, and he gave many speeches and made extensive use of television interviews. Those were the building blocks of his remarkable comeback to elder-statesman status.

The scandal known as Watergate also continues to transition into its historical context. Unlike earlier political scandals—the Teapot Dome scandal, for example, which gradually faded from public consciousness and became a historical footnote—Watergate took hold. Earlier scandals usually involved personal enrichment or sexual misconduct. Watergate was presented as subverting an election and creating a constitutional crisis. It was also the first scandal with the mass electronic media in place to spread it and dumb it down. From then on, any new political scandal has become known as a "-gate." Ironically, among the first to use it was Bill Safire, a former speechwriter for President Nixon, who used it in 1974 when he referred to "Vietgate." He was, he later explained, "seeking to minimize the relative importance of the crimes committed by Richard Nixon with this silliness." Instead it became part of American culture, applied to any potential scandal, ranging from the Clinton Travelgate, President Clinton's travel office scandal; and Nannygate, which sunk two of Clinton's attorney general appointments; to the cultural Nipplegate, when Janet Jackson's bare breast was exposed for an instant during the 2004 Super Bowl halftime show.

When I was publishing *Success,* my office was in the *Sun-Times* building in Chicago. One afternoon in 1980 I had left the office to get a haircut. As the elevator doors opened, I saw a group of reporters who had gathered in the lobby and were talking to G. Gordon Liddy. Gordon Liddy and Howard Hunt had been involved in the planning and execution of the Democratic headquarters burglary in the Watergate Hotel. Liddy had served more than four years in prison for his role in that burglary. In his bestselling book *Will,* he claimed he and Hunt had planned to murder columnist Jack Anderson after hearing Nixon say that someone had to get rid of him—though anyone would know Nixon didn't mean that literally. The president had never met Gordon Liddy, nor had I ever met him, but as I stepped off the elevator, I certainly recognized him. He had just published his book, and he was obviously there at the *Sun-Times* to publicize it. I waited until he had finished speaking to the group, then approached him and introduced myself. Then I invited him up to my office for a cup of coffee.

We sat talking for more than half an hour. He could not have been more interesting. His reputation was that of a no-nonsense, somewhat mysterious ex-CIA operative. Actually his reputation was worse: He was viewed as semi-crazy. A nut case. He once held his hand over an open-flame candle to prove the strength of his "will." Liddy appeared very fit, articulate, incredibly self-confident, and actually reasonable. Toward the end of our meeting he asked me, "Do you ever see the president?"

"Sometimes a couple of times a year," I replied. "I either go over to his office in New Jersey or we'll bump into each other at a dinner or a reunion or something."

He looked at me seriously and said, "I want you to give him a message for me."

"Sure," I said.

Gordon went on: "You tell him, if there is ever anything he wants me to do for him, I'm available." He paused, then added emphatically, "And I will do it!"

I didn't respond. But it was a message I never delivered.

18

WHAT I KNOW NOW THAT I DIDN'T KNOW THEN

While through the decades Watergate has remained the background music of my life, popping up from time to time, it never has been the grand theme. Long periods would pass during which I never thought about it. I cannot, and do not, expect to see Watergate disappear. It is part of our political history. In the passage of years, I have learned things that I feel are important to add to the story. I know things now that I didn't know then. In his 1982 response to my daughter Kimberly, Bob Haldeman had noted, "There are far more unanswered questions [about Watergate] than there are correct answers at this point. And they may never be answered—although I think that over the years more and more will gradually become known."

Bob was absolutely right about more bits and pieces of history becoming known. There have been more tapes released, more revelations, and the important perspective time brings—which have all added significantly to my understanding of "Watergate."

When I've gotten together with members of the greater Nixon network and good friends, we would discuss it, just like everyone else, trying to understand exactly what had happened, who had played what roles. It has never ceased to surprise me that those of us caught in the whirlwind do not know any more about what actually took place than some journalists and professors. In the ensuing decades, we have continually uncovered information that many of us knew nothing about.

For example, I had maintained in my interviews with the government prosecutors that Bob Haldeman had never heard the name Donald Segretti. I believed that completely. I swore to it. It was only years later that I was surprised to learn of the existence of documentation in which Bob tells Gordon Strachan to put Don Segretti under Gordon Liddy's direction. Whether or not Bob knew the details of Segretti's activities, he knew of his existence.

There always was something more. In the spring of 2020, I received a phone call from a researcher in London who told me he had become aware that at some point Segretti had gone to Florida to meet with Howard Hunt and Liddy. That made no sense to me. Why would Don have done that? If it had happened, I knew nothing about it. "Let me check it out," I said, and sent Don an email asking if that meeting took place. "Yes," he wrote back. *Good God,* I thought. *How much more had been going on that I knew nothing about?*

Even after all these decades, there remain secrets to be uncovered. Thus far, for example, we have learned little about the CIA's role in Watergate. I know that one or more books on the subject are now being written. We know that charts G. Gordon Liddy used to present his illegal plan to Attorney General John Mitchell, White House Council John Dean, and Deputy Campaign Manager Jeb Magruder were produced at the CIA. We know Bernard Barker and Howard Hunt of the White House Plumbers unit, operatives who broke into Daniel Ellsberg's psychiatrist's office, had been on the CIA payroll. We know the film from the pictures they took at the psychiatrist's office was developed and printed by the CIA. We know Hunt and Barker were also part of the planning for the Watergate break-in and in fact were caught, prosecuted, and imprisoned. Last, CIA Director Richard Helms, a JFK and LBJ appointee, had a somewhat adversarial, less-than-friendly relationship with President Nixon. There is more to be investigated to ascertain the CIA's precise role in Watergate. It is not conceivable that the CIA leadership did not know what was happening with current and former personnel. Should the director of the CIA have said something to the president?

Given that Nixon was a political lightning rod, there are many misconceptions about the man. This is especially true when it comes to defining him by the more conventionally accepted view of how he handled Watergate. *What in the world was Nixon thinking?* is perhaps the common question. One cannot understand Nixon's role in Watergate without understanding how he thought and what he had experienced in his decades of political life.

President Nixon, over the twenty years between his resignation and his death, took responsibility for not pushing his staff hard enough for full disclosure during the cover-up.

Why didn't the president immediately demand to get to the bottom of the investigation? Where was the accountability for the break-in that clearly had ties to the Committee to Reelect the President? When was the cover-up initiated?

In 2019, I was providing information and answering questions for a proposed television miniseries about Richard Nixon based on the book *Being Nixon* by author Evan Thomas. Ron Bass, the talented screenwriter who wrote the Academy Award–winning film *Rain Man,* was creating the series and asked me a question about Watergate and Nixon that I had thought about countless times in the previous decades. "Dwight, what I really want to know is what was the trigger? What was that date, or occasion, that exact moment when Nixon decided he had to cover this up? What was the singular ah-ha moment that changed everything?" Ron Bass was looking, as so many other writers and historians before him have, for that one dramatic scene—the guilty moment—where the writer can say, "See, he just covered it up!"

The real answer to that question probably goes back to Nixon's historic press conference in 1962, in which he bitterly told the media, "You won't have Dick Nixon to kick around anymore!" Until recently I never understood how psychologically revealing that remark would turn out to be. It was a liberating, spontaneous moment for him. At that moment, he believed, he had nothing more to lose. That was

Richard Nixon expressing his well-founded pent-up frustrations with the adverse press coverage he had been receiving for his entire political life. The continual and unrelenting attacks on his character and career, much of it very personal, set in place an almost automatic response to political attacks, a response conditioned by hundreds of moments of allegations.

My answer to Ron Bass's question was that there was no beginning, no one moment when a White House decision was made that the break-in at the Watergate had to be covered up. John Dean told the Ervin committee that they automatically began covering up, but he was talking about the people who were at risk of prosecution, among them Mitchell, Magruder, and himself.

Immediately after the break-in, if the president did anything wrong, it was that he was playing for time to get a better grasp of the problem and he was being given bad information. He had been told by his White House Counsel John Dean that no one in the White House had been involved. In fact, that simply was not true. However, because John Dean himself was involved, that was the story he told the president. It would be nine long months later, as the story slowly unfolded, before Dean told the president the truth: a White House aide, Gordon Strachan, did, in fact, know in advance about the break-in and he himself, John Dean, might also have had some culpability. (See Exhibits 4A and 4C in the Appendix on pages 430 and 439.) It is my belief that it was Dean's continual and successful efforts to protect himself from implication that precluded him from telling the president the truth. For those nine months, the president was blind to the facts and every step he took, or didn't take, seems to reflect that.

Once Dean had falsely reassured the president that no one in the White House was involved in the break-in, the president, Haldeman, and Ehrlichman viewed it as a Mitchell and Magruder campaign-management problem. It was embarrassing and needed containment. In the first few days after the break-in, true to his political style and modus operandi, the president suggested solutions, offered ideas, wondered about what could or could not be done—"what would be right" and "what would be wrong." It was as if he was dealing with a piece of legislation or some abstract concept instead of a crime. In fact, I don't think he saw it as a real crime but rather as political excess committed by overly enthusiastic and misdirected campaign workers. As a result, the maneuvering, the fix-it part of his thinking, was all playing out on a political level and not a criminal one. For such an intelligent man, the president's vision was clouded by his past experiences. When decisive leadership called for "Who did this? Why? Fire them," he didn't have it in him to ask those tough probing questions. Instead, he defaulted to his contemplative rehashing what-if-it-is-this-or-maybe-it-is-that style, searching for an answer, thinking out loud, looking for a way out—all caught on an invisible and largely ignored taping system.

There is no question that there was a real crime and that it was being covered up. However, people in positions of power were not thinking criminally. They were thinking, as Haldeman clearly believed, "containment," political containment. Richard Nixon responded instinctively based on everything that had happened to him in his political career. His first thought must have been, *Here they come. They're coming after me again.* This wasn't paranoia. They really had come after him in the past and they *were* coming after him again. But rather than putting that feeling aside and focusing on how to best handle the situation, he made the worst possible decision. He started fighting back. Worse, he did so without knowing the facts. The president was being misled and wrongly advised by John Dean. His trusted counsel was providing the president with incomplete and often misleading information in an apparent effort to save himself—not to faithfully advise the president. In fact, on March 21, 1973—nine months after the break-in—Dean starts the important "Cancer on the Presidency" meeting by admitting that the time had come for the president to know all the facts. (See Exhibit 4D in the Appendix on page 443.)

Until writing this book, I had not spent much time really focusing on the details of John Dean's involvement in Watergate. I knew he was critical to the story and what happened to the president. I also knew the role he had played in my situation with Segretti, but not the full story of his involvement. Even now, I don't believe we know the full story. Only more time will sort out more of the truth.

I do know for my story, which is forever tied to the president's, that John Dean's role needs more academic attention. The truths of Watergate are far from black-and-white. The conventional assumption that Richard Nixon represented evil and John Dean honor and integrity is unquestionably a myth. Those who are antagonistic toward the president and what unfolded need not pardon Nixon in their thoughts. Rather they need to focus on what John Dean did, and didn't do, as the president's counsel, what he knew and when he knew it. I am an admitted partisan on this issue, a loyalist, and my views are understandably suspect. But there is much to consider, many questions remaining to be answered, among other things, the role John Dean, the CIA, and perhaps others played.

Evidence incriminating John Dean is contained in the March 13– March 21, 1973, tapes. In the tapes, Dean can be heard discouraging the president from putting out the full truth of what they knew to the public (even though the president was suggesting that he thought it was a good idea to put it all out there). It was Dean who encouraged the president to throw Segretti and me under the bus with the hope that with this sacrifice the main Watergate story would evaporate. (See Exhibit 4B in the Appendix on page 436.) We can hear Dean talking about Segretti's "pranks" as "humorous," "nothing evil, nothing vicious, nothing bad, nothing . . ." (See Exhibits 4A and 4C in the Appendix on pages 430 and 439.) Dean also tosses Magruder and Strachan under the bus, taking no responsibility himself for having pushed for the break-in.

These tapes were in the hands of the prosecutors. However, the prosecutors had absolutely no interest in undermining John Dean, who was their lead prosecution witness. Instead, they had every reason to sit on those tapes and not have them come out at trial. The public was unaware of those tapes until they became public in 1995 in response to a private lawsuit. I was not aware of them until 2020.

Imagine, after all that time, through all the headlines, Dean led off a March 21, 1973, Oval Office meeting (nine months after the June 17, 1972, break-in) telling the president, *"The reason I thought we ought to talk this morning is because, in our conversations, I have the impression that you don't know everything I know—and it makes it very difficult for you to make judgments that only you can make."* This is the president being informed by his White House Counsel—for the first time—how Watergate started. Dean went on: *"I think that there's no doubt about the seriousness of the problem we've got. We have a cancer within—close to the presidency, that's growing. It's growing daily. It's compounding. It grows geometrically now because it compounds itself."* This was the real beginning of the end. At some point, this had gotten beyond Dean's ability to control it. Secretly, about ten days after this conversation, Dean turned on the president, hired a criminal defense lawyer, and began cooperating with the prosecutors.

Over the many years since Watergate, I have given countless talks and always welcomed questions afterward. Often for interest, I would offer up a thought that I've long held: If one of three men had been alive there would never have been a Watergate. Those three men are former Presidents Dwight Eisenhower and Lyndon Baines Johnson, and Senator Everett Dirksen of Illinois.

When Eisenhower was president he had a chief aide named Sherman Adams, a former governor of New Hampshire. It was said, "Adams is the man you want to see if you want to see Eisenhower." Adams resigned under fire for accepting a vicuña coat from an old friend who was having problems with the government. Eisenhower didn't try to save Adams. In fact, Eisenhower ordered him fired and then tasked Vice President Nixon with the extremely unpleasant and controversial job of doing it. Similarly in 1964, President Johnson's key White House aide, Walter Jenkins, was arrested for "disorderly conduct." Jenkins was forced to resign. As for Dirksen, the veteran of years of political wars and consequences, Nixon had the highest respect for Dirksen's political judgment. I believe Nixon would have listened to each of them. They would have told him early on, without his even having to ask for their advice, "Dick, cut your losses. Call those involved into your office, get the facts, and fire those responsible, and do it today!" Containment wouldn't have even been on the table for consideration.

Containment, by definition "keeping something within limits," is a managerial term, not a political one. It was natural to a management pro such as Haldeman to use that term, and it was logical that Nixon would be thinking that way, too. It matched his nonconfrontational style. But the bottom line is Watergate was a political-legal problem. Adding "legal" to the "political" makes an issue "white hot"—something to be addressed and disposed of quickly before it burns you, before it consumes you.

Some conspiracists contend that the president had a plan and didn't care about the Constitution or the rule of law, and would do anything to advance his own interests and screw his enemies. That's nonsense. No such plan existed, nor was there ever any intention to do so. Among the more logical theories is that there was concern that the FBI investigation was going to uncover the sources of the burglars' cash and thereby reveal big Democratic donors who had been promised anonymity and had a legal right to remain anonymous. And then there was Nixon's possible hesitation to ask the tough questions, arguably most of it being due to his fear that the answers would lead to John Mitchell, his former attorney general and his campaign manager. Mitchell was Nixon's friend. Mitchell had tried to beg off even coming to Washington because he felt it would destroy his wife, Martha. Nixon had said, "I'm asking you as your president." I believe this reason for Nixon's hesitation, which speaks to his loyalty to Mitchell, might be the most accurate view. Again, I believe Eisenhower or Johnson would have convinced him to put that loyalty aside. The presidency was at stake.

But none of this would have happened without the involvement of

John Dean. Whether intentional or simply inept, rather than putting out the growing fire, he fed it. It was Dean to whom Haldeman had assigned responsibility for developing a campaign-intelligence plan and who had recruited and hired Gordon Liddy for that purpose. It was Dean who from the earliest moments of the planning had been there for Liddy's presentations to Mitchell and Magruder. It was Dean who knew that Liddy's campaign-intelligence plan included proposed break-ins. It was Dean who finally admits to the president, on March 17, 1973, that he himself could be culpable because "I've been all over this thing like a blanket." (See Exhibit 4C in the Appendix on page 439.)

On that March 17, 1973, tape, the president decided that Chapin has "just got to take the heat." The president clearly understood the depth of my loyalty and was confident I would sacrifice my career for him. My response years later, when I heard him talking about throwing Segretti and me overboard, was "Well, that's Nixon." Without much doubt, if I had been aware of this conversation during that period, when I was fighting for my freedom, I would have felt differently. Undoubtedly I would have responded with great anger and disappointment. But these many years later, I read these transcripts and realize it was Nixon flailing for an answer, as he was inclined to do. Time dulls the pain of him throwing me overboard. But it was not that one sentence that was important. Far more consequential was the fact that in March 1973, immediately before flipping on the president, Dean was suggesting a dishonest path to the president. He was suggesting that Chapin and Segretti be sacrificed in order to distract from Watergate. My belief is the fact that the president even considered following Dean's suggestion is proof of how confused he was by the entire Watergate matter at that juncture.

John Dean once characterized himself as the "Desk Officer" for the Watergate cover-up. *Desk Officer* is a State Department term for someone who is charged with keeping abreast of all developments within a given country, so they can quickly and thoroughly respond to questions from their superiors. He may not be making the actual decisions, but that Desk Officer is responsible for briefing those who are. By claiming this title, Dean was confirming that he was at the very center of the cover-up, that he was not an innocent bystander caught up in the events.

The FBI had a different view. They didn't use the term *Desk Officer*. Though I don't believe the Bureau's analysis was ever made public, the FBI clearly understood Dean's role in Watergate. On July 5, 1974, a "Watergate Investigation—OPE Analysis" was provided in a "memo to the [FBI] director." From that report: "While Dean's role as the master manipulator of the cover-up was unknown and, in fact, the cover-up itself was unknown during the investigation, obviously the furnishing to Dean by Mr. Gray [Acting Director of the FBI] of our reports allowed Dean the total opportunity to plan a course of action to thwart the FBI's investigation and grand jury inquiry." (See Exhibit 1 in the Appendix on page 419.) The role of John Dean as the "master manipulator" certainly was unknown to President Nixon, who, most unfortunately, trusted his counsel.

To control the flow of information, Dean managed to insert himself at the center of the White House response. But to be "the master manipulator" he needed to know as much as possible about what was going on. That's why—as is obvious in hindsight—even after I had left the White House, he would call me at United Airlines to keep tabs on my situation. It also explains why months earlier he was sitting in on my initial FBI interviews.

What I did not know—what no one knew—was that Dean's lawyer had opened discussions with career prosecutors at the very beginning of April 1973, while he was still White House Counsel.

Dean's deal with the prosecutors launched what was to become his solely owned cottage industry, "The Vilification of Richard Nixon— founded in 1973." Dean has spent fifty years attempting to shred the integrity of Richard Nixon as well as so many of the good and dedicated people who worked in the administration. For those same fifty years, the media has served as his megaphone. Because it contradicts the popular narrative, it is never mentioned by the talking heads that Dean is a disbarred lawyer and an admitted felon. Dean has worked to achieve the phony image of one led astray but, just in the nick of time, saw the light and changed his ways—more of a Boy Scout or a whistle-blowing hero caught in a nest of vipers, a contrast to the "evil" President Nixon. One of the more humorous aspects of Dean's cottage industry is that in recent years he has lectured to lawyers—as part of their required continuing education—on legal ethics.

Ironically, I was one of the people who originally vetted Dean for the White House Counsel position and, with some reservations, told Haldeman he would fit into the White House. That was my mistake. After interviewing Dean in 1970, I wrote to Haldeman: "John Dean is a very smooth, cool, calculating, tough, and probably very self-centered individual. I like him." But, I continued: *"I have a real hang-up with the degree of commitment that he would have to the president—something that I feel that the person who is Counsel to the President should have. Maybe it is his arrogance—I am not sure."*

Like so many of his former colleagues, I did like John Dean. But my original caveat, my concerns about the depth of his commitment to the president, proved to be accurate. For years, until researching this book, I had no depth of understanding or appreciation for Dean's involvement in the whole Watergate mess. While I sensed he was culpable, I didn't fully appreciate the depth of his involvement in Watergate—from recruiting Gordon Liddy to preparing a campaign intelligence plan through the cover-up.

Others saw him more clearly. Bill Safire, who worked at the White House as a speechwriter, became a good friend of mine. No one would accuse Safire of being a partisan player, so his understanding of the impact of Watergate on our history matters. Upon leaving the White House in 1973, he went on to become a Pulitzer Prize–winning columnist, appearing regularly on the *New York Times* op-ed page. For twenty years his column was must reading for both Republicans and

Democrats. Bill saw the depth of Dean's deceit. On June 18, 1973, shortly after leaving the White House, he published "Gunga Dean." Here are the closing lines from Safire's parody of the Kipling poem:

Yes, it's Dean! Dean! Dean!
Star of everybody's television screen.
You will claim that you obeyed,
But the truth is you betrayed,
A far better man than you are, Gunga Dean!
(See full "Gunga Dean" poem in Exhibit 2 in the Appendix on page 424.)

The esteemed publishing legend Alice Mayhew also held Dean in low regard. Ms. Mayhew, a senior editor at Simon and Schuster, had edited Dean's book *Blind Ambition*. In the process of writing his book *Silent Coup,* Len Colodny went through John Dean's Senate testimony and compared it with what Dean had written in *Blind Ambition*. Colodny found many inconsistencies between the two. When Colodny interviewed Dean, he asked Dean about the differences. Dean tried to explain them away by telling Colodny that those were things his editors made him put in his book. When Colodny asked Mayhew about Dean's claim, she responded that Dean had lied and she said she would never work with him again. In fact, her disgust with Dean was included in her obituary, as published by the *New York Times* in February 2020: "In an interview with Len Colodny, co-author of *Silent Coup: The Removal of a President,* about Mr. Dean's claim that his editors had told him to include false information in *Blind Ambition* (reissued in 2009), Ms. Mayhew said: 'That's a lie. LIE. That is spelled L-I-E.'" (See Exhibit 3 in the Appendix on page 426.)

One additional aspect of Watergate that I believe has been historically overlooked is the political motives behind it. It was perhaps the last, desperate attempt to revive the presidential prospects of Teddy Kennedy. Both of Senator Kennedy's older brothers, John and Bobby, had been assassinated—John in 1963 and Bobby in 1968. It was the alumni of both of his brothers' political organizations, including people like Archibald Cox, who pushed hardest to resurrect Ted Kennedy. Since Chappaquiddick Teddy was damaged goods, but he was the only pathway back into power for the hundreds of Kennedy loyalists. In order to bring back Teddy, destroying Nixon became the Democrats number-one mission. Incredibly, all forty-three of the lead prosecutors were Democrats and many were formerly associated in some way, or friendly with, the Kennedys.

The prosecutorial efforts against Nixon, starting in the House and Senate, were strategized and led by Kennedy and his supporters. Kennedy's Senate subcommittee took the original lead in the investigation of Watergate. As the story developed and became more serious, Senator Mike Mansfield, the Senate Majority Leader, told Kennedy that it was too politically sensitive for him to directly manage, and it was, therefore, with Kennedy's agreement, moved so Senator Sam Ervin took over the leadership.

These were the people who pursued Nixon, and with the 1976 election of Jimmy Carter, they achieved their objectives.

There were crimes committed during Watergate. But the pursuit of the president was political, first and foremost.

In 1973, I was sitting at home in Chicago watching Gordon Strachan's testimony before the Senate Watergate Committee. Since that day, I have been bothered by the advice he offered when asked what he might say to young people contemplating public service. "My advice," he replied, "would be to stay away."

John Ehrlichman offered different guidance when asked the same question. "Politics," he said, "is only as honest as the people involved in it," adding that his advice would be different from Strachan's. "I hope they come and test their ideas and convictions in this marketplace," Mr. Ehrlichman said. "We did our best. I hope they come here and do better." But, he added, they should keep their "eyes open." John Ehrlichman's Secret Service code name was, appropriately, "Wisdom."

Over the decades when I've been asked by younger people about going to Washington to work, I have always encouraged them to do so.

John Ehrlichman had that challenge right.

Yes! Go to Washington. Go and do better. Get in that arena. Seize the opportunity and make a difference.

★ 19 ★

DEBT OF HONOR

What might have been? I rarely think about that. I have always lived in the present. But had Richard Nixon been allowed to complete his second term in office, the world would have been very different.

And my life? I was so fortunate. After working for W. Clement Stone for fifteen years, we sold *Success* to another publishing company. I accepted a job at the public relations firm Hill and Knowlton, which coincidently was owned by J. Walter Thompson, where I had started with Bob Haldeman so many years earlier. I was living in Hong Kong, running our business in Asia.

In 1988, recently back in the country from running the Hill and Knowlton Asia operations, I took a page from the life of my mentor and friend Tex McCrary, and I became a strategic communications consultant. I ventured out on my own as Chapin Enterprises, independent of any corporate ties and assuming responsibility to be my own boss. It was one of the best business decisions I ever made.

For the next thirty years I worked as a consultant, with individuals, with companies, and with associations referred to me by, or run by, friends and acquaintances. I loved my work. It was filled with variety and exceptional assignments, from crisis communication to solving organizational and complicated and sensitive personnel situations. I moved from one assignment to the next, always busy and having the time of my life. Looking back, there is no doubt, those game planning sessions in the White House Roosevelt Room had given me a base of experience and a way of dissecting issues and problems—and then solutions for resolving them. They provided me with the thinking and tools for what became my life's work.

Susie and I divorced. We had been married for thirty years and been together as a couple since the ninth grade. To our family and friends it was always "Susie and Dwight." Our divorce hit each of us, and our daughters too, in different ways. It was a difficult and sad time for all of us, for our family and for our close friends. For my entire life, even after the divorce, when it came to Watergate, Susie always came to my defense. Several years after our divorce, she had seen John Dean on a talk show. Susie emailed: "Don't ever forget you wanted to put out the truth and he wanted to check you into Walter Reed Hospital and hide you." Susie had lived it all too. She knew the truth and was always out front expressing it. If asked to describe her, I would say loyal, loving, empathetic, a great friend to so many, and a fighter. Susie was a fighter. I was always amazed by the fact that when she was born, she weighed less than one pound. Susie fought from her first breath to live. She had two exceptional daughters, four equally exceptional grandchildren, wonderful friends, and "Smitty," a husband she loved. All of them are a tribute to her and what she gave to each of us.

Our daughters Kimberly and Tracy married two superb men, Dan and Jeff. Wonderful grandchildren arrived, and life got better as time healed wounds. When Jack was born, Kimberly asked me what I would like my grandson to call me. My answer was "Gramps." But it turned out little Jack couldn't quite enunciate "Gramps" and my name came out as "Pipps." For Jack, his sister Emily, his cousins Chase and Matthew, the "Pipps" name has fit perfectly. It was the best name ever! Now the entire family, and even some friends, call me "Pipps"!

Terry Decker Goodson, who—along with Nell Yates—had worked for me at the White House, reentered my life in 1990. She eventually brought her children and extended family. Then along came their spouses and even more grandchildren. Terry's former husband, Peter, and I became trusted friends. We are all now a huge and extended family, which just keeps growing. I am deeply grateful for all the loved ones who are in my life.

Through Terry, I discovered the East End of Long Island. Never in the world would I have believed that Long Island could be so beautiful. Maybe it is the rural nature of the fields that remind me of my youth and farming in Kansas. But Kansas has no such spectacular beaches. Our entire family benefited from moving out and living on the East End for a few years. While we finally decided to move "back to civilization"—the New York–Connecticut metro area—our visits to the East End have continued in the summer. Those visits spark wonderful lasting memories of so many great times.

Tracy and I danced at her wedding. The music began, "Fairy tales can come true, it can happen to you, if you are among the very young at heart. Here is the best part, you'll have a head start if you are among . . ." Tracy had picked the song. It had always been significant and important to me, before Tracy's dance and after. I believed the words of the song. It embodies what "Nano Chapie," my grandmother Chapin, was working to instill in her grandson when she gave me Dr. Peale's *The Power of Positive Thinking.* Thank you, Nano, *for knowing that the gift of the right attitude could shape my life.* Maybe that's why I loved publishing *Success: The Magazine with a Positive Mental Attitude.*

In 1998, I attended a Landmark Forum, an "idea-tuning" weekend, for some mind and soul expansion. Our group worked the forum exercises over the weekend. We were instructed to come back on Tuesday with a new idea: "How do I want to stand before the world?" We were told to bring something to demonstrate our idea. I arrived with my new business card. My former card had said, "Dwight Chapin, President, Chapin Enterprises." My new card gave my name and then, under it, two words, "Value Creator." That was it. I decided that for the next chapter of my life I wanted to be known—and to "stand before the world"—as a "Value Creator." In everything I do personally, with my family, in business—in every which way—I want to add value, to be a contributor, to be a builder, to give by adding value to everything. It's a mindset, an attitude, and it has paid great dividends.

The year 2013 marked the centennial anniversary of Richard Nixon's birth. A decision had been made to use that occasion for a major fundraising effort and to renovate the exhibit area of the Nixon Presidential Library in Yorba Linda, California. I was invited to participate and lead the renovation efforts by friends and former Nixon colleagues Ron Walker, Sandy Quinn, and Fred Malek. Ron was the chairman of the Nixon Foundation Board. Sandy was the president of the foundation. Fred was the chairman of the Centennial Campaign. It was my last consulting assignment before retiring, and was it ever fun. I had come full circle.

My life in the orbit of Richard Nixon began that summer in 1962, that fateful day when I went to be interviewed by Herb Kalmbach and Bob Haldeman and was hired to be a Nixon field man. Almost sixty years later, having lived virtually my entire life as a "Nixon Man," I was gifted with the library renovation assignment.

At the suggestion of William Baribault, the new Nixon Foundation president, the board set up an oversight committee. Baribault requested that I prepare a set of guidelines for the project. For the most part, the board and Baribault allowed me significant authority and lots of running room. I reached out to Frank Gannon, a great friend, a historian, and an expert on all things Nixon as well as a consultant to the foundation. Frank was not only our substance expert but he became my trusted partner and made a priceless contribution. I served as the ringmaster of our circus, designated to crack the bullwhip and keep things moving. We did our best to include ideas and recommendations from our supportive Nixon alumni group, the Nixon family, and experts on modern museums. The renovation project took almost four years to complete. It involved well over a hundred participants. Every step we took had to be approved by our National Archives and Records Administration partner. The Archivist of the United States, David Ferriero, harnessed his bureaucratic organization and endorsed our "no delays" plan. David

Ferriero was a hero, a Democrat in the Obama administration, prodding the bureaucracy to get the Nixon Library project completed on time. Mike Ellzey had been brought aboard by Ferriero to represent him on site, and we also owe Mike significant thanks.

We hired an incredible project manager, Dennis Irvine, who brought us in on budget. We retained the services of Thinkwell, a top-tier attractions design firm. Cortina Productions produced our interactives, videos, and orientation film. We had recruited an incredible team with an important assignment: Tell the story of Richard Nixon's life.

Our mission statement read in part:

> *President Nixon was unique among presidents. The story of his life is one of inspiration, challenges, and persistence. He influenced American and world affairs for a half century. President Nixon was one of the most intelligent, insightful, and visionary presidents in the history of the nation. He also is the only president to ever resign. His story and that of his administration are of historic importance to future generations and it is the foundation's responsibility to tell that story—honestly, completely, and unequivocally!*

Working through the renovation project those four years let me relive my earlier days with Richard Nixon. I call it a gift, but it was much more. The total immersion into what we were creating helped me understand more fully what a unique and special man Richard Nixon was. We worked with his entire life, not just Watergate and not just China.

I have a plaque on my bookshelf, a quote from one of his speeches: *"I ask you to join in a high adventure—one as rich as humanity itself, and as exciting as the times we live in."* I joined him in that adventure he proclaimed, and it surely lived up to the billing. I have always worn my participation in the Nixon administration as a badge of honor. I've always focused, not on the failures, but on our accomplishments.

It became clear to me that my memories are not necessarily those of my family. I was so proud of my efforts on behalf of the renovation that Terry and I invited my two daughters, their husbands, four grandchildren, and other relatives to Yorba Linda to tour the newly renovated library. The orientation film, a thirteen-minute spectacular production, is the first thing a guest sees upon entering. We all watched the informative and dramatic film. I, of course, was watching it for the hundredth time because Frank Gannon and I had worked for months on producing it. I knew every word and was very excited to share it with my family who were there.

When the movie ended, I knew that something was wrong.

Huge tears were streaming down Kimberly's face. For several seconds, she literally couldn't talk.

"What's wrong, dear?" I asked

Very softly, she choked out, "It's the memories."

I can only imagine what Kimberly, and Tracy too, experienced in those days. They were little girls. They couldn't have completely understood what was happening to our family. They must have been scared. The media was camped out on our front yard for days on end. Their dad went to prison. The kids at school may not have been so kind. Their mother was putting up a strong front and working to keep things "normal." Those were Kimberly's real and emotional memories, in contrast to what I was assuming she would feel as I had extended my *"Welcome to the great new Nixon Library!"* Seeing her reaction helped me, once again, understand and feel the pain that my family experienced.

It's been an extraordinary journey. Even today, even after all these years, people still recognize my name. They don't quite know exactly where I fit, just that I had something to do with Richard Nixon, something to do with Watergate.

I knew Richard Nixon as just a man. I know what a smart, sensitive, caring man he was. Yes, President Richard Nixon. When I got out of Lompoc, Susie and I took the girls to see him in San Clemente, before he and Mrs. Nixon moved back to New York. He fumbled around when we entered his office. He was awkward, saying inconsequential things to try and make conversation. Inside I smiled. It was familiar.

He was a little clueless in trying to converse with Kim and Tracy, and he had difficulty looking at Susie and me. Then, after a few minutes, he shifted to what he had planned. Undoubtedly, he had envisioned this time before the four of us arrived for our visit. The former president looked at the girls and said, "Now, I want to share something with you. Your dad made a real contribution to our country. I want you to know that." How nice. He meant it. It was his way. Thank you, Mr. President. The girls might not remember it. I've never forgotten it.

In February of 1976, I was still in Lompoc, hoping to be released soon. A letter arrived from the former president, who was in San Clemente. It was a short note, signed with his "RN." He was getting ready to visit China again, he wrote, and was thinking back to our historic trip four years earlier. Obviously I was on his mind. He felt compelled to reach out to me in prison. That was thoughtful. He was remembering, again. It was his way.

Sometimes I am asked, "Why aren't you bitter?" and "Don't you feel angry about the way you were treated?" I guess the honest answer is, at times, "Yes." But really, why should I feel that way? As I've said, I was given an incredible gift. All of it, even prison, has made my life extraordinary. I just wish it didn't have the price tag called Watergate.

Richard Nixon's impact on my life was incalculable. At the Nixon Presidential Library, one of our films ends with the president delivering one of his favorite thoughts. It was inspired by President Charles de Gaulle of France telling President Nixon of a favorite quote from Sophocles: "One must wait until the evening to see how splendid the day has been." For me, now in the evening of my life, how very splendid my association with Richard Nixon has made my life.

I was a young man when Watergate erupted. Often I have reflected how painful it was for the older men who had to live with Watergate as the capstone of their careers. For me, it was my base, my early years. It afforded me a gift like few men are privileged to receive. I honor that. As my friend and Nixon colleague Fred Malek would often remind all of us, "We have a *Debt of Honor* to Richard Nixon." I believe virtually all my Nixon friends feel the same way. We were honored to have served Richard Nixon.

A question I am still asked, after all this time and all that happened: Did I "like" Richard Nixon?

Liking him was never part of my job description. "Like" implies a certain level of personal relationship. We were friendly, but we were never friends. He was my boss. I was his aide. I was next to him in the foxhole, doing my duty. Richard Nixon was a man of many layers. I was more fortunate than most people to have seen some of them stripped away, but only some of them. What I am left with, after all this time, is enormous respect and admiration—and awe. Whatever the detractors say, whatever the writers of history say, he was a decent man who set out to do the most good for the most people. When I look back on those days, when I close my eyes and picture him in that easy chair, surrounded by his yellow pads, working tirelessly for the American people, my answer, without hesitation, is: Yes, I liked him.

He was kind to me, as was Mrs. Nixon. I reciprocated then, and I still do today, with loyalty.

I told my grandson Matthew my story was complicated because it was. It became important to me to write this book. I don't mean important in an ego sense but important in whatever it adds to the historical perspective of Richard Nixon. And yet, even more important than that, I wanted Matthew, the fourteen other grandchildren Terry and I share, and our incredibly large extended family to understand a little more of what happened. Why I went to prison. Why I love the life I have lived. And why I continue to be so loyal and hold the deepest respect for the great American I was honored to serve, President Richard Nixon.

Dwight Chapin
RIVERSIDE, CT, 2022

ACKNOWLEDGMENTS

DWIGHT CHAPIN

William "Bill" Safire was a friend of mine. We served together in the Nixon White House where Bill was a speechwriter. He went on to become a Pulitzer Prize–winning *New York Times* columnist. One afternoon in 2003, I visited Bill's office, seeking his advice on an idea I had for a novel I was thinking of writing, based on Richard Nixon and Howard Hughes. "Dwight," Bill said, "you have the stories, but you're not a writer. You need to work with a writer." Bill planted the seed of thought that afternoon.

Sixteen years later in 2019, my wife, Terry, and I were visiting a beach house for rent in Amagansett, New York. One of the couple who were currently renting the property was reading the recently released *Unfreedom of the Press* by Mark Levin. We ended up in a discussion about the book and the current state of politics in our country. Our realtor, Michael Schultz, was listening and said, "Dwight, you should write a book." I responded with something along the lines of "I'd like to, but I'm not a writer." Then I mentioned the sage advice Bill Safire had offered. Schultz immediately said, "We had dinner just last night with one of the top ghostwriters in the country. I'll introduce you." I took Schultz up on the invitation the very next day, and that's how I met David Fisher. The connection with Michael Schultz, which led to the connection with David Fisher, felt divinely inspired. "Good vibrations" have surrounded this book, continually, from the git-go.

David, Terry, and I had three long breakfasts to explore our chemistry with the idea of working together. At our very first meeting, David explained his role. He would indeed be "the writer," but I would be "the author." David stressed his belief that the undertaking had to be "a collaborative partnership." It would be the story of my experiences, with my feelings, and in my voice. I would provide the substance. David would use his craft to weave the stories together in a coherent format. Through our collaboration, David's creativity and great writing skill made the narrative come alive. He delivered big-time. And I will be forever grateful to him. And also grateful for Laura, David's energetic and knowing wife, who supported David's enthusiastic immersion in our project.

A word about our process or, said differently, how in the world could you remember so much after fifty years or more? Here is how. David interviewed me in about thirty sessions. The first dozen or so were three hours or longer, and in person. After COVID-19 came along, we switched to telephone interviews, two to three hours in length. All the sessions were recorded and transcribed, providing us with more than eight hundred pages of transcripts. I also had dozens upon dozens of letters and memorandums that had been exchanged with Bob Haldeman. Additionally, at various times, I had kept personal journals. And then there were the thousands of documents in the Nixon Library archives, along with the Nixon tapes. Bottom line, we had a treasure trove of material plus my memory of events, people, and the times. Our biggest problem was in whittling down and deciding which of the materials would be included in the book. David used his unique indexing system for organizing it all. That is how and why we were able to tell this story in such detail.

Terry Decker Goodson, with whom I now share my life, was a devoted advocate of the project from day one. Dedicated to me, she has been what my Secret Service name was, my "Watchdog." She not only knows how to edit and spell but also knew most of my White House story and the people in it. Terry worked with the historian and Nixon tapes expert, Luke Nichter, ensuring the accuracy of all the tape excerpts we utilized. Thank you, Luke. And for Terry, there is no salute that adequately recognizes the love she has given to me and this book.

Along with Terry, seven other trusted people read the first-draft manuscript before it went off to William Morrow's publishing team. With deep appreciation, I thank them all. The first two read each chapter after our rough editing—Mark Decker Sr., my brother-in-law, and Roger Lew, my good friend. Mark, a poet and writer himself, offered advice and wisdom every step of the way. Two agents at the Javelin Literary Agency, Matt Latimer and Dylan Colligan, commented on the chapters. Next, Frank Gannon—friend, historian, and Nixon "expert"—checked and re-checked my facts and offered his critique and expertise. That was followed by Jack Carley, another friend, superb lawyer, and fellow Nixon traveler, who gave it the first of the legal reads. Sandy Quinn, the seventh reader, had started it all. Truth be known, Sandy had rushed me into the Sigma Chi fraternity the summer of 1960 using "politics" as the worm on the hook. Sandy knew my story as well as the Nixon story and was, like the other seven, totally honest in his appraisal of our draft. Each reader offered positive suggestions. It was remarkable how each reviewer provided different insights and perspectives that worked to energize my thinking and enrich the manuscript.

You might note that among those who encouraged me I have not put immediate family members. While my stepchildren—Taylor, Peter and Mark—and their spouses did encourage me, Susie's and my daughters—Kimberly and Tracy—were less enthusiastic. That's very important. There are parts of this book where you will read how our family was hurt. There was heartbreak. Some emotional scars remain to this day. It was tough for the girls. But they did read the first draft of the manuscript and weighed in with knowing comments and suggestions. The good news was that by the end of the process both girls, with some continuing tribulations, I know, lovingly supported me. What more could I ask?

The Watergate sections were read several times by Geoff Shepard, former White House colleague and author of several Watergate books. He is the Nixon Foundation's presiding expert on Watergate. I thank Geoff very much.

The book *Silent Coup* is a Watergate classic. Its co-author Len

Colodny was most gracious with his time, providing a great deal of education on the roots of the scandal by directing us to relevant tapes and testimony. Len donated all of his papers to the Colodny Collection at Texas A&M. Len passed at the very end of this project. To Len I send a particular salute of affection and appreciation. Len introduced us to Ray Locker, author of *Haig's Coup*. Ray, a former reporter for *USA Today*, was not just gracious with his time and expertise but was an incredible source of information and a first-class detective of all things Watergate. We appreciate how both Len and Ray helped make what I had lived through clearer to us without, in my opinion, any ulterior motive other than that the truth be brought forward.

There are some great books referenced in the Recommended Sources on President Nixon section of this book. I thank all the authors of those books, which greatly assisted with reminding and re-educating me in many instances of facts and many things Nixon.

David Young was Henry Kissinger's able assistant and assigned to work with John Ehrlichman on the investigation of the Pentagon spy ring. I thank David for confirming the details surrounding that incredible saga and for reviewing that section of my book for accuracy. The spying on the president and Kissinger is an extraordinary piece of White House history. Hopefully, David will write the story in full, with the consequences and the lessons learned underscored.

The editing, shaping, and publishing of this book is the work of the great team that publisher Liate Stehlik and associate publisher Ben Steinberg have assembled at William Morrow, HarperCollins. From the outset, editor Mauro DiPreta has been the trusted guide. He was always encouraging, never critical, but always persuasive when differing views emerged in the process. Mauro is gifted, and I was told, and I was to find, one of the best editors in all of book publishing. He was definitely the perfect editor for me. Mauro's assistant, Vedika Khanna, is the person who cracked the whip nicely and put up with my barrage of questions and concerns. Bonni Leon-Berman did the sensational interior design. For cover design and art, I thank Ploy Siripant and Jeanne

Reina. And for the tedious production work, Pamela Barricklow, Andrea Molitor, Dale Rohrbaugh, Bob Costillo, and Aryana Hendrawan. On the publicity front, I salute Kayleigh George, Kelly Rudolph, and Rhina Garcia, and for the legal work, thanks go to Beth Silfin and the insightful Kyran Cassidy. A great group of professionals.

Keith Urbahn and Matt Latimer started the literary agency Javelin in 2011. Terry and I talked with them that first year. It took us six years to get my book idea together and then Matt and Keith made it better. They have been the backbone of this project, believing I had a story to tell, a real book, and encouraging me along the way. Shortly after David Fisher and I first met, the Javelin men endorsed the wisdom of our "collaborative" partnership. Along with Dylan Colligan, Elizabeth Aucamp, and the other Javelin team members, they delivered on everything—the business arrangements, story positioning, issue resolutions, marketing, every nuance of the published copy of the book that you are reading. Hungry, hard-driving, and ethical players, it is no wonder they are redefining what a great book and public relations agency can accomplish. Thank you, Javelin.

As I talked with David Fisher about our collaboration, an especially talented man showed up. Hugh Hewitt was named the president and CEO of the Richard Nixon Foundation. Upon hearing the idea for this book, Hugh immediately became an advocate. Hugh was looking for ways to bring about a renewed look at President Nixon. He felt that those of us who really knew Nixon needed to speak out. Hugh was not advocating a whitewashing but a telling of the truths of the Richard Nixon—the man, the president—we had known. One of Hugh's first calls was to Javelin in support of the book. I am deeply grateful to Hugh and to the board of the Richard Nixon Foundation for their support. At no time did anyone associated with the Nixon Foundation offer suggestions as to what should be in the book, nor did I ask them to review anything I had written.

I want to single out two additional people at the Nixon Foundation: Jim Byron, the executive vice president of the Nixon Foundation, for his incredible and loyal support on my behalf, and Jason Schwartz, for his research assistance and the hours he spent in helping me locate the photographs and other material I wanted to include in my book.

I am also indebted to many friends who provided encouragement and voiced support along the way: Mike Woodson, Jann Duval, Mike Paulin, Red Cavaney, Phil and Sandi Bonnell, Tim and Kathy Kilduff, Marsha Burger, Sue Hoyt, Anne "Banany" Dearborn, John R. Brown III, James Rosen, John O'Connor, Bob Bostock, Bruce Herschensohn, Ken Khachigian, Carole McMahon Butcher, the Rittenhouse family, Molly Decker, Joe Lopez, Chis Nordyck, Marlene and Pat Pavelski, Jeff Donfeld, Don and Liza Segretti, Pat and Shelley Buchanan, Kip and Lisa Barnett, Missie Motz, Michael Schultz, Linda Giannettino, Greg D'Angelo, Marilyn Lew, Henry Cashen, Steve Bull, and David and Jane Bruen.

The president's scheduling operation was masterfully managed by David Parker. We became lifelong friends. David passed during the writing of this book, and I miss him greatly. Hugh Sloan, a man of the highest integrity, served loyally alongside David. Their able assistant was Barbara Franklin. Mary Francis Widener, Helen Donaldson, and Mary Rawlins served loyally, too. Helen's and Mary's White House days reached back to the Eisenhower era.

We established the first White House Advance Office with Ron Walker as director. Ron is now a legend. That does not happen solo. Ron's advance team and office staff are legendary, too. Ron and I both received praise for the efforts of that team. From the secretaries—Karen Reitz Hart Fuller, Julie Rowe Cooke, Sally Brinkerhoff Hartwig, and Marsha Griswold Smith—to Mike Schrauth, Mike Duval, Red Cavaney, Dewey Clower, John Foust, Alan Hall, and all the outstanding advance men who served on a volunteer basis, it was a talented group of people who always made President Nixon's travel and appearances look fantastic, as they executed brilliantly. No White House has had a better advance operation.

As the book makes clear, that "advance" competence was best exemplified in our administration of the China and Russia trips. There were many who deserve a salute. I wish I could name them all. I believe Ron Walker would agree that it was the ability of the two of us to work with a singleness of purpose that made the advance aspects of the China and Russia trips successful. Others who contributed significantly include Ron's and my dear friend, Tim Elbourne; Gerry Warren, the deputy press secretary; all the volunteer advance men; the incredible and able military aides, most especially Marine Major Jack Brennan and Army LTC Vern Coffey; the Secret Service agents; and the White House Communications Agency who sent their finest. There were dozens who contributed, and all are deserving of praise and recognition.

My legal defense was expensive. I gratefully thank once again the people who contributed to my "Chapin defense fund," many of whom I didn't know personally. We raised approximately $200,000 in 1973 dollars, which today is the equivalent of $1,225,000. I particularly thank three friends, Dick Howard, Bill Cudlip, and Bill Carruthers, who were the trustees, and who collected and administered the fund. All monies were paid to my lawyers. No regrets. My lawyers did a fine job against formidable odds.

As I trust the book confirms, no words can express the depth of my feelings about my former White House colleagues, some of the best friends and most trusted people in my life. With them I want to include all those others who served the president and Nixon family over their decades of political, public, and private life. The Nixons always attracted gifted and loyal people to their campaigns and staffs. I was the beneficiary, becoming lifelong friends with so many.

At USC, lifelong friendships were also made. Some of those men came along with me to Washington and served our government with distinction. Mike Guhin worked in the 1962 and 1968 campaigns, joined Henry Kissinger's National Security Council staff, and then moved to the State Department, serving many administrations as an expert on multilateral arms negotiations while achieving ambassador rank. John Shlaes first worked in the 1968 campaign and then went to Washington as a deputy director of the Peace Corps. Jess Hill and Harvey Harris both served in the Department of Labor at OSHA. Dick Howard was at the Commerce Department and then the White House. Red Cavaney was a 1972 Nixon advance man and then ran the Advance Office for President Ford. My best friend, "best man," and Sigma Chi fraternity brother, Phil Bonnell, worked for the United States Information Agency.

Gratitude is a state of mind, and I want to mention a man, a friend to many, for this recognition. I will just call him Bill W. He doesn't want or seek publicity. He insists on staying behind the scenes, but he literally saved my life thirty-one years ago. Thank you, Bill, and thanks to the millions who carry on your program.

To my mother; father; sister, Linda; Linda's husband, David Bruen; and most important, to Susie, Kimberly, and Tracy. They lived it all; the highs of my young life at the time, and the lows. They were so proud, and then they, too, were heartbroken and hurt. We all recovered or, perhaps more accurately, are still recovering from the ordeal, each in our own way. To the three remaining, and all the loved ones who comprise our family, I love you.

My mentor Herm Stein taught me many years ago from *Science and Health and Key to the Scriptures* by Mary Baker Eddy, Divine Truth, Life, and Love—Inspires, Illuminates, Designates, and Leads the Way. For me, *it has and it does.*

DAVID FISHER

Every project brings with it new and different challenges and relationships, as well in many cases the opportunity to work with people you know and respect. This book fulfilled each of those parameters. I have long been fascinated by Richard Nixon. I lived through this period. This gave me the opportunity to explore and learn, and to come away from it with long-missing clarity and some important insights. More than that though, I had the privilege of working with Dwight Chapin and Terry Goodson. It was a fascinating journey, as Dwight and I explored his history together and perhaps brought new emotions to it. It would be impossible not to be grateful to Dwight and Terry for their extraordinary work ethic, their commitment to historic accuracy, their candor and caring, and their friendship.

I also had the pleasure of working once again with the great and wonderful editor Mauro DiPreta, who understands how to make life easier for writers while pushing gently for more and better—while also meeting deadlines. Mauro also has the advantage of being assisted by Vedika Khanna, who has been persistent and always good-natured about putting all the pieces together and making the details work. I am thankful to her.

This was my first opportunity to work with the good people at Javelin. That, too, was impressive. Each literary agent reinvents publishing of necessity and, in this case, with passion. They were always there to answer the phones on the first ring and to do what was necessary, often going much further than I would have expected.

I also owe a great debt of gratitude to Michael Schultz, who envisioned this project and put me together with Dwight. His foresight and great nature make it clear to me that if I were in the Hamptons real estate market he would be the man I would want to deal with.

Finally, and first always, is my wife, Laura, who creates the life we lead together; who makes it possible for me to do what I do; who somehow always figures out what needs to be done and how to do it. There is no me, there is only us. Us, of course, and our sons, Taylor and Beau, and Beau's Jeanne, and always our small doghter, Willow Bay, who does anything but.

RECOMMENDED SOURCES ON PRESIDENT NIXON

Books

RN: The Memoirs of Richard Nixon by President Richard Nixon

Richard M. Nixon: A Life in Full by Conrad Black

Being Nixon: A Man Divided by Evan Thomas

Richard Nixon: The Life by John A. Farrell

With Nixon by Raymond Price

The Haldeman Diaries: Inside the Nixon White House by H. R. Haldeman

The Ends of Power by H. R. Haldeman

The Greatest Comeback: How Richard Nixon Rose from Defeat to Create the New Majority by Patrick J. Buchanan

Nixon's White House Wars: The Battles That Made and Broke a President and Divided America Forever by Patrick J. Buchanan

Silent Coup: The Removal of a President by Len Colodny and Robert Gettlin

The Nixon Conspiracy: Watergate and the Plot to Remove the President by Geoff Shepard

The Real Watergate Scandal: Collusion, Conspiracy, and the Plot That Brought Nixon Down by Geoff Shepard

The Secret Plot to Make Ted Kennedy President by Geoff Shepard

The Making of the President 1968 by Theodore H. White

Witness to Power: The Nixon Years by John Ehrlichman

The Strong Man: John Mitchell and the Secrets of Watergate by James Rosen

Making It Perfectly Clear: An Inside Account of Nixon's Love-Hate Relationship with the Media by Herbert Klein

Nixon and Mao: The Week That Changed the World by Margaret MacMillan

Haig's Coup: How Richard Nixon's Closest Aide Forced Him from Office by Ray Locker

Leak: Why Mark Felt Became Deep Throat by Max Holland

The Nixon Tapes: 1971–1972 by Douglas Brinkley and Luke A. Nichter

The Nixon Tapes: 1973 by Douglas Brinkley and Luke A. Nichter

The Last Liberal Republican by John Roy Price

Websites

Shepard on Watergate: shepardonwatergate.com

The Colodny Collection at Texas A&M University: www.watergate.com/colodny
-collection/texas-a-m-university

Luke A. Nichter Nixon Tape Collection: NixonTapes.org

APPENDIX

EXHIBIT 1: FBI REPORT JULY 5, 1974

To "The Director" of the FBI Cover Memorandum. Includes Dean as "Master Manipulator."

UNITED STATES GOVERNMENT

Memorandum

TO : THE DIRECTOR   DATE: 7/5/74

FROM : O. T. JACOBSON

SUBJECT : WATERGATE INVESTIGATION – OPE ANALYSIS

James walter mccord

          Pursuant to the Director's instructions on 5/14/74 for the Office of Planning and Evaluation (OPE) to conduct a complete analysis of the FBI's conduct of the Watergate and related investigations the enclosed study has been prepared. The General Investigative Division participated in major portions of this study.

          In view of the immense scope of the Watergate investigations, it was necessary for OPE to narrow the focus of this analysis to those areas of the investigations which have caused critical commentary relating to the Bureau's performance. Therefore, the OPE staff undertook a review of selected materials which provided a comprehensive cross section of commentary regarding these investigations. The materials reviewed included "White House Transcripts", proceedings of the Senate Watergate Committee; confirmation testimony before the Senate Judiciary Committee on the nomination of L. Patrick Gray III to be FBI Director, Earl J. Silbert to be U. S. Attorney for the District of Columbia, and William D. Ruckelshaus to be Deputy Attorney General. Numerous books and articles relating to the Watergate matters were also reviewed. In addition, Inspection reports, summary memoranda, and selected file materials were reviewed and analyzed as to content.

Enclosure

1 - Mr. Callahan (Encl.)
1 - Mr. Adams (Encl.)
1 - Mr. Gebhardt (Encl.)
1 - Mr. Jacobson
1 - Mr. Sheets
1 - Mr. Revell

OBR/imt
(7)

REC-84

12 JUL 23 1974

13-081

CONTINUED - OVER

67 JUL 24 1974

"ENCLOSURE IN BULKY ROOM"
1B 873 JEH

ALL INFORMATION CONTAINED
HEREIN IS UNCLASSIFIED
DATE 7/16/80 BY SP4 JRM/DAS

Memorandum to The Director
RE: WATERGATE INVESTIGATION -
    OPE ANALYSIS

that the actions of former Attorney Generals Mitchell and Kleindienst
served to thwart and/or impede the Bureau's investigative effort. The
actions of John W. Dean at the White House and Jeb S. Magruder at the
Committee to Re-Elect the President were purposefully designed to mislead and thwart the Bureau's legitimate line of inquiry. At every stage
of the investigation there were contrived covers placed in order to mislead
the investigators.

In spite of the most serious impediments posed in this
investigation, the professional approach used by the Bureau and the
perseverance of our investigative personnel were the ultimate key to the
solution of not only the Watergate break-in but the cover up itself.

Those most closely associated with the Bureau's efforts
including Acting U. S. Attorney Earl Silbert, Assistant Attorney General
Henry Petersen, former Acting Director Ruckelshaus and the Special
Prosecutor's Office have on several occasions praised the Bureau's
investigative performance in these cases. The direction given to Bureau
investigations by the U. S. Attorney's Office and the Criminal Division
of the Department of Justice has been the subject of much criticism due to
a clear intent to initially steer away from political issues. Acting U. S.
Attorney Silbert and Assistant Attorney General Petersen have borne the
brunt of most of this criticism. The FBI followed well established
Departmental policies in these areas and did vigorously pursue cases
when requested to do so by the Department and/or the Special Prosecutor.
All information developed indicating any possible violations of Federal
law was properly referred to the Department.

In OPE's view the Bureau has a legitimate and compelling
defense in all but three of the areas of criticism. In these three areas
the facts must speak for themselves as no adequate explanation can be
rendered due to the circumstances involved.

Page 5 of the report.

The Inspection Division completed its analysis of the activities of former Acting Director Gray on June 26, 1973. Ten specific allegations were addressed in the analysis set forth in a memorandum which is twelve pages in length. The most significant aspect of the Inspection staff's analysis appears to be the following observations:

"In considering possible impediments to obtaining the full facts of the Watergate case the furnishing of numerous FBI reports and other communications by Gray to Dean must be considered. . . It is true there is no evidence in the files indicating this action by Gray impeded our investigation from an investigator's standpoint. Access by Dean to our investigation would logically indicate to him what information had been developed and which would enable him to work out strategy to cover up the case. Likewise, the destruction by Gray of documents apparently furnished him from Hunt's safe would have impeded the investigation although this cannot be stated positively since we do not know what specific material he destroyed, if any."[7]

On April 10, 1974, the Inspection Division's analysis of Mr. Gray's activities relating to the Watergate investigation were furnished to the Special Prosecutor's Office along with 32 other Bureau

Page 8 of the report.

IV. AREAS OF CRITICISM AND COMMENTS

1. Allowing John Dean to sit in on interviews of White House personnel; submitting copies and/or reports of the FBI investigative results to Dean, and clearing proposed investigative activity through Dean.[9]

COMMENTS: On June 19, 1972, WFO by teletype requested authority to interview Charles W. Colson since information had been developed that Hunt had worked for Colson at the White House. On June 22, 1972, Mr. Gray telephonically authorized then Assistant Director Bates to have WFO contact John Dean to set up interview with Colson. Dean subsequently indicated he would sit in on interviews of White House personnel and all requests for investigation at the White House had to be cleared through him.

Criticism of FBI interviews in the presence of Dean and clearing proposed investigative activities through him is justified. However, there appeared no alternative to WFO and to the Accounting and Fraud Section to following this procedure since the decision concerning this apparently had been made between Mr. Gray and Dean, and neither Bureau supervisors nor field agents were in a position to overrule decisions of the Acting Director.

With respect to the submitting of copies of FBI reports to Dean, this is probably the most serious blunder from an investigative

Page 10 of the report.

standpoint made by Mr. Gray. The facts concerning this development
became known outside Mr. Gray's staff for the first time on February 5,
1973. This is long after the substantive investigation into the Democratic
National Committee Headquarters (DNCH) break-in was completed and,
in fact, was after the trial of those originally implicated was completed.
While Dean's role as the master manipulator of the cover up was unknown
and, in fact, the cover up itself was unknown during the investigation,
obviously the furnishing to Dean by Mr. Gray of our reports allowed
Dean the total opportunity to plan a course of action to thwart the FBI's
investigation and grand jury inquiry. There was no way that FBI
personnel could have avoided this situation since it was unknown that
Mr. Gray was furnishing the reports to Dean.

The principal lesson to be learned from this is that rarely
should we conduct interviews in the presence of an attorney and never
should we allow the same attorney to sit in on all interviews relative to
a certain situation. Further, FBI reports should be disseminated only
to the prosecutor and certainly never to the White House.

Page 11 of the report.

EXHIBIT 2: "GUNGA DEAN"
—June 18, 1973, William Safire Poem in the *New York Times*
(From The New York Times. ©1973 The New York Times
Company. All rights reserved. Used under license.)

WASHINGTON.
You may talk o' Hunt and Liddy
When you're feelin' gay and giddy
And you think you have th' White House in your sights,
But when your side is achin'
To prove Nixon said "Go break in"
You need an aide who sat there at the heights.
Now in D.C.'s sunny clime
Where I used to spend my time
A-servin' of the public, sight unseen,
Of all the crewcut crew
The straightest lace I knew
Was the man in charge of ethics, Gunga Dean.
     He was "Dean! Dean! Dean!
   "You smoothie of a lawyer, keep us clean!
     "With your ardor never dampened
     "We'll see rectitude is rampant
   "For no scandal can deflect us, Gunga Dean."
Nixon entered the campaign
And considered it insane
To concern himself with breakin' any rules,
For a-watchin' the committee
And its forty-million kitty
Was his counselor from all the finest schools.
But while leading lambs to slaughter
Came the shockin' gate o' water
And all the district fuzz began to fly.
To give him true reports.
Of any White House torts
Nixon wrongly chose an implicated guy.

It was "Dean! Dean! Dean!
  "I want the deepest probe you've ever seen!'
    "Don't blow anybody's cover
    "But try and soon discover
  "If CREEP did anything illegal, Gunga Dean."
For six long months Dean battled
(Nobody caught had tattled)
And kept sendin' word he had the problem solved.

ESSAY
When the Oval Office queried
Dean would smile, and with eyes bleuried,
Say: "No one in the White House was involved."
Then McCord untied his knot
And the story went to pot
And the hunter was the hunted sudden-ly;
Dean ran out hell-for-leather,
Said: "We were in it altogether,
"—And nobody makes a scapegoat out of me."
    Then it was "Dean! Dean! Dean!
  "For your testimony we are very keen!
    "Point the finger, show who's sleazy,
    "And we'll see the judge goes easy.
  "Here's your chance to cop a plea, Gunga Dean."
"Thanks, but I'll not need ya.
"I've got contacts in the media
"Who'll print my leaks until the price has risen.
"I'll use them for my ends,
"'According to Dean's friends,'
"For the likes of me does not belong in prison."
He would sing out any tune
To hear Sirica say "immune"
("No less than forty times I've made the scene!")
Justice balked, but Senate crumbled,
To Ervin's saving arms he tumbled,

And now they cannot jail you, Gunga Dean.
    So it's Dean! Dean! Dean!
  Smear your leader, save your skin and vent your spleen!
    Though the Fifth Amendment aids you,
    By the TV that parades you—
You will never drag down Nixon, Gunga Dean.
    Yes, it's Dean! Dean! Dean!
    Star of everybody's television screen.
    You will claim that you obeyed,
    But the truth is you betrayed
A far better man than you are, Gunga Dean!

EXHIBIT 3: OBITUARY OF ALICE MAYHEW—February 4, 2020, *New York Times*

Alice Mayhew, Who Edited a Who's Who of Writers, Dies at 87

At Simon & Schuster, best sellers were her stock in trade. She popularized the nonfiction political page turner, starting with "All the President's Men."
By Anita Gates
Published Feb. 4, 2020 Updated Feb. 5, 2020

Alice Mayhew, a widely admired editor who shepherded into print best sellers by a veritable who's who of writers—along the way popularizing the Washington political narrative, beginning with "All the President's Men" in 1974—died on Tuesday at her home in Manhattan. She was 87.

The death was confirmed by Simon & Schuster, where she had been a vice president and editorial director.

"All the President's Men," the Washington Post reporters Bob Woodward and Carl Bernstein's account of how they uncovered the truth about the Watergate burglary and the subsequent White House effort to cover it up, became an immediate best seller and had a decided impact on American history. Published on June 15, 1974 (no advance copies had been provided, even for reviewers), it accelerated a growing public disapproval of President Richard M. Nixon's actions and helped fuel a congressional drive toward impeachment that led to Nixon's resignation 55 days later.

Ms. Mayhew also worked with notable public figures, including President Jimmy Carter ("A Full Life: Reflections at Ninety," 2015) and the Supreme Court justice Ruth Bader Ginsburg ("My Own Words," 2017).

The countless best sellers that Ms. Mayhew edited include John Dean's "Blind Ambition: The White House Years" (1976); Taylor Branch's "Pillar of Fire: America in the King Years" (1998); Walter Isaacson's books, including "Steve Jobs" (2011) and "Leonardo da Vinci" (2017); David Brooks's "On Paradise Drive: How We Live Now (and Always Have) in the Future Tense" (2004), an examination of contemporary American society; Diane McWhorter's Pulitzer Prize-winning civil rights history, "Carry Me Home" (2001); and the first volumes of Sidney Blumenthal's political biography of Abraham Lincoln, beginning with "A Self-Made Man" (2016).

In 2014, when Simon & Schuster celebrated its 90th anniversary by having staff members vote for their 90 favorite titles over those years, almost one-third of the books (29) had been edited by Ms. Mayhew.

Mr. Woodward's "Fear: Trump in the White House" (2018) was, as he noted in the acknowledgments, his 19th book with her.

Ms. Mayhew's books occasionally dealt with the lighter side of political or popular culture. She edited Kitty Kelley's gossipy biography "Nancy Reagan" (1991) and two memoirs by the fashion designer Diane von Furstenberg.

Though Ms. Mayhew was highly regarded, her own life was something of a closed book, so rigorously did she defend her privacy. When The New York Times ran an article about her in 2004 with the headline "Muse of the Beltway Book," she declined to be interviewed. The article relied on the observations of those who worked with her, some of whom said her greatest talents lay in conceptualization and structure.

"She is particularly adept at unearthing submerged themes," the Times article concluded, "developing swift transitions, unsentimentally pruning away digressions, even when—especially when—they are hundreds of pages long. Mayhew's faith in chronological organization is said to be nearly religious."

Alice E. Mayhew was born on June 14, 1932, in Brooklyn, the daughter of Alice and Leonard S. Mayhew. Alice grew up in the Bronx and had an older brother, Leonard F. Mayhew, who was her neighbor in Sag Harbor, N.Y., on Long Island, where she also had a home. He died in 2012. Simon & Schuster said she left no immediate survivors.

Ms. Mayhew joined Simon & Schuster in 1971. One of her early successes there was "Our Bodies, Our Selves" (1973), the feminist classic assembled by the Boston Women's Health Book Collective. What began as a 193-page course booklet on stapled newsprint sold, in the Simon & Schuster version, at least 4.5 million copies worldwide.

Just a sampling of her other authors, many of them historians and journalists, would include, in no particular order, Betty Friedan, Frances Fitzgerald, Michael Beschloss, Steven Brill, E. J. Dionne, J. Anthony Lukas, Kati Marton, Richard Reeves, Evan Thomas, David Gergen, Jill Abramson, David Herbert Donald, Robert Gates, Fred Kaplan, Sylvia Nasar, William Shawcross, James B. Stewart, Amy Wilentz, Joe Conason, Mark Whitaker, Harold Holzer, Connie Bruck, Jonathan Alter, Jennet Conant, Richard Engel, David Maraniss and Sally Bedell Smith.

Ms. Mayhew's reputation was sterling, but her career was not untouched by scandal. In 2002, the historians Stephen E. Ambrose and Doris Kearns Goodwin, both Mayhew authors, were accused of plagiarism. Ms. Goodwin acknowledged that in 1987 Simon & Schuster settled with an author over accusations of plagiarism in a book she had written about the Kennedy family. Mr. Ambrose was found to have lifted, without using quotation marks, passages from another book, though he had footnoted them.

The twist with the Ambrose episode, as the gossip site Gawker reported, was that the book Mr. Ambrose had mined, Robert Sam Anson's "Exile: The Unquiet Oblivion of Richard M. Nixon," had also been edited by Ms. Mayhew.

In 2008, Priscilla Painton became Simon & Schuster's executive editor, taking over many of Ms. Mayhew's duties. But Ms. Mayhew continued to acquire and edit titles.

While Ms. Mayhew firmly avoided talking about herself, she was considerably more straightforward when discussing others.

In an interview with Len Colodny, co-author of "Silent Coup: The Removal of a President," about Mr. Dean's claim that his editors had told him to include false information in "Blind Ambition" (reissued in 2009), Ms. Mayhew said: "That's a lie. L-I-E. That is spelled L-I-E."

EXHIBITS 4A TO 4D:
THE MARCH 13, 1973, TO MARCH 21, 1973, TAPE SEGMENTS

These tape exhibits contain segments from the March 13, 1973, to the March 21, 1973, Oval Office tapes. *The segments selected are those only relevant to my story.* These segments are a minuscule part of the entire tape collection. Those interested in a deeper understanding or who want to listen to more detail are encouraged to visit the tape website Nixontapes.org or find other sources. For clarity, it will be helpful if you read the transcript while listening to a specific tape. Luke Nichter's transcription books are an excellent source for accurate transcripts. (See Recommended Sources on President Nixon.)

The March 13 to March 17 tapes were not made available to the public until 1995, as the result of a private lawsuit.

All use of these transcripts of tape excerpts is made possible by permission granted by Luke A. Nichter. All segments have been verified for accuracy.

EXHIBIT 4A: FROM THE MARCH 13, 1973, OVAL OFFICE MEETING—Richard Nixon and John Dean

To listen to this segment as you read the transcript, go to Nixon Tapes.org, then to "audio & transcripts," then to "John W Dean III," then to 3/13/73—OVAL 878-014b.

Author's Note: John Dean had been telling the president for nine months— since the June 17, 1972, break-in—that no one in the White House knew in advance about the Watergate operation. Dean finally tells the president here that actually Gordon Strachan, who was on the White House staff, knew in advance. And, of course, I believe Dean himself knew in advance, though he doesn't confess that.

At 00:22:

NIXON: They're really—let's face it, after—I think they are really after Haldeman.

DEAN: Haldeman and Mitchell.

NIXON: Mitchell—I mean, Colson is not a big enough name for them. He really isn't. You know, he is a thorn in their side, but Colson's name bothers them none. So they get Colson. They're after Haldeman and after Mitchell. Don't you think so?

DEAN: That's right. Or they'd take Ehrlichman if they could drag him in but they've been unable to drag him in in any way.

NIXON: Ultimately, Haldeman's problem is Chapin, isn't it?

DEAN: Bob's problem is circumstantial.

NIXON: What I meant is, looking at the circumstantial, I don't know that anything—Bob had nothing—didn't know any of those people, like the Hunts and all that bunch. Colson did. But Bob did know Chapin.

DEAN: That's right.

NIXON: Now, what—now however the hell much Chapin knew I'll be goddamned. I don't know.

DEAN: Well, Chapin didn't know anything about the Watergate, and—

NIXON: You don't think so?

DEAN: No. Absolutely not.

NIXON: Did Strachan?

DEAN: Yes.

NIXON: He knew?

DEAN: Yes.

NIXON: About the Watergate?

DEAN: Yes.

NIXON: Well, then, Bob knew. He probably told Bob then. He may not have. He may not have.

DEAN: He was judicious in what he relayed, and—but Strachan is as tough as nails. I—

NIXON: What'll he say? Just go in and say he didn't know?

DEAN: He'll go in and stonewall it and say, "I don't know anything about what you are talking about." He has already done it twice, as you know, in interviews.

Author's Note: As the conversation continues, Dean tells the president, "They would have a hell of a time proving that Strachan had knowledge of it, though." John Dean had no idea that there was a recording device in the Oval Office. As it turns out, it's easy to prove that Strachan had knowledge of it: John Dean's own words, as recorded in the Oval Office, prove it!

NIXON: Yeah. I guess he should, shouldn't he? In the interests of—why, I suppose we can't call that justice, can we? We can't call it [unclear].

DEAN: Well, it—

NIXON: The point is, how do you justify that?

DEAN: It's a personal loyalty with him [meaning Gordon Strachan]. He doesn't want it any other way. He didn't have to be told. He didn't have to be asked. It just is something that he found is the way he wanted to handle the situation.

NIXON: But he knew? He knew about Watergate? Strachan did?

DEAN: Mm-hmm.

NIXON: I'll be damned. Well, that's the problem in Bob's case, isn't it? It's not Chapin then, but Strachan. Because Strachan worked for him.

DEAN: Mm-hmm. They would have one hell of a time proving that Strachan had knowledge of it, though.

Author's Note: In the following segment of the same conversation, Segretti's name comes up. You can hear in the conversation that Nixon is still unclear as to what Watergate was actually about—because his White House Counsel, John Dean, had not been giving him accurate information.

Continuing at 4:50:

NIXON: Bob must have known about Segretti.

DEAN: Well, I—Segretti really wasn't involved in the intelligence gathering to speak of at all.

NIXON: Oh, he wasn't?

DEAN: No, he wasn't. He was out just—he was out—

NIXON: Who the hell was gathering intelligence?

DEAN: That was Liddy and his outfit.

NIXON: I see. Apart from Watergate?

DEAN: That's—well, that's right. That was part of their whole— Watergate was part of intelligence gathering, and this—

NIXON: Well, that's a perfectly legitimate thing. I guess that's what it was.

DEAN: What happened is they—

NIXON: What a stupid thing. Pointless. That was the stupid thing.

DEAN: That was incredible. That's right. That's right.

NIXON: I wouldn't want to think that Mitchell would allow—would have allowed this kind of operation to be in the committee.

DEAN: I don't think he knew it was there.

NIXON: You kidding?

DEAN: I don't—

NIXON: You don't think Mitchell knew about this thing?

DEAN: Oh, no, no, no. Don't mis— I don't think he knew that people— I think he knew that Liddy was out intelligence gathering.

NIXON: Well?

DEAN: I don't think he knew that Liddy would use a fellow like Mc-Cord, for God's sake, who worked for the Committee. I can't believe that. You know, that—

NIXON: Hunt? Did Mitchell know Hunt?

DEAN: I don't think Mitchell knew about Hunt either.

Author's Note: A couple of minutes later, in the same conversation, the president goes back to the idea of putting all information out. John Dean advises re: "White House involvement in the Watergate" that he thinks "there is just none . . . people here [in the White House] just did not know that that was going to be done." (That statement contradicts what he told the president a couple of minutes earlier in the same conversation, when he said that Gordon Strachan, who was on the White House staff, did know in advance.) Dean continues to advise that it's too late to put all the information out, that there would be "a certain domino situation" and that "there are going to be a lot of problems if everything starts falling." Dean himself couldn't afford for all the information to be put out. If it had been, Dean would have clearly been seen in the middle of both the plan to break into the Watergate and the subsequent cover-up—and he would no doubt have been one of the dominos to fall. As for Segretti's work, Nixon says there was nothing "sinister" about it. Dean says it was, in fact, "quite humorous."

Continuing at 7:47:

NIXON: Is it too late to, frankly, go the hangout road? Yes, it is.

DEAN: I think it is. I think—here's the—the hangout road—

NIXON: The hangout road's going to be rejected by—somebody on your staff has rejected it.

DEAN: It was kicked around. Bob and I, and—

NIXON: I know Ehrlichman always felt that it should be hangout. [unclear]

DEAN: Well, I think I convinced him why—that he wouldn't want to hang out either. There is a certain domino situation here. If some things start going, a lot of other things are going to start going, and there are going to be a lot of problems if everything starts falling. So there are dangers, Mr. President. I'd be less than candid if I didn't tell you there are. There's a reason for us not—not everyone going up and testifying.

NIXON: I see. Oh, no, no, no, no, no. I didn't mean go up and have them testifying. I meant—

DEAN: Well, I mean just—they're just starting to hang out and say, "Here's our story—"

NIXON: I mean putting the story out to PR buddies somewhere. "Here's the story, the true story about Watergate [. . .]"

DEAN: They would never believe it.

NIXON: That's the point.

DEAN: The point is—the two things they are working on, on Watergate—

NIXON: Who is "they"? The press?

DEAN: The press—

NIXON: The Democrats?

DEAN: The Democrats, the intellectuals—

NIXON: The Packwoods [recent criticism by Senator Packwood]?

DEAN: Right. Right. "They" would never buy it, as far as, one, White House involvement in the Watergate, which I think there is just none—for that incident that occurred over in the Democratic National Committee headquarters. People just—here would—did not know that that was going to be done. I think there are some people who saw the fruits of it, but that's another story. I am talking about the criminal conspiracy to go in there. The other thing is that—the Segretti thing. You hang that out, they wouldn't believe that. They wouldn't believe that Chapin acted on his own to put his old friend [unclear] Segretti in to be a Dick Tuck on somebody else's campaign. They would have to paint it into something more sinister, something more involved—a part of a general plan.

NIXON: Shit, it's not sinister at all. None of it is.

DEAN: No.

NIXON: Segretti's stuff hasn't been a bit sinister.

DEAN: It's quite humorous, as a matter of fact.

EXHIBIT 4B: FROM A MARCH 16, 1973, PHONE CALL— Richard Nixon and John Dean—8:14 to 8:23 P.M.

To listen to this segment as you read the transcript, go to Nixon Tapes.org, then to "audio & transcripts," then to "John W Dean III," then to 3/16/73—WHT 037-134.

Author's Note: After telling the president three days earlier, on March 13, that Gordon Strachan knew about Watergate in advance, Dean goes back to his original story, saying that "there was not a scintilla of evidence in the investigation that led anywhere to the White House." He then suggests to the president that the way he could extricate himself from the Watergate mess was to put the attention on Segretti because, while it's "a little embarrassing, it's not evil. It's nothing."

At 6:44:

DEAN: A lot of the—a lot of my conclusions were based on the fact that there was not a scintilla of evidence in the investigation that led anywhere to the White House.

NIXON: Mm-hmm.

DEAN: There's nothing in the FBI file that indicates anybody in the White House was involved.

NIXON: Mm-hmm.

DEAN: There's nothing in what was presented before the grand jury indicating—

NIXON: Mm-hmm.

DEAN: —White House involvement.

NIXON: Well, just saying some of those things could be helpful.

DEAN: That's right.

NIXON: See? It could be helpful—

DEAN: [unclear]

NIXON: And then we just put it out and then let, let the committee try to prove otherwise.

DEAN: And I understand that they will not get the grand jury minutes, which is good because the grand jury is even more thorough than the FBI.

NIXON: Mm-hmm.

DEAN: The committee's starting ten paces behind, and Ervin does not, I'm told, have a total disposition for what he's doing. He just doesn't relish it. He wants to find out things. He's—

NIXON: Why not?

DEAN: He's more excited about the confrontation on executive privilege, I think, than he is about what else he might find.

NIXON: We would welcome that, wouldn't we?

DEAN: Oh, he'd love that.

NIXON: Well, so would we.

DEAN: Mm-hmm.

NIXON: I mean, let's have it. Particularly if it's on you—oh, no, he won't have it on you. He'll—

DEAN: No, I don't think he'll [laughs] bite for that—

NIXON: On Chapin, huh?

DEAN: Chapin or Colson.

NIXON: Mm-hmm.

DEAN: I think that the other part of the report that we can probably put out with even greater detail than, say, Watergate is Segretti. And that—

NIXON: That I would like.

DEAN: And that—you see, that would put us in a very forthcoming posture.

NIXON: Mm-hmm.

DEAN: Here's—

NIXON: We could point out that the one case has now been determined by the courts, and that we have nothing to indicate that the White House was involved. Now, second, with regard to Segretti, let's lay all this—let's lay it all out. Here it is.

DEAN: Now, sure, it's a little embarrassing—

NIXON: The problem there—

DEAN: It's nothing evil. It's nothing—

NIXON: Well, it's less embarrassing than what's been charged, and the innuendo.

DEAN: That's right.

NIXON: Of course, I realize the major problem there is the financing, but even that—

DEAN: That's going to have to be answered well before Ervin—

NIXON: That's gonna come out. That's right, so you—

DEAN: —so we might as well leave it out—

NIXON: Yeah. That's right. So, you can think about it. Okay?

DEAN: All right, sir. Well—

NIXON: Fine.

DEAN: We will win! [laughs]"

Excerpt from *The Nixon Tapes: 1973* (With Audio Clips) (Enhanced Edition), Douglas Brinkley & Luke A. Nichter, https://books .apple.com/us/book/the-nixon-tapes-1973-with-audio-clips-enhanced -edition/id1396139825. This material may be protected by copyright.

EXHIBIT 4C: FROM THE MARCH 17, 1973, OVAL OFFICE MEETING—Richard Nixon and John Dean

To listen to this segment as you read the transcript, go to Nixon Tapes.org, then to "audio & transcripts," then to "John W Dean III," then to 3/17/73—OVAL 882-012b.

Author's Note: When the president asks who could be vulnerable in the Watergate incident, Dean offers, for the first time, that he—Dean—could be, which surprises the president who immediately assumes that Dean didn't have any foreknowledge of the break-in. When Jeb Magruder's name comes up, Dean expresses concern that Magruder would not go down without dragging many others down with him—which seems to concern Dean, who likely was thinking that he, Dean, would be among those dragged down. The president clearly had no idea why there had been a break-in at the Watergate, wonders what kind of "intelligence" they were hoping to find in the Democratic National Committee headquarters there—and wonders who was pushing for the break-in.

At 32:04:

NIXON: Now, you were saying too, ah, what really, where the, this thing leads, I mean in terms of the vulnerabilities and so forth. It's your view that the vulnerables are basically Mitchell, Colson, Haldeman, indirectly, possibly directly, and of course, the second level, as far as the White House is concerned, Chapin.

DEAN: And I'd say Dean, to a degree.

NIXON: You? Why?

DEAN: Well, because I've been all over this thing like a blanket.

NIXON: I know, I know, but you know all about it, but you didn't—you were in it after the deed was done.

DEAN: That's correct that I have no foreknowledge . . .

NIXON: Here's the whole point, here's the whole point. My point is that your problem is you, you have no problem. All the others that have

participated in the goddamned thing, and therefore are potentially subject to criminal liability. You're not. That's the difference.

DEAN: That's right.

(Pause)

NIXON: And on that score, of course, we have to know where we are.

DEAN: And on . . .

NIXON: Everybody—Magruder I understand knows, told some people
that Haldeman knows, told other people that, ah, Colson knows [unin-
telligible].

DEAN: Oh Jeb, is ah, Jeb is a good man. But if Jeb ever sees himself
sinking, he will reach out to grab everybody he can get hold of.

NIXON: Will he?

DEAN: Yes, and I think the unfortunate thing in this whole thing, Jeb
is the most responsible man for the whole incident.

NIXON: [Unintelligible]

*Author's Note: Dean tells the president in the following segment of this con-
versation that Gordon Liddy told him that Gordon Strachan was the only
person in the White House who knew of the Watergate break-in in advance.
Dean did not testify that way before the Senate Watergate Committee. In his
testimony before the committee, Dean testified that Gordon Liddy told him
that no one in the White House knew of the Watergate break-in in advance.*

DEAN: Well, let me tell you, one, after it happened and on, on
Monday—I—didn't take me very long to put the pieces together what
had occurred, ah, I got ahold of Liddy and I said, "Gordon, I want to
know who in the White House is involved in this." And he said, "John,
nobody is involved or has knowledge, that I know of. Ah, that we were
going in or the like, with one exception and it was a lower level person."

NIXON: Strachan?

DEAN: Strachan. Ah, he said, "I don't really know if he, how much he
knew." And I said, "Well why in the hell did it happen?" And he said,

"Magruder pushed me without mercy to go in there. Magruder said I had to go in there. He had to do this . . ."

NIXON: Who pushed Magruder?

DEAN: That's . . .

NIXON: Colson?

DEAN: That's—that what Jeb . . .

NIXON: Colson, did Colson push Magruder though?

DEAN: Now that's where there's two stories.

NIXON: That's my point, I don't, I think, I—Colson can push, but he didn't know Magruder that well.

DEAN: No.

NIXON: And had very damn little confidence in him. Uh . . .

DEAN: Right.

NIXON: So maybe that one can come from here. Is that your point?

DEAN: That's, ah, that's . . .

NIXON: Think Haldeman pushed him?

DEAN: Well, I think what happened is that on sort of a tickler . . .

NIXON: I can't believe Haldeman would push Magruder.

DEAN: No, I don't think that happened.

NIXON: I don't think [unintelligible]—maybe Chapin did.

DEAN: No, I think Strachan did. Because Strachan just had it on his tickler. He was supposed to be gathering intelligence and talking to Jeb and saying what, where is it and why isn't it coming in? You haven't produced it.

NIXON: Intelligence problems? What were they worried about? They worried about, as I understand it, the San Diego demonstrations. I'm too sure of, but I guess everybody around here except me worried about them.

Author's Note: Shortly thereafter the president and Dean talk about ending the Watergate matter by shifting the blame to Segretti and me, knowing that Segretti's "Dick Tuck–like pranks" are of lesser consequence than Watergate. The president says that "Chapin and all of them have just got to take the heat." The segment then goes on to Dean's characterization of Segretti's activities as "just not that serious."

Continuing at 36:39:

NIXON: I think what you've got to do, to the extent that you can, John, is cut her off at the pass. And you cut off at the pass. Liddy and his bunch just did this as part of their job.

Author's Note: "Cut her off at the pass" is not referring to a specific person. It's simply an expression the president is using.

DEAN: They were out on a lark. They went beyond any assignment they ever had.

NIXON: Now on the Segretti thing, I think you've just got to—Chapin and all of them have just got to take the heat. Look, you've got to admit the facts, John, and . . .

DEAN: That's right.

NIXON: And that's our—and that's that. And Kalmbach paid him. And paid a lot of people. I, I just think on Segretti, no matter how bad it is—it isn't nearly as bad as people think it was. Espionage, sabotage, shit.

DEAN: The intent, when Segretti was hired, was nothing evil, nothing vicious, nothing bad, nothing. Not espionage, not sabotage. It was pranksterism that got out of hand and we know that. And I think we can lay our story out there. Ah, I have no problem with the Segretti thing. It's just not that serious . . .

Excerpts from *The Nixon Tapes: 1973* (With Audio Clips) (Enhanced Edition), Douglas Brinkley & Luke A. Nichter, https://books.apple.com/us/book/the-nixon-tapes-1973-with-audio-clips-enhanced-edition/id1396139825. This material may be protected by copyright. This transcript is courtesy of Luke A. Nichter.

EXHIBIT 4D: FROM A MARCH 21, 1973, OVAL OFFICE MEETING—Richard Nixon and John Dean

To listen to this segment as you read the transcript, go to Nixon Tapes.org, then to "audio & transcripts," then to "John W Dean III," then to 3/21/73—OVAL 886-008a.

Author's Note: This is from the "cancer on the presidency" conversation. Dean tells the president he "thought we ought to talk this morning" because he has "the impression" that the president doesn't know everything he, Dean, knows. If Dean hasn't been telling the president everything he knows, then of course the president would not know what he knows. Dean continues— nine months after the June 17, 1972, break-in—to tell him the "basic facts," clearly information that one would think the White House Counsel would have told the president from the beginning. Among his pronouncements, Dean says they're being blackmailed. It is a couple of weeks after this conversation that Dean decides to jump ship and hires his own criminal defense attorney.

At 5:52:

DEAN: The reason I thought we ought to talk this morning is because in our conversations, I have the impression that you don't know everything I know—

NIXON: That's right.

DEAN: —and it makes it very difficult for you to make judgments that only you can make—

NIXON: That's right.

DEAN: —on some of these things and I thought that—

NIXON: You've got—in other words, I've got to know why you feel that something—

DEAN: Well, let me—

NIXON: —that we shouldn't unravel something.

DEAN: Let me give you my overall first.

NIXON: In other words, your judgment as to where it stands, and where we go now.

DEAN: I think that there's no doubt about the seriousness of the problem we're—we've got. We have a cancer—within—close to the presidency, that's growing. It's growing daily. It's compounding. It grows geometrically now, because it compounds itself. That'll be clear as I explain, you know, some of the details of why it is. And it basically is because, one, we're being blackmailed; two, people are going to start perjuring themselves very quickly that have not had to perjure themselves to protect other people and the like. And that is just—and there is no assurance—

NIXON: That it won't bust.

DEAN: That that won't bust.

NIXON: True.

DEAN: So let me give you the sort of basic facts, talking first about the Watergate, and then about Segretti, and then about some of the peripheral items that have come up. First of all, on the Watergate: How did it all start? Where did it start? It started with an instruction to me from Bob Haldeman to see if we couldn't set up a perfectly legitimate campaign intelligence operation over at the reelection committee.

NIXON: Mm-hmm.

Author's Note: The reader can continue to listen as Dean goes on to explain to the president—in great detail—his version of events relating to the June 17, 1972, break-in and the involvement of the various players. The meeting lasted about 97 minutes and was recorded on two tapes. About 57 minutes into the meeting, the president asked Haldeman to join them, which Haldeman did (at 1:06 in the second tape).

The conclusion of the meeting (beginning at 37:46 on the second tape):

As John Dean gave his explanation of events to the president and Haldeman, it became evident to them that Dean himself could be implicated in the Watergate debacle as "a principal." At that point, the president, Haldeman, and

Dean concluded that an outside "special counsel" was needed, "for the purpose of conducting an investigation" and, as the president says, "to get to the bottom of the goddamn thing." They decided that Henry Petersen at the Department of Justice would be a good candidate. The meeting ended with the decision to approach Petersen to conduct the investigation. It was just days later, after Dean left this meeting, that he hired his own criminal defense attorney and began to work with the prosecutors and against the president.

To me, the president sounds calm as he is listening to Dean and asking questions, while Dean sounds unsettled as he offers his explanations. However, readers can make their own judgment by listening to their conversation themselves.

The two tapes that comprise this 97-minute meeting can be found by going online to nixontapes.org, then to "audio & transcripts," then to "John W. Dean III," then to 3/21/1973. The first of the two tapes is "OVAL 886-008a." The second is "OVAL 886-008b." It will be much easier to understand the audio if readers read a transcript of it as they listen.

I have found Brinkley & Nichter's transcriptions to be excellent and accurate, and recommend them.

EXHIBIT 5: AUGUST 28, 1972, FBI REPORT, INTERVIEW
OF CHAPIN AND STRACHAN, DEAN PRESENT

FEDERAL BUREAU OF INVESTIGATION
COMMUNICATIONS SECTION

AUG 28 1972

NR914 WF PLAIN

6:58PM IMMEDIATE 8-28-72 ALM

TELETYPE

TO ACTING DIRECTOR (139-4089)

FROM WASHINGTON FIELD (139-166) (P) 3P

JAMES WALTER MC CORD, JR., ETAL; BURGLARY, DEMOCRATIC NATIONAL

COMMITTEE HEADQUARTERS, WASHINGTON, D.C. JUNE SEVENTEEN SEVENTY-TWO.
Interception of Communications
IOC; OO: WFO.
Office of Origin: Washington Field Office

Reference

RE WFO TELETYPE TO BUREAU TODAY.

SUMMARY OF INVESTIGATION.

CHARLES COLSON AND SECRETARY JOAN HALL FURNISHED SWORN

DEPOSITIONS TODAY AT DEPARTMENT OF JUSTICE. NO ADDITIONAL

INFORMATION OF VALUE OBTAINED.

THIS EVENING, DWIGHT CHAPIN AND GORDON STRACHAN INTERVIEWED

AT EXECUTIVE OFFICE BUILDING IN PRESENCE OF JOHN W. DEAN,

COUNSEL TO THE PRESIDENT. BOTH INTERVIEWED RE GUIDANCE OF

DONALD HENRY SEGRETTI AND HIS ACTIVITES IN REGARDS TO DEMOCRATIC

CANDIDATES.

BOTH ADMITTED KNOWING SEGRETTI SINCE COLLEGE DAYS IN CALIFORNIA.

BOTH LAST MET WITH SEGRETTI IN JUNE SEVENTY-TWO WHEN HE CALLED

AND SAID FBI WAS LOOKING TO TALK WITH HIM. ASKED THEM WHAT THE FBI

WANTED. NEITHER COULD TELL HIM. BOTH TOLD HIM BETTER TALK

TO FBI AND FIND OUT WHAT ITS ALL ABOUT.

CHAPIN ADMITS GIVING SEGRETTI JOB OF HARRASSING DEMOCRATIC

END PAGE ONE

18 SEP 22 1972

ALL INFORMATION CONTAINED
HEREIN IS UNCLASSIFIED
DATE 4|16|80 BY SP3 TAJ/DJS

6 7 MAR 1973

PAGE TWO

CANDIDATES AND SEGRETTI DID THIS ON HIS OWN WITHOUT ANY SPECIFIC

GUIDANCE FROM CHAPIN OR STRACHAN.

WHEN PRESSED ABOUT FEES OR COMPENSATION FOR SEGRETTI'S WORK,

CHAPIN SAID FEES OR PAYMENT WERE ARRANGED THROUGH HERBERT KOMBACH, *KALMBAC*

AN ATTORNEY ON THE WEST COAST, IN LOS ANGELES. AT THIS POINT

DEAN INTERJECTED THAT KOMBACH IS A VERY CLOSE PERSONAL FRIEND OF

THE PRESIDENT'S. CHAPIN SAID KOMBACH DID NOT KNOW WHAT SEGRETTI

WAS BEING PAID FOR. CHAPIN SAID MAYBE ONLY ONCE OR TWICE, SEGRETTI

CALLED HIM AND TOLD HIM HOW SUCCESSFUL HE WAS IN ACCOMPLISHING A

CERTAIN FEAT, LIKE CHANGING A TELEPHONE NUMBER OF THE DEMOCRATIC

CANDIDATES OFFICE AND THINGS ALONG THAT NATURE.

WHEN ASKED ABOUT ED WARREN AND THEIR KNOWLEDGE OF HIM,

BOTH STRACHAN AND CHAPIN DENIED KNOWING ANYONE BY THAT NAME OR ANYONE

EVER USING THAT NAME. THEY BOTH DENIED EVER TELLING SEGRETTI THAT

SOMEONE NAMED WARREN WOULD BE CONTACTING HIM.

STRACHAN DID ADMIT TALKING WITH GEORGE G. LIDDY IN LATE

FEBRUARY OR MARCH, SEVENTY TWO. LIDDY WAS UPSET SINCE SOMEONE WAS

HARASSING SURROGATE
~~HARASSING~~ A ~~SURROGATE~~ CANDIDATE OF THE REPUBLICANS AND HAD CALLED

THE WHITE HOUSE TRYING TO TOUCH BASE WITH SOMEONE WHO MIGHT KNOW

END PAGE TWO

PAGE THREE

THIS. STRACHAN SAID HE RECALLS TELLING LIDDY ABOUT A MAN HE HAD
WORKING FOR HIM, BUT CANNOT POSITIVELY SAY HE DID NOT TELL LIDDY
SEGRETTI'S NAME AND PRESENT LOCATION. HE DID ADMIT GIVING A PHYSICAL
DESCRIPTION TO LIDDY FOR SOME REASON, BUT CANNOT RECALL WHY HE
DID THAT.

    STRACHAN DID NOT RECEIVE ANY REPORT FROM SEGRETTI
NOR HAS HE HAD CONTACT WITH HIM MORE THAN A HALF A DOZEN
TIMES.

    INVESTIGATION CONTINUING.

END

HOLD

MRF FBI WA DC

3

EXHIBIT 6: LETTER FROM THEODORE H. WHITE,
AUTHOR OF *THE MAKING OF THE PRESIDENT 1968*

White is returning my handwritten notes from Election Day, saying, "You're an amateur historian." The first three pages of my notes are below. Note on page two—aboard the airplane with Tricia, Julie, and David Eisenhower present—Nixon gives his wife an Election Day gift—"Diamond and Pearl Pin and ear rings."

THEODORE H. WHITE   168 EAST 64 STREET   NEW YORK 21, N. Y.

December 9, 1968

Mr. Dwight Chapin,
Staff of President-Elect, Richard M. Nixon,
39th Floor,
The Pierre Hotel,
New York.

Dear Dwight:

I'm sorry for keeping these so long; but wanted to wait until you were back in town so they would not get lost.

They are magnificent historical data; you're an amateur historian; and you should keep them for delivery to the archives in Washington at some future date. All my thanks to you.

The President said we had best wait until all the cabinet is chosen for our next session; so I am standing by. He also said that he would let me glance at the Kissinger-Lindsay memo on re-organization of the White House if it were of interest to me; which, indeed, it is. I'll telephone you on both matters later this week.

All best. And again my gratitude,

Teddy White

Chrisffl. Chapin
10 Rippowam
Cos Cos, Conn.

November 5, 1968
Los Angeles, California
Century Plaza Hotel

1:25 AM u/s RN turned in for the night

7:20 RN came into announce he won up
PST - said he wanted to use lamp
- ask departure time
- said he slept pretty well

7:45 Breakfast - hot oatmeal, juice, milk,
coffee
ask to see HRH & ~~Frank~~ Le Garment

8:15 Made Calls -
- John Mitchell (12 min)
- Norman Chandler (10 min)
- Mr. DDE (12 min)
- Murry Chotiner (10 min)
- Ed Nixon (6 min.)
- Manny Stow (5 min)

- During this period both HRH
& John Ehrlichman were in
to see him.

Handwritten notes from Election Day 1968. Page 1 of 12

9:15   Depart Suite for car &
       airport.
       Ron Ziegler rode to airport

9:45 - Aprox Arrive Airport board plane
       - Picture only - no press -
       - RN change to Sport Coat
       - coffee

10:00 RN walks through plane &
       Shakes hands - Calls the
       family up to front cabin area

       - Presents Mrs. N with a
         gift - Diamond & Pearl
         Pin & ear rings. (David,
         Tricia & Julie present.)

       - Reviewed the election
         possibilities with the family
         Chances on winning & loosing
         - what would happen either
         way - a preparation

Handwritten notes from Election Day 1968. Page 2 of 12.

(30) 10:20 to   Met with Jim Keogh,
     10:50   Pat Buchanan, Bill Safire,
                     and Ray Price

(40) 10:55 to   Met with Len Garment,
     11:35   Frank Shakespeare, Paul Keyes
                     Bud Wilkinson & Roger Ailes

     (Note: At 11:15 Ellsworth saw RN with
       a message — also mentioned vote very
       heavy — heavy in Philadelphia)

     11:35   Garment ask for a couple
                     of minutes alone with RN

     11:38   Met with Finch, Ellsworth,
                     Herb Klein & McWhorter —
                     HRH invited but wouldn't
                     go.

     (Note: At this time RN had three
       Blend Dubonets on the rocks.

Handwritten notes from Election Day 1968. Page 3 of 12.

INDEX

Abplanalp, Bob, 63, 65, 302
Abrams, Creighton, 176–77, 194
Adams, Sherman, 391
Agnew, Judy, 312, 375
Agnew, Spiro, 71–73, 102, 113–15,
    139, 172, 174, 311–13, 374
Ailes, Roger, 53–55, 169
Allen, George, 163–64
Allin, Mort, 156
All the President's Men (Bernstein and
    Woodward), 314
Anderson, Bob, 370
Anderson, Jack, 113, 115–16,
    271–76
Annenberg, Walter, 177
appointments secretary position,
    154–77
    media strategy and, 155–57,
        167–74
    Nixon's family and, 166–67
    official visitors and, 157–64
    "Open Door Hour," 164–65
    Pat Nixon's schedule and, 174–75
    photo opportunities and, 164
    pranks, alcoholism, and, 175–77
    visits/calls initiated by Nixon,
        165–66
Atkins, Ollie, 163, 165, 292
Austria trip, 279, 284, 297

Bachman, Kathy, 204
Baker, Howard, 149
Baker, Jim, 134, 376
Ball, Hiram, 14
Baribault, William, 402
Barker, Bernard, 386

Bass, Ron, 387–88
Beam, Jacob, 278, 282
Beecher, William, 125
Being Nixon (Thomas), 387
Bernstein, Carl, 313–14, 320–21,
    338, 356
Black, Hugo, 148
Blackmun, Harry, 148
Bonnell, Phil, 8
Bradley, Ed, 7
Brennan, Jack, 308
Brezhnev, Leonid, 282, 286, 287–89,
    292
Broder, David, 190
Brokaw, Tom, 254
Brown, Pat, 15, 60, 86, 145–46, 150
Buchanan, Patrick J.
    appointment scheduling and, 156,
        169, 176
    book by, 355
    China trip and, 233, 261, 268–69
    Huston Plan, 214
    post-Watergate life of, 376–77
    presidential campaigns and, 31, 36,
        37, 44, 50, 51, 56, 60, 62, 74, 75,
        79
Buckley, William F., 254
Bull, Stephen, 107, 162, 168, 191,
    204, 213, 216
Bumgardner, Bruce, 176
Burns, Arthur, 98, 99, 143
Bush, Barbara, 376
Bush, George H. W., 376
Bush, George W., 381
Butterfield, Alexander, 107, 157–58,
    168, 204, 337

Carley, Jack, 381
Carlson, Eddie, 330–32, 333, 342
Carruthers, William, 169, 310, 376
Carswell, G. Harrold, 148
Carter, Jimmy, 134, 367, 397
Cashen, Henry, 161–62, 175–76,
 188, 227–28, 299–300, 336, 360
Cashen, Leslie, 299
Chamberlain, Neville, 198
Chamberlain, Wilt, 66–67
Chambers, Whittaker, 10, 150
Chapin, B. R. (uncle), 13, 25
Chapin, Dwight. *See also* Watergate
alcoholism of, 175–77
as appointments secretary, 154–77
 (*see also* appointments secretary
 position)
career trajectory of, 1–3, 14–19, 262
Chapin Enterprises, 399, 401
China trip selection of, 234 (*see also*
 China trip)
as Deputy Assistant, 155, 168–70
early biography of, 3–14, 20
early White House role of, 117–18,
 122, 130–32 (*see also* first
 hundred days)
FBI report (August 28, 1972), 311,
 445–48
Haldeman's relationship with, 2,
 3, 6, 14–18, 21–23, 30, 40–41,
 130–32, 142, 204–6, 212–13,
 225–26
JWT jobs of, 20–34, 38
late career of, 399–406
marriage and children of (*see
 individual names of family members*)
Moynihan on, 181
as Nixon's personal aide, 34–37 (*see
 also* presidential election [1968])
office proximity to Nixon, x, 73,
 92, 204

parents of, 3–7, 10–12, 14, 21, 38,
 223, 339–40, 369, 389, 401
political pranks by, 14, 61–62, 162,
 175–77, 215–19
presidential campaign roles of,
 24–37
Stone Enterprises jobs of, 350–52,
 358–59, 364, 368–72, 376, 383,
 399, 401
Ten Outstanding Young Men
 award, 181, 225–26
White House role change (1971),
 203–7
Chapin, Dwight ("Pop,"
 grandfather), 4, 310, 339–40
Chapin, Kimberly (daughter)
childhood of, 28, 29, 176, 267,
 339, 352, 357–58, 363, 385, 400,
 404–5
father's post-Watergate life and,
 377–82
marriage and children of, 401
Chapin, Linda (sister), 6, 399
Chapin, Matthew (grandson), xi,
 405
Chapin, "Nano Chapie"
 (grandmother), 339–40, 401
Chapin, Ross (cousin), 191
Chapin, Sheldon (brother), 4
Chapin, Susie Howland (ex-wife)
courtship and marriage of, 9, 12
divorce of, 319, 400
Dwight's early career and, 5, 22,
 25, 29, 32, 45–46, 85, 87, 91–92,
 102–3, 176, 226
Dwight's trial, conviction,
 incarceration and, 267, 339, 346,
 348, 350, 352, 357–58, 363, 365
Watergate and impact on, 299, 310,
 317, 318, 323, 325, 330–31, 400,
 404–5

Chapin, Tracy (daughter)
childhood of, 176, 267, 299, 339, 352, 357–58, 363, 400, 404–5
father's post-Watergate life and, 371, 379, 381–82
marriage and children of, xi, 401
characterization of Nixon, 133–53, 178–202. *See also* media coverage of Nixon administration
accomplishments vs., 179–81
Agnew and, 113–15, 139
"Berlin Wall" image, 157, 188
Chief of Staff and, 133–37, 139–42, 145–47, 151
decision-making and, 139, 142–49, 151–53
"don't have Nixon to kick around" speech, 1–3, 18–19, 85, 387
Eisenhower and, 128–30
EOB office preferred by, 104, 128, 138–40, 214
by Haldeman, 344–45
Humphrey and, 89–90
Huston Plan of, 214–15
as introvert, 40–41, 178–79, 183, 201
legacy of, xi–xii, 402–6
memoranda protocol, 136–37, 157
mistrust of intelligence agencies, 192–94
mistrust of military leaders, 194
political enemies and paranoia accusations, 89–90, 149–51, 187, 389
Rebozo and, 122–23
San Jose incident and "V sign" of, 209–12
sports interest, 183–85
tape recordings and, 104, 140–41, 181–83, 185–88, 207–8, 307, 331, 337, 388–90, 393, 429–45

"thinking time" of, 79–80, 137–40, 214–15
"Tricky Dick," 315–16
Vietnam War and, 184–85, 188–92, 194–202
White House staff on, 118–20
"Checkers speech" (Nixon), 31–32, 88
Cheney, Dick, 134
Chennault, Anna, 78–79, 93
Chiang Kai-shek, 232
China trip, 253–76
advance planning for trip, 229–39, 253–54
first advance trip (October 1971), 222, 239–47
joint communique issued, 247, 252, 262–63, 268–70, 277
Kissinger's Pakistan trip and, 231, 271
military spy ring suspicion following trip, 271–76
Nixon's meetings in, 253–68
pandas as gift from, 258–59
post-Watergate business exploration in, 372–73
Russia's culture vs. China, 277–78, 280–81, 288
second advance trip (December 1971), 246–52
Vietnam War and, 224, 238, 241, 243, 245, 247–49
Chisholm, Shirley, 345
Chotiner, Murray, 25, 32
Chou En-lai
China advance trips, 222, 230–31, 241–45
Kissinger on, 241, 285
Nixon's meetings with, 254–56, 259–60, 262–65, 266, 268, 270
Chuang Tse-tung, 230

Churchill, Winston, 86, 198
CIA, 192, 194, 246, 278, 386, 390
Cliburn, Van, 288–89
Clinton, Bill, 383
Coffey, Vernon, 228–29, 308
Cole, Ken, 175–76
Cole, Nat King, 154
Colodny, Len, 273, 304, 396
Colson, Chuck
  incarceration of, 356–57
  Watergate break-in and
    investigation, 300–301, 307, 320,
    326, 327
  White House work of, 139, 161,
    169, 207, 361
Committee to Reelect the President
    (CRP), 303–10, 316–18. *See also*
    Watergate
Congress
  election (1966) of, 37
  official White House visitors from,
    158–59
  Senate Watergate hearings, 149,
    325, 336, 337, 388, 396–97
Connally, John, 375–76
Council for Urban Affairs, 179–80
Cowan, Glenn, 230
Cox, Archibald, 336, 337, 397
Cox, Ed, 260, 298

Daley, Richard, 14, 32, 83–84
Dart, Justin, 329–30
Davies, John, 82
Dean, John
  Blind Ambition, 396
  Chapin hospitalization suggested
    by, 319, 400
  FBI report (July 5, 1974), 394,
    419–23
  "Gunga Dean" (Safire), 395–96,
    424–26

  incarceration of, 357, 362
  Mayhew on, 396, 426–29
  "the Plumbers" and, 217
  tape recordings, Oval Office
    (March 13–21, 1973), 307, 331,
    388–90, 393, 429–45
  Watergate break-in and
    investigation, 301–2, 303–8,
    310–11, 313, 315, 317, 318–21,
    323–24, 327
  Watergate charges and plea, 330,
    331, 333, 335, 344
  Watergate role of, 386, 388–96,
    400
Dean, Mo, 357
Deaver, Mike, 170
"Deep Throat," 313–15
De Gaulle, Charles, 86, 87, 129,
    290, 405
DelConte, Ken, 13
Democratic Convention (1968), 75
Democratic headquarters break-in.
  See Watergate
Dewey, Tom, 31–32, 160
Diamond, Neil, 361
Dirksen, Everett, 43–44, 391–92
Disney, Walt, 22, 52
Disraeli, Benjamin, 322
Dobrynin, Anatoly, 100, 122
domestic policy
  accomplishments, 179–81
  antidrug program, 161
  Domestic Council, 179–80
  "southern strategy," 151–53
  Supreme Court, 148–49
Donfeld, Jeff, 162, 186
Douglas, Helen Gahagan, 10
Douglas, Mike, 53
Duberstein, Ken, 134
Duggan, Tom, 19
Dulles, John Foster, 255

Duncan, Bill, 66, 69, 229, 288
Duval, Mike, 370

Eagleburger, Larry, 222
Edge of the Sword, The (De Gaulle), 87
Ehrlichman, John
  appointment scheduling and, 157,
    171
  campaign (1968) and, 75, 83–84
  Chapin and, 335, 343, 363
  China trip and, 233–34
  domestic policy and, 179, 180
  firing of, 334–35
  first-term transition/first hundred
    days, 97, 101, 113, 115–18
  Jewish vote and, 186
  Kissinger and, 224
  Nixon's gubernatorial campaign
    and, 15, 17
  Nixon's working style and, 136,
    139, 146
  Pakistan story in *Post* and, 272,
    274–75
  "the Plumbers" and, 215
  post-Watergate life of, 373, 374–75,
    377–78
  Rome trip and, 227–28
  unanswered Watergate questions
    and, 388, 397–98
  Watergate break-in and
    investigation, 301, 304–5, 307–9,
    318, 320, 326, 327
Eisenhower, David, 46, 88, 129, 184,
  189, 298
Eisenhower, Dwight
  death of, 128–30
  King and, 63
  Nixon and, 10–11, 31, 86, 88, 133,
    143, 150, 391, 392
Eisenhower, Mamie, 129
Eisenhower, Milton, 48–49

Elbourne, Tim
  campaign (1968) and, 70
  Chapin's prison visit from, 358
  China trip and, 235, 237, 241, 242
  press office role of, 13, 195, 225
Ellsberg, Daniel, 215–17, 304, 386
Ellzey, Mike, 403
Ervin, Sam, 325, 336, 397
Evans, John, 175–76
Evans, Rowland, 117
Evans, Tom, 50

FBI. *See also* Hoover, J. Edgar
  "black bag operations," 215
  "Deep Throat," 313–15
  on homosexuality, 116–17
  Watergate investigation, 310–11,
    316–17, 320, 321, 394, 419–23,
    445–48
Felt, Mark, 116, 314–15, 321
Ferriero, David, 402–3
Fielding, Fred, 321
Fielding, Lewis, 216, 304, 305
Finch, Bob, 25, 27, 50, 96
first hundred days, 110–32
  Cambodia invasion, 122–25, 148,
    198, 201
  concept of, 110–11
  Eisenhower's death, 128–30
  European trip, 117–18, 126–27
  homosexuality investigation,
    115–17
  staff and working relationships,
    111–15, 117–22, 130–32
  West Wing remodeling, 125–28, 221
first term. *See* Nixon's first term
Fisher, Max, 185
Flanigan, Peter, 36, 50
Fleming, Ian, 332
Fonda, Jane, 192
Ford, Gerald, 134, 169, 325

foreign policy. *See also* China trip;
    Russia trip; Vietnam War
  ABM system, 142–43
  Israel and Yom Kippur War, 139,
    186, 187
  North Korea crisis (1969), 144–49
  Rome trip, 227–29
Fortas, Abe, 148
Frankel, Max, 254
Frost, David, 366
Fulbright, William, 93

Gallup, George, Jr., 81–82
Gannon, Frank, 148, 402, 404
Garment, Len, 36, 44, 50, 51, 62,
    149, 185
Gesell, Gerhard, 362, 363
Gettlin, Robert, 273, 304, 396
Goldwater, Barry, 26–28, 33, 73, 93
Goode, Mark, 169, 310, 313, 374
Goodearle, Roy, 59, 102, 113,
    114–15, 227–28, 374, 377
Goodpaster, Andrew, 135
Goodson, Terry Decker, 204,
    400–401
Gore, Louise, 72
Graham, Billy, 5, 34, 73, 83, 156,
    186, 270, 355
Gray, Pat, 314–15, 394
Greene, Bobbie, 185
Greenspan, Alan, 185
Griffin, Shelia, 299
Gromyko, Andrei, 285
Guhin, Mike, 17, 346
"Gunga Dean" (Safire), 395–96,
    424–26

Haig, Alexander
  Chapin and, 342
  China trip and, 231
  first hundred days and, 122, 124

Kissinger and, 222
  military spy ring suspicion and,
    273–76
  Nixon's working style and, 134
  Vietnam War and, 192–93
  Watergate and, 314
Haldeman, Betty, 21
Haldeman, Harry Robbins ("H. R.,"
    "Bob")
  campaign (1964), 27–28
  campaign (1968), 29–30, 36–38,
    50–53, 55–56, 69–71, 74–76,
    83–84
  Chapin's firing by, 328–29, 332
  Chapin's relationship with, 2, 3, 6,
    14–18, 21–23, 76, 130–32, 142,
    204–6, 212–13, 225–26
  Chapin's trial and conviction, 333,
    334, 335, 338, 339, 342, 344
  characterization of, 21–22, 91
  charges against and incarceration,
    356, 358, 364, 365, 372–73
  Chief of Staff role of, 133–37,
    139–42, 145–47, 151
  China trip and, 231, 232, 234, 237,
    238–39, 254–56, 259, 260, 262,
    266, 268, 270
  firing of, 334–35
  first hundred days and, 110, 114–17,
    119–20, 122, 124–26, 129–32
  first-term transition and, 91, 94, 97,
    99, 100–102, 103–9
  The Haldeman Diaries, 257
  at JWT, 20–34
  Nixon's appointment scheduling and,
    155–56, 157, 162, 167–68, 173–77
  Nixon's working style and, 187, 197,
    200–202
  Pakistan story in *Post* and, 271, 276
  "the Plumbers" and, 215–21, 224,
    271–76

post-Watergate life of, 377–79
Russia trip and, 283–85, 292, 295
on tape recordings, 183
unanswered Watergate questions
    and, 385, 386, 388, 393
Vietnam War and, 192–93, 207–8,
    210–14
Watergate break-in and
    investigation, 300–301, 304–7,
    309, 316, 318–20, 322–27
Woods and, 53, 100
young staff of, 265
Haldeman, Jo, 21, 127, 292, 293,
    301, 326
Han Hsu, 256, 258–60, 266–67, 269
Harlan, John Marshall, 148
Harlow, Bryce, 97, 99–100, 105, 136,
    143, 158, 332, 355, 361
Harriman, Averell, 78
Harris, Harvey, 13
Harris, Lou, 81
Harvey, Paul, 369
Haynsworth, Clement, 148
Helenas (Chapin's maternal
    grandparents), 3
Helms, Richard, 214, 386
Herschensohn, Bruce, 185, 320, 346
Hesburgh, Father, 173–74
Higby, Larry, 75, 83, 115–17,
    126–28, 131, 300–301, 306
Hill & Knowlton, 399
Hiss, Alger, 10, 19, 150
Hite, Kathleen, 12, 154
Hoover, J. Edgar, 8, 93, 116–17, 201,
    214–15, 305, 314
Hope, Bob, 176–77
Hope, Delores, 177
House Un-American Activities
    Committee (HUAC), 10–11, 150
Howard, Dick, 165, 323, 353,
    359–60, 365, 372

Howard, Marsha, 165, 323, 353, 365
Hughes, Donald, 98, 228, 235
Hullin, Tod, 191
Humphrey, Hubert, 68, 79–82, 85,
    89–90, 341
Humphrey, Muriel, 89, 90
Hunt, E. Howard, 301, 304, 305,
    308, 383, 386
Huntley, Chet, 226
Huston, Tom, 214

image of Nixon. See appointments
    secretary position;
    characterization of Nixon; media
    coverage of Nixon administration
Iran trip, 283, 294–96
Irvine, Dennis, 403

J. Walter Thompson (JWT), 20–34,
    38, 225–26, 399
Jackson, Robert, 149
Jaffe, Jerome, 185
Javits, Jacob, 187
Jaworski, Leon, 337–38, 343
Jaycees, 181, 225–26
Jenkins, Walter, 115–16, 391
Jiang Qing, 254
Johnson, Lyndon Baines
    election (1960), 32
    election (1964), 26
    Jenkins and homosexuality scandal,
        115–16, 391
    Nixon's transition to office, 93, 94,
        102, 104
    presidential campaign (1968) and,
        33, 35, 47, 68, 69, 78–81, 87, 89
    Vietnam War and, 190, 191, 194,
        195
    working style of, 133, 139, 144
Jones, Jim, 225
Jurgensen, Sonny, 223

Kalmbach, Herbert
  Chapin and, 14, 15, 20, 329, 341,
    344, 350–51, 357
  Watergate break-in and
    investigation, 308, 311
Keach, Stacy, 9
Kehrli, Bruce, 191, 307–8
Kendall, Don, 107–8
Kennedy, Edward "Ted," 65, 160–61,
    396–97
Kennedy, Jackie, 65–66
Kennedy, John F.
  assassination of, 25–26
  campaign expectations (1964), 17
  Cuban Missile Crisis and, 145–46
  election (1960), 12, 14, 60, 150
  family visits to White House of, 167
  1960 election of, 77, 81, 86, 89
Kennedy, Robert F., 65, 68–69
Kent State University, 71, 196
Keyes, Paul, 27, 270
KGB, 282, 287–88, 291–92
Khrushchev, Nikita, 11, 146
Kilberg, Bill, 185
Killgallon, Bill (W. C. Killgallon's
    son), 34
Killgallon, W. C., 34
Kim Il-sung, 146
King, Coretta Scott, 62–64, 118–19
King, Martin Luther, Jr., 62–67, 69
King, Martin Luther, Sr., 62–64
Kinsley, Michael, 377
Kissinger, Henry
  appointment scheduling and, 174
  campaign (1968) and, 87
  Chapin and, 342, 361
  China trip preparation by, 231–47
    (see also China trip)
  first hundred days and, 111–12,
    118–19, 122, 124–25
  Nixon characterized by, 111–12

Nixon in China with, 253–55, 256,
    259, 260, 262, 264–66, 268,
    270–71
  Nixon on Jews and, 185, 187
  Nixon's first term and, 94–95, 97,
    100, 101
  Nixon's working style and, 136,
    139, 145–47
  Nuclear Weapons and Foreign Policy,
    95
  Pakistan story in Post and, 271,
    273, 275
  Russia trip and, 277–79, 282, 283,
    285, 290–91
  Vietnam War and, 192–94, 215,
    219–24
Klein, Herb, 115–17, 169, 184, 265,
    303
Kleindienst, Dick, 307, 326, 327
Kopechne, Mary Jo, 160
Kosygin, Alexei, 288, 289, 292–93
Kramer, Mike, 8
Krogh, Egil "Bud," 162–63, 176,
    197, 215, 272, 303
Kurtis, Bill, 371

Laird, Melvin, 96, 147, 194, 274
Lasker, Bunny, 185
Leddel, Bart, 13
Liberace, 8
Liddy, G. Gordon, 303–10, 316–18,
    383–86, 393, 395
Lillie, Mildred, 148–49
Limbaugh, Rush, 377
Lincoln Memorial, Nixon at,
    196–202
Lodge, Henry Cabot, 190–91
Lombardo, Guy, 165–66
Lord, Winston, 241, 256
Luce, Clare Boothe, 94–95
Lucky, Jane, 64

Magruder, Jeb, 217, 303–7, 327, 357, 362, 386, 388, 390, 393
Mahan, Jann, 370, 376
Making It Perfectly Clear (Klein), 265
Making of the President 1960/1968, The (White), 112
Making of the President 1968, The (White), 79, 83
Malek, Fred, 169, 402, 405
Mangold, Rob, 330, 331
Mansfield, Mike, 158, 191, 397
Mao Tse-tung, 230, 232, 242, 253, 256–57, 260, 262, 264, 269
Mayhew, Alice, 396, 426–29
McCarthy, Eugene, 66, 68, 190
McCarthy, Joseph, 11, 150
McCord, James, 305
McCrary, Tex
  appointment scheduling and, 172–73
  Chapin and post–White House correspondence, 363
  China trip and, 261
  later career of, 399
  Russia trip and, 284, 297
  on Vietnam publicity, 184
  Watergate break-in and investigation, 310, 315–16, 319
McGovern, George, 218–19, 317, 322
media coverage of Nixon administration. See also *Washington Post*; Watergate
  accusations of homosexuality among staff, 115–17
  Agnew and, 114–15, 311–13
  China trip and, 232, 236–38, 261, 267–68
  on Martha Mitchell, 121–22
  Nixon's media strategy, 112–13, 155–56, 226
  for Russia trip, 279, 291–92

White House press accommodations, 126
Meir, Golda, 187
Mitchell, John
  antiwar protests and, 212
  campaign (1968) and, 44, 50, 58, 62, 74, 75, 77, 83–85
  Chapin and, 331, 364
  first hundred days and, 115–16, 120–22
  first-term transition and, 95, 96
  on Huston Plan, 215
  as Nixon's law partner, 31
  Nixon's working style and, 148–49, 152
  Pakistan story in *Post* and, 274–75
  post-Watergate life of, 377–78
  unanswered Watergate questions and, 386, 388, 392–93
  Watergate break-in and investigation, 303–5, 320
Mitchell, Martha, 85, 120–22, 392
Mondale, Walter, 81
Moore, Dick
  antiwar protests and, 212–13
  appointment scheduling and, 169
  Chapin and, 181, 330, 336
  first hundred days and, 121
  Nixon's working style and, 149
  post-Watergate life of, 376
  Watergate break-in and investigation, 310, 317, 318, 320, 324
Moorer, Thomas, 272, 274–75
Morgan, Ed, 57, 175–76, 362
Mosbacher, Bus, 101, 234
Moss, Dan, 13
Mountbatten, Lord, 129
Moynihan, Daniel Patrick, 97–98, 99, 172, 173, 174, 179, 180–81
Murdock, David, 373

Murphy, George, 209–10
Muskie, Ed, 89, 218, 317, 341, 345

National Security Agency (NSA), 192
National Security Council. *See*
    Kissinger, Henry
New York Times, Pentagon Papers
    and, 215
Nixon, Julie (daughter)
  campaign (1968) and, 46, 58,
    82–84, 88
  father's appointment scheduling
    and, 167
  father's China trip and, 298
  father's Russia trip and, 298
  marriage of, 129, 189
  Pat, 258–59
  Woods and, 30
Nixon, Pat (wife)
  appointment scheduling and, 166,
    174–75, 177
  campaign (1968) and, 45, 46, 53, 55,
    58, 59, 69, 74–75, 80, 83, 88
  Chapin's post-Watergate meeting
    with, 405–6
  China trip and, 235, 254–56,
    258–60, 261, 269
  daughter Julie's marriage, 189
  election (1964) and, 26
  election (1968) and, 30–32
  husband's gubernatorial campaign
    and, 19
  husband's working style and, 149
  Russia trip and, 2, 283, 284, 289
Nixon, Richard. *See also* Chapin,
    Dwight; characterization of
    Nixon; China trip; domestic
    policy; first hundred days; foreign
    policy; Haldeman, Harry Robbins
    ("H. R.," "Bob"); media coverage
    of Nixon administration; Nixon's

first term; presidential election
    (1968); Russia trip; Vietnam War;
    Watergate
  back taxes paid by, 344
  campaign (1960), 60, 77, 81, 86,
    89–90, 150
  campaign (1964), 24–28, 33
  Chapin hired as personal aide by,
    34–37
  Chapin's post-Watergate meeting
    with, 405–6
  "Checkers speech," 31–32, 88
  gubernatorial campaign, 1–2, 15–19
  House Un-American Activities
    Committee and, 10–11, 150
  law career of, 31, 44, 261
  media strategy of, 97, 98
  military spy ring suspicions, 271–76
  Presidential Library of, 402–4
  San Clemente home of, 107,
    171–72, 203
  as vice president, 10–11, 133, 211
  Watergate role of, 385–95, 397, 399
Nixon, Tricia (daughter)
  campaign (1968) and, 58, 82, 83
  Donfield and, 186
  father's appointment scheduling
    and, 156, 167
  father's Russia trip and, 298
  Woods and, 30
Nixon's first term, 91–109. *See also*
    first hundred days
  first week of, 106–9
  inauguration and swearing in of
    staff, 100–106
  transition process and, 91–100
Nixon Tapes, The (Nichter), 182–83
Nofziger, Lyn, 169
Novak, Robert, 117
Nuclear Weapons and Foreign Policy
    (Kissinger), 95

Oates, Jim, 369
O'Donnell, Kenny, 181
Ogilvie, Richard, 71, 331
Ohio National Guard, 71, 196
One of Us (Wicker), 179

Pahlavi, Farah (empress consort of
    Iran), 294
Pahlavi, Mohammad Reza (shah of
    Iran), 283, 294
Pakistan, 231, 271–76
Parker, David, 157, 168
Paterno, Joe, 185
Paulin, Mike, 14
Paul VI (pope), 227–29
Peale, Norman Vincent, 5, 369–70,
    401
Peale, Ruth, 370
Pearson, Drew, 113
Pennsylvania Avenue Development
    Corporation, 181
Pentagon Papers, 215, 304
Pepsi, 107–8
Percy, Chuck, 48–49, 158–59
Percy, Sharon, 48
Pham Van Dong, 189, 192
PJB from the Right (newsletter), 377
Podgorny, Nikolai, 288, 292–93
Poland trip, 283, 296
Pompidou, Georges, 271, 346
Powell, Lewis, 149
Power of Positive Thinking, The
    (Peale), 5, 369–70, 401
presidential election (1968), 40–67,
    68–90
  advisors to, 44, 49–53
  Agnew chosen as Nixon's running
    mate, 71–73
  campaign staff, 75–77
  Chapin's personal aide role in,
    40–46, 56–58

election of Nixon, 82–90
media strategy, 41, 53–56
"New Nixon" theme of, 36, 48, 60,
    179 (*see also* characterization of
    Nixon)
Nixon's decision to run, 46–58
nomination of Nixon, 73–75, 183
primaries, 58–67
security for candidates during,
    69–71
Vietnam War and unrest during,
    68–69, 77–82
presidential election (1972). *See also*
    Watergate
Committee to Reelect the President
    (CRP), 303–10, 316–18
Republican Convention, 309
president's style. *See* characterization
    of Nixon
Presley, Elvis, 161–63
Price, John, 179
Price, Ray (military general), 294–95
Price, Ray (speechwriter)
  campaign (1968) and, 44, 50, 51,
    54, 56, 62, 74
  confused with General Price,
    294–95
  With Nixon, 60
  post–White House role of, 260, 261

Quinn, Sandy, 13, 15, 402

Radford, Charles, 273, 274
Ramirez, Lou, 9, 13
Rast, Bob, 373
Rather, Dan, 254
Reagan, Nancy, 45
Reagan, Ronald
  antiwar protests and, 209–10
  communication skills of, 169, 170
  election (1980), 44–45, 376

Reagan, Ronald (*cont.*)
  presidential campaign (1968) and,
    33, 48, 60, 61, 67, 71
  staffers of, 13, 102, 370
  on *Success* cover, 371
Rebozo, Bebe, 42, 64–67, 75,
  122–23, 302
Redstone, Sumner, 188
Rehnquist, William, 149
Rhodes, James, 70
Richardson, Elliot L., 337
Rick, John, 6
Rivers, Mendel, 146
Robinson, Rembrandt, 273
Rockefeller, Jay, 48
Rockefeller, Nelson, 33–34, 48,
  61–62, 67, 71, 94, 95, 174, 193
Rogers, William
  China trip and, 234, 241, 254, 255,
    256, 260, 262, 266
  first hundred days and, 122
  Kissinger and, 224
  Nixon's working style and, 147
  Russia trip and, 285, 290–91
  Secretary of State appointment of,
    101
  Vietnam War and, 192–93
Romney, George, 48, 61, 71, 96
Roosevelt, Franklin Delano, 129, 277
Rosen, James, 274
Rowley, Jim, 69
Ruckelshaus, William D., 337
Rumsfeld, Don, 75, 134, 174, 179,
  373
Rush, Kenneth, 193
Russell, Dick, 158
Russia trip, 277–98
  advance trip, 278–83
  Austria trip and, 279, 284, 297
  China's culture vs. Russia, 277–78,
    280–81, 288

  China trip and planning for,
    238, 254, 266, 269, 272,
    274, 277
  gift exchange, 288
  Iran trip and, 283, 294–96
  KGB, 282, 287–88, 291–92
  Nixon's meetings, 284–94
  Poland trip and, 283, 296
  return to U.S. from, 297–98
  SALT and, 143, 277, 283, 286,
    288–91, 299, 322
Ruwe, Nick, 15–17, 56, 63–66, 101–2

Safire, William
  appointment scheduling and, 169,
    174
  campaign (1968) and, 44
  Chapin and, 342
  first hundred days and, 114
  first-term transition and, 95
  "-gate" used by, 383
  "Gunga Dean," 395–96, 424–26
  Kissinger and, 222–23
  Nixon on Jews and, 185
  Watergate break-in and
    investigation, 310
St. John, Jill, 223–24
SALT (Strategic Arms Limitation
  Treaty), 143, 277, 283, 286,
  288–91, 299, 322
Sanchez, Fina, 45
Sanchez, Manolo, 45, 46, 196–97,
  200–201
Saperstein, Michael, 188
"Saturday Night Massacre," 337
Sawyer, Diane, 258, 371
Scarney, Shelley, 31
Schrauth, Mike, 370
Schreiber, Taft, 185
Schuller, Robert, 369, 370
Scott, Al, 54

Scowcroft, Brent, 277, 295, 342
Scranton, William, 71
Sears, John, 36, 37, 44–45, 50
Secret Service and security. *See* presidential election (1968); *individual names of trips*
Segretti, Donald
Chapin's hiring of, 334–35
Chapin's trial and conviction, 331, 337, 338, 340–41, 342, 343–46
"Dick Tuck" political tricks by, 302, 317–18, 325, 381
incarceration of, 362
"the Plumbers" and, 217–19
unanswered Watergate questions and, 386, 390, 393
at USC, 13–14
Watergate break-in events and investigation, 302–3, 306, 308, 310–11, 314–20, 321, 325
Semple, Bob, 319
Shafer, Ray, 71
Shakespeare, Frank, 51, 54
Shell, Joe, 26
Shultz, George, 96, 152, 180
Sidey, Hugh, 132
Sidley, Toni, 204
Sihanouk, Norodom (prince of Cambodia), 124
Silent Coup (Colodny and Gettlin), 273, 304, 396
Sinatra, Barbara, 312
Sinatra, Frank, 311–12
Sinatra, Nancy, 7
Skinner, Sam, 134
Sloan, Hugh, 308–9, 311
Smathers, George, 122
Smith, Gerard, 290–91, 299
Smith, Hedrick, 124–25
Smith, Howard K., 19

Smith, Sandy, 314
Soviet Union. *See* Russia trip
Stans, Maurice, 50, 97, 308
State Department, Nixon's distrust of, 285, 291. *See also* Rogers, William
Stein, Ben, 186
Stein, Herb, 185
Stein, Herm, 340, 353, 357, 360
Stein, Jake, 336, 338–39, 342, 343–47, 362
Stennis, John, 158
Stoessel, Walter, 193
Stone, Jessie, 351
Stone, Milburn, 154
Stone, W. Clement, 350–52, 358–59, 364, 368–72, 376, 399
Storm, Gale, 8
Strachan, Gordon
FBI report (August 28, 1972), 311, 445–48
"the Plumbers" and, 217–19
unanswered Watergate questions and, 386, 388, 390, 397
Watergate break-in and investigation, 306, 307, 310–11, 316, 317, 325, 327
Strategic Arms Limitation Treaty (SALT), 143, 277, 283, 286, 288–91, 299, 322
Stuart, Robert, 330–31
Success (magazine), 351, 368, 369, 371, 376, 383, 399, 401
Sullivan, Bill, 314

Table Tennis Association (Chinese), 230–31, 252
Taiwan, 232–33, 251, 252, 256, 262–63, 268–70, 277
Talman, William, 8
Tanaka, Kakuei, 310

tape recordings by Nixon
on antiwar protesters, 207–8
on Jews, 185–88
Oval Office (March 13–21,
1973), 307, 331, 388–90,
393, 429–45
placement of, 104
"abuse of power" tapes, 181–83
Watergate hearings on, 337
Taylor, Bob, 70, 71, 210, 235, 256,
284, 295, 297
Teeter, Bob, 82
Ten Outstanding Young Men
(Jaycees), 181, 225–26
Thieu, Nguyen Van, 78
Thomas, Evan, 387
Timmons, William, 158, 310, 373
Tkach, Walter, 2, 176
Trento, Joe, 115
Truman, Harry, 10, 105, 160, 236
Tuck, Dick, 61, 216–18, 341
Turnbo, Chuck, 358–59

United Airlines, 330–33, 341–42
University of Southern California
(USC), 8–9, 11–14, 20, 175, 217

Vesco, Robert, 167
Vietnam War, 203–24
antiwar protests, 68–69, 77–82,
184–85, 188–92, 194–202,
207–15
Cambodia invasion, 122–25, 148,
198, 201
China trip and, 224, 238, 241, 243,
245, 247–49
FBI investigations and, 93–94
Hanoi/Haiphong bombing, 282
Kent State shootings and, 71, 196
Kissinger's White House role and,
219–24

North Korea crisis (1969) and,
144–49
Percy on, 158–59
presidential campaign (1964) and, 33
presidential campaign (1968) and,
35–36
Watergate publicity and, 322
White House on public perception
of, 203–7
Volpe, John, 71, 96

Walker, Anne, 165, 323, 369
Walker, Ronald
antiwar protests and, 209, 210
appointment scheduling and, 165,
168–69, 176
Chapin's trial and conviction, 346
China trip and, 235, 259–60
Nixon Library and, 402
post-Watergate life of, 369
presidential campaign (1968) and,
69–70
in Russia trip, 287, 294
Watergate break-in and
investigation, 323
White House advance office and,
194–95
Wallace, George, 62, 69, 173, 174
Wallace, Mike, 35–36, 60, 83
Walters, Barbara, 254
Warren, Earl, 106, 109
Warren, Jerry, 169, 175–76
Washington Post
on Chapin as "Mr. Nice Guy," 131
Pakistan story by, 271–76
on Watergate, 313–15, 317–18, 321,
338, 343, 356
Wasserman, Lew, 329
Watergate, 299–327, 328–47,
348–66, 385–98. See also tape
recordings

break-in events, 299–302
Chapin's grand jury testimony, 333–34
Chapin's implication and firing, 318–33
Chapin's incarceration, 352–65
Chapin's indictment, 336–42
Chapin's subsequent job with Stone Enterprises, 350–52, 358–59, 364, 368–72, 376, 383, 399, 401
Chapin's trial and conviction, 302–3, 342–47
Chapin's trial and incarceration, xi–xii, 3, 14, 267, 302–3, 336–47, 352, 357–58, 363, 365
CRP's role, 303–10, 316–18
exhibits on, 419–52
FBI investigation, 310–11, 316–17, 320, 321
Haldeman's and Ehrlichman's firing, 334–35
incarceration of other administration officials, 356–57, 362
Nixon's resignation, 348–50, 365–66
post-Watergate lives of Nixon alumni, 367–84
"Saturday Night Massacre," 337
Senate hearings on, 149, 325, 336, 337, 388, 396–97
special prosecutors, 336–38, 343
"the Plumbers" and, 215–21, 224, 271–76, 304, 305, 386
unanswered questions about, 385–98
Washington Post on, 313–15, 317–18, 321, 338, 343, 356
Weicker, Lowell, 336
Weigold, Chuck, 370
Welander, Robert O., 273

Wells, Ida, 304
Westmoreland, William, 194
Whitaker, John, 34, 36, 64–65, 227, 343
White, Theodore "Teddy," 79, 83, 112, 254
White House. *See also* appointments secretary position
Camp David retreat from, 129
Executive Protective Service Police, 127
office layout, x
organization chart, xiii–ix
West Wing remodel, 125–28, 221
Wicker, Tom, 179
Wilkinson, Bud, 55
Will (Liddy), 383
Wilson, Pete, 15
Windon, Bernie, 373
With Nixon (Price), 60
Woodruff, Judy, 182
Woods, Arthur, 331
Woods, Rose Mary
antiwar protests and, 211
campaign (1968) and, 30–31, 37, 41, 43, 47, 50, 52–53, 74, 80, 88
characterization of, 31
China trip and, 261, 268, 269
first hundred days and, 110, 123
first-term transition and, 100, 104, 106, 108
Haldeman and, 53, 100
Nixon's gubernatorial campaign and, 15
office location of, 204
Rome trip and, 228
in Russia, 284–85
Woodson, Mike, 175
Woodward, Bob, 313–14, 320–21, 338, 356

Yates, Nell
appointment scheduling and, 161,
162–63
Chapin's post–White House
correspondence, 356
Chapin's trial and conviction, 343
China trip and, 235
first hundred days and, 115
first-term transition and, 105
office location of, 204
in Russia, 286–87
Watergate break-in and
investigation, 312
Yeamans, Lenore, 16
Yorty, Sam, 11
Young, David, 215, 272–73, 275

Zboril, Chuck, 69
Ziegler, Ron

antiwar protests and, 210, 211
appointment scheduling and, 177
campaign (1968) and, 69–70
China trip and, 232, 256, 257,
258, 267
first hundred days and, 119–20
first-term transition and, 98, 102,
108–9
at JWT, 20, 22, 24
Nixon's gubernatorial campaign
and, 15
Russia trip and, 2
Ten Outstanding Young Men
award, 225–26
Watergate break-in and
investigation, 300–301, 317, 318
White House press office role of,
13
Zumwalt, Elmo, 273, 275